MW01051469

TOLSTOY IN CONTEXT

Likened to a second Tsar in Russia and attaining prophet-like status around the globe, Tolstoy made an impact on literature and the arts, religion, philosophy, and politics. His novels and stories both responded to and helped to reshape the European and Russian literary traditions. His nonfiction incensed readers and drew a massive following, making Tolstoy an important religious force as well as a stubborn polemicist in many fields. Through his involvement with Gandhi and the Indian independence movement, his aid in relocating the Doukhobors to Canada, his correspondence with American abolitionists, and his polemics with scientists in the periodical press, Tolstoy engaged a vast array of national and international contexts of his time in his life and thought. This volume introduces those contexts and situates Tolstoy – the man and the writer – in the rich and tumultuous period in which his intellectual and creative output came to fruition.

ANNA A. BERMAN is Assistant Professor of Slavonic Studies at the University of Cambridge and a fellow of Clare College. Her research focuses on the nineteenth-century Russian and English novel and issues of kinship and family. She is the author of *The Family Novel in Russia and England, 1800–1880* (2022) and *Siblings in Tolstoy and Dostoevsky: The Path to Universal Brotherhood* (2015) and has also published articles on Tolstoy, Dostoevsky, Russian opera, the relationship of science and literature, and the family novel as a genre.

TOLSTOY IN CONTEXT

EDITED BY

ANNA A. BERMAN

University of Cambridge

CAMBRIDGE
UNIVERSITY PRESS

CAMBRIDGE
UNIVERSITY PRESS

Shaftesbury Road, Cambridge CB2 8EA, United Kingdom

One Liberty Plaza, 20th Floor, New York, NY 10006, USA

477 Williamstown Road, Port Melbourne, VIC 3207, Australia

314–321, 3rd Floor, Plot 3, Splendor Forum, Jasola District Centre, New Delhi – 110025, India

103 Penang Road, #05–06/07, Visioncrest Commercial, Singapore 238467

Cambridge University Press is part of Cambridge University Press & Assessment,
a department of the University of Cambridge.

We share the University's mission to contribute to society through the pursuit of
education, learning and research at the highest international levels of excellence.

www.cambridge.org
Information on this title: www.cambridge.org/9781108479240

DOI: 10.1017/9781108782876

First published 2022

A catalogue record for this publication is available from the British Library.

Library of Congress Cataloging-in-Publication Data
NAMES: Berman, Anna A., editor.
TITLE: Tolstoy in context / edited by Anna A Berman.
DESCRIPTION: Cambridge, United Kingdom ; New York, NY : Cambridge University Press, 2022. |
Includes bibliographical references and index.
IDENTIFIERS: LCCN 2021060633 (print) | LCCN 2021060634 (ebook) | ISBN 9781108479240
(hardback) | ISBN 9781108749510 (paperback) | ISBN 9781108782876 (epub)
SUBJECTS: LCSH: Tolstoy, Leo, graf, 1828–1910. | Tolstoy, Leo, graf, 1828–1910–Political and social
views. | Tolstoy, Leo, graf, 1828–1910–Influence. | Authors, Russian–19th century–Biography. |
Russia–Social conditions–1801–1917. | Russia–Intellectual life–1801–1917.
CLASSIFICATION: LCC PG3385 .T855 2020 (print) | LCC PG3385 (ebook) |
DDC 891.73/3 [B]–dc23/eng/20220204
LC record available at https://lccn.loc.gov/2021060633
LC ebook record available at https://lccn.loc.gov/2021060634

ISBN 978-1-108-47924-0 Hardback

Contents

Figures

Notes on Contributors

GALINA ALEKSEEVA, Ph.D. (Russian Academy of Sciences, Institute of World Literature, 1997), is Academic Director, State Museum-Estate of Leo Tolstoy at Yasnaya Polyana, a member of the Slavic Research Group at the University of Ottawa (Canada), and a member of the Academic Council of the State Museum of Tolstoy in Moscow. She is the author of over 150 academic publications, including the book *American Dialogues of Leo Tolstoy* (*Amerikanskie dialogi L'va Tolstogo*, 2010), and the *Annotated Catalogue of Tolstoy's Personal Library*, vol. III: *Books in Foreign Languages* in 2 parts (1999).

CHARLOTTE ALSTON is Professor in History at Northumbria University. She is the author of books and articles on the international influence of Tolstoy's thought, the Russian revolutions and civil war, and the post-First World War peace settlements. Her 2014 book *Tolstoy and His Disciples: The History of a Radical International Movement* explores the operation of international Tolstoyan networks, and the ways in which Tolstoy's ideas were received and developed in different national contexts.

CAROL APOLLONIO is a Professor of the Practice of Slavic and Eurasian Studies at Duke University, specializing in nineteenth-century Russian prose literature, post-Soviet writing, and literary translation. Her books include *Dostoevsky's Secrets* (2009), *Simply Chekhov* (2020), *Chekhov's Letters* (co-edited with Radislav Lapushin), and *The New Russian Dostoevsky* (ed. and trans.). She holds a Chekhov bicentennial medal (2010) from the Russian Ministry of Culture and a Dostoevsky bicentennial medal, awarded in July 2021. She also translates from Japanese and Russian, most recently Alisa Ganieva's novel *Offended Sensibilities*. In 2019 she blogged across Siberia "in Chekhov's footprints" (https://sites.duke.edu/chekhovsfootprints).

ROSAMUND BARTLETT is a writer, translator, and lecturer who until 2006 was Reader in Russian at the University of Durham. She is the author of *Tolstoy: A Russian Life* (2010), longlisted for the 2011 Samuel Johnson Prize, the UK's premier award for nonfiction, and wrote the Introduction and Notes for her new Oxford World's Classics translation of *Anna Karenina* (2014). She is also a biographer and translator of Chekhov, and has published widely on Russian music, art, and cultural history. Her article on Chekhov and Tolstoy is forthcoming in the Cambridge volume *Chekhov in Context*.

ANNA A. BERMAN is Assistant Professor of Slavonic Studies at the University of Cambridge and a fellow of Clare College. Her research focuses on the nineteenth-century Russian and English novel and issues of kinship and family. She is the author of *The Family Novel in Russia and England, 1800–1880* (2022) and *Siblings in Tolstoy and Dostoevsky: The Path to Universal Brotherhood* (2015) and has also published articles on Tolstoy, Dostoevsky, Russian opera, the relationship of science and literature, and the family novel as a genre.

TATIANA BORISOVA is Associate Professor of History at the National Research University Higher School of Economics in St. Petersburg, Russia. She holds Ph.D. degrees in history (St. Petersburg Institute of History, Russian Academy of Sciences) and Law (University of Turku). She has published widely on the Russian legal tradition and the cultural history of Russian law. Her most recent publications include *Russia's Legal Trajectories* (2018) (with Jane Burbank), and *The Civic Religion of Anatolii Koni* (2021). She co-edited *The Legal Dimension in Cold-War Interactions: Some Notes from the Field* (2012). She is currently working on a monograph entitled '*For My Enemies, the Law': A Cultural History of Law and Justice in Russia, 1866–1881.*

ALEXANDER BURRY is Associate Professor of Slavic and East European Languages and Cultures at Ohio State University. He is the author of *Multi-Mediated Dostoevsky: Transposing Novels into Opera, Film, and Drama* (2011), and the co-editor, with Frederick H. White, of *Border Crossings: Russian Literature into Film* (2016) and *Approaches to Teaching Dostoevsky's Crime and Punishment* (2022) with Michael R. Katz. His current book *Legacies of the Stone Guest: The Don Juan Legend in Russian Literature*, is forthcoming in 2023.

CARYL EMERSON is A. Watson Armour III University Professor Emeritus of Slavic Languages and Literatures at Princeton University. Her scholarship has focused on the Russian classics (Pushkin, Tolstoy, Dostoevsky), Mikhail Bakhtin, and Russian music and opera. Recent projects include the Russian modernist Sigizmund Krzhizhanovsky (1887–1950) and the allegorical historical novelist Vladimir Sharov (1952–2018).

SIBELAN FORRESTER is Susan W. Lippincott Professor of Modern and Classical Languages and Russian at Swarthmore College. She works on Russian poetry, women's and gender studies, folklore and folk magic, science fiction, and theory and practice of translation, with published translations of fiction, poetry, and scholarly prose from Croatian, Russian, Serbian, and Ukrainian. She is co-editor of *Times of Mobility: Transnational Literature and Gender in Translation* (2019) and *Silver Age Poetry: Texts and Contexts* (2015), among others, and editor of *A Companion to Marina Cvetaeva: Approaches to a Major Russian Poet* (2016).

ELENA FRATTO is Assistant Professor in the Department of Slavic Languages and Literatures at Princeton University. She is the author of *Medical Storyworlds: Health, Illness, and Bodies in Russian and European Literature at the Turn of the Twentieth Century* (2021) and co-editor of *Russian Literature of the Anthropocene* (special double issue of *Russian Literature*, 2020). She has also published on literature and science, Russian Formalism, and theories of narrative. Her current project investigates the concept of "metabolism" as energy transformation in Russian literature and culture at the beginning of the twentieth century.

MELISSA FRAZIER is Professor of Russian language and literature and Associate Dean of the College at Sarah Lawrence College. Her book *Romantic Encounters: Readers, Writers and the Library for Reading* (2007) was awarded the Jean-Pierre Barricelli Book Prize for "excellence in the field of Romanticism scholarship" by the International Conference on Romanticism. She is working on a new project on Dostoevsky and the nineteenth-century intersections of literature and science, tentatively titled *Signs of the Material World: Dostoevsky and Nineteenth-Century Science*. Current interests include Russian realism; the nineteenth-century novel in a comparative context; and the intersections of literature, philosophy, and science.

EMILY FREY is Assistant Professor of Music at Brandeis University. Her research on opera, literature, and culture in nineteenth-century Russia has been published in the *Journal of the American Musicological Society*,

19th-Century Music, and several edited collections. An advocate of interdisciplinary teaching and research, Emily has held faculty positions in Music, Russian, and Comparative Literature. She is currently finishing her first book, *Russian Opera and Realism*.

MICHAEL D. GORDIN is Rosengarten Professor of Modern and Contemporary History at Princeton University. He specializes in the history of modern science, especially in Russia and the Soviet Union. He is the author of several books, including *A Well-Ordered Thing: Dmitrii Mendeleev and the Shadow of the Periodic Table* (2004, 2019), *Scientific Babel: How Science Was Done Before and After Global English* (2015), and *Einstein in Bohemia* (2020).

DANIEL GREEN received his Ph.D. from Harvard University in 2018 and has since taught at the Universities of Oxford and Cambridge. His interests include material culture, semiotics, the history of censorship, intellectual thought, and narrative theory. He is writing a book on the relationship between literature and dress culture in the reign of Nicholas I.

BELLA GRIGORYAN is Associate Professor of Slavic Languages and Literatures at the University of Pittsburgh. She works on eighteenth- and nineteenth-century Russian literature with a particular interest in the interplay between political history and the arts. She is the author of *Noble Subjects: The Russian Novel and the Gentry, 1762–1861* (2018) as well as articles about Karamzin, Pushkin, Dostoevsky, and Goncharov, among others.

G.M. HAMBURG is the Otho M. Behr Professor of History at Claremont McKenna College, where he specializes in the history of modern Russian politics and intellectual life. His recent books include *Russia's Path toward Enlightenment: Faith, Politics, and Reason, 1500–1801* (2016) and, as editor, *Russia in War and Revolution: The Memoirs of Fyodor Sergeyevich Olferieff* (2021). He is editor, with Semion Lyandres, of the *Journal of Modern Russian History and Historiography*.

HILDE HOOGENBOOM is Associate Professor of Russian at Arizona State University, and studies nineteenth-century Russian literary, intellectual, and book history using digital humanities. An expert on Catherine the Great, she co-translated her memoirs from French. Other publications include *Noble Sentiment and the Rise of Russian Novels* (forthcoming), supported by the National Humanities Center and Social Sciences

Research Council; archival letters by the three Khvoshchinskaia sisters; an essay collection on gender; and articles on women writers. A board member of the Association of Women in Slavic Studies, she is past president of the Eighteenth-Century Russian Studies Association.

ANNE HRUSKA is a Senior Instructor at Stanford Online High School, where she teaches courses on Russian and English literature, as well as workshops on online pedagogy. She received her Ph.D. from the University of California at Berkeley, and has taught at Berkeley, the University of Missouri at Columbia, the Pedagogical Institute in Saratov, and Stanford University. She has published several articles on nineteenth-century Russian literature, especially focusing on serfdom, emancipation, and family.

CHLOË KITZINGER is Assistant Professor of Russian at Rutgers University. Her research and teaching focus on the nineteenth- and twentieth-century Russian, European, and American novel and on narrative and literary theory. She is the author of *Mimetic Lives: Tolstoy, Dostoevsky, and Character in the Novel* (2021) and has also published essays and articles on Tolstoy, Dostoevsky, Nabokov, and Bely. Her other academic interests include seriality, translation studies, and science fiction.

LIZA KNAPP wrote *Leo Tolstoy: A Very Short Introduction* (2019) and *Anna Karenina and Others: Tolstoy's Labyrinth of Plots* (2016); she co-edited the MLA *Approaches to Teaching Anna Karenina* (2003). She teaches in the Slavic Department of Columbia University and taught in the Slavic Department of the University of California at Berkeley.

TONY H. LIN received his Ph.D. from the University of California at Berkeley and is Assistant Professor of the Practice and the Russian/Slavic Coordinator at Boston College. He has won numerous grants (such as Fulbright-Hays DDRA, IIE Fulbright Research Fellowship, DAAD, NEH, Critical Language Scholarship, Department of State Title VIII grant) to study and live in Russia, Poland, Germany, and France. He has published on Russian literature and music, Polish theater, and Chopin's literary representations. Prior to Boston College, he has taught at UC Berkeley, Connecticut College, and the University of Pittsburgh. He is also an accomplished pianist, having graduated from Northwestern University's School of Music with a degree in piano performance and given numerous recitals in the United States and Europe.

ANNE LOUNSBERY is Professor of Russian literature and Chair of the Department of Russian and Slavic Studies at New York University. Her publications include the books *Life Is Elsewhere: Symbolic Geography in the Russian Provinces* (2019) and *Thin Culture, High Art: Gogol, Hawthorne, and Authorship in Nineteenth-Century Russia and America* (2007, Russian translation 2021), as well as numerous articles on the Russian, European, and African American literary traditions. She is currently writing a book on how Russian texts have imagined the bourgeoisie.

JEFF LOVE is Research Professor of German and Russian at Clemson University. He is the author of *The Black Circle: A Life of Alexandre Kojève* (2018), *Tolstoy: A Guide for the Perplexed* (2008), and *The Overcoming of History in War and Peace* (2004). He has also published a translation of Alexandre Kojève's *Atheism* (2018), an annotated translation (with Johannes Schmidt) of F.W.J. Schelling's *Philosophical Investigations into the Essence of Human Freedom* (2006), a co-edited volume, *Nietzsche and Dostoevsky: Philosophy, Morality, Tragedy* (2016), and an edited volume, *Heidegger in Russia and Eastern Europe* (2017). His most recent work is a translation of António Lobo Antunes' novel *Until Stones Become Lighter than Water* (2019).

VERONIKA MAKAROVA received her Ph.D. in Linguistics from St. Petersburg University, Russia, in 1992. Before taking her current position of Professor at the Department of Linguistics, University of Saskatchewan, Canada, she worked at universities in Russia, Japan, and Scotland. Her research addresses bilingualism/multilingualism, language and culture, Russian immigrant studies, Russian-as-a-heritage-language studies, and Canadian Doukhobor (Spirit Wrestlers) language and culture. She has published over 100 research articles and is an author or (co)editor of five books, including *The Chronicles of Spirit Wrestlers' Immigration to Canada: God is Not in Might, but in Truth* (2019), *Linguistic Universe: An Introduction to Linguistics* (2015), *Russian Language Studies in North America: The New Perspectives from Theoretical and Applied Linguistics* (2012).

INESSA MEDZHIBOVSKAYA (Professor of Literary and Liberal Studies at Eugene Lang College and the New School for Social Research in New York City) is the author of *Tolstoy and the Religious Culture of His Time* (2008), *Tolstoy's On Life: From the Archival History of Russian Philosophy* (2019), and *L.N. Tolstoy* in the Oxford Bibliographies online (2021);

and editor of *Tolstoy and His Problems: Views from the Twenty-First Century* (2018), Tolstoy's *On Life* (2018), and three other volumes on Tolstoy's art and thought. Her new book *Tolstoy as Philosopher* is coming out in October 2022. She is also completing *Tolstoy and the Fates of the Twentieth Century*, a big archival project with Princeton University Press.

PRISCILLA MEYER received her Ph.D. from Princeton University and was Professor of Russian Literature at Wesleyan University for 50 years. Her books include *Dostoevsky and Gogol: Prose and Criticism* (1979), *Find What the Sailor Has Hidden: Nabokov's Pale Fire* (1988), *How the Russians Read the French: Lermontov, Dostoevsky and Tolstoy* (2008), and *Nabokov and Indeterminacy: The Case of The Real Life of Sebastian Knight* (2018). She wrote the foreword to the Signet classics edition of *Anna Karenina*.

DANIEL MOULIN-STOŻEK is Assistant Professor at the University of Cambridge Faculty of Education and Fellow in Education at Jesus College, Cambridge. He works in the fields of religious studies, ethics, and the philosophy of education. His interest in Tolstoy's philosophy was first kindled when he found a 1930s pocket edition of *On Life* in a local library.

THOMAS NEWLIN is Professor of Russian at Oberlin College, where he is also affiliated with the Environmental Studies Program. He is author of *The Voice in the Garden: Andrei Bolotov and the Anxieties of Russian Pastoral, 1738–1833*. He has published articles on Tolstoy in *Slavic Review* and *Russian Review*, and is currently working on a book titled *Tolstoy: A Natural History*.

WILLIAM NICKELL is a comparative cultural historian and specialist on Tolstoy at the University of Chicago, where he is Associate Professor of Russian Literature and Chair of Slavic Languages and Literatures. His forthcoming companion volume for *War and Peace* will be a guide for its lone readers, offering background, close readings, and interpretive strategies. It follows *The Death of Tolstoy: Russia on the Eve, Astapovo Station, 1910*, which uses media coverage of the dramatic story of Tolstoy's death as a lens for examining Russian culture in the years between the Russian revolutions of 1905 and 1917. His work in cultural history focuses on media studies, cultural production, and medical aesthetics.

DONNA TUSSING ORWIN is a professor in the Department of Slavic Languages and Literatures at the University of Toronto and a fellow of the Royal Society of Canada. A specialist on Leo Tolstoy and Russian psychological prose, she has published three monographs, four edited volumes, and many articles. She was editor of *Tolstoy Studies Journal* from 1997 to 2005. She also works on war and Russian culture, and is completing an anthology of primary sources on this subject for Columbia University Press. She is a 2008 recipient of the Pushkin Medal for her contribution "to the study and popularisation of Russian language and culture."

RANDALL A. POOLE is Professor of Intellectual History at the College of St. Scholastica and a fellow of the Center for the Study of Law and Religion at Emory University. He is the translator and editor of *Problems of Idealism: Essays in Russian Social Philosophy* (2003) and co-editor of five other volumes, including *A History of Russian Philosophy, 1830–1930: Faith, Reason, and the Defense of Human Dignity* (2010), *Religious Freedom in Modern Russia* (2018), and *The Oxford Handbook of Russian Religious Thought* (2020). He is also the author of many articles and book chapters on Russian intellectual history, philosophy, and religion.

FRANCESCA SILANO is Assistant Professor of History at Houghton University. She has published a number of articles on the history of the Russian Orthodox Church in late Imperial and early Soviet Russia. She is also co-editor of a forthcoming volume on religion and the Russian Revolution. She is currently completing a monograph on the clash between Patriarch Tikhon, the leader of the Russian Orthodox Church from 1917 to 1925, and the fledgling Soviet state.

SUVIJ SUDERSHAN is a Ph.D. candidate in the English Department at Yale University. His field of study is comparative literature, with a particular focus on the vernacular – Hindi, Urdu, and Bengali – and anglophone writings of twentieth-century South Asia. His M.A. thesis researched how urbanization in post-1990s India has been represented through changing images of "small towns" in novelistic fiction. His work has been published in *The Economic and Political Weekly* and *Africa Is a Country*.

MARIA TAROUTINA received a Ph.D. in Art History from Yale University and is Associate Professor of Art History at Yale–NUS College in Singapore. She is the author of *The Icon and the Square: Russian*

Modernism and the Russo-Byzantine Revival, which was awarded the 2019 USC Book Prize in Literary and Cultural Studies by the Association for Slavic, East European, and Eurasian Studies. She has also co-edited two volumes, *Byzantium/Modernism: The Byzantine as Method in Modernity* (2015) and *New Narratives of Russian and East European Art: Between Traditions and Revolutions* (2019). Her work has been featured in the *Slavic Review*, *Tretyakov Gallery Magazine*, and *Experiment: A Journal of Russian Culture*. She is currently working on two new book projects: a monograph on Mikhail Vrubel, and a study of Russian orientalist painting, tentatively titled *Exotic Aesthetics: Art, Race, and Representation in Imperial Russia*.

JULIA VAINGURT is Associate Professor of Russian Studies at the University of Illinois at Chicago. She is the author of *Wonderlands of the Avant-Garde: Technology and the Arts in Russia of the 1920s* (2013) and co-editor, with Colleen McQuillen, of *The Human Reimagined: Posthumanism in Russia* (2018) and, with William Nickell, of *Nestandart: Zabytye eksperimenty v sovetskoi kul'ture, 1934–1964* (2021).

MARGARITA VAYSMAN is Lecturer (Assistant Professor) and Head of the Russian Department at the University of St Andrews, Scotland. She is the author of *Self-Conscious Realism: Metafiction and the Nineteenth-Century Russian Novel* (2021) and editor of the collected volume *Russkii realizm: Obschestvo, znanie, povestvovanie* (2019). She specializes in Russian and Ukrainian literary history, celebrity, and gender studies.

ILYA VINITSKY is a professor of Russian in the Slavic Department at Princeton University. His main fields of expertise are Russian Romanticism, Tolstoy, Dostoevsky, and the history of emotions. His books include *Vasily Zhukovsky's Romanticism and the Emotional History of Russia* (2015), *Ghostly Paradoxes: Modern Spiritualism and Russian Culture in the Age of Realism* (2009), *A Cultural History of Russian Literature*, co-written with Andrew Wachtel (2009), and *The Count of Sardinia: Dmitry Khvostov and Russian Culture* (2017, in Russian). He is currently working on a book about the cultural values of mystifications, including a chapter on forgeries of Tolstoy's works.

ANDREI ZORIN is a professor and Chair of Russian at the University of Oxford, and Fellow of New College. He works on the history of Russian literature and culture in the eighteenth and nineteenth centuries. He has published *Leo Tolstoy: A Critical Life* (2020), *On the Periphery of Europe: The Self-Invention of the Russian Elite, 1762–1825* (2018, co-authored with Andreas Schönle), *The Emergence of a Hero: Russian Emotional Culture of the Late Eighteenth to early Nineteenth Centuries* (2016, in Russian), *By Fables Alone: Russian Literature and Official Ideology in Late Eighteenth- and Early Nineteenth-Century Russia* (2014 in English, 2001 in Russian).

Preface

Lev Tolstoy was not only a very great writer but also – with the rise of new forms of mass media at the end of the nineteenth century – the first to enjoy world celebrity during his lifetime. It would be difficult to overstate the reach of his influence; likened to a second Tsar in Russia and attaining prophet-like status around the globe, Tolstoy made an impact on literature and the arts, religion, philosophy, and politics. His novels and shorter fiction both responded to and helped to reshape the European and Russian literary traditions. His nonfiction incensed readers and drew a massive following, turning Tolstoy into an important religious force as well as a stubborn polemicist in many fields. He was an indefatigable letter-writer in four languages. From his famous correspondence with Gandhi and his impact on the Indian independence movement to his aid in relocating the Doukhobors to Canada, from his correspondence with abolitionists in America to his polemics with scientists in the periodical press, Tolstoy's life and thought engaged a vast array of national and international contexts of his times. The aim of this volume is to introduce readers to those contexts and to situate Tolstoy – the man and the writer – in the rich and tumultuous period in which his thought and creative output came to fruition.

Tolstoy was born in 1828 on his family's gentry estate that ran on serf labor. He died in 1910, less than a decade before the Bolshevik Revolution. This gargantuan life – eighty-two years – was characterized by abundance: wealth and privilege, fecund family with dozens of children and grandchildren, voluminous output of writing, vociferous reading in many fields, and tremendous guilt and self-torment. To fully appreciate Tolstoy's writing and beliefs as well as the impact they had, one needs to be familiar with the historical realities in which he lived – social, cultural, political, scientific – as well as the intellectual waters he swam in through his reading, correspondence, and face-to-face discussions. His contacts were numerous even when he was ensconced on his estate, where the family hosted a constant stream of visitors from many countries. This breadth of context is a tall order for a single volume to cover.

Tolstoy's life and writing are difficult to separate. Therefore, the volume opens with a section on "The Man" that provides necessary biographical background: an overview of the life, with attention to the way Tolstoy's outlook was shaped by his constant awareness of death. Tolstoy's noble ancestry and the rights and privileges presumed by it were crucial to forming his worldview, as was the experience of family life on his beloved family estate of Yasnaya Polyana.

During Tolstoy's very long life, the structure of Russian society and politics changed radically. Thus, the second section, "Russian Social and Political Contexts," is the longest, introducing the reader to the essential historical, political, and cultural features of the Russian landscape. Tolstoy was at one and the same time a great radical and a great conservative. The chapters in this section contextualize his idiosyncratic views by exploring his fraught relationship with the Orthodox Church, the legal and political systems, and shifting discourse about the "Woman Question." The contexts span from major historical events and institutions, like "War and the Military" or "Emancipation and the Great Reforms," to the more intimate, but no less significant topics of "Clothing" or "The Family." Chapters in this and later sections are designed to help readers better appreciate the references and allusions that appear in Tolstoy's works (e.g. the significance of characters' sartorial choices, mentions of the new zemstvo governing bodies, Darwinian theory, or Buddhist ideas).

The third section covers "Literature, the Arts, and Intellectual Life," arguably Tolstoy's primary profession. This section looks at education, Russian literary evolution, European literature, and also at other art media about which Tolstoy had passionate opinions, from theater to music to the visual arts. It is followed by a closely related section on "Science and Technology." Tolstoy wrote a series of articles that treated art and science together, and his critiques of both were based on the same principles.

The final two sections of the volume pan out in space and time, first to the broader world context in "Beyond Russia," and then to "Tolstoy's Afterlife." Tolstoy actively corresponded in several languages with famous persons and causes around the world, so the "Beyond Russia" chapters explore both what he absorbed from these contacts and also what he contributed to various international movements. And finally, "Tolstoy's Afterlife" attends to Tolstoy's words and ideas as they reach us today. It begins with the colossal Soviet project of creating a "Complete Works," which resulted in the ninety-volume scholarly edition that Tolstoy scholars rely on for accessing Tolstoy's writings. It then turns to translation and the challenge facing those who create English-language versions of Tolstoy's texts. Yet text is not the only means of engaging with the creative legacy of Tolstoy. The final chapters explore Tolstoy's evolving position and stature in world culture as his works are adapted into different media – film, opera, musical, etc. – and as he, in turn, becomes the subject of films, biographies, and artworks.

Readers may be surprised not to find a section devoted specifically to religion. This is by design, and is in keeping with Tolstoy's own views. Tolstoy saw religion as integral to all aspects of life. Focusing primarily on its moral and ethical components, he believed religious convictions should inform the projects of science and art and the shaping of societal institutions. Several chapters – "The Russian Orthodox Church," "Eastern Religions," "English Varieties of Religious Experience" – are explicitly about Tolstoy's relationship with various world religions, but his religious views also feature prominently in the chapters on the Tolstoyans, Pacifism, and the Doukhobors, India, science, and the arts. Indeed, the religious quest is present in all chapters of this volume as they address the basic Tolstoyan questions: how must I live? and what must I do? The answer is always informed by the context.

Acknowledgments

This volume was written in 2020–1, one of the most challenging times imaginable for scholars. I am deeply grateful to the thirty-eight contributors who came together to produce this book, overcoming countless obstacles: losing access to their offices and books, canceled research trips to Russia, lack of childcare, the time burden of revamping and teaching courses by remote delivery, caretaking duties for relatives, and fights with the coronavirus. The volume is a testament to their dedication to Tolstoy.

I am especially grateful to Caryl Emerson, Donna Orwin, and Inessa Medzhibovskaya, who offered expert feedback on many aspects of the volume from the preface to further readings. Rose FitzPatrick provided meticulous copy-editing for citations and transliterations.

Thanks to Bethany Thomas, George Laver, and their team at Cambridge University Press for expertly guiding the volume through the publication process. Katie Idle offered invaluable help in navigating image permissions. And finally, thank you to my family and friends for benevolently humoring my constant references to Tolstoy in all contexts.

Anna A. Berman

Note on Citations, Translations, and Transliterations

Unless otherwise noted, all citations of Tolstoy's texts in Russian are from the Jubilee Edition, whose history is described in Chapter 35: *Polnoe sobranie sochinenii (iubileinoe izdanie)*, 90 vols. (Moscow: Gosudarstvennoe izdatel'stvo "Khudozhestvennaia literatura", 1928–59). They are included parenthetically in the text with volume and page number (e.g. 19:348). For the long works – *War and Peace* and *Anna Karenina* – the volume, part, and chapter number are also indicated to facilitate locating passages in different editions.

There is no universally agreed-upon standard English translation of Tolstoy's works, so contributors have made their own choices when citing from translations. These are indicated in the chapter endnotes.

Transliterations in the body of the text and notes follow the Library of Congress system, except in the case of proper names, for which we are using a modified system to make them more familiar to anglophone readers. The –y ending is used instead of –ii and –ya instead of -ia (e.g. Volkonsky, Tolstaya) and Ya/Yu is used instead of Ia/Iu at the start of names (e.g. Yasnaya Polyana). At the end of names, -ai/-ei is used instead of –ay/-ey (e.g. Nikolai, Timofei). The letter ë is transliterated as yo (i.e. Fyodor, Pyotr). In the middle of names x is used instead of ks (Alexander). Soft signs are omitted (e.g. Nikolenka, not Nikolen'ka). Well-known spellings are used for famous names (e.g. Tchaikovsky instead of Chaikovsky), and Tsars' names are anglicized (Nicholas II, Peter the Great).

Chronology

This chronology is designed to place Tolstoy's life and works in the context of Russian and world history and literature. The left column provides key events in Tolstoy's life and writing. The center column provides the Russian historical and literary context, and the right column expands to the wider world. Entries are highly selective, focusing on the events most important to Tolstoy and the topics covered in this volume. For a more detailed chronology of Tolstoy's life without the wider world context, see *The Cambridge Companion to Tolstoy*.

Date	Tolstoy's Life and Works	Russian Literature and History	World Literature and History
1825		Nicholas I ascends the throne (r. 1825–1855); Decembrist uprising	
1828	Lev Nikolaevich Tolstoy born August 28 at the family estate of Yasnaya Polyana		
1830	Death of Tolstoy's mother, Maria Nikolaevna née Volkonskaya	Polish Rebellion (1830–31)	
1832			George Sand's first novel *Indiana*
1834		Beginning of Imam Shamil's rebellion in the Caucasus (lasts until 1859)	
1836	Tolstoy family moves to Moscow	P. Ia. Chadaaev's *First Philosophical Letter* published in *Telescope*	
1837	Death of Tolstoy's father, Nikolai Ilyich Tolstoy; Lev and his siblings placed under the care of aunts	Death of Pushkin	Start of Queen Victoria's reign in England (reigns 1837–1901); commercial telegraph patented
			Stendhal's *The Charterhouse of Parma*
1839	Moves with siblings to Kazan		
1841			
1842		Gogol's *Dead Souls*; Construction begins on the railway line linking Moscow and St. Petersburg (completed 1851)	
1844	Enters the university in Kazan, first studying oriental languages, then transferring to the Faculty of Law		
1846		Dostoevsky publishes his first novel, *Poor Folk*	

(cont.)

Date	Tolstoy's Life and Works	Russian Literature and History	World Literature and History
1847	Begins keeping first diary while hospitalized for venereal disease; May, withdraws from the university and returns to Yasnaya Polyana, which he has inherited	Herzen emigrates, first to Italy and then ultimately settles in London (1852)	Thackeray's *Vanity Fair* (1847–48); Charlotte Brontë's *Jane Eyre*
1848	(1848–9) Spends time in Moscow and St. Petersburg, then returns to Yasnaya Polyana to open a school for peasant children		Revolutions across Europe; Publication of Marx and Engels' *The Communist Manifesto*
1849			Dickens' *David Copperfield* (1849–50)
1851	April, travels to the Caucasus with older brother, Nikolai, who is serving as an artillery officer; begins writing *Childhood*		
1852	Joins the artillery in the North Caucasus as a cadet; *Childhood* published		Stowe's *Uncle Tom's Cabin*
1853		Start of the Crimean War (1853–56); Herzen set up the Free Russian Press in London	
1854	Promoted to ensign; loses the ancestral house at Yasnaya Polyana as a gambling debt; November, transferred to the Crimean front; *Boyhood* published		
1855	Participates in the defense of Sevastopol; Publishes "Sevastopol in December" and "Sevastopol in May"; November, moves to St. Petersburg, where he lives with Turgenev	Death of Nicholas I; Alexander II takes the throne (reigns 1855–81)	Trollope's *The Warden*, first in the Barchester chronicles; Whitman's *Leaves of Grass*

1856	Death of brother, Dmitry, from tuberculosis; sends in his resignation from the army; publishes "A Landowner's Morning"	Turgenev publishes his first novel, *Rudin*	Flaubert's *Madame Bovary*
1857	Travels in Europe; March 25, deeply affected by witnessing an execution in Paris; *Youth* published	Herzen and Ogaryov begin publishing a weekly newspaper, *The Bell* (1857–67)	Start of British Empire in India (Crown rule lasts 1858–1947)
1858	Begins affair with peasant at Yasnaya Polyana, Aksinya Bazykina, which continues up to his marriage; she bears him an illegitimate son, Timofei, who becomes a coachman on the estate		
1859	"Three Deaths" and *Family Happiness* published	Goncharov's *Oblomov*	George Eliot's *Adam Bede*; Darwin's *On the Origin of Species* (first translated into Russian 1864)
1860	Death of brother, Nikolai, from tuberculosis while he and Tolstoy are traveling together in Europe		
1861		Emancipation of the serfs	Outbreak of the American Civil War (1861–1865)
1862	Working on pedagogy and his journal, *Yasnaya Polyana*; many schools for peasants set up in his area; while away visiting Samara province to drink *kumys* for his health, the authorities raid *Yasnaya Polyana* to look for radical materials; September 16, proposes to Sofia Andreevna Behrs (age 18); the couple marries September 23	Turgenev's *Fathers and Children*	Hugo's *Les Misérables*

Date	Tolstoy's Life and Works	Russian Literature and History	World Literature and History
1863	June 28, birth of son Sergei, first of thirteen children borne by Sofia Andreevna (ten live to adulthood); publishes *The Cossacks*; begins work on *War and Peace*	N. G. Chernyshevsky's *What Is to Be Done?*; Sechenov's *Reflexes of the Brain*	US President Lincoln issues the Emancipation Proclamation
1864		Establishment of *Zemstvo* governing bodies; Judicial reform	Trollope's *Can You Forgive Her?* (1864–65), first of the Palliser novels
1865	*The Year 1805* (roughly the first volume of what would become *War and Peace*) published in *Russian Herald*		
1866		Dostoevsky's *Crime and Punishment* (overlaps with *War and Peace* in the *Russian Herald*)	
1867	Changes title to *War and Peace*; visits battlefield at Borodino		Zola's *Thérèse Raquin*
1869	*War and Peace* published in six volumes; experiences his "Arzamas terror" while spending the night there on the way to visit land for purchase	Mendeleev formulates the Periodic Table of Elements	J. S. Mill's *The Subjection of Women*
1870	Has the first idea for *Anna Karenina*		Outbreak of the Franco-Prussian War (1870–1)
1871		First exhibition by the *Peredvizhniki* ("The Wanderers")	Eliot's *Middlemarch* (1871–72); Darwin's *The Descent of Man* (first Russian translation the same year)
1872	Seeing the body of a neighbor's mistress who has thrown herself under a train gives Tolstoy the idea for the ending of *Anna Karenina*; publishes "Prisoner of the Caucasus" and "God Sees the Truth But Waits"		

1873	Begins writing *Anna Karenina*	First Impressionist exhibition in Paris
1874	Made a member of the Academy of Sciences	Premier of Musorgsky's opera *Boris Godunov*
1875	*Anna Karenina* begins serial publication in *Russian Herald*; continues serial publication through 1877, but editor Katkov refuses to publish Part VIII	
1876		Alexander Graham Bell patents the telephone; Wagner's *Ring Cycle* first performed in its entirety
1877		Russo-Turkish War (1877–78); Premier of Tchaikovsky's *Swan Lake* — Edison invents the phonograph; Zola's *L'Assommoir* (from *Les Rougon-Macquart* series, 1871–93)
1878	*Anna Karenina* published as single edition, including Part VIII; undergoing spiritual crisis	
1879	Writes most of *Confession*, though the work is not completed until 1882	
1880	Begins writing a *Translation and Harmonization of the Four Gospels*	Dostoevsky's final novel, *The Brothers Karamazov*
1881	Deeply saddened by the death of Dostoevsky (even though the two had never met)	Assassination of Alexander II by terrorists; Alexander III becomes Tsar (reigns 1881–94); wave of pogroms — James' *The Portrait of a Lady*
1882	Participates in the Moscow census, which provides the material for several works on urban poverty; *A Confession* banned from publication in Russia, but begins circulating illegally (eventually published in Geneva, 1884)	Abolition of the state monopoly on theater — Beginning of the Triple Alliance of Germany, Austria-Hungary, and Italy (lasted on and off until 1915)

(*cont.*)

Date	Tolstoy's Life and Works	Russian Literature and History	World Literature and History
1883	Gives Sofia Andreevna the legal right to conduct his business affairs; meets Vladimir Chertkov, who will become his most important disciple		
1884	Establishes publishing house, The Intermediary, with Chertkov; *What I Believe* published in January, but then the copies seized from printing house in February (it does not appear in Russia until 1906)		
1885		First congress of the Society of Russian Physicians	Guy de Maupassant's *Bel-Ami*
1886	*The Death of Ivan Ilyich* and "How Much Land Does a Man Need?" published		
1887	*The Power of Darkness* published		Conan Doyle's first Sherlock Holmes story
1888	First meets Aylmer Maude, who will become his major English language biographer and also translator; March, birth of last child, Ivan (Vanya); December, birth of first grandchild, Anna (daughter of his son Ilya)		
1889	Writes *The Kreutzer Sonata* and begins work on his final novel, *Resurrection*		Completion of the Eiffel Tower

1891	Becomes a vegetarian; gives up alcohol; renounces copyright on all his works published before 1881; beginning September 1891 (through June 1893) the Tolstoy family organizes and participates in famine relief in the Tula, Riazan, and Orlov provinces	Severe famine in the provinces
1892	Finishes writing *The Kingdom of God is Within You* (sends it abroad for publication)	Premier of Tchaikovsky's *Nutcracker*
1894		Death of Alexander III; Nicholas II becomes Tsar (reigns 1894–1917)
1895	Learns to ride a bicycle; first meets Chekhov	Doukhobors' Burning of the Weapons (June 29–30)
1896	Begins writing *Hadji Murat*	Premier of Chekhov's *The Seagull*
1898	Publishes *What Is Art?*; finishes work on *Father Sergius* (published posthumously)	
1899	Publishes *Resurrection* and donates the proceeds to help the Doukhobors emigrate to Canada	
1901	Formally separated from the Russian Orthodox Church	
1903	Protests pogroms against the Jews in Kishinev; working on *Hadji Murat* (will continue to work on it at least through 1905, published posthumously)	Split of the Russian Social Democratic Labour Party into Bolshevik and Menshevik factions
1904	Writes anti-war tract "Bethink Yourselves!" in response to the outbreak of the Russo-Japanese War; August 23, death of brother Sergei	Outbreak of the Russo-Japanese War (1904–05)

(cont.)

Date	Tolstoy's Life and Works	Russian Literature and History	World Literature and History
1905		Blood Sunday leads to the Revolution of 1905; Establishment of the first State Duma of the Russian Empire (dissolved 1906)	Einstein publishes his theory of relativity; Upton Sinclair's *The Jungle*
1908	Receives dictaphone from Thomas Edison; publishes "I Cannot Be Silent," arguing against the death penalty		
1909	Writes a will giving rights to all his works to his daughter Alexandra, who is on bad terms with Sofia Andreevna and closely aligned with Chertkov		Gandhi's *Indian Home Rule*
1910	October 28, flight from home in the middle of the night; October 31 takes ill on the train and disembarks at the station Astapovo; dies at the stationmaster's home November 7 with a crowd of international news media waiting outside; buried at his estate of Yasnaya Polyana		Gandhi establishes "Tolstoy Farm" in South Africa (1910–1913)

PART I

The Man

CHAPTER I

The Life

Andrei Zorin

Readers often expect the "lives" of famous authors to explain their "works." In Tolstoy's case the reverse perspective is arguably even more essential since he always regarded his prose and philosophical writings as means for personal development. Moreover, in his "lived experience" Tolstoy embodied the fundamental Romantic mythology of the modern age, which synthesizes the biblical myths of the Lost Paradise and the Prodigal Son with the classical myth of the Golden Age. According to M.H. Abrams, Romantic vision "represents man's fall from happy unity into the evil of increasing division and suffering as an indispensable stage on his route back towards the lost unity and happiness of the origin."[1] Tolstoy's life was full of abrupt ruptures perceived both as an exile and as an escape. He longed to leave behind the confines of his social upbringing, his earthly pursuits and fame, his family, and finally his mortal body in an ardent desire to return home to the eternal and universal unity of "general life." His vision of this unity underwent many changes but his urge to join it was always unwavering.

Count Lev Nikolaevich Tolstoy was born on August 28, 1828 on his family estate of Yasnaya Polyana, near the city of Tula, located 120 miles south of Moscow. The expansive and beautiful estate initially belonged to his maternal grandfather Prince Sergei Volkonsky, a scion of one of the most aristocratic families in the Russian Empire (see Chapter 3). The marriage to Princess Maria Volkonskaya, a rich heiress, saved Count Nikolai Tolstoy, the writer's father, who was mired in debt, from imminent ruin. Lev was the fourth and last son of the couple. Tolstoy's mother died two years later after giving birth to her only daughter. Young Lev did not remember his mother, but always cherished her memory and, as he confessed, "in his middle age ... prayed to her soul and asked her for help" (34:354).

This loss, followed by the sudden death of his father in 1837 when young Tolstoy was not yet nine years of age, had a huge impact on the

sensitive boy known to his relatives as a "cry baby." Lev lagged behind his
siblings in his studies and felt his physical unattractiveness very strongly;
until his marriage he was not sure that any woman could fall in love with
such an ugly person. In memoirs from the latter years of his life, Tolstoy
wrote that "since the time he remembered himself, the death of his mother
had already cast its shadow upon the life of the family," but at the same
time described his childhood as "bright, tender, poetic, loving, mysterious," a time full of "true anticipation or retrospective feeling of the real
depth of life" (34:354, 375). The latter perspective reflects the Romantic
notion of childhood as a time of paradisical innocence, fullness of being,
and union with God and nature.

Primordial bliss was to be ended, however, by original sin. Tolstoy was
expelled from his paradise in 1841 when his aunt and legal guardian
Alexandra Osten-Saken died at Yasnaya Polyana. As a result, he and his
siblings were transferred to the city of Kazan to live under the guardianship
of another aunt, Polina Yushkova. Here he spent his teenage years, a
period marked by the conflict between his powerful sexuality and his no
less powerful desire for chastity. Having been introduced to paid sex by his
elder brother at the age of fifteen, Tolstoy recalled weeping after losing his
virginity. The fall implied efforts at redemption and self-improvement. In
Kazan, Tolstoy began the diaries he would keep on and off for more than
sixty years. He subjected his deeds, thoughts, and desires to harsh scrutiny,
condemning his own self for a failure to abide by the highest moral ideals
he had set.

Kazan was a university city and home to a huge Tatar population, the
biggest Muslim minority in Russia. In 1844 Tolstoy was admitted to the
Faculty of Oriental Languages. He excelled at languages but performed
poorly in many other subjects. Paradoxically for the future author of the
one of the most famous historical novels to have ever been written, he
struggled with Russian history, and was reluctant to memorize dates and
names that made no sense to him. To avoid resitting his exams, he
transferred to the Law Faculty but did not succeed there either. In
1847 when the family estates were divided between the five siblings,
Tolstoy inherited Yasnaya Polyana and headed there without completing
his course.

A military career was the natural choice for a Russian nobleman. In
1851, after four years of a mostly dissipated life between Yasnaya Polyana,
Tula, and Moscow, Tolstoy joined his officer brother Nikolai and set off
for the Caucasus where Russia was fighting rebellious local tribes. He spent
more than two years in the Cossack settlement of Starogladkovskaya, first

as an intern of sorts, and then as an artillery officer participating in raids and clashes. Wild mountain nature and the primitive life shared by the Cossacks and the tribesmen became for him the new incarnation of his Lost Paradise. Tolstoy's daily routine in Starogladkovskaya allowed him time for leisure that he used not only for gambling and womanizing, but also for literary pursuits. His story *Childhood* published in 1852 in *Sovremennik* (*The Contemporary*), the most popular literary magazine in Russia, brought him national fame (see Chapter 16).

In 1853 the Crimean War began. Tolstoy applied for a transfer to the battlefield and in November 1854 he joined Russian troops in Sevastopol, besieged by the Anglo-French coalition. Tolstoy was a brave and diligent, but not very disciplined, officer (see Chapter 11). Often he used to leave his brigade on quiet days to participate in clashes elsewhere and constantly argued with his superiors. This military experience was much more horrifying than anything he could have seen in the Caucasus and gave rise to the passionate pacifism that inspired his *Sevastopol Stories*. The publication of this cycle transformed an aspiring beginner into an acknowledged star of Russian literature. In the autumn of 1855 Tolstoy left military service and went to St. Petersburg to enjoy his newly acquired literary glory. On his way he lost an enormous sum at the card table and had to sell the mansion at Yasnaya Polyana to pay the debt – the house was disassembled and moved to the neighboring estate. For the rest of his life Tolstoy lived in one of the remaining two wings of the manor.

In St. Petersburg, Tolstoy was greeted by the leading authors of the day, and he both enjoyed and loathed his newfound fame. In 1857 he went for a European tour. In Paris he enjoyed theatres and concerts but became critical of "mechanistic" European civilization more generally. Appalled by witnessing a public execution, he rejected not only capital punishment, but the modern state that legislated institutionalized violence; he described the state "as a conspiracy not only to exploit, but above all to corrupt its citizens" (60:168). He left Paris for Switzerland to wander in the mountains in the footsteps of his beloved Rousseau, then went to Germany but, having lost a lot of money at the roulette table in Baden-Baden, had to cut his trip short and return to Russia.

Russian society was preparing for the imminent abolition of serfdom. Tolstoy tried to create an ideal model of emancipation on his estate but encountered the nearly fatal inability of educated nobles and peasants to understand each other. To overcome this gap in communication, he launched a major educational program for peasant children. He opened a school in Yasnaya Polyana and more than twenty in neighboring villages, launched a pedagogical magazine, and tried to organize a national society for education (see Chapter 17). Asserting his identity as an educator, he stopped publishing literary works and tried to conceal his writings from his friends. In 1860 he left Russia to study the practices of popular schools in Europe, an experience which left him profoundly disappointed since he witnessed how Europeans were using the same disciplinary methods he had observed and loathed at home.

The emancipation manifesto of February 19, 1861 caught him on his way back. Having arrived at Yasnaya Polyana, he accepted the position of civic arbiter responsible for resolving conflicts between newly emancipated peasants and landlords. He mostly failed in this office as peasants would not listen to his arguments, while nobles hated him with a passion; in spring 1862 he resigned from this post. His successful pedagogical activities also had to stop. In July, at a time when he was absent from his estate, his property was raided by the gendarmes searching for illegal printing presses. Nothing suspicious was found, but the police turned the house and the village upside down, scared his relatives, and read his intimate papers. The incensed writer even considered leaving Russia forever, but instead made an entirely different, but no less momentous, decision.

In Romantic mythology a soul exiled from the paradise of childhood had a chance to regain the fullness of being through love. In the house of his friend, the Moscow doctor Andrei Behrs, Tolstoy was captivated by a vision of the happy family he had never had a chance to experience. In August 1862 he asked a perennial question in his diary: whether his feeling for Andrei's daughter, the then eighteen-year-old Sofia Behrs, "a child" as he called her, amounted to "true love." He quickly answered in the affirmative but was still afraid to propose as he "demanded from marriage something terrible, impossible" – to be loved as he could love (83:4). Finally, he handed Sofia a letter pleading with her to make her decision without haste. She accepted, as she later confessed, without having read the letter in question apart from the sentence "Do you want to be my wife?"[2] Contrary to all customs, the wedding at Tolstoy's insistence took place a week after the engagement. According to Sofia's memoirs, the marriage was consummated in the sleeping carriage taking the couple from Moscow to Yasnaya Polyana. Their first child, Sergei, was born in June 1863 followed by twelve other siblings, five of whom died in childhood.

Having closed his school, Tolstoy shared his time between running his estate and writing. He aspired to establish direct bonds with the peasants, personally performing all managerial duties. In the novel he started to write at this time, he brought together family chronicle and national epic to describe the same ideal bond that, as he believed, emerged between peasants and nobles during the war of 1812. Sofia helped him in both endeavors, keeping financial records and copying drafts of his novel. The first installment of *War and Peace* appeared in 1865 in the journal *Russkii Vestnik* (*Russian Herald*), though Tolstoy would soon switch to publishing new installments in book form. The publication was completed in 1869. Some critics were confused by the novelty of the text, but the public was more than enthusiastic. While the results of Tolstoy's agricultural entrepreneurship were mixed, his novel enjoyed a major success which solidified his reputation as a leading Russian writer of the time and significantly enhanced the well-being of his family.

However, Tolstoy was deeply dissatisfied by his work and even called his novel "verbose nonsense." In August 1869 he travelled to Penza province to buy land. In the coach inn at the little town of Arzamas he fell into a state of unbearable panic. The acute feeling of his mortality rendered life and its endeavors useless. This crisis led to a prolonged depression and was aggravated by family problems. In 1871 Sofia gave birth to their fifth child. The pregnancy and the delivery were extremely difficult, and the doctors strongly advised against further pregnancies, but Tolstoy adamantly refused to hear about any contraceptive measures since he considered them an abomination worse than death. Sofia gave birth to eight more children, but the resentment caused by her husband's stance never completely healed.

Struggling with a feeling of failure in his mission, Tolstoy reverted to pedagogical activities. He reopened in his house the school for peasant children and composed an "ABC Book" that included new methods in the teaching of basic literacy, and a primer containing texts which gave rudimentary lessons in the natural sciences and morality. The reaction of the pedagogical community to his innovations was mostly negative, but the lower classes acquired the books for their children with great zeal. In Tolstoy's lifetime the collected print runs of both publications exceeded 2 million copies.

At the same time, he could not completely leave literature behind. Tolstoy initially thought about writing dramatic works and studied Ancient Greek to better appreciate classical tragedy. Following this, he planned and drafted historical novels about the time of Peter the Great and the exile of the Decembrists in Siberia. However, in 1873 he found himself writing a new novel about life in contemporary high society. The publication of *Anna Karenina* started in January 1875 in the *Russian Herald* and continued for two years. Tolstoy kept re-editing and rewriting his drafts, and the slow rhythm of the publication process also gave the impression that the action was unfolding in real time. The narrative absorbed political, social, and cultural events happening in Russia, including the beginning of the war with the Ottoman Porte. In the last chapter, Tolstoy resoundingly attacked the war and its proponents. The militaristic *Russian Herald* discontinued the publication, and the last installment was published separately in book form.

Despite the ire of progressive critics irritated by Tolstoy's patriarchal views and interest in high society, the excitement of the public and the commercial success of *Anna Karenina* were unheard of in the annals of Russian literature. The following year saw the first French translation of *War and Peace*, which added an international dimension to Tolstoy's fame. And yet, the author was plunged into the deepest existential crisis he had ever experienced. Tolstoy called his novel "dull and vulgar" and later, in his *Confessions*, wrote about how his life was brought to a virtual standstill by a simple question he kept asking himself: "Very well; you will be more famous than Gogol and Pushkin or Shakespeare or Molière or all the writers in the world – and what of it? And I had no reply at all" (23:11).

Neither love, family, nor literature could provide an answer to his question, and Tolstoy turned to religion. Much like Levin in the final pages of *Anna Karenina*, he embraced the faith of his forefathers and the peasants that, as he believed, gave them the ability to accept mortality. His Orthodoxy was fervent and passionate: he fasted, withstood long Church services which involved constant bowing and praying on his knees, made a pilgrimage to Kiev to kiss the relics of the first Russian saints, visited monasteries, and talked to Church elders. Very soon, however, he discovered that Church dogmas and rituals could not satisfy his reason and conscience.

In 1855, in Sevastopol, Tolstoy dreamed about starting "a religion of Christ without mysticism" (47:37), and a quarter of a century later he embarked on this mission. He studied Hebrew and biblical Greek, and devoured enormous amounts of theological literature. He wrote *Confessions*, where he told the history of his conversion, a refutation of the most popular Orthodox catechism, and prepared a new translation and digest of the Gospels. In less than five years he developed a comprehensive religious, moral, political, and economic philosophy that he summarized in his treatise *What I Believe*, a work published, and immediately banned, in 1884. In the spirit of the Sermon on the Mount, Tolstoy preached benevolence towards all humans, chastity, a rejection of all obligations to state authorities and tribal patriotism. These commands and taboos were all based on the principle of nonviolence, a practice that he regarded as the main tenet of his teachings.

In 1881 the need to educate his elder children compelled Tolstoy to buy a house in Moscow. Deeply shocked by sights of urban poverty and hoping to better understand the roots of this social evil as well as the ways to alleviate it, he volunteered to take part in the census of 1882 in one of the most dangerous parts of Moscow, an area which was full of shelters for the homeless and the outcast. For a while he considered launching a major philanthropic initiative, but it failed from the very beginning. In his essay *What Then Must We Do?*, Tolstoy blamed the misery of the poor on the way of life led by the leisured classes, a life based on property rights, coercive taxation, and legitimized violence. He could no longer believe in the necessity or possibility of a bond between the educated elite and the impoverished majority, and instead suggested that the rich should adopt peasant lifestyles and habits.

It took Tolstoy several years to overhaul his own way of life. He began working in the fields and wearing peasant clothes, and he grew a peasant-style beard. He gradually became a vegetarian, and renounced drinking, smoking, and hunting. He dismissed his personal servants and started bringing water to the house on his own, cutting wood, and cleaning his room. He explained each step of this process in passionate articles. His family and his friends were skeptical and even outright hostile, but his teachings and example quickly and powerfully resonated both in Russia and beyond its borders. In 1883 Tolstoy met Vladimir Chertkov, also a converted descendant of a rich and aristocratic family. Chertkov became his most devoted and trusted disciple and his closest confidant. On Tolstoy's advice, he organized Intermediary (Posrednik), a publishing house that specialized in cheap editions of various literature for the public. Chertkov's connections with several British evangelicals helped spread Tolstoy's word globally, and the success of Tolstoy's novels increased the public attention to his teachings. By the end of the 1880s Tolstoy had become the most famous living author in the world and the natural leader for many existing sects and communes practicing agricultural labor and nonviolence.

Tolstoy's glory reached its zenith during the famine of 1891. Overcoming his skepticism toward philanthropy, Tolstoy appealed to individuals and organizations around the world for financial support for the needy, coordinated the relief plan, and published regular reports about the distribution of monetary funds. The enormous sum he and his wife managed to collect in several months allowed them to open 250 kitchens feeding 14,000 adults and several thousand children. A significant part of the donations came from Britain and the USA, with Quakers being especially generous. Russian authorities were fearful of the level of Tolstoy's activity, but could not stop him. The only person deeply dissatisfied was Tolstoy himself who called his relief work "stupid." Incredible human suffering made his own relatively comfortable life especially unbearable in his own eyes.

In 1891 Tolstoy managed to convince his wife to renounce the copyright for all his works published after 1881, the year of his conversion. His earlier publications, including the two great novels, remained her exclusive property. In the following year he renounced his rights as a landowner, but transferred ownership not to the peasants, but to Sofia and their children. This tortured compromise did not satisfy either party. To avoid family conflicts, Tolstoy stopped publishing fiction, the sole exception being the novel *Resurrection*, the income from which he donated to help in the resettling of thousands of persecuted Doukhobors to Canada (see Chapter 29). *Resurrection* was published simultaneously in 1898 in a censured version in Russia and in unredacted form abroad; it was immediately translated into the major European languages. In a year, it reached more readers worldwide than Tolstoy's two great novels did in twenty.

The full version of the novel contained scathing attacks on the Orthodox Church. For a long period, the Russian Church and government had persecuted his friends and followers but did not touch Tolstoy himself for fear of making him a martyr. In 1900 the Holy Synod finally decided to take action (see Chapter 8). The edict, which amounted to a de facto excommunication even if the word itself was not used, expressed a wish for the sinner to repent and return to the bosom of the Church. In his reply Tolstoy stated that he no more could do that "than a flying bird can re-enter the eggshell from which it has emerged" (34:247). This final split with the official Church only gave more power to his voice. During the Russo-Japanese war of 1904–5 and the revolution that erupted after the defeat of the Russian army, he became the only moral authority able to stand above the fray; Tolstoy condemned both sides. He was sure that neither half-hearted political concessions nor "guns, cannons and executions" could save the government, which should at least "admit its sins before the people and try to redeem itself." At the same time, he accused the revolutionaries of being ready "to blow up, destroy and kill" (36:304, 306), and urged millions of Russian peasants not to revert to violence but to start a peaceful campaign of civil disobedience. In 1908, shocked by news of executions of the rebellious peasants, he wrote the pamphlet

I Cannot Be Silent – a passionate denunciation of capital punishment. Tolstoy ended this piece by expressing his desire to be finally imprisoned or hanged like the nameless peasants he was writing about.

In the meantime, the situation in his family became outright tragic. Sofia hated the Tolstoyans who surrounded her husband and especially despised Chertkov, who returned to Russia in 1908 after ten years of exile in Britain. She insisted on controlling Tolstoy's contacts, reading his diaries, staging and censuring his photo ops. Some of their sons threatened to start legal proceedings against their father to invalidate his decision regarding the renouncement of copyright for his works which, in any case, was legal only until Tolstoy's death. To protect free access to his writings, and following Chertkov's advice, Tolstoy drew up a will where he bequeathed all the rights of his works to his daughter, Alexandra, and appointed Chertkov his literary executor. Unable to sustain the tumult that would ensue in the family, Tolstoy signed the document secretly. However, the news regarding the will soon came into the open and the family crisis was aggravated once more: Sofia threatened suicide and repeatedly claimed that she had the necessary means to kill herself at her disposal.

Since his religious conversion, Tolstoy had cherished the idea of leaving home and joining the crowds of wanderers, pilgrims, and beggars that sustained themselves through daily labor and alms. Nonetheless, he stayed with his family, believing that Christian love manifests itself only through love to those who are close to you. On the night of October 28, 1910, after Sofia had searched his room in search of the papers she thought he was hiding, Tolstoy's patience had run its course. He left early the following morning, accompanied by his doctor, and follower, Dushan Makovitsky. Tolstoy did not know where he was heading to; he was only sure that he wanted to spend his last days in a peasant hut, far away from a Tolstoyan commune. Leadership was thus something he resolutely left behind. He visited his sister, Maria, at Shamordino Convent where she was living as a nun, and then, together with Makovitsky and Tolstoy's daughter Alexandra who had joined them, boarded a train heading south. On the train he fell ill, and his companions had to help him disembark at Astapovo railway station.

When recovering from nearly terminal illness in 1886, Tolstoy wrote *On Life*, a treatise where he claimed that any individual existence is just a tiny particle of life, and that death is a necessary and liberating union with the source of universal and eternal love. In the last decades of his life, he was on the very brink of death at least five times. He became accustomed to it and was always "packing for transition" (57:185), as he put it in one of his letters. Tolstoy's one and everlasting wish was to be left to experience this sacred moment alone. This wish was not granted. His death became one of the first global media events, a manifestation of a modernity that he always loathed.

Notes

1 M.H. Abrams, *Natural Supernaturalism: Tradition and Revolution in Romantic Literature* (New York: W.W. Norton, 1973), 201.
2 S.A. Tolstaya, *Dnevniki*, 2 vols. (Moscow: Khudozhestvennaia literature, 1978), vol. II, 489.

CHAPTER 2

The Death

William Nickell

Tolstoy's death was the most spectacular and strange of all Russian deaths. It brought to a close the author's obsession with mortality and long struggle to overcome his fear of it – one that Rilke called a "fear permeated with grandeur, a fugue of fear almost, a huge construction, a tower of fear with gangways, staircases and ledges with no railings and precipices on every side."[1]

Tolstoy entered this tower in his literary debut, *Childhood* (1852), which builds toward the death of the young protagonist's mother. Nikolenka is initiated into the depths of self-consciousness as he realizes that his grief is corrupted by his awareness that it is exalted by others, who are full of sympathy for the orphan. This egoism is tied directly to the problem of death itself, as the nanny, Natalya Savishna, who is unsusceptible to affectations of grieving, prays to join the mother in death. *Childhood* closes with this second death, which introduces a contrast that Tolstoy would continue to trace to the end of his career: where the mother's death is harrowing and brings emotional crisis to the whole family, the nanny's, lacking self-pity, is calm and accepting.

Tolstoy found himself rooted, however, in the consciousness of the mother, and over the course of his career continually tried to write his way out of it. The 1858 story "Three Deaths," which had initially been titled simply "Death," took up this task explicitly. A noblewoman dies miserably and makes everyone suffer her torments, while a peasant awaits his death unquestioningly; the woman flees death, frantically seeking a miracle cure, while the peasant gives up his boots, accepting that he will never need them again. The third death, of a tree falling sublimely in an indifferent forest, figures as the ideal – but it was that of the peasant that Tolstoy continued to cultivate as a model. In a letter of May 1, 1858, he explained the story in terms of truth: the noblewoman lives according to the lies of society and the Church, the peasant looks death in the face, while the tree dies most honestly of all (60:265). Ego-driven self-consciousness, which Tolstoy believes is particular to the propertied classes, obscures the inexorable truth.

In *War and Peace* (1865–9), Andrei Bolkonsky faces his own three deaths, presumed dead at Austerlitz, badly wounded at Borodino, and finally passing in a humble village during the collective flight from Moscow. In the first case he is cut down magnificently beneath an infinite sky that he has seen for the first time, feeling "nothing except silence, tranquility" (9:341/Vol. 1, Pt. 3, Ch. 16).[2] But he is drawn back into life by Napoleon himself, a lion of earthly ambition, and left to contemplate "the insignificance of everything I can comprehend and the grandeur of something incomprehensible but most important" (9:355/Vol. 1, Pt. 3, Ch. 19). When death finally comes, its nearness does not inspire fear: "Twice he had experienced that frightful, tormenting feeling of the fear of death, the end, and now he no longer understood it" (12:60/Vol. 4, Pt. 1, Ch. 16). He watches Natasha worship reverently at the altar of his life, but she is unable to comprehend the sacrament he is taking. Even as she knits at his bedside to provide the "soft silence" he wants, she pulls at him, wanting him to live a life he knows he must accept as lost.

Natasha is still subsumed in the noise of life, which in Tolstoy's works always conflicts with dying: the grieving in *Childhood*, the desperate search for a cure in "Three Deaths," the struggle for the Bezukhov fortune in *War and Peace*, the societal commotion in *The Death of Ivan Ilyich* (1886). But Tolstoy also understood that he himself was not ready for the silence of death, and pointed as evidence to an incident in Arzamas in 1869, when he had woken in the middle of the night in a vault-like room, feeling a terrifying sense of death's presence. Continued thought of inevitable death led to serious bouts with depression, as recounted in *Anna Karenina* (1875–8), which is known as a novel of adultery, but is also a study of suicide – one committed (Anna), another failed (Vronsky), and a third averted by hiding the rope (Levin). Levin is saved through his desperate commitment to find meaning in collective labor, but we are not certain that death can become as natural to him – and to Tolstoy – as the reaping of the grass, which falls effortlessly when the scythe finds the rhythm of the peasants working together in the field.

Tolstoy confronts this doubt bluntly in the *Confession* (1879–82), a long meditation detailing the triumph of death in captivating his mind: "No matter how much you say to me 'you can't understand the meaning of life – don't think, live,' I cannot do that, because I have done that too long already. Now I cannot not see the days and nights running along and leading me to death. I see that alone, because that alone is the truth.

Everything else is a lie" (23:14). Wisdom is found in Socrates, Schopenhauer, Solomon, and Buddha, but the way out is found in imitation of the peasants, who, "in complete contrast to my ignorance," understand the meaning of life and death, and see in it not vanity, but good (23:40).

Confession was but the first part of a four-work cycle, completed in 1884, setting forth a new confessional practice that drew upon folk and wisdom traditions and eschewed the values and beliefs of Tolstoy's own class. He renounced his copyright and rejected the novel as a form ill-suited to preserving the common trust of this knowledge, and began writing simpler literary works, often in the mode of the parable. "How Much Land Does a Man Need?" (1886), which James Joyce called the greatest work in literature, made the economy of Tolstoy's poetics of death clear: the peasant who covets property dies in literal pursuit of it, his body needing only enough land for burial. The apogee of this tendency is found in Alyosha the Pot, who, in the story of the same name, gives up his plans to marry after his master objects, and then in the same manner, when fatally injured, relinquishes his life: "But why not? Will we just live then? It has to happen sometime" (36:57).

Even in works more consistent with his former style, Tolstoy continued to develop this worldview, including in the most influential of his treatments of death, *The Death of Ivan Ilyich*. This long story is part of the world literary canon, and is widely read as a therapeutic guide for its understanding of the stages of grief and the possibility of finding peace in dying. It includes the elements of Tolstoy's essential death fable: the educated, worldly man, a successful jurist, learns through his illness that his former concerns are the stuff of vanity, and becomes increasingly alienated from a family that is still caught up in that world. Understanding comes from the servant Gerasim, a *muzhik*, or peasant of the most common stock, who is an effective caregiver because he does what is necessary in a matter-of-fact way, explaining to a colleague of Ivan Ilyich's: "We'll all come to it someday" (26:68/46).[3] He is the only one who does not lie about what is happening, and thus earns the trust of Ivan Ilyich and is able to comfort him.

The culmination of this effort to bring his view of death into clearer focus is found in the series of wisdom anthologies Tolstoy produced in his last years, beginning with the *Calendar of Proverbs for 1887*, where characteristic Tolstoyan perspectives are found in the authentic language of the folk saying ("The shirt is close to the body, and death closer still"; "To fear death is to not live in the world"). Tolstoy considered these anthologies his most important work, and he focused intensively on them in the 1900s, producing *Thoughts of Wise People for Every Day* (1903), *A Circle of Readings* (1906–8), and *Path of Life* in his last year, 1910, during which he also revised *For Every Day*.[4] He described *Path of Life* as a final synthesis of this project, writing V.A. Posse that it contained the most important thoughts of all, organized in a specific order that had its own intrinsic meaning (45:7–8). The chapters progress toward a group titled "Death," "After Death," and the final section "Life is Good." The "path of life" led toward death, and the anthology insisted that it should be walked with that destination always in mind.

These later works now drew from a global wisdom tradition, which lent credence to Tolstoy's belief in the universality of his discoveries. Tolstoy continued to be convinced that the peasant way of life lent itself to understanding this wisdom, however, and his work to assimilate the language of death wisdom into his own was interwoven with a doctrine of renunciation of privilege and the pursuit of the moral life. This was not only the right way to prepare for death, but also the right way to live, and he continually tried to instill this principle in others.[5] It was death itself which best taught this lesson. On June 16, 1909, Tolstoy told his doctor, Dushan Makovitsky, that being old makes you surprised that people do not think about death, and that it was important even for children to be taught to do so. "If they thought about it, they would see that it is unavoidable. Then the meaning of life would be different; they would lead not just a bodily life, which ends. They would seek a different meaning, which doesn't end with death. They would live morally."[6]

Tolstoy's diaries and notebooks reveal that he himself kept to this advice, developing a set of spiritual maxims that he repeated like a meditation. This catechism is repetitive: he formulates and reformulates, at times simply in a reflexive pattern of writing down his thoughts, but at others clearly working to refine them. This is a confessional practice – the written equivalent of the repetitive prayers of the hesychast or Buddhist – but where others speak a learned prayer, Tolstoy notes down his thoughts as a series of iterative discoveries. "Nearer and nearer I feel the approach of death. Without a doubt my life, and likewise, probably, everyone's becomes more spiritual with the years" (58:33). "How imperceptibly and easily I approach death. And again I am only thankful" (58:66). But these repetitions and reformulations at times suggest that his meditations are in fact unquiet; one frequent formulation was that death was like sleep, through which one lost consciousness on a daily basis – one of many efforts to domesticate death, making it seem natural and unworthy of fear (58:24). What appears in the published works as secured in the wisdom of the ages is in his notebooks provisional, as he struggles with his words and unsilenced uncertainties. On September 7, 1910, just two months before Tolstoy died, Makovitsky observed that even if Tolstoy was mentally prepared for death, he was still physically afraid of it, as evidenced by his hypochondriacal anxiety that he might be developing gangrene.[7]

Tolstoy was approaching death as a confessional problem, and wanted to describe his attitude toward it honestly – as an abiding and overwhelming anxiety, and then as an overcome concern. In his anthological works, the sections on death are full of protest against such anxiety, and represent great effort to overcome it and to help others achieve the same attitude. Trying to both raise consciousness of death and dispel the anxiety that accompanies it, Tolstoy sometimes comes across as a grim reaper, harvesting for the reader an endless series of memento mori. He wrote of the benefit of thinking about the possibility that one could die at any moment (58:16). And, as opposed to monastic tradition, in which such quietism was seen as a practice to be cultivated by a select few who found virtue in pursuing it, Tolstoy suggested that it was necessary for everyone.

He knew that the equanimity he was cultivating was in fact rare among people of his own class – but he found evidence for it in the villages around his estate. Tolstoy visited the deathbeds of nearby peasants, such as Andrei Maslov, a former student at his school, who reported that it was not difficult to await death.[8] In 1908 he made an agreement with his friend and kindred spirit, Maria Schmidt, who was ill and speaking openly about her death: she should summon him if she were going to die, and he would do the same.[9] This death pact was another way of enforcing his commitment to walk this quiet path to the end. On another occasion, feeling weak, he told Schmidt that he would be happy to die, exchanging the "energetic work of thought" for "calm harmony."[10]

At some points such eagerness may have been an index of depression, as Tolstoy's spiritual ruminations were at times mixed with expressions of world-weariness.[11] In April 1909 he expressed shame that he sometimes wished for death – for emancipation from this "disgusting assemblage of atoms."[12] The ideal was not eagerness, but indifference, which became a metric for measuring Tolstoy's spiritual preparedness for death. On February 26, 1910 he observed in his diary: "I am preparing for death, but badly. I'm not indifferent" (58:20). A month later, he appeared to be improving on this front, noting in his diary on March 31: "on the matter of indifference: I do not desire nor do I fear either life or death" (58:31). Pyotr Struve visited Yasnaya Polyana in 1909, and found that, though Tolstoy was physically fit enough to live for years, he was already distant from this world. "Spiritually and in spirit he is already there, where most people arrive only via the grave ... I saw with my own eyes and with trembling sensed that the living Tolstoy stood outside of 'life.'"[13]

But Tolstoy's family life at this time militated against such quiet withdrawal, as a long-standing battle over his estate built toward a climax. He had written a will naming Vladimir Chertkov his literary executor, causing increased strain in his relations with his wife; at the same time, his health was declining. On September 1, 1910 he wrote, and crossed out: "God, my father. ~~I know, th[at] you sent me.~~ Help ~~me do what you want. I will try~~" (58:214). He left his home in the middle of the night on October 28, writing his wife that he was doing what old men of his age usually do: abandoning worldly life to spend his last days in solitude and quiet. The newspapers soon learned of his disappearance, and his family and followers, journalists and the police took up pursuit, finally tracking him down at the remote railway station of Astapovo. He had fallen ill on the train, his destination unknown. Seeking solitude, Tolstoy had provoked the first modern media sensation in Russia, with the press setting up shop right outside the home where he lay dying. Telegraph equipment was brought by train, and the newspapers offered a steady stream of bulletins on his condition. He died ten days after leaving home, at the eye of a storm: secret police, Church officials, and six doctors were in attendance, as was his family. Yet his wife was denied access to preserve his health and peace, creating a scandal that was fully exploited by the papers.

The Orthodox Church, anxious to preserve one of its all-embracing sacraments, made a concerted effort to administer last rites, hoping – as they had in 1901 when they announced Tolstoy's departure from the fold – that the approach of death would cause the lost soul to renounce his heretical views (see Chapter 8). But these overtures were rejected on both occasions, as Tolstoy remained true to his vision of the deathbed as a place of universal, yet personal, confession, where the dying find their own way, without the guidance of a priest or the structure of a ritual, with death itself as the teacher. As unorthodox as his death appeared from outside, it was consistent within the world of his confessional writing, diaries, and letters, where he described persuasive doubts and yearning for faith. And it was consistent with his literary works, where the lessons of the dead are so often incommunicable to the world around. The world surrounding Tolstoy on his deathbed bustled its way forward, reading for its own meanings as it scrambled to acquire his legacy, arguing over whether his departure had been a sincere confessional moment or the final performance of a carefully cultivated persona. Tolstoy had summoned this attention just as persuasively as he had shunned it. He had invited Maria Schmidt to witness his death, but it was the Russian public that came to see what he would make of it.

It is not hard to understand why. Was any other modern death so abundantly anticipated, so forcefully imagined, so repeatedly rehearsed? Had any other writer set such a stage for his end, or written so evocatively of what was at stake? In the passage with which this chapter began, written on the five-year anniversary of Tolstoy's death, Rilke concluded by asking whether the force with which Tolstoy had experienced and described the "tower of fear" surrounding death might have become "its sure foundation, landscape and sky and the wind and flight of birds around it . . ." He evokes "Three Deaths," but also Tolstoy's grave, a simple mound above ground, with no marker but the monument of writing that leads the way there.

Notes

1 Rainer Maria Rilke, "Letter to Lotte Hepner, 8 November 1915," in *Letters of Rainer Maria Rilke*, ed. and trans. Jane Bannard Greene and M.D. Herter Norton, 2 vols. (New York: W.W. Norton, 1945), vol. II, 150–1.
2 *War and Peace*, trans. Richard Pevear and Larissa Volokhonsky (New York: Alfred A. Knopf, 2007).
3 *The Death of Ivan Ilyich and Other Stories*, trans. Richard Pevear and Larissa Volokhonsky (New York: Alfred A. Knopf, 2009).
4 See his letter to N.N. Gusev of June 25, 1910 (82:61).
5 An example: in February 1910 Yu. P. Loktin wrote Tolstoy that after reading his works he had become indifferent to both death and money. Tolstoy had sent *For Every Day*, and wrote Loktin that his response made him very, very happy (58:329, 81:277, 283).
6 S.A. Makashin, M.B. Khrapchenko, and V.P. Shcherbina (eds.), *"Iasnopolianskie zapiski" D. P. Makovitskogo*, Literaturnoe Nasledstvo 90:3 (Moscow: Nauka, 1979), 442.
7 Ibid., 4:345.
8 Ibid., 3:238.
9 Ibid., 3:67.
10 Ibid., 3:94.
11 See Gary Jahn, "Tolstoj's Vision of the Power of Death and 'How Much Land Does a Man Need?'" *Slavic and East European Journal* 22:4 (1978), 442–53.
12 Makashin, Khrapchenko, and Shcherbina (eds.), *"Iasnopolianskie zapiski"*, 3:392.
13 Petr Struve, "Smysl' smerti Tolstogo," in *Russkie mysliteli o L've Tolstom* (Tula: Izdatel'skii dom Yasnaya Polyana, 2002), 227–8.

CHAPTER 3

Tolstoy's Family

Rosamund Bartlett

With his ancestry dating back possibly to the fourteenth century, and statesmen and military leaders amongst his many distinguished forebears, Tolstoy had good reason to feel proud of his family. The disdain the old-world Russian noble Levin expresses in *Anna Karenina* (1875–8) for nouveau riche aristocrats like Vronsky, who lack breeding and cannot point back to three or four generations, largely expresses Tolstoy's own sentiments. Whether it is the nostalgic celebration of patriarchal values in *War and Peace* (1865–9), or the dogged championing of them in the face of their erosion by the forces of modernity in *Anna Karenina*, one only has to turn a few pages of Tolstoy's great fictional masterpieces to realize that family is his great theme. Tolstoy drew on the members of his own family, past and present, to breathe flesh and blood into the iconic characters of his two great novels, and he also found inspiration in the reassuring surroundings of his home at Yasnaya Polyana, whose heirlooms were a constant reminder of his family's history. He certainly had plenty of material. As the title of an exhibition held at Yasnaya Polyana in 2008 proclaimed: "The history of the Tolstoy family is the history of Russia." The catalogue quotes the words of the popular nineteenth-century historian Vasily Kliuchevsky: "Almost all the noble families elevated under Peter and Catherine degenerated. The Tolstoy family is an exception. This family has shown particular vitality."[1]

The Tolstoy vitality engendered a complicated genealogy, comprising the titled branch and the untitled branch, which themselves both have senior and cadet lines. There is the Tver branch of the Tolstoys, and also the Kutuzov branch, formed when Praskovya Golenishchev-Kutuzov, daughter of the famous Field-Marshal, married Matvei Tolstoy. In 1859, Kutuzov's third grandson Pavel Mikhailovich was allowed by Alexander II to acquire the rare triple-barreled surname of Golenishchev-Kutuzov-Tolstoy. Then there are the Osterman-Tolstoys, and the Tolstoy-Miloslavskys, who were given permission by Nicholas II to adopt their double-barreled surname in 1910. This was to recognize their descent from the female line of the old *boyar* Ivan Miloslavsky, and prevent the ancient name from dying out. Lev Nikolaevich belonged to the senior titled branch of the family, as did the poet Alexei Konstantinovich Tolstoy, the artist Fyodor Petrovich Tolstoy, and Alexei Nikolaevich Tolstoy, who later became a celebrated Soviet writer.

Whether or not the Tolstoys' mythical fourteenth-century ancestor ever existed remains open to doubt, but the family can certainly trace its lineage back to Andrei Kharitonovich, who moved to Moscow in the early fifteenth century. His rotund physical shape apparently earned him the nickname of *tolstyi* (the Russian adjective for "fat"), which gave rise to the family's illustrious surname of Tolstoy. In 1682, Russian families were obliged to register their genealogy with the state in order to legitimize their claim to noble status, and one of the six signatories who submitted the Tolstoys' early family history to the heraldry office in Moscow was the court servant Pyotr Andreevich (1645–1729). A few decades later he would become the first Count Tolstoy. A brilliant man of immense energy, he was sent by Peter I to study navigation and ship-building in Italy, and became one of the first Russians to don Western dress when he returned to old Muscovy. In 1701, he was appointed as Russia's first ambassador to Constantinople, where he served for thirteen years.

In 1717, Pyotr Andreevich was entrusted with the most delicate and challenging of missions: to go to Naples and persuade the Tsar's errant son Alexei, the heir to the throne, to return to Russia. Hostile to his father's reforms, Alexei had sought refuge in Vienna with his brother-in-law Emperor Charles VI, who stationed him out of harm's way in Naples in order to avert a diplomatic crisis. Pyotr Andreevich had to resort to guile and cunning, but his mission was successful. Upon the tsarevich Alexei's return to Russia, he was immediately thrown into the dungeon of the Peter and Paul Fortress and interrogated for treason; he died soon afterwards. For his role in this affair, Pyotr Tolstoy was showered with riches by the grateful Tsar, who decorated him, appointed him senator, and gave him extensive lands.

By the time he was made a Count, on the day of the coronation of Peter's wife Catherine I as Empress in 1724, Pyotr Andreevich was one of the most powerful men in Russia. But his later political machinations were to be his undoing. In 1727, two years after Peter the Great died, he was himself arrested and imprisoned in the Peter and Paul Fortress. At the age of eighty-two, Pyotr Andreevich was shorn of his title, his decorations, and his lands, and sentenced to life exile in the Solovetsky Monastery prison,

Figure 1   Tolstoy family crest. Reproduced by permission of gerbovnik.ru.

located on an island near the Arctic Circle. With its harsh climate, it was a particularly bleak place to serve a sentence. Pyotr Andreevich's son Ivan, who accompanied him into exile, died the year after they arrived. Within eight months, Pyotr Andreevich was also dead.

The Tolstoy family's position improved when Peter the Great's daughter Elizabeth became Empress. By 1760 she had returned all the Tolstoy family estates to Ivan Petrovich's widow, as well as Pyotr Andreevich's title. It was at this time that the Tolstoy family crest was designed (Figure 1), consisting of a shield supported by two borzoi dogs, signifying loyalty and swiftness in attaining results. The shield, divided into seven segments, features at its centre a crossed gold sword and a silver arrow running through a golden key, as a symbol of the family's long history. In the top left-hand corner is half of the Russian imperial eagle, and next to it on a silver background is the blue St. Andrew Cross which Pyotr Andreevich was awarded in 1722. In the bottom right-hand corner, the seven towers topped with crescents recall Pyotr Andreevich's incarceration in Constantinople's Yedikule Fortress while Russia was at war against the

Ottoman Empire, and his role in securing victory. Ivan Tolstoy's second son Andrei Ivanovich, a loyal and fiscally astute servant of the state, was Tolstoy's great-grandfather. The profligate and sybaritic Ilya Andreevich, Tolstoy's grandfather, was very different. He and his wife Pelageya Nikolaevna lived in some style (even despatching linen to Amsterdam to be laundered), and it is not hard to see their shadows behind the figures of Count and Countess Rostov in *War and Peace*. Ilya Andreevich's extravagant lifestyle eventually led him into debt.

Tolstoy's father, Nikolai Ilyich, born in 1794, was the eldest of Ilya Andreevich's and Pelageya Nikolaevna's four sons. When Napoleon invaded Russia in 1812, Nikolai Tolstoy served with distinction, but struggled as a civilian. After all the family debts had been paid off, Nikolai Ilyich was forced to lead a modest life in Moscow and find a job. When Tolstoy describes the position Nikolai Rostov finds himself in after the death of the old Count in *War and Peace,* he is essentially telling the story of his father, who in 1821 took up a very minor appointment in Moscow's military bureaucracy. The magic solution for Tolstoy's father, as for Nikolai Rostov, was a rich bride. In the novel she appears as Princess Marya Bolkonskaya; in real life she was Princess Maria Volkonskaya.

Compared to the Volkonskys, who were descended from the legendary Scandinavian settler Riurik, the ninth-century founder of Russia, the Tolstoys were mere parvenus as a noble family. Tolstoy's maternal ancestors, who took their name from the Volkona River near Kaluga, could trace their roots back to at least the thirteenth century. The life story of Tolstoy's distant cousin Prince Sergei Grigorievich Volkonsky, a hero of 1812 who became a Decembrist, is intimately connected with the genesis of *War and Peace*.

It was through Tolstoy's mother, Maria Volkonskaya, that Nikolay Ilyich's family came to be connected with the estate of Yasnaya Polyana. Tolstoy's maternal great-grandfather Major General Sergei Fyodorovich Volkonsky originally bought Yasnaya Polyana, and it was inherited by Tolstoy's maternal grandfather Nikolai Sergeevich Volkonsky (1753–1821) in 1784. He was a widower when he brought his seven-year-old daughter Maria to live there, and for the remaining two decades of his life, he devoted himself to her upbringing, and to creating the idyllic surroundings which would later become instrumental to his grandson's creativity. It was Nikolai Volkonsky who transformed Yasnaya Polyana from a fairly ordinary piece of land into a carefully landscaped estate, complete with ponds, gardens, paths, and imposing manor house, when he retired from the army in 1799.

Yasnaya Polyana would be Maria Volkonskaya's home for the rest of her life. At the age of thirty-two, she probably thought she would never marry, but she was introduced by relatives to Nikolai Tolstoy, who was four years her junior and a distant relative. They married in June 1822. By the time Lev Nikolaevich Tolstoy was born in 1828, Yasnaya Polyana was quite crowded, as Nikolai Tolstoy brought various members of his family to live at the estate after marrying Maria Volkonskaya. Apart from his venerable mother Pelageya Nikolaevna, there were his younger sister Alexandra Ilyinichna and his distant "aunt" Tatiana Alexandrovna Ergolskaya. Lev Tolstoy's arrival followed that of his elder brothers Nikolai, Sergei, and Dmitry, who were born in 1823, 1826, and 1827. Maria Nikolaevna died in 1830, not long after the birth of her only daughter, also christened Maria. Nikolay Ilyich was by all accounts an attentive husband, and he became a conscientious father as a single parent, devoted to his children, but he himself died seven years later.

During his early childhood, Lev Tolstoy had the opportunity to meet Count Fyodor Ivanovich (1782–1846), his uncle-once-removed, whose life became so shrouded in legend and prurient gossip that it is difficult to establish the veracity of the many stories which circulated about him. He fought his first duel at the age of seventeen, soon after joining the elite Preobrazhensky Guards regiment in St. Petersburg, but two years later, he escaped the confines of military life by securing a berth on Adam von Krusenstern's ship *Nadezhda*, whose mission was to complete the first Russian round-the-world expedition. While visiting a Polynesian island in the South Pacific, he decided to emulate the natives by having his body completely covered in tattoos. After being ordered to leave the ship, he spent time with native tribes on Sitka Island in southern Alaska, then part of the colony called "Russian America," which is how he came to acquire his nickname of "Tolstoy the American."

Fyodor Ivanovich was the living embodiment of what Tolstoy defined as the cardinal family trait of *dikost'*, a word which can mean "wildness," but also shyness or eccentricity. When applying this word to members of his family, Tolstoy liked further to define *dikost'* as the quality of possessing passion, daring, originality, and independence of thought, as well as propensity for doing the opposite of everyone else. Tolstoy himself certainly went against the grain in almost everything he did as an adult, and perceived *dikost'* not only in many of his ancestors, but also in some of his contemporaries – even his very prim and proper first cousin once removed, who was a spirited but nevertheless very poised lady-in-waiting at the imperial court.

The five orphaned Tolstoys, who were brought up by their uncle and aunt in Kazan, were very different from each other, but all inherited the Tolstoyan *dikost'* in some way. Nikolai, the eldest, revered by his youngest siblings, served in the military and dabbled in literature, but never fulfilled his early promise, and died at the age of twenty-nine of tuberculosis. Dmitry, the most eccentric and "unloved" of the brothers, also died young from tuberculosis. When it became clear he had not long to live, he abandoned his ascetic life of extreme moral purity for one of debauchery, and mistreated the former prostitute who became his common-law wife. Tolstoy drew on aspects of Dmitry when creating the character of Levin's brother Nikolai in *Anna Karenina*. Sergei, whom Tolstoy idolized in his youth, was the most dashing of the brothers, and highly talented, but was also wayward. His eventual marriage to the gypsy girl he pursued in his youth was deeply unhappy.

Tolstoy was outlived only by his younger sister Maria, who also suffered from depression, like Sergei. After fleeing abroad from an abusive marriage to a distant relative from the Tolstoy family, with whom she had three children, "Masha" entered into a relationship with an impoverished Swedish aristocrat who abandoned her after she gave birth to their daughter Elena. Despite the prospect of social disgrace, she sought her brother Lev's help in obtaining a divorce, before her husband's death conveniently made her a widow. However, she still faced the stigma of having an illegitimate child. Legitimacy in imperial Russia was only open to subjects who had been baptized, and whose parents had been married in the Orthodox Church. Masha openly admitted to her brother that she was too ashamed to bring Elena back to Russia with her. This was one of the backdrops against which Tolstoy embarked on the early chapters of his novel of marital breakdown, *Anna Karenina*, and Masha directly identified with his heroine in a letter she sent him in 1876. When Elena eventually moved to Russia after completing her education in Switzerland, she adopted the patronymic of Sergeevna, which was derived from the name of her uncle rather than that of her father. Masha found solace in religion, becoming a nun in her late fifties, which did not prevent her remaining close to her brother Lev, even after his denunciation of the Russian Orthodox Church.

Tolstoy's own family life, while outwardly conventional and certainly more successful, at least initially, was no less complicated than that of his siblings. Before his marriage, he fathered an illegitimate son with Aksinya Bazykina, a young peasant girl on his estate. Timofei later worked for him as a coachman, and his presence, as well as that of his mother, was a subject of extreme discomfort for Tolstoy's young bride Sofia Andreevna Behrs, who became Tolstoy's wife in 1862. She came from a far less aristocratic family, was half his age, and the marriage was completely on his terms. Sonya thus had to consent to marry at precipitate speed, for example, and read accounts of amorous conquests in her fiancé's diaries before her wedding. Then she had to cut herself off from Moscow, where she had grown up, settle in the countryside, and devote herself to motherhood. Tolstoy plundered his and Sofia Andreevna's experiences to tell the story of Levin and Kitty's courtship and the first years of their marriage in *Anna Karenina*, in which he even fictionalized the ambivalence he felt toward his own children when they were small babies.

Tolstoy was a devoted husband in the first decade of his marriage, and a good father to his eldest children Sergei, Tatiana, Ilya, Lev, and Maria, who were all born between 1863 and 1871. The first three were even drafted into helping teach the local peasant children when Tolstoy briefly reopened his Yasnaya Polyana school in 1872. The rest of the decade, however, when he was writing *Anna Karenina*, was overshadowed by death – of his children Pyotr, Nikolai, and Varvara in early infancy, of his young niece Dasha, and of both his aunts, who had lived at Yasnaya Polyana in their old age, and represented the last living link with his parents. As if this were not enough, two of his sisters-in-law suffered stillbirths during this period, and his wife nearly died of peritonitis.

Tolstoy's relationship with his family was notably different when he emerged from the depression and existential crisis which ensued, particularly after he began to live according to his newfound Christian principles. His thirteenth and final child with Sofia Andreevna, Ivan, was born in 1888 – the year in which he became a grandfather at the age of sixty. From this point, he became an increasingly absent father as his religious crusade gained momentum and he acquired numerous followers. Even Tolstoy's eldest children felt neglected in one way or another, but the problem was particularly acute with his younger offspring, who hardly saw their father while they were growing up. Tolstoy's son Andrei, for example, was expelled from school for destroying a picture of the Tsar. He then went on to lead a dissolute life, running up large debts, pursuing first a peasant girl, then a Georgian princess, and becoming a serial philanderer, all of which shocked his father.

Despite renouncing his aristocratic title of Count and dressing like a peasant, Tolstoy retained a deep reverence for his ancestry and its illustrious past heritage until his dying day. Sofia Andreevna had not accompanied him on his spiritual journey, however, and Tolstoy's relationship with his wife steadily worsened. Cracks in the marriage had started to appear in the 1880s, and the rift created a fault line within the family, with the sons generally siding with their mother, and the daughters remaining fiercely loyal to their father. It was particularly painful for Sofia Andreevna to find herself supplanted in her husband's affections by his disciple Vladimir Chertkov in the last years of their marriage. Tolstoy's mission as an evangelist for the gospel of universal brotherly love proved tragically incompatible with the more mundane business of maintaining a loving environment within his own immediate family.

Note

1 *Istoriya roda Tolstykh – istoriya Rossii. Katalog vystavki* (Tula: Izdatel'skii dom "Yasnaya Polyana," 2008).

CHAPTER 4

Estate Culture and Yasnaya Polyana

Hilde Hoogenboom

A biography of Tolstoy's life and works is also a biography of his family estate of Yasnaya Polyana. In 1858, he wrote that, "It is hard for me to imagine Russia or my relationship to her without my own Yasnaya Polyana. Without Yasnaya Polyana perhaps I will see the general laws that are needed in my fatherland more clearly, but I will not love it to distraction" (5:262). These often-quoted words reveal a deeper meaning in their context – the fragment, "A Month in the Country," about the impending emancipation of the serfs. Serfdom made Tolstoy's Yasnaya Polyana possible, but justice argued that 50 million serfs should be freed with "their" land.

Tolstoy felt Russia's central conflict deeply as an aristocrat and noble servitor, a landowner and estate manager, a religious family man, and a writer. With 233 male serfs, a distillery, aviary, orchards, creamery, and forests, Yasnaya Polyana was the great constant in the life and history of the Tolstoys. It became a cultural beacon as readers everywhere pictured Russian country life through Tolstoy's evocations of hunting, mushroom picking, and farming. It was the bustling stage where Sofia Andreevna Tolstaya photographed her family, and where Tolstoy posed for Russia's leading painter Ilya Repin (see Chapter 39). A steady stream of Russians and foreigners made pilgrimages to Tolstoy at Yasnaya Polyana.

Yet Tolstoy soon came to loathe property – his property – as a great evil. His self-censure was equal to his ambitions to acquire property. After squandering half his inheritance on gambling in the 1850s, by the 1860s, now married and with a growing family, Tolstoy invested the profits from his publications by buying land nearby and, in the early 1870s, in Samara, contributing to gentrification and the poverty and famine there that he documented. By the 1880s, the family bought a second home to winter in Moscow, and summered at Yasnaya Polyana. In three decades, he invested 100,000 rubles and quintupled his inheritance, re-establishing his parents' and grandparents' fortunes.[1]

But in 1883, Tolstoy stepped away from his business life by giving his eminently capable wife power of attorney to manage his estates and publish his novels. Already in 1884, he began to threaten to leave Sofia Andreevna and Yasnaya Polyana, arguing that they should give up the Samara income to the peasants there and manage on the minimal income from Yasnaya Polyana. In 1891, Tolstoy divided all his land, valued at 550,000 rubles, to provide an inheritance for her and their ten children, leaving himself 2,000 rubles and royalties from his play *The Fruits of Enlightenment*. Still, he received letters and read articles in the press that, with reason, accused him of being a hypocrite for living off peasant labor at Yasnaya Polyana, which brought in 2,000–3,000 rubles annually (49:122). On October 28, 1910, shortly before he died, Tolstoy decided to leave Sofia Andreevna and Yasnaya Polyana for the last time. In his will, he asked that the family's land be given to the peasants. The estate proved to be a fruitful blessing and a curse to Tolstoy.

Located 120 miles south of Moscow, beyond Tula, Yasnaya Polyana became a national icon only because of its famous inhabitant. Well-known estates belonged to the wealthiest noble families. Estate culture thrived in the eighteenth century under Catherine the Great, at Tsarskoe Selo and her other properties. In and around St. Petersburg and Moscow and beyond, nobles staged their connections to the court on their estates. In this golden age of the nobility, Catherine made gifts of newly conquered lands with serfs that allowed her grandees to rival the royal palaces and gardens. They looked to Europe's power houses and their grounds, while provincial nobles modeled themselves on the court.

Yasnaya Polyana bears the traces of the European neoclassical architecture that dominated wealthier estates, with their neo-Palladian rectangles and squares, columns, pediments, and large flanking wings. Features included conservatories, churches, hunting lodges, stables, pavilions, grottos, temples, mausoleums, bridges, and gates. Nobles added oriental and neo-Gothic details and structures to vary their imperial stages. The enormous Sheremetev estates at Kuskovo and Ostankino had especially grand halls and dining rooms. Crowds gathered for balls and meals, with concerts, plays, and ballet by guests and serf ensembles. Visitors toured the manicured French gardens and "natural" English parks. Ha-has disguised the fences between these pleasure grounds and the working pastures and fields. There, the free labor of hundreds and thousands of field serfs, along with that of hundreds of house serfs, serf artisans, and serf gardeners, built and staffed the estates and their culture.[2]

Yasnaya Polyana embodied Tolstoy's elite noble ancestry, of which he was very proud. In 1763, Tolstoy's maternal great-grandfather Major General Prince Sergei Fyodorovich Volkonsky purchased Yasnaya Polyana by the Voronka River for his wife. Originally named Yasennaya Polyana for its many ash trees (*yaseni*), over time it became Yasnaya Polyana, or Clear Glade.[3] Their son, infantry general Prince Nikolai Sergeevich Volkonsky, married Princess Ekaterina Dmitrievna Trubetskaya. When she died in 1799, he retired with their only child Maria Nikolaevna to Yasnaya Polyana, which had 159 serfs and a carpet factory. With revenues from nearby estates, Volkonsky added nineteen buildings, including two orangeries, stables, coach house, bath house, summer house, and quarters for house serfs. A formal French garden with pollarded lime trees by the house led to an English park with a series of ponds ringed by rose bushes and a ha-ha. In the gardens and at home, a small serf orchestra played the music he loved. Set along the road from Tula, two squat towers with an iron gate opened to a wide birch-tree-lined alley to the house. When he died in 1821, Volkonsky had built the wings and the first floor of the central house.

In 1822, now a thirty-two-year-old heiress with 800 serfs on several estates, Princess Maria Nikolaevna Volkonskaya suddenly married the impoverished younger Count Nikolai Ilyich Tolstoy. By 1824, Tolstoy's parents lived at Yasnaya Polyana and finished the second floor of the central house, which no longer exists. Tolstoy and his four siblings were born and raised in a thirty-two-room mansion. After Tolstoy's mother died in 1830, his father nearly doubled the number of serfs, recouping the half-million-ruble losses of Tolstoy's grandfather.[4] To put this into perspective, few nobles owned settled estates. Most had less than one hundred (male) serfs and, like Bazarov's parents in Ivan Turgenev's *Fathers and Children* (1862), these nobles worked with their serfs. Tolstoy and his parents, like Turgenev, who had 1,925 serfs, belonged to the 3 percent of nobles who owned over 500 serfs.[5]

This was the Tolstoy family inheritance that the four brothers and their younger sister Maria divided equally in 1847. Their correspondence attests that throughout their lives, they visited and helped each other with debts, mortgages, sales, and purchases of land.[6] As the youngest son, Tolstoy inherited the main house and its mortgaged village Yasnaya Polyana (233 male serfs), and four other villages: Yasenki (17 serfs), Yagodnaya (38 serfs), Mostovaya Pustosh (18 serfs), and Malaya Vorotynka (22 serfs), totaling 4,000 acres and 330 serfs, plus 4,000 rubles from Nikolai and Sergei (5:344). Soon, Sergei and Lev would inherit the properties of their

brothers Dmitry and Nikolai, who died young. Tolstoy inherited
Nikolskoe and Plotitsyna, north of Yasnaya Polyana, doubling his wealth
to about 600 serfs.[7]

Tolstoy experienced coming into his inheritance of Yasnaya Polyana at
age nineteen as an ethical epiphany of his duty to others. Leaving Kazan
University and returning to Yasnaya Polyana, Tolstoy began a diary, where
he famously chronicled his struggle to live a virtuous life, provide for his
serfs, and use his talents for the good of Russia.[8] He channeled misgivings
about serfdom into lifelong projects to educate peasants.

But Tolstoy soon left for St. Petersburg and Moscow, becoming an
absentee landlord who gambled away half his inheritance. Tolstoy regularly asked his brothers to sell forests, villages, and finally, in 1854, the
central house at Yasnaya Polyana. This was the imposing three-story
central rectangle completed by his father, with the usual pediment, eight
two-story columns, and large hall. Minus its two wings, the big house was
sold for 5,000 rubles to a neighboring landowner, Gorokhov, who moved
it to Dolgoe, about 10 miles away. Tolstoy visited the house once, in 1897,
and drew its plan. Peasants bought it in 1911, and by 1913, they dismantled it for salvage. A foundation stone at Yasnaya Polyana marks where it
once stood. There, the Tolstoys built a plain two-room guest cottage in
1888, grandly called the Pavilion.[9]

After the Crimean War (1853–6), Tolstoy resigned his officer's commission and returned to his estate, now reduced by half, and settled into
careers as a landowner, educator, and writer. When the eighteen-year-old
Tolstaya arrived the day after their wedding in 1862, she found a plain,
dilapidated estate run according to Tolstoy's belief in simplicity. Tolstaya
took over the kitchen, the house, and the accounts. Kitchen staff now wore
white and uniformed butlers with white gloves served meals. But the house
vodka remained an infusion of peppermint, anise, and bitter orange.
Meanwhile, Tolstoy oversaw a team of teachers to educate the peasants,
learned agriculture, bought and bred animals, and tended his beehives.

Husband and wife discovered a shared passion for planting varieties of
trees, increasing the forests from 500 to 1,200 acres – her daughters'
dowry, Tolstaya would say. Tolstoy planted an apple orchard in honor
of their first child Sergei, and more followed, totaling 100 acres. They
celebrated name days with picnics in the woods. Family and guests went
walking, driving, riding, sledding, and hunting. There were sports –
croquet, skittles, bowling (gorodki), gymnastics, skating, and in the
1890s, tennis and cycling. Masters and peasants went swimming in
the Great Pond along the main drive, or they took the Bathing Path to

the bath house to swim and fish in the Voronka River. The nearby village of Yasnaya Polyana had 120 huts, some of stone and some with iron roofs, where 700 peasants, whom Tolstoy knew, lived. Initially, Tolstaya was friendly with peasants, but ended relations after she took over management in 1883 because she felt guilty about enforcing laws against them.[10] While Tolstoy evoked estate life in his fiction, from the late 1880s Tolstaya documented their life in approximately 1,000 glass plate photographs taken with a large portable Kodak camera. A serious amateur, she did her own developing and printing at Yasnaya Polyana.[11]

On Sundays, the family went through the woods to the seventeenth-century Church of St. Nicholas on the Kochak River, where Tolstoy's grandparents, parents, siblings, aunts, children, wife, and his valet Ilya Sidorkov are buried. Excommunicated by the Orthodox Church in 1901, Tolstoy lies alone in unconsecrated ground in the Old Reserve forest along the path he took to go swimming in the river.[12]

The comfortable country house where the Tolstoys raised their family was the remaining two-story rectangular right wing of the original mansion. A small central pediment and Palladian window divide regular rows of five windows upstairs and downstairs on each side. As Tolstoy's literary fortunes improved, Tolstaya added a small two-story wood addition in 1866, where Tolstoy moved his study from the pantry "under the vaults" to the "room for the new arrivals," with his father's Persian walnut desk and the leather couch on which he had been born. A large two-story brick addition from 1871 contained the new parquet-floored parlor, with a "corner for serious conversations" and two pianos. The left wing of the original house, where peasants were schooled from 1859 to 1862, became known as Kuzminsky House, after Tolstaya's beloved younger sister Tanya Kuzminskaya, who visited summers with her eight children.[13] Foreigners were amazed at the spartan furnishings, while readers of Tolstoy's tracts against property were surprised at the luxuries. Both had good reason.

When he married, Tolstoy understood, like Count Nikolai Rostov in *War and Peace*, that he had to restore the family finances. Readers imagine Tolstoy only toiling in the fields with the peasants – thanks to Levin in *Anna Karenina*, and Repin's much-reproduced painting (see Figure 12). But their emancipation had forced Tolstoy to learn the economics of estate management. In April 1856, after talking with friends on the emancipation commissions, Tolstoy offered his serfs a contract similar to the forty-nine-year contracts they would soon sign: he would convert their required labor to dues and over twenty-four years, their dues would pay off his mortgage of 20,000 rubles, allowing him to free them (5:243–5). Although peasants preferred paying dues, serfs rejected his plan because they expected the Emperor to free them with "their" land.

Everywhere, the family fortunes depended on the estates and Tolstoy's publications, which were intertwined in the infamous dramas over manuscripts and copyrights. After 1883, Tolstaya managed his estates and pre-1881 publications with his power of attorney and promise of the copyrights, allowing Tolstoy to publish religious works with his wealthy acolyte Vladimir Chertkov. After 1891, Yasnaya Polyana belonged to Tolstaya and their youngest son Ivan. When he soon died, four sons, who all needed money, became co-owners with Tolstaya. In 1908, Chertkov returned from exile in England and, with the Tolstoys' youngest daughter Alexandra, secretly became Tolstoy's literary executor with sole possession of the manuscripts and copyrights. Tensions escalated in the month before Tolstoy left home because Tolstaya had to decline an offer of 1 million rubles for the copyrights, which would have provided for Yasnaya Polyana and their thirty-eight dependents.[14]

The Tolstoys strove to preserve Yasnaya Polyana because the estate embodied the whole of the family's existence – their life together, their history, and Tolstoy's literary legacy. Letters, diaries, and memoirs record the comings and goings of four generations of family, extended family members, and visitors, not to mention the servants (who lived in Volkonsky House), the nursemaids, nannies, and tutors. The cook, Nikolai Mikhailovich Rumiantsev, had been Tolstoy's grandfather's cook and flautist in his orchestra. His grandmother's maid Agafya Mikhailovna was the "dogs' governess." Only when Tolstoy died would Yasnaya Polyana seem empty.

Tolstoy's daughter Alexandra fulfilled his final request to give their land to the peasants. Using the profits from a three-volume edition of his censored works, she purchased 1,620 acres of Yasnaya Polyana's 2,230 acres from her mother and four brothers for 400,000 rubles (double its value), with the provision that the brothers could first sell the timber. Her mother used her share to buy out her sons, becoming sole owner of the house and surrounding 540 acres, where she remained until her death in 1919.

Alexandra returned from World War I with three Orders of St. George and the rank of colonel for her service as a nurse, and became a kommissar in charge of Yasnaya Polyana. She succeeded in having it designated a museum in 1921. Unlike most estates, Yasnaya Polyana survived the Revolution and then World War II, in the capable hands of the Tolstoys' granddaughter Sofia Andreevna Tolstaya-Esenina (1900–57).[15]

The current director since 1994, Tolstoy's great-great-grandson Vladimir Ilych Tolstoy, became an advisor to President Vladimir Putin in 2012, on Russia's cultural soft power at home and abroad. Meanwhile, Tolstoy's great-great-great grandson Ilya is producing honey and apple juice from the thirty-three varieties that Tolstoy planted, under the brand name Yasnaya Polyana.

The scholar Boris Eikhenbaum recognized that for Tolstoy, the "remarkable tactician and strategist, . . . Yasnaya Polyana was a comfortable vantage point, the elevated spot from which he surveyed and measured the march of history."[16] It continues to provide a place from which to view the march of history.

Notes

1 Sofia Andreevna Tolstaya, *My Life*, ed. Andrew Donskov, trans. John Woodsworth and Arkadi Klioutchanski (University of Ottawa Press, 2010), 101–2, 172–3, 245, 266; David Moon, *The Abolition of Serfdom in Russia, 1762–1907* (New York: Routledge, 2002), 101; Rosamund Bartlett, *Tolstoy: A Russian Life* (London: Profile, 2010), 209, 212, 227; Henri Troyat, *Tolstoy*, trans. Nancy Amphoux (New York: Grove Press, 1967), 284.

2 P.R. Roosevelt, *Life on the Russian Country Estate: A Social and Cultural History* (New Haven, CT: Yale University Press, 1995), chaps 2–3.

3 Bartlett, *Tolstoy: A Russian Life*, 22.

4 Ibid., 24–30, 38; Nina Nikitina, *A Tour of the Estate with Lev Tolstoy* (Tula: Izd. Dom Iasnaia Poliana, 2004), 69–76.

5 Moon, *Abolition of Serfdom*, 13, 17, 45–6; M.G. Mulhall, *The Dictionary of Statistics*, 4th edn (London: George Routledge, 1899), 541.

6 N.A. Kalinina, V.V. Lozbiakova, and T.G. Nikiforova (eds.), *Perepiska L.N. Tolstogo s sestroi i brat'iami*, Perepiska russkikh pisatelei (Moscow: Khudozhestvennaia literatura, 1990); Nikitina, *Tour of the Estate*, 199–205.

7 Bartlett, *Tolstoy: A Russian Life*, 82, 144; Kalinina et al. (eds.), *Perepiska L.N. Tolstogo s sestroi*, 35n3–4, 210n2, 211.

8 June 25, 1853, June 24, 1854, *Tolstoy's Diaries*, trans. R.F. Christian, 2 vols. (London: Athlone Press, 1985), vol. 1, 68, 88.

9 Kalinina et al. (eds.), *Perepiska L.N. Tolstogo s sestroi*, 41, 57, 105n3, 117n2, 123n3, 137, 139n14, 141, 149n3, 177n5; Nikitina, *Tour of the Estate*, 76–9; S.M. Borisov, *Iasnaia Poliana, Fotoal'bom* (Moscow: Sovetskaia Rossiia, 1978), 30.

10 Nikitina, *Tour of the Estate*, 186, 160–5, 186–98, 102–9, 152–8, 167–73; Tolstaya, *My Life*, 65, 67, 107, 101, 102, 113.

11 S.A. Tolstaya and Leah Bendavid-Val, *Song Without Words: The Photographs & Diaries of Countess Sophia Tolstoy* (Washington, D.C.: National Geographic, 2007), 227–28.

12 Nikitina, *A Tour of the Estate*, 174–82.
13 Borisov, *Iasnaia Poliana, Fotoal'bom*, 122–23, 128, 156–57, 228–29; Tolstaya, *My Life*, 135–6, 173–4; Nikitina, *Tour of the Estate*, 91, 62–8.
14 Bartlett, *Tolstoy: A Russian Life*, 410–11; Tolstaya and Bendavid-Val, *Song Without Words*, 236; Troyat, *Tolstoy*, 663.
15 Nikitina, *Tour of the Estate*, 51–3, 161, 221–3, 247–63; Borisov, *Iasnaia Poliana, Fotoal'bom*, 70–3; Bartlett, *Tolstoy: A Russian Life*, 156, 419, 420–1.
16 Boris Eikhenbaum, "The Literary Career of Lev Tolstoi," in Gary Kern (ed.), *The Young Tolstoi* (Ann Arbor, MI: Ardis, 1972), 136.

PART II

Russian Social and Political Contexts

CHAPTER 5

Peasants and Folklore

Sibelan Forrester

By the end of his life, Lev Nikolaevich Tolstoy had become so strongly associated with Russian peasants that one style of traditional men's peasant shirt was called a "tolstovka." For a man who was not a peasant to dress like one meant acting like the author. Tolstoy's relationship with peasants has several aspects: the consequences of his own wealth, noble rank, and class background; his depictions of peasants in literary works and other writings; and his actions on behalf of peasants and communication with them. Since Russian folklore is so strongly associated with peasants, it is no wonder that Tolstoy also had a closely engaged relationship with folklore (Russian and otherwise), using many folk plots in his primers and favoring the simple oral style he found in folk narratives for his teaching tales.

Tolstoy's family and class situation meant that his relationship to individual peasants and to the peasantry as a whole was structurally determined from the moment he was born: his family had serfs working in their city and country houses and in their fields, in the same positions as peasant laborers or nannies he encountered elsewhere. As he grew up Tolstoy pursued a stereotypical young male aristocrat's sexual relationships with peasant women (and with the prostitutes whose colloquial job title, *devka*, was also the standard term for an unmarried peasant girl). He long regretted that in his late teens he had "seduced" an innocent servant, who was dismissed from her position in his aunt's house as a result. In his early thirties he had a child with one of his own serfs, the married peasant Aksinya Bazykina, not long before his marriage to Sofia Behrs. Everyone on his estate knew who the boy was as he grew up. Like his initial sexual experience with a prostitute, Tolstoy's class position left him with something of a sense of original sin, though he saw the sin more as the fact that he had been exploiting peasant labor while living in luxury and idleness than in the ways he had exploited peasant women sexually. He considered wanting and especially having sex with them as a moral failing, rather than a class issue.

At the same time, Tolstoy was always sensitive to the poverty of many Russian peasants, including those on his own estate, and the bad moral consequences of that poverty. His early story "A Landowner's Morning" (1856) lays out both the poor condition of the titular landowner's village and the peasants' resistance to change. The protagonist's suffering seems to echo Tolstoy's own.

> Nekhliudov had long known, not by rumors, not by believing the words of others, but in practice, the whole extreme level of poverty in which his peasants lived; but all that actuality was so hard to reconcile with his whole upbringing, mentality, and way of life that he would against his will forget the truth, and every time when, as now, he was reminded of it in a striking and palpable way, his heart would feel unbearably heavy and sad, as if the recollection of some unredeemed crime he had committed were tormenting him. (4:134)

(Unlike Turgenev's *Sportsman's Sketches*, this and many of Tolstoy's stories about peasants do not specify where the village is located; his peasants are generalized and typical.) In the largely autobiographical work *Childhood* (1852), the protagonist narrator describes the peasant house serfs as part of an idyllic family past in which their servitude is unproblematic: here Tolstoy has the sunny attitude of a master comfortable with his reliance on (and often blindness to) the domestic and emotional labor of the servants around him.

Later in his career, Tolstoy was inspired by the simple religious faith of peasants at a time when many Russian intellectuals considered the peasants all but pagan and ignorant of the central tenets of Orthodoxy. He wrote in his *Confession* (1882):

> I began to get closer to believers among the poor, simple, uneducated people, with pilgrims, monks, sectarians, peasants. The catechism of these simple folk was also Christian, like the catechism of supposed believers from our social class ... In opposition to what I saw in our circles, where life without faith is possible and where barely one in a thousand will declare himself a believer, in their circles barely one in a thousand was not a believer. (23:39)

Tolstoy enjoyed walking to a nearby monastery along with the largely peasant pilgrims on the main road near his estate, returning home feeling refreshed and inspired by their example and his own sense of participation.

In the late 1850s Tolstoy founded a school on his estate for peasant children, whom he viewed in Rousseau's terms of natural goodness (see Chapter 17). As teachers, he hired students who had been expelled from university for their political opinions and activities, though his diary suggests that he was generally dissatisfied with their work. Tolstoy did quite a bit of teaching himself, and he founded a journal (*Yasnaya Polyana*, "Bright Meadow," also the name of his estate) to publish pedagogical articles related to the peasant schools. Tolstoy was an adult (in his thirties) when the serfs were liberated in 1861, and his final government service was as a local official carrying out the provisions of that change. Thus, the greater part of Tolstoy's long life was lived after the emancipation, but still under the shadow of serfdom and the class relations it had cemented – a deep division in Russian society. Though he often sought to teach peasants, especially peasant children, Tolstoy also welcomed peasant thinkers and seekers whose beliefs fit his own tendency toward Christian anarchism, including the Doukhobor Pyotr Verigin. Tolstoy's daughter Alexandra, in an article that highlights his strong connection with the peasantry, shows him singling out the importance of two other peasant philosophers, Timofei Bondarev and Vasily Sutaev.[1]

Tolstoy also sought out direct information about peasants' lives: his long article "Slavery of Our Time" (1900) recounts what peasant laborers from Tula, Oryol, and Voronezh told him about their punishing and poorly paid work on the Moscow railroad. Here testimony about the real conditions of peasant life shades into journalism, always tied to strong moral concern. The suffering and oppression of the laborers obligate the educated reader to make changes in response.

> It would seem that, knowing [the harm done to workers] (and it is impossible not to know), for us, the people who take advantage of this labor that costs human lives, if we are not beasts, it would be impossible to remain calm for even one minute, but meanwhile we, people of means, liberal, humane, very sensitive to the sufferings not only of people but also of animals, take advantage without ceasing of such labor, we strive to get richer and richer, i.e. to take advantage more and more of such labor, and we remain entirely calm. (34:151)

Tolstoy's various statements about diet emphasize that peasants who did heavy physical labor genuinely needed to eat the meat and other rich foods that for idle aristocrats merely tickled their sensual desires. Late in his life, and after his death, socialist theorists traced a short line from his focus on "exploiter and exploited in rural Russia," as Gyorgy Lukács put it, to the class analysis of socialism and Marxism.[2] For this and other reasons, Tolstoy was a highly regarded writer on peasant issues throughout the Soviet period, when so much of the pre-Revolutionary canon was overturned.

Tolstoy depicts peasants in literary works and other writings as a variety of types and individuals: some are crafty, others open and sincere. Probably the most famous example is the idealized (and tellingly androgynous) Platon Karataev in *War and Peace*, a wise though untutored peasant counterpart of Kutuzov in understanding how a human fate should fit the larger frame of life and history, and for Pierre Bezukhov "the strongest and dearest recollection and personification of everything Russian, kind and round" (12:48/Vol. 4, Pt. 1, Ch. 13). Tolstoy at times shows a peasant as an idealized noble savage, implausibly pure in sexual feelings and simple in character: during haymaking, in *Anna Karenina*, Konstantin Levin sees one very young couple, only recently married, discovering their love for each other while still very shy about sexual relations – a contrast to Tolstoy's own sexual initiation, and perhaps an unrealistic view of how a peasant child living in a one-room hut would think and feel about sex. In the early story "Three Deaths" (1859), Tolstoy depicts peasants with a much more realistic, less troubled attitude about death, and far less squeamish or in denial than aristocrats when dealing with mortality. *The Death of Ivan Ilyich* (1886) focuses firmly on the upper-class Ivan Ilyich and his mortality. We never hear how bored the peasant servant Gerasim must have been, or how his young limbs must have cramped as he sat there so long holding Ivan Ilyich's feet. To his credit, Ivan Ilyich does appreciate the service.

As groups, however, peasants in Tolstoy's writing appear much less attractive. The upper-class characters from whose point of view Tolstoy's earlier prose fiction is usually told often grow uneasy as they try to evaluate these faceless groups and their uncooperative behavior, more powerful as they present a united front. Poor, well-intentioned Princess Marya Bolkonskaya in *War and Peace* is unable to communicate with her peasants, who assert their own lack of education and will not be forthright with her (though they respond well to the forceful approach of her eventual husband, Nikolai Rostov). Levin struggles to get his peasants to follow the forward-thinking farming techniques he has read about in Western European journals. As long as he is trying to compel changes in their practice, they resist, break things, or simply forget to do as he has requested; it is unclear how much resistance comes from the peasants themselves and how much from the layer of management intervening between the landowner and the actual peasant laborers. A well-intentioned landowner's disappointment after trying to "make the peasants happy" suggests a frustrating inability to understand their lives and opinions.

Like many Russian authors, Tolstoy has the sense that even in the upper classes women (natural, spontaneous, emotional) are closer to the folk than (rational, intellectual, educated) men. In a much-cited scene from *War and Peace*, Natasha Rostova performs a dance in precisely the folk style without ever having done it before:

> Where, how, and when had this little countess, brought up by an émigré Frenchwoman, sucked this spirit in from the Russian air she breathed, where had she gotten these ways, which should have been long supplanted by the *pas de châle*? Yet that spirit and these ways were those very inimitable, unstudied Russian ones which the uncle expected of her. (10:267/Vol. 2, Pt. 4, Ch. 7)

The narrator notes that her brother, Nikolai, and the others present were worried that she would embarrass herself; Nikolai himself, of course, does not dance. Yet the folk dance emerges as a spontaneous product of Natasha's unspoiled human nature, explicitly showing that she understands peasant women and indeed all Russians. This in turn suggests that a peasant dance is artless and reflects tradition only in the sense that all the peasants, and maybe all "unspoiled" women, know how to do it. In a famous passage from *What Is Art?* (1897), Tolstoy asserts that peasant women's singing is true art, comparing it favorably to the late works of Beethoven (30:144–5). A good woman like Natasha is close to the peasants because of her closeness to nature; this means she will breastfeed her own children as peasant women do, and as Tolstoy's own wife did, rather than exploit a peasant wet nurse. It is the "Uncle" they have stopped to visit who is living with a peasant woman and thus blurring class boundaries (becoming déclassé himself).

For Tolstoy, peasants are good largely because they live in nature, or at least in the more natural setting of the Russian village, far from the city with its many sources of corruption. Over time, the exemplary peasants Tolstoy depicts tend to be less often women and more often men. In the late story "Alyosha the Pot" (1905), the simple, almost holy peasant hero whose dedication to work and obedience embodies genuine active love is supported by concrete details about the bad situation of peasants. Alyosha's father comes to town to collect all his wages, which are probably needed for taxes and to pay off the family's debt for the land received in the emancipation.

Tolstoy felt that (at least for him personally) doing peasant things made a person from the upper class better: we see Levin enjoying a moment of "flow" as he mows with the local peasants (who work on his farm but are no longer his serfs), and Tolstoy himself enjoyed peasant crafts and tasks, making boots or ploughing. (Russian popular culture at the time played with the contradictions: one anecdote has him coming outside to plough as his butler says, "The ploughing is served.") His growing worldwide fame helped bring issues facing the Russian peasantry into public discourse, though some (especially people from lower-class backgrounds, such as Anton Chekhov, Maksim Gorky, or Ilya Repin) were troubled by the tensions they saw between his ambitions and his play at living like a peasant. Tolstoy himself called Chekhov's story *Peasants* "a sin before the people," saying that Chekhov had not looked into the soul of the people (though Chekhov's grandfather had been a serf).

The Count did not always keep in mind that his own class identity necessarily impacted the way peasants (and others) could speak to him and how much they would trust him. Just as the peasant-style *tolstovka*, unremarkable on a genuine peasant (at a moment when young peasants were shifting to town clothing when they could get it), marked a man from any other social class with a particular set of politics, rather than signifying that he came from the Tula region, Tolstoy tended to treat the peasants of Russia as homogeneous. They formed a social class whose lifestyle and simple relationship to life and death had a great deal to offer but who (for him) possessed no remarkable specific culture; at its extreme, the peasant lifestyle and worldview might well be replaced with the rational morality he favored and considered a more perfected form of natural goodness.

Consistent with his principles, Tolstoy took action many times on behalf of peasants: he offered financial help to victims of famines (especially peasants); he was interested in the Molokan sect, communicated cordially with the Doukhobors (see Chapter 29), and helped them emigrate to Canada, designating a substantial part of the revenue from his novel *Resurrection* (1899). He was courteous to peasant sectarians (in writing and in person), and they respected and valued him, sometimes writing him to express their ideas and engage in discussion. If a peasant wrote to Tolstoy, he would be sure to answer the letter, though he often neglected letters from others. He approved of nonviolence and dietary restrictions, but not of ideas like voluntary self-castration (practiced by the Skoptsy sect on the basis of the biblical idea of making oneself a eunuch for the sake of God). His concern about peasants' poverty resulted in articles like "What Is to Be Done?" (1906) and "The Slavery of Our Times" (1900).

Besides his concern for peasants' poverty, Tolstoy valued Russian folklore, which since the eighteenth century had been most closely associated with the peasantry, and he often borrowed from folklore or wrote in a simple style that he associated with folk narratives. Many of the teaching tales or tales in the primers he composed for peasant children were based on folklore plots. At the same time, Tolstoy would strip away stylistic ornamentation from folktales, leaving bare moral narratives quite different from Alexander Pushkin's joyous verse versions of folktales, which followed the originals to the point of reproducing three identical repetitions at the appropriate places. The aesthetics of folklore did not especially interest Tolstoy, or else he saw clarity and simplicity – a kind of anti-aesthetic – as characteristic; indeed, a stylish oral narrative must have seemed to share the artsy features he eventually rejected in his own writing. Art – be it decoration of a useful object or entertainment from a bewitching song or narrative – might be suspect even if created by peasants. Just as the peasant was "closer to nature" than an educated upper-class man, any ornamentation in peasant folklore threatened to ruin the universality that made it accessible to any unspoiled observer. Tolstoy's attitude toward the plots he borrowed from elite writers was just the same: a plot was common property, which should be retold in the simplest and clearest manner for greatest impact. Recent readers have sometimes found Tolstoy's stories for children upsettingly naturalistic and unsuitable for family use, given their rather bare presentation of death and misfortune.[3] Well-known examples of his simplified narration of folk plots include the "folk" stories "Where There Is Love, There Is God" (1885) and "What Do People Live By" (1885).

Tolstoy's connections with peasants – writing to and for them, dressing like them, learning the crafts they practiced – were so famous that for some readers they almost overshadowed his writings and actions. At the same time, his willingness to do peasant work and be seen doing it both established and advertised his moral authority. He was sometimes therefore seen as competing with various revolutionary groups, both for connections with the working class (largely former peasants) and for authority with the rural peasantry. These connections explain why even a figure like Vladimir Lenin admired his insight into peasant thoughts and expression. In his article "Marx and Tolstoy" (1911), Plekhanov granted the writer a high level of authority, though he saw Tolstoy's conclusions as wrong. The approval expressed by these important Marxists helps to explain Tolstoy's continuing popularity as an author of fiction, a literary classic, throughout the Soviet period.

Notes

1 Alexandra Tolstoy, "Tolstoy and the Russian Peasant," *Russian Review*, 19:2 (April 1960), 150–6.
2 Gyorgy Lukács, *Studies in European Realism*, with an Introduction by Alfred Kazin (New York: Grosset & Dunlap, 1964), 129.
3 See John Byron Kuhner, "Leo Tolstoy's Children's Stories Will Devastate Your Children and Make You Want to Die," *LA Review of Books*, April 26, 2020, https://lareviewofbooks.org/article/leo-tolstoys-childrens-stories-will-devas tate-your-children-and-make-you-want-to-die (accessed May 3, 2020).

CHAPTER 6

The Great Reforms

Anne Hruska

The term "The Great Reforms" refers to a series of reforms instituted under Alexander II, each of which brought Russian societal structures more in line with those in Europe. Taken together, these reforms affected every aspect of Russian public life. The most important of the Great Reforms, especially where Tolstoy and his works are concerned, were the ending of serfdom in 1861, the reform of the legal system in 1864, and the creation of a system of local self-government called the zemstvo (1864). Other major reforms included reformation of the system of censorship (1865), the creation of city councils in urban areas (1870), and reform of the military system (1874).[1]

Tolstoy's reaction to the Great Reforms was complex and ambivalent. Both in his personal life and in his literary works, the reforms are connected with tensions between love and freedom, justice and social stability. In Tolstoy's writing, the reforms often reveal his conflicted thinking about his own role as a nobleman, elevated through wealth, power, and education above the peasantry. While Tolstoy's thinking develops over the course of his life, the fundamental tensions connected with the Great Reforms largely remain constant. This chapter will focus especially on the end of serfdom, which was a defining political moment for Tolstoy, and which was reflected in his work throughout his life. It will also discuss the zemstvo, and Tolstoy's own brief involvement with his local zemstvo, as opposed to his tendency to reject the zemstvo as a meaningful institution in his writing. Chapter 9 in this volume has more information on the reforms of the legal system.

Serfdom

Serfdom was fundamental to Russian social and economic structures in the early to middle nineteenth century. Originated during the fifteenth century, it was formally recognized in the law code of 1649, which tied the serfs to the land without right to leave it unless given permission by the landowner. During the reigns of Peter I and Catherine II, serfdom was increasingly codified and extended to include more peasants. By 1861 there were about 22 million nobility-owned serfs in Russia, as well as about 22 million state peasants and 3 million appanage peasants (meaning peasants belonging to the royal family). Combined, this made for about 68 percent of the population. The word *pomeshchik* in Russian means "landowner," but it also means the owner of the serfs who worked the land. While not all noblemen owned serfs, only the hereditary nobility had that right. Serfs belonged to the land, which the landowners owned; they were not allowed to travel, marry, or make other major life decisions without the permission of the landowner. Serfs were subject to all kinds of violence and humiliation, including beatings, rapes, and forced family separation. While Russian serfdom resembled American slavery in this way, one particularly important difference is that serfdom did not depend on the ideology of white supremacy, and thus the physical brutality of serfdom was less consistent. It depended on the whim of the landowner, who might be violent or relatively passive. But in either case, every major aspect of serfs' lives was always outside their own control. In any work of Tolstoy's that is written or (like *War and Peace*) set before 1861, one can assume that all domestic servants, farm laborers, and common soldiers, except for Cossacks, are serfs.

Landowners had a quota of recruits that they were required to send to the army, and they could choose which serfs to conscript, sometimes sending them as punishment. Richer serfs could buy exemptions for themselves or for family members. In *War and Peace*, the idealized peasant Platon Karataev tells Pierre that he was conscripted as punishment for taking wood. Since the term of service in the army for a common soldier was twenty-five years, conscription was a terrifying prospect. Even if the soldier survived his term and returned home, he could expect that everyone he had known would be either dead or changed beyond recognition.

Both serfs and landowners had duties to each other. At least nominally, landowners were supposed to take care of their serfs in times of famine, and also to give their serfs allotments of land that they could use for their own needs. Serfs could pay their duty to their owners in the form of *obrok* (also called quit-rent, meaning payment in money) or *barshchina* (also called corvée, payment through work on the nobleman's estate, usually about three days a week). *Obrok* was widely considered to be the less onerous system, because it allowed more liberty to the serfs, while *barshchina* gave more reasons for the landowner to interfere in the peasants' daily life. *Barshchina* was the more common system; only about one third of estates used *obrok* alone. At the end of *War and Peace*, Nikolai Rostov's serfs are on the *barshchina* system, as were Tolstoy's own serfs until 1857.

Tolstoy himself owned serfs until the official emancipation. When his parents' property was divided between Tolstoy and his siblings, he inherited 330 male serfs along with the estate at Yasnaya Polyana. In 1858, Tolstoy was in the top 20 percent of landowners, those who owned 100–500 serfs (his father had been in the top 3 percent of landowners, with over 500 serfs, and with future acquisitions, Tolstoy regained that status).[2] In his early writings, Tolstoy tended to write about serfdom as a fundamentally unjust structure – and yet one that is connected with love and familial stability. In his diary in 1854, Tolstoy wrote "It is true that slavery [meaning serfdom] is an evil – but it is an extremely lovable evil" (47:4). This outrageous statement makes at least a kind of twisted sense if one considers the example of Natalia Savishna in *Childhood* (1852), who embodies the loving injustice of serfdom. Deprived by her masters of her own chance to marry and have a family of her own, Natalia Savishna instead envelops her owners' children in her unconditional love.

Tolstoy's writing, both before and after the emancipation, glosses over the brutality of serfdom. When Nikolai Rostov puts down a serf rebellion on Princess Marya's estate in *War and Peace*, he does so with minimal but effective violence; soon the ringleaders are tied up and the estate is restored to what the novel seems to ask us to perceive as the proper order of things. In the first epilogue, Nikolai Rostov breaks his signet ring punching a disobedient serf; this act is described as problematic only because it makes his wife sad. Likewise, old Bolkonsky raises his stick at his steward Alpatych, who flinches but then, "frightened at his impudence in avoiding the blow, approached the prince bowing his balding head submissively" (9:263–4/Vol. 1, Pt. 3, Ch. 3). If this were a Dostoevsky novel, the blow would land and the cruelty underlying the system would be made explicit. Since it is not, Bolkonsky only threatens to strike but does not follow through. In this way *War and Peace* acknowledges the violence and coercion at the heart of serfdom, but never shows its effects in detail.

Tolstoy was more disturbed by the poverty serfdom caused than by the violence. In "A Landowner's Morning" (1856), Nekhliudov sees the desperate poverty among his serfs, but proves unable to address it. Tolstoy's least conflicted depictions of serfdom avoid the problem of poverty almost entirely. For all of Nikolai Rostov's freedom with his fists, we are told that the peasants love him, and even come from neighboring areas to ask him to buy them, because he provides for their needs. As the peasants put it, "He was a master . . . First he took care of the peasants, and then himself" (12:257/Epilogue, Pt. 1, Ch. 6). Only later in his life, such as in *Resurrection* (1899), does Tolstoy again depict poverty as a relic of serfdom.

Emancipation

The beginning of the end of serfdom came in an 1856 speech by the new Tsar Alexander II, in which he proclaimed that "it is better to start to abolish serfdom from above, than to wait for that time when it starts to abolish itself from below."[3] The official emancipation occurred a full five years later, on February 19, 1861. Alexander II put much of the responsibility for structuring the reforms on the landowners, giving them permission to elect local committees to plan the process, and what freedom would look like for the serfs. While the end of serfdom drastically changed the structure of Russian society, structural injustices and class advantages were carefully preserved in the post-serfdom system.

Soon after Alexander II's 1856 speech, Tolstoy told his serfs that he wanted to free them, but that "this cannot be done at once" (5:243). Instead, Tolstoy proposed that the serfs would be released from *barshchina*, but would pay him rent for the land they worked, receiving this land outright in twenty-four years, after the mortgage for Tolstoy's estate was paid. He was surprised to find that the serfs rejected his offer. Tolstoy learned that the serfs believed that they were going to be given full freedom, which for them meant freedom with the full right to the land they had been working, and which they needed to survive. Furthermore, Tolstoy was hurt that the serfs did not trust him, as landowner, to protect their interests. He also was frightened by the prospect of a peasant uprising if the emancipation did not satisfy them. In one letter Tolstoy writes, "Landowners are now facing the following question: your land or your life" (5:256). In another, he predicts, "This will end with our throats being cut" (60:89). Many other noblemen shared this fear.

Tolstoy was also concerned that emancipation would not solve the true problems, poverty and exploitation. In the letter where he framed the question as "your land or your life," Tolstoy also claimed the poverty of freed serfs without land could not be worse than the current situation, when the destitute serf "dies from hunger on his own land, which doesn't feed him and which he has no means to cultivate" (5:255). This (unsent) letter reacts conservatively to the project of emancipation, defending the class interests of the landowners; however, a fundamental awareness of injustice is buried beneath the defensiveness. Tolstoy understands that the emancipation as organized by the nobility is likely to be unfair to the freed serfs, and unlikely to solve the problem of peasant poverty. In this, Tolstoy is actually in a kind of agreement with radicals like Nikolai Chernyshevsky, who hoped that reaction against this injustice would trigger revolution.

The terms of the emancipation as set out in the statutes of February 19, 1861 gave serfs immediate personal freedom: they could now no longer be bought or sold, and had the right to marry and buy or sell property without permission, although they still could not own passports or travel independently. Peasants would be allowed to pay in installments for the allotments of land they needed to live. After forty-nine years of payment, they would own the land outright. Former household serfs were not included in the granting of land, and could be released by their former owners with nothing.[4] As David Moon writes, "Many observers noted that peasants' initial reactions to the Proclamation were a mixture of incomprehension and disappointment."[5] The serfs had been freed, but the fundamental class structure and economic hardships remained much the same.

The reform created the office of the "peace mediator": the intermediary between the peasantry and the landholders who helped to resolve conflicts over land distribution and payment. Tolstoy was appointed a peace mediator in 1861, and at first enjoyed it, writing, "Mediation is interesting and fascinating, but the one bad thing about it is that now all the nobility hate me with all the force of their souls" (60:405). In 1862 he resigned in frustration, after a letter signed by all the nobility of his district complained that he always favored the peasants.

Many of Tolstoy's major works make implicit or explicit reference to emancipation and the fears and problems connected to it. In *Family Happiness* (1859) the heroine's husband is absorbed in "gentry business" (5:77) that is implied to be connected with preparations for the end of serfdom. *War and Peace* is set in 1805–20, well before the emancipation, but it reflects emancipation in its concerns with freedom, structure, and rebellion. The first epilogue hints at the impending doomed Decembrist uprising of 1825, which had emancipation as one of its goals. Pierre and Denisov discuss a secret society and even the possibility of "revolt" (12:285/Epilogue, Pt. 1, Ch. 14), while Rostov declares that he will fight against them if need be. In this way the epilogue engages with a pervasive question of *War and Peace*: to what degree political freedom is possible, or even desirable, and to what degree one can still find internal freedom even within oppressive structures. In post-emancipation *Anna Karenina* (1878) the old order has been disrupted, but the new one has not yet fully taken shape. Levin's attempts to figure out how to live in a family work in parallel with his attempts to find a way to farm with the peasants, now that serfdom has ended. Levin longs to join with the peasantry (and even considers marrying a peasant woman), yet he also fears the loss of his noble status in the changing post-emancipation society. In *Anna Karenina*, the social uncertainty in the wake of serfdom helps frame the larger problem of the place of the individual in the social world.

Zemstvo

Serfdom put the responsibility on landholders to establish and maintain order within their own estates. With serfdom's end, tsarist officials recognized the need to create units of local government. The zemstvos (from the word *zemlia*, meaning "land") were established in 1864 to create a system connecting the newly freed peasants to the larger tsarist government. The zemstvo was supposed to take care of local needs, including education, famine relief, trade, and public health. Each zemstvo was divided into two levels. The local population elected deputies at the district level; the district assembly then elected deputies for the provincial level. Eligibility to vote was based on three kinds of property ownership: privately owned land, urban real estate, and peasant allotment land. Each of these three groups were able to elect a specific number of delegates. Many male peasants over twenty-five thus had the right to vote, and yet because of the structure of voting, and because members of the nobility tended to have more leisure to attend meetings, the nobility was disproportionately represented in the zemstvo.

Tolstoy was involved with his local zemstvo in the 1870s as part of his work on education. In 1874 he was elected as a member of the council of education at the district level, and then in 1877 to the provincial level for a three-year term, although he stopped participating after two years. In *Anna Karenina*, Levin, like Tolstoy, becomes disenchanted with the zemstvo, telling Stiva that he is no longer a zemstvo member because "I have quarreled with everyone and don't go to meetings anymore" (18:21/ Pt. 1, Ch. 5). Levin and his brothers argue repeatedly about the usefulness of the zemstvo as a social institution.

In an 1891 article "On Hunger," Tolstoy articulates a different problem with the zemstvo: that it still works within a framework of class hierarchy, and thus cannot really solve anything. Writing about attempts of the zemstvos to help the starving peasantry during the famine of 1891,

Tolstoy explains that dire poverty has always existed in Russia, "before and after emancipation" (29:105). As an example of the acts of desperation caused by poverty, he mentions stealing wood from the master's forest "under threat of beating and imprisonment" (29:93) – the very crime for which Platon Karataev was forced into conscription. In order to be able to change things in a meaningful way, the higher classes would "need first of all to see the cold and hungry man, create straightforward relations with him, destroy the barriers that had separated us from him" (29:109) – which is something the structure of the zemstvo does not allow them to do.

Resurrection (1899) offers an example of what a true rectification of the wrongs of class separation would look like. The hero Nekhliudov (a name that Tolstoy used multiple times in his works, but that echoes especially the bemused hero of "Morning of a Landowner") offers to give the land on one of his estates to the peasants. Unlike Tolstoy in his abortive attempt to free his serfs before the emancipation, and unlike Princess Marya during the serf rebellion in *War and Peace*, Nekhliudov is able to enter into a meaningful conversation with the peasants, in such a way that they no longer suspect him of trying to manipulate or cheat them; instead, they realize that, as one peasant woman phrases it, "the master has begun to think of his soul, and is acting for its salvation" (32:231/Pt. 2, Ch. 9). While Nekhliudov is never able to fully transcend his own class status and join this this larger community, he does here embody Tolstoy's vision of connecting in a truthful and individual way, outside of bureaucratic structure, to correct the evil of dire poverty, the terrible legacy of serfdom in post-emancipation Russia.

Notes

1 For a more in-depth explanation of the Great Reforms, see W. Bruce Lincoln, *The Great Reforms: Autocracy, Bureaucracy, and the Politics of Change in Imperial Russia* (DeKalb: Northern Illinois University Press, 1990).
2 David Moon, *The Abolition of Serfdom in Russia, 1762–1907* (New York: Longman, 2001), 17.
3 For the full speech, see ibid. The translation here is his.
4 For a fuller breakdown of the complex terms of the 1861 statute, see ibid., 69–82.
5 Ibid., 88.

CHAPTER 7

Nobility and the Russian Class System

Bella Grigoryan

> What they were looking for remains unknown. Some friend of yours, a filthy colonel, read all my letters and diaries ... he read two sets of correspondence for whose secrecy I would have given everything in the world – and went away, saying he had found nothing *suspicious*. It is my good fortune, and that of your friend, that I wasn't there – I would have killed him!

So wrote Lev Tolstoy to his longtime correspondent the countess and lady-in-waiting Alexandra Andreevna Tolstaya, after gendarmes searched Yasnaya Polyana, looking for evidence of subversive activity in 1862, when Russia saw a wave of student protests. Claiming to have long been "completely indifferent to the government" and "even more indifferent to the present-day liberals," Tolstoy added that he now had "anger and revulsion, almost loathing for that dear government which makes searches of my property looking for [equipment] for publishing the proclamations of [émigré revolutionary political thinker and activist Alexander] Herzen, which I scorn, which, from boredom, I haven't the patience to read" (60:428–30).[1] Such was Tolstoy's offense at the search that in a subsequent letter he considered selling his estates and leaving Russia. Eventually, he wrote a letter to the Tsar Alexander II, asking for an explanation. Throughout Tolstoy's correspondence in the summer of 1862, most galling for him is the awareness that even a nobleman has no stable and guaranteed rights to privacy and inviolability of person and property. The gendarmes' search of his property is painful because it reveals the fundamental insecurity of noble status and privileges.

Tolstoy was born into a noble family of considerable standing (see Chapter 3). The family of his mother – princess Maria Nikolaevna Volkonskaya – was among the nation's oldest aristocratic families, able to trace its lineage to Riurik, the legendary Varangian ruler of early medieval Rus. In Russia, as elsewhere, the verifiable longevity of noble clans conferred status, although this did not always translate to greater economic or political power. The family of the writer's father – count Nikolai Ilyich Tolstoy – was also an old aristocratic clan; the Tolstoys' ancestor Pyotr Andreevich had been made a hereditary Count in 1724 by decree of Peter I, at the coronation of Catherine I. In the nineteenth century, one might have said that the Tolstoys were an old noble family and not particularly prominent, despite being titled. The age and respectability of a clan were more important than imported titles (Baron, Count), which were given with relative liberality throughout the eighteenth century and could even mark the recipient as something of an upstart.

Throughout Tolstoy's lifetime (1828–1910) subjects of the Russian Empire were inscribed into a social estate or, in Russian, *soslovie*, a term that anglophone historians have hesitated to translate as social class. Given that the Russian estates system persisted until the 1917 revolutions, the historians' decision not to equate, even rhetorically, estates with social class highlights a peculiarity of Russian sociohistorical progress: its divergence from trends ascendant in Western Europe, and especially France, where estates gave way to class much earlier, at the end of the *ancien régime*. The French origins of the concept of class date to the immediate aftermath of 1789, when jurists began to replace "estates" with "class"; in England, the word "class" was in use even earlier. By contrast, in Russia estates – not class – continued to define the legal ramifications of residency and determine the availability of various political, economic, and social experiences.

From a juridical standpoint, the estates provided a mediating system between the state and its subjects. Russian subjects were granted privileges and were required to fulfill obligations not as individuals, but as members of a social estate. The law, in other words, viewed and treated Russian subjects through the lens of *soslovie*. Belonging to a particular social estate meant a legal identity, which could also carry a social and a political dimension, as well as one or another kind of access to assets and economic well-being, especially insofar that the *soslovie* system governed such privileges as the right to engage in industry and commerce, as well as the right to own and use land and natural resources. The Russian social estates legally defined included the following categories of imperial subjects (among others): the nobility, the merchantry, townspeople, clergy, and peasants. Either legally or socially (or sometimes both), each of these categories was internally subdivided farther, making for finer distinctions, so that, taking some of the more salient categorizations to provide two examples, a peasant owned by the state would be distinguished from a serf owned by a landowner, just as an aristocrat who could trace his lineage to the medieval period would be sharply differentiated from an individual who had attained personal (as opposed to hereditary) nobility through state service. Boundaries between the estates were not impermeable, and it remained possible and sometimes advantageous to move between social estates; to leave one estate to become inscribed in another was neither easy, nor prohibitively difficult. The permeability of estate boundaries, as well as the relative breakdown or hybridization of the estates in Tolstoy's lifetime, was all but announced by the arrival of the paradigmatic mid-nineteenth-century figure of the *raznochinets*, literally, a person of various ranks, represented often by the educated children of clergy who did not pursue a religious vocation and began to gain prominence in Russian intellectual life and public discourse by the 1840s, to become a major force by the 1860s.

Without question, the nobility was the social estate endowed with the greatest, farthest-ranging privileges. The nobility was distinguished from the other estates in many ways, perhaps the most important of which was the right to own land populated by serfs. Only a noble could be a serf- and landowner or, in Russian, a *pomeshchik*. Despite the estate's shared privileges, the nobility had a high degree of internal heterogeneity when it came to such matters as modes of sociability, access to power and to polite society, relationship to the provinces, and connection to the cultural and political centers (e.g., Moscow, St. Petersburg), as well as scope of property (assets, income, and debt). The number of male serfs owned served as shorthand for wealth. During the middle decades of the nineteenth century the noble economic elite was small: only about 3 percent of nobles owned more than 500 male serfs, and only 1 percent owned more than 1,000. The middling category of nobles, those who owned between 100 and 500 serfs, comprised between 16 and 22 percent of the noble population. As Katherine Antonova explains, the "remaining roughly 80 percent of all nobles were those who owned fewer than 101 souls, and could thus be described as poor."[2] Both noble men and women exercised control over property and noblewomen retained a legal claim to their property after marriage. Tolstoy's mother entered her marriage with a dowry that included the estate Yasnaya Polyana, where Tolstoy would spend much of his life, and some 800 serfs, of whom Tolstoy would inherit some 300 when his parents' properties were distributed among the heirs.

As for the history of landownership, the etymology of the word *pomeshchik* – with its suggestion of *pomeshchennyi*, meaning "someone placed" – points to the likely medieval origins of upper-crust landholding as probably temporary compensation for service, usually in a military capacity. The feudal Russian nobles had little in the way of stable privileges. As with so many aspects of Russian culture and history, the reign of Peter I would reshape the picture. The Emperor reorganized what had been varied Russian elites into a single aggregate social and political body, the *dvorianstvo*, the term suggesting proximity to the court (*dvor*). Still more impactful was Peter I's introduction of the Table of Ranks in 1722, which articulated noblemen's service obligations to the state and made nobles into servitors, splitting them into three categories according to their engagement in the military, civil service, or at court. One could regard the Table of Ranks as a measure that coerced the elite into more structured forms of state service. To the extent that it replaced the feudal system of *mestnichestvo* (which determined a man's right to occupy a position via complicated calculations of individual and clan seniority), one could also view the Table as a meritocratic equalizer that made upward mobility available to capable and enterprising persons.

The old Russian elites retained their power in the post-Petrine period to a significant degree; however, the eighteenth century saw noble upstarts, whose meteoric rise became the stuff of gossip and legend. Throughout the Table's existence, attaining various ranks in the military, civil, and court service conferred either personal or hereditary nobility. The ranks required for the conferral of nobility kept rising in successive reigns, in correspondence with a desire to curb the number of newly "made" nobles. Nevertheless, the Table of Ranks meant that the nobility had become somewhat open to newcomers. The Petrine system continued to shape the Russian elites for the rest of the imperial period; with some revisions, the Table of Ranks survived for nearly 200 years, until the 1917 revolutions. A man's rank determined specific forms of address (e.g., your excellency, your high excellency) and therefore structured common exchanges via epistolary correspondence, as well as everyday social and personal interactions. Tolstoy retired from military service at the relatively low rank of lieutenant.

The relationship between the nobility and the state underwent another major shift in 1762 when Peter III's very short reign (six months that ended in a coup) saw the royal promulgation of a manifesto that liberated nobles from what had been obligatory state service. No doubt in the long-range history of the nobility (and of Russia) this was a piece of consequential legislation; in its long aftermath the nobility's self-fashioning and self-understanding were recalibrated. Historians' appraisals of the tangible short-term impact of the nobility's emancipation from service to the state vary, when it comes to the extent to which nobles took advantage of their newly gained right to retire whenever they liked. (The right to retire after some years of service had been gained in increments, as the period between 1722 and 1762 saw the gradual lightening of the noble corporate lifelong obligation to serve.) Even as state service ceased to be a legal obligation, that a nobleman should serve in some capacity remained a social expectation. A non-serving nobleman could not, for example, be addressed by a rank-based honorific in official correspondence. Tolstoy's own *Anna Karenina* (1875–8) registers shifting attitudes to state service in the figures of Konstantin Levin, who is viewed, at the novel's beginning, as an oddity in part because he does not serve the state and does little other than mind his ancestral estate; of Vronsky, who causes something of a scandal when he leaves a brilliant military career to pursue a personal passion; and of Oblonsky, whose move from a good government service post to a job in a grotesquely hybrid amalgamated railways and banking company signals a shift toward a new mode of both social and economic relations, enabled by the ascendancy of Russian capitalism.

If the nineteenth century saw the gradual incorporation of the nobility into emerging capitalist relations, the latter decades of the eighteenth century came close to providing the nobility with something like rights guaranteed in legal discourse. Peter III's manifesto was affirmed and amplified by Catherine II's 1785 Charter to the Nobility, which confirmed the nobles' exemption from obligatory state service and granted the empire's highest estate a range of privileges that included the right to a trial by peers, the right to assembly, freedom from corporal punishment, and various forms of control over property, including extensive control over serfs. Some would see in Catherine's legislation the inception of a veritable golden age for the nobility. Others would point to the empress's habit of governing through favoritism and her attendant tendency to elevate specific individuals, endowing them with political power and granting extensive economic assets (in the form, for example, of country estates) as proof that even under Russia's most enlightened monarch, noble privileges remained subject to the whim of the autocrat.

A review of the subsequent reigns supports the latter interpretation. Catherine's son Paul I undid much of his mother's legislation and subjected nobles to what many perceived as an insulting degree of surveillance and supervision, particularly in his attempts at military reform. Catherine's grandson Alexander I was seen as more like Catherine than Paul, in a positive sense, and was therefore greeted with a good deal of enthusiasm, which, nevertheless, turned to discontent from both the conservative and radical wings of the nobility in the years to come. Alexander I's unexpected death in 1825 prompted the Decembrist Revolt, in which members of some of the oldest aristocratic families participated. How to explain that a small group of Russian nobles staged a revolt at Senate Square to demand the end of serfdom and a constitution?

The famed parting of the ways between the educated elite and the state was precipitated by the 1762 emancipation of the nobility from service: the state no longer *needed* the nobles. Then, following the post-1789 shift in Russian autocratic rule toward a greater degree of repression of private enterprise and independent activity, cultural historians note an inward turn among the educated nobility. The inward turn could be expressed in retirement from service, the cultivation of domestic pursuits, as well as in an interest in personal growth, mysticism, and membership in the Masonic lodges. Tolstoy's *War and Peace*, which began as a book about the Decembrists, explores this phenomenon through many of its male noble characters, especially Pierre Bezukhov.

In the more immediate context, the Decembrists' views were shaped by their relatively recent exposure to West European culture and politics in the course of the Napoleonic campaigns; the contrast between the state of affairs at home and abroad may have been instructive. In any event, as the war neared its end, there was an expectation of extensive state-sponsored changes on all sides of the period's political spectrum. However, in the direct aftermath of 1812 the Russian elites were polarized on the subject of reform, with the Decembrists comprising a small but, in the realm of Russian intellectual history, highly impactful minority of the educated public. The temptation to see the Decembrists as typical nobles must be resisted. We are dealing with a small number of noblemen whose political position did not represent the views of the estate, which tended toward conservatism. Moreover, throughout the period of the Russian imperial nobility's existence, it would be difficult and perhaps inadvisable to speak about anything like a corporate noble identity, a set of views held by all or most nobles, or a shared sense of noble politics. The Russian nobility was a social estate with a great deal of internal heterogeneity when it came to such things as education, social formation, and political outlook.

Ultimately, whether Tolstoy's life and work may be read through the lens of noble history is an open question; the lens may reveal some preoccupations while obscuring others. As is well known, Tolstoy all but renounced his nobleman's privileges. Famously, the Count spent a good deal of his adult life dressed in the clothes of a peasant, much as he did not usually manage to pass for one (see Chapter 13). While many peasants appear to have recognized Tolstoy as someone who was not one of their own, educated contemporaries recall a highly charismatic nobility ever perceptible in Tolstoy's bearing, brought into even sharper relief by his simple clothes and homemade shoes.[3] Tolstoy came to engage in various forms of peasant labor: making boots, ploughing, doing household chores, tidying his own room, and emptying his own chamber pot. He found the nobles' ownership of land populated by serfs disturbing, even after the long-awaited 1861 emancipation of the serfs by a royal edict, whose preparatory stages he had judged a violation of noble property rights in 1856 (see Chapter 6). Eventually, Tolstoy came to see all property ownership as immoral. Late in life he transferred the ownership of his various properties to members of his family, including his wife, Sofia Andreevna. This means that during the last years of his life, Tolstoy had neither legal control over, nor legal rights to, what had been his mother's ancestral property; this was probably an especially frustrating circumstance when, in the years following the 1905 revolution, his wife summoned police guards to protect their woods from peasants who were cutting down trees. By that time, Tolstoy was a radical pacifist likely to have objected to the gendarmes at Yasnaya Polyana for reasons quite different from his indignation at the violation of noble privileges during the search of 1862.

Notes

1 The letter is quoted and discussed in Kathryn B. Feuer, *Tolstoy and the Genesis of War and Peace*, ed. Robin Feuer Miller and Donna Tussing Orwin (Ithaca, NY: Cornell University Press, 1996), 184–5 (translation altered).

2 Katherine Pickering Antonova, *An Ordinary Marriage: The World of a Gentry Family in Provincial Russia* (Oxford University Press, 2013), 27. See also Jerome Blum, *Lord and Peasant in Russia: From the Ninth to the Nineteenth Century* (Princeton University Press, 1971), 367–70.

3 Thomas Newlin, "Peasant Dreams, Peasant Nightmares: On Tolstoy and Cross-Dressing," *Russian Review* 78 (October 2019), 595–618.

CHAPTER 8

The Russian Orthodox Church

Francesca Silano

In February 1901, the Holy Synod, the body that governed the Russian Orthodox Church, published a resolution decrying the fact that Leo Tolstoy, who had been baptized in the faith, had "openly denied before all the Mother who nurtured and educated him – the Orthodox Church." In so doing, Tolstoy had "alienated himself" (*ottorg sebia sam*) from the Church. For this reason, the Church could no longer consider him a member unless he repented and expressed a desire to renew his communion with it. Tolstoy had publicly mocked some of the core dogmas of Orthodoxy and rejected the sacraments, including the most sacred one: the Eucharist, even satirizing it in his last novel *Resurrection* (1899). The Synod claimed that it was necessary to correct those who were being led astray by Tolstoy's teachings and to admonish Tolstoy himself who, as an elderly man, risked dying "having rejected the blessings and prayers of the Church and all communion with Her."[1]

This message set off a storm in the media and in Russian society as revolutionaries, journalists, Orthodox believers, and prominent members of the intelligentsia debated its meaning. Tolstoy received thousands of letters and telegrams; some called for his conversion and repentance (sometimes even threatening violence against him), others encouraged him in his beliefs, and still others claimed that the author was aiding the Church by forcing it to awaken from its "slumber."[2]

Tolstoy wrote a public response to the Synod and to his correspondents in the spring of 1901, protesting that he had been singled out among other "educated people" who "share[d] the same disbelief." He provided an account of his own beliefs and spiritual journey, explaining how he had, indeed, "renounced the Church," precisely out of a desire to serve the Lord. He had decided to separate himself from the Church and from "the communion with people which was inexpressibly dear to me," only after carefully studying Church doctrine and strictly following all the Church's teachings for a whole year. At this point, he determined that "the theory of the Church doctrine is an insidious and harmful lie." Tolstoy concluded by saying that even as his beliefs might offend others, "I can just as little change them as my body ... I do not believe my faith to be the one indubitable truth for all time, but I see no other that is simpler, clearer, and meets all the demands of my reason and my heart ... I cannot return to that from which, with such suffering, I have escaped, just like a flying bird cannot re-enter the eggshell from which it has emerged" (34:245–53).

The bishops referred to the Church as Tolstoy's "Mother" in their message; in presenting himself as a bird who had grown beyond the safety of the nest, Tolstoy revealed that he too conceived of himself as a child of the Church, albeit one who had left the nest. Indeed, the mother–child metaphor is the one that best captures the relationship between Tolstoy and the Orthodox Church, and it is the key to understanding the place of the Church in his writings, and the crucial role he played in the life of the Orthodox Church of his time. Scholars have underestimated or misunderstood this relationship, often preferring to behold the "flying bird" than to consider the "eggshell" in the nest, not least because they assume the Orthodox Church to have been a mere handmaid of the state, a decrepit institution that could not have imparted much to a man whose philosophies seemed to be more indebted to Schopenhauer than to saints.

Yet, Tolstoy, as the bishops argued in their message, had been baptized and educated in the Church; he came from an Orthodox family and lived in an environment where church bells marked the passing of time and where Orthodox feasts determined the yearly calendar. In his two most famous novels, *War and Peace* (1865–9) and *Anna Karenina* (1875–8), both Natasha and Levin receive crucial insights in the course of the Orthodox liturgy. Even as his relationship with the Church waxed and waned, culminating in the 1901 controversy, Tolstoy continued to be influenced by his Orthodox roots.

For its part, the Orthodox Church of Tolstoy's time found itself in many of the same dilemmas as a mother in the face of a rebellious child. As the author exposed its weaknesses, railed against its injustices, and forged his own religious path in the world, the Church – in the form of its clergy, lay people, and institutional leadership – was alternately aggrieved, angered, saddened, thoughtfully reflective, and, some might argue, reformed by his rebellion. The remainder of this chapter lays out some of the essential aspects of this relationship, revealing how its dynamics profoundly shaped Tolstoy, his writing, and the Church of his time.

In Russian, the word for "orthodox" (*pravoslavie*) is literally translated as "right glory." The Eastern Orthodox Church in general, and the Russian

Orthodox Church specifically, has traditionally seen itself as possessing the sole true means of glorifying God. It professes Jesus Christ to be the son of God. It is convinced that human history will eventually come to an end, at which point Christ will return in glory. Until such time, the Church has the task of guiding the people of God in correctly glorifying him and preparing for Christ's return. In this sense, the Orthodox Church in Russia, although bound to a specific country, has always made normative and universal claims for all of humanity.

Russia's long association with Orthodoxy began in 988 when Vladimir, the Grand Prince of Kiev, was baptized into the Byzantine Church. Over the next 600 years, the Church developed in tandem with the fledgling Russian state until 1589, when the Russian Church declared itself auto-cephalous, that is, self-governing, under the leadership of its own patriarch. Tsar Peter the Great (r. 1682–1725) used state laws to ensure the confor-mity of all Orthodox subjects with Church law; but he also firmly established the Church's subordinacy to the state. After the death of Patriarch Adrian in 1700, Peter forbade the election of a new patriarch and ordered instead that the Church be governed by a Holy Synod consisting of a group of bishops and a lay over-procurator who served as the liaison between the bishops and the tsar. The extent to which the Church was formally subjected to the state has been hotly debated by scholars, and it is certainly not the case that the Church was a mere department of the state. It cannot be denied though that with the passing of time, the Church's proximity to the state, combined with the growing authority of the lay over-procurator over Synodal affairs, undermined its authority in public life.[3]

The Church, however, was far from a moribund institution, especially in the nineteenth century. A monastic revival saw the number of nuns and monks rise tenfold between 1825 and 1917. The number of monasteries doubled over this period to 1,000, becoming sites to which an increasing number of pilgrims traveled each year.[4] The most noted of these was Optina Pustyn, the home to numerous *startsy* (spiritual elders), who became important figures of consolation, wisdom, and leadership for many Orthodox faithful and intellectuals, including Tolstoy, who continued to visit the monastery even after he had turned his back on the Church.[5]

The monastic revival also led to impressive efforts on the part of monks and groups of Orthodox scholars to translate into Russian and to dissem-inate texts written by the first Christian thinkers, whose writings are known as patristic texts. These translations enabled Tolstoy to make a careful study of patristic thought when he was developing his own responses to the Orthodox Church in the 1870s. This mass translation effort reflected another important current in Orthodox life: the development of an Orthodox academic world, best represented by the flowering of the Church's four theological academies in Kiev, Moscow, St. Petersburg, and Kazan, which trained the best and brightest clerical and lay Orthodox thinkers of the day. The academies became vibrant centers of discussion and debate about the state of Orthodoxy in Russian life. Students were introduced to the translated patristic texts, but also to emerging (and often Western) historical, philosophical, and archeological methods that allowed them to reflect upon Orthodoxy in new ways.

This last development is essential to understanding the relationship between the Church and Tolstoy; for many of the clerics who served as his interlocutors, and, in particular, Antony (Vadkovsky) (1846–1912), the head of the Synod at the time of its break with Tolstoy, were shaped by this academic context. These men were deeply interested in the relationship between Orthodox and secular thought and were aware of the challenges that modern philosophy and science posed to the Church with its normative claims. People like Vadkovsky, who was the rector of the St. Petersburg Theological Academy from 1887 to 1892, encouraged students to develop Orthodox responses to the challenges of modern life.

Just as Church intellectuals were undertaking these efforts, Tolstoy was poking holes in their arguments. In *A Confession*, written between 1879 and 1882, he described his tortured relationship with the Church. His decision to spend a year following the Church's teachings, he explained, was inspired by his admiration for the faith of the peasants: "I united myself with my forefathers: the father, mother, and grandparents I loved ... I united myself also with millions of the common people, whom I respected."[6] This experience of unity with believers past and present allowed him for some time to "conceal from myself the contradictions and obscurities of the doctrine," and above all, all those doctrines that were based on miraculous occurrences. He also found it impossible to accept the Church's normative claims. Having encountered good people of different creeds, he thought it cruel that the Church could condemn alternative forms of worship.[7]

By 1879, Tolstoy had resolved to separate the truth from the falsehoods in the Orthodox faith. He did so by engaging in a careful study of Orthodox doctrine, and through debates and discussions with some of the most important Orthodox figures of the day, including the monks of Optina and at least three of the leading hierarchs of the Orthodox Church.[8] In other words, the author's battles with the Orthodox Church were made possible in part because of the vitality of Orthodox life. Tolstoy dedicated much of his work in the 1880s to systematically refuting the Orthodox Church's teachings through his rewriting of the Gospels, his setting out of his own creed, and his numerous challenges to the Orthodox clergy. This rebellion, once begun, played out across the pages of his collected works, the public press, and the journals of Orthodox academia.

Tolstoy embodied many of the ideas that Orthodox academics knew they had to respond to in order to demonstrate the credibility of Orthodoxy in modern times. The future Patriarch Tikhon (1865–1925), who served as the head of the Orthodox Church during the first years of Bolshevik rule, devoted most of his academic writing to engaging with Tolstoy's ideas. Leading preachers of the day addressed Tolstoy in their homilies and writings, publishing 85 books and booklets, along with 260 articles.[9] Some of these authors condemned the Count outright for heresy, while others, like Tikhon (who had been trained under Antony at the St. Petersburg Academy), aimed to demonstrate how the Church could reasonably respond to Tolstoy's modern objections. In a certain sense, then, Tolstoy and Orthodox thinkers needed each other. Tolstoy's works provided some Church commentators with the opportunity to demonstrate the relevance of Christianity to modern people. Conversely, the Church provided Tolstoy with an opponent against whose teachings he could construct his own religious worldview. And so, in the 1880s and 1890s Tolstoy continued to publish defamatory remarks about the Church, yet the Synod made no attempt to excommunicate him, despite the calls of some clergyman for it to act.[10] What, then, prompted the members of the Synod to write their 1901 resolution against the Count?

In early February 1901, members of the newly formed Religious-Philosophical Group made up of leading members of the clergy and intelligentsia gathered in St. Petersburg for one of a series of meetings that would occur regularly until 1903. Their goal was to discuss and bridge the growing gap between the secular Russian intelligentsia and the Orthodox Church. By this point, Antony, now Metropolitan of St. Petersburg, was the leading hierarch on the Holy Synod, and he strongly supported the meetings. At the February gathering, the attendees discussed Tolstoy, and one of the priests, Grigory Petrov, argued that Tolstoy was to Russia what Virgil was to Dante – a guide who could lead Russia through the spiritual darkness of the times to the gates of heaven.[11]

It was only at this point, when it looked like even Orthodox clergymen risked being led astray by Tolstoy, that Antony, as head of the Synod, felt he had no choice but to publicly and authoritatively denounce Tolstoy's teachings.[12] Petrov's comments had also made it clear that the Orthodox clergy could not be trusted to defend Orthodox teaching; therefore, Orthodox believers were at increased risk of being confused by Tolstoy and his supporters. The Synod's 1901 message, then, was primarily an educational act aimed both at Tolstoy and at Orthodox believers in general: it served to clarify the Church's teachings and to explain where Tolstoy had contradicted that teaching. So concerned were the members of the Synod about not appearing to punish Tolstoy that they deliberately avoided the word "excommunication" in the message, emphasizing that Tolstoy had already separated himself by his own choice, and that the door was open for him should he elect to return.[13]

For the next nine years, hierarchs, clergymen, and Orthodox lay believers would devote their time and energy to pleading with their brother to come home. Although it is difficult to discern the ultimate intentions of all of these figures, the idea that they all acted for the cynical reason of being able to claim Tolstoy as a repentant convert and thus boost the public image of the Orthodox Church seems implausible. At least some appear to have been moved by a sincere wish to see Tolstoy return to the Mother's fold, convinced as they were that life – and death – outside of it was no life at all. "There is no life without the sun, there is no life without Christ," wrote Metropolitan Antony to Tolstoy's wife in one of a series of letters the two exchanged. The bishop urged Sofia to make every effort to ensure that the Count repented before his death so that he could receive the Eucharist "which gives peace, joy and life to the believing soul."[14]

It was precisely this insistence that he not die without repenting that Tolstoy found so vexing. After receiving a visit from the Bishop of Tula in January of 1909, the Count wrote in his diary: "It is especially unpleasant that he asked to be informed when I was dying." He even worried that the Church would try to persuade people that he had repented before dying. "And for this reason," he continued, as insurance against what might happen after his death, "I pronounce … that to return to the Church, to receive communion before dying I cannot do … and thus everything that will be said about my deathbed repentance and confession is a lie."[15]

On October 27, 1910, Tolstoy set out on the journey that would take him to his death in the Astapovo station, but he went first to Optina Pustyn. During his brief respite at the monastery guest house, one account claims that Tolstoy twice set out to meet with the elders and twice changed his mind, setting off for the forest instead.[16] The prodigal son, it seems, did not want to return home, but he could not entirely forget his mother. Similarly, Metropolitan Antony could not forget Tolstoy. At the news that

Tolstoy was dying at the station, Antony made a series of desperate attempts to have the Count reconciled with the Church, culminating in his final appeal to Tolstoy that was published in the newspapers: "From the very first moment of your break with the Church I have prayed and do pray unceasingly that the Lord will return you to the Church ... I beseech you now to make your peace with the Church and with the Orthodox Russian people. May the Lord bless and keep you."[17] The same newspapers reported that the Metropolitan cried upon hearing of the Count's death. The mother and the child were never reconciled, but these tableaux of the final moments of Leo Tolstoy's life reveal that they were forever intertwined.

Notes

1 "Opredelenie Sv. Sinoda ot 20–22 fevralia 1901 goda, s poslaniem vernym chadam Pravoslavnyia Grekorossiiskiia Tserkvi o grafa L've Nikolaeviche Tolstom," *Tserkovnye vedomosti* 8 (1901), 46–8.

2 Alexandra Tolstoy, *Tolstoy: A Life of My Father*, trans. Elizabeth Reynolds Hapgood (New York: Harper & Brothers, 1953), 412.

3 Scott M. Kenworthy and Alexander S. Agadjanian, *Understanding World Christianity: Russia* (Minneapolis: Fortress Press, 2021), 118–20.

4 Ibid., 122–4.

5 Pål Kolstø, "The Elder at Iasnaia Poliana: Lev Tolstoi and the Orthodox *Starets* Tradition," *Kritika* 9:3 (Summer 2008), 533–44.

6 Leo Tolstoy, *A Confession and What I Believe*, trans. Aylmer Maude (London: Oxford University Press, 1920), 83.

7 Ibid., 89–92.

8 Prot. Georgii Orekhanov, *Lev Tolstoy "prorok bez chesti": khronika katastrofy* (Moscow: Voskresenie, 2016), 133–9.

9 Pål Kolstø, "The Demonized Double: The Image of Lev Tolstoi in Russian Orthodox Polemics," *Slavic Review* 65:2 (Summer 2006), 305.

10 Orekhanov, *Lev Tolstoy "prorok bez chesti,"* 461–7.

11 Kolstø, "The Demonized Double," 310–11.

12 Orekhanov, *Lev Tolstoy "prorok bez chesti"*, 467–8.

13 Ibid., 480–2.

14 Ibid., 527–8.

15 Quoted in William Nickell, "Transfigurations of Tolstoy's Final Journey: The Church and the Media in 1910," *Tolstoy Studies Journal* 18 (2006), 35.

16 Kolstø, "Elder at Iasnaia Poliana," 540.

17 Nickell, "Transfigurations of Tolstoy's Final Journey," 39.

CHAPTER 9

Law

Tatiana Borisova

On December 8, 1908, Tolstoy's wife Sofia Andreevna wrote in her diary that peasants had broken the locks on several buildings at their estate and stolen honey. "I hate the people threatening our lives nowadays. I hate the executions and the inability of the government," she lamented.[1] She wished for authorities who could protect her property and maintain order. A diary entry seven months later made a related point. Pleased to be helping copy her husband's prose, Sofia Andreevna was upset by what he had written: he again made his readers sympathize with a revolutionary. Indirectly, she was irritated that her spouse was attacking the law and the government institutions that enforce it – the very sources of the stability she craved. She explained Tolstoy's motives quite bluntly: "although he masks it with Christianity, without a doubt he supports revolution, while hating everything that is put above us by fate, that is – authorities."[2] This chapter examines the implications of Sofia Andreevna's insight: that her husband's ideology was weakening the legitimacy of imperial legality. Beginning with an overview of the state of Russia's legal system, the chapter examines Tolstoy's first encounters with the law as a student at Kazan University, his evaluation of public access to justice after the liberal reforms of the 1860s to 1870s, and his ideas of rule of law in general.

Tolstoy lived in a very turbulent epoch of Russian legal history. The expansion of liberal ideology and capitalism pushed all the monarchies of Europe to modernize their legal institutions in order to achieve economic growth. In the Russian Empire, the challenges of legal modernization were particularly complex. For centuries Russian law operated as a multiplicity of regional legal orders and Tsar's codes and edicts enforced by imperial civil servants and local intermediaries. This legal system was based on social stratification in which different social groups – religious, ethnic, and estate – had different obligations in exchange for special "privileges" guaranteed by the Tsar. These privileges included a variety of conflict resolution methods. Having such a patchwork legal system across the

Empire made it difficult to efficiently administer both public expenditure and government revenue, which Russia desperately needed in its military and economic rivalry with other empires.

Starting during Peter the Great's reign in the early eighteenth century, many initiatives were undertaken to modernize economic and legal institutions. These efforts were twofold. Practically, they involved adopting institutions and practices from Europe and adjusting them to Russian realities. On the ideological level, Russian subjects' access to justice and their compliance with newly adopted law became a part of a civic religion that Peter and his followers attempted to impose. In opposition to the discourse of natural law and inherent rights, Peter offered a model in which loyal subjects' service to the Tsar and Fatherland would be rewarded with order, safety, and clemency. The development of administrative techniques along with expertise in theoretical jurisprudence in Russian universities, established at the beginning of the nineteenth century, pushed forward Peter's plan for the systematization of Russian law. Finally, in 1835, the codification plan was realized in the fifteen volumes of the *Digest of Laws of the Russian Empire*. The Digest systematized the privileges of each estate and stipulated the general procedures for criminal and civil law.

In 1847, as a nineteen-year-old law student at Kazan University, Tolstoy had to go through many volumes of the *Digest*, which was used as a textbook on Russian law. He had a dual motivation for choosing to study law: the prestigious career as a diplomat it could guarantee for a young nobleman, and his substantial interest in the subject. From childhood, Tolstoy had a sharp eye for injustice and the sorrows of life around him. In a letter to a close friend he confessed that "probably the only kind feature" of his character was his sensitivity.[3] This sensitivity enabled him to recognize early in life the moral conflict between the "right feelings" that he had, and the "wrong doings" dictated by the conventions of society. While studying in Kazan, Tolstoy started keeping a diary, a lifelong practice that he initiated in the hopes of achieving self-improvement via numerous self-imposed regulations and resolutions. His legal studies were an important basis for this obsession with rules.

On March 18, 1847, the second day of his diary writing, Tolstoy made an entry on his law term paper. The assignment was to analyze a famous Russian historical document: Catherine the Great's *Instruction to the Legislative Commission of 1767 (Nakaz)* (46:4). The *Instruction* was a compilation of Enlightenment legal ideas that Catherine borrowed mostly from Montesquieu and other Encyclopédistes and some thoughts of her own. She wrote it for the Legislative Commission of representatives of the estates, who were to work out a plan for the codification of Russian law. However, Catherine dissolved the Legislative Commission before a draft of the Code had been prepared. Historians today consider the whole project a smart political move by Catherine, but in the nineteenth century, the *Instruction* was romanticized as an example of the goodwill of the enlightened sovereign who listened to her people and shared "civilized" humanistic ideas about natural rights and equality before the law.

Tolstoy was deeply skeptical of such romantic thinking about the Russian autocracy and its legality. While studying the *Instruction*, he noted the tension between what he called "fashionable revolutionary ideas" of natural law and the "despotic realities" of governance in the Russian Empire (46:27). In his diary he underlined that Catherine failed to balance this tension. In particular, Tolstoy criticized Catherine's approach to freedom of speech and political crime, something that he would push to the edge in his lifelong literary career. In the "Instruction" Catherine proposed that speeches against the government "should not be punished by death" because of the difficulty of proving this crime, but those who write letters of this kind "should be punished by death" (46:24). Tolstoy responded to this passage in his diary: "This stipulation proves clearly that in a despotic state the monarch cannot hope for the loyalty of citizens. Why not? Because in despotism there is no [social] contract" (46:24). By social contract he meant the interconnection of rights and duties shared by both the rulers and the ruled. This interconnection is unknown for despotic rulers, he wrote, since they "became rulers by force" (46:24). For young Tolstoy, Catherine advocating capital punishment for written speeches against the government proved that violence was the best way to keep the power that comes from force. At the same time, the absence of a contract in a despotic regime exempted the subjects from a duty to be loyal to the government. Tolstoy withdrew from the university after his second year, but already in his analysis of the "Instruction" he had learned the major lesson of Russian jurisprudence: it was up to the sovereign to make, change, and adjust the existing law according to perceived challenges to his or her omnipotence.

Disappointed in law as a field of independent expertise, Tolstoy became more interested in true power, which he believed one could find in oneself by understanding the purpose of life. In order to obtain this power, he turned to literature, which he found to be much stronger than law. In his writing he could criticize both the social and political systems in which people participated and the way they had been conditioned not to recognize the horrors of these systems. The most disturbing example Tolstoy witnessed personally was people being forced to serve in the army during war and told that it was their sacred duty to kill. Believing, like his hero Jean-Jacques Rousseau (1712–78), that the conditions of society corrupt people's natural goodness, Tolstoy made it his mission to save people from such false ideas and actions being legally and socially imposed upon them.

The shameful defeat in the Crimean War in 1855 forced Emperor Alexander II to change Russia's isolationist agenda and to undertake an ambitious program of "Great Reforms" aimed at modernizing Russia's social and political institutions (see Chapter 6). The Russian public received significant legal recognition from the reforms; the sovereign's absolute authority, which was carried out by numerous civil servants, now had to coexist with public participation in courts (the introduction of trial by jury), institutions of self-governance (the zemstvos), and cultural and educational institutions. The opportunity for public debates and participation in governance was something the Russian educated class cherished and for which it had many hopes.

Despite the seeming gains, however, gradually the tensions between autocratic principles of administration and public involvement in decision-making became clearer. Tolstoy worked to dismantle the illusion of power that the new public regime of autocratic legality gave to the educated elite. His writing became an influential critique of the Russian tsars, their unjust laws, and the cynical civil servants enforcing them, together with priests from the Russian Orthodox Church who legitimized all these institutions. Drawing attention to the conflict between tsarist laws and true justice, he helped convince his readers that the Kingdom of God had been forgotten in the Russian Empire.

Tolstoy's short novella The Death of Ivan Ilyich (1886) offers the most condensed form of this critique. Ivan Ilyich, a middle-aged judge, has made a successful career as one of the so-called new people who carried out the Great Reforms. Tolstoy contrasts the procedural purity of Ivan Ilyich's service in court to the moral compromises that define the rest of his life climbing the career ladder and enjoying the bourgeois niceties and vices of upper-class existence. "It was all done with clean hands, in clean shirts, with French words, and above all in the highest society, consequently with the approval of highly placed people" (26:35). In court he decides people's destinies with full self-assurance, never doubting his own importance or the institution he serves. But on his death bed, Ivan Ilyich realizes that he did not really live until he was dying and saw the falseness of everything that filled his life. Tolstoy juxtaposes Ivan Ilyich's striving for high-paid positions, which he filled with "clean hands" and lip service to justice, to the truly helpful life of his uneducated servant, Gerasim. While Ivan Ilyich had devoted himself to the false and corrupted law of man, Gerasim helps him understand and accept the higher law of God. Humbled, Ivan Ilyich is finally able to embrace his mortality.

In his literature, Tolstoy addressed different aspects of this conflict between the false laws of the government and the true laws of God, in particular when he wrote about crimes and trials in The Kreutzer Sonata (1889), The Power of Darkness (1886), and The Living Corpse (1900). His last novel, Resurrection (1899), provided an epic picture of the Russian justice system. It was inspired by a real story that his friend Justice A.F. Koni told him from his practice: a member of the jury was to sentence a girl whom he had seduced and left pregnant years earlier. He tried to lift her punishment by getting married to her while she was imprisoned, but she died in prison.

Tolstoy revised the story to sharpen the moral conflict. While serving on a jury, the nobleman Dmitry Nekhliudov realizes that he himself is the guilty party: his affair years earlier with a young servant, Katiusha Maslova, left her pregnant and pushed her to become a prostitute. She is now accused of murdering a client, and despite her innocence, the "decent" jurors convict her. Their "shirts and hands are clean," just like Ivan Ilyich's. Nekhliudov, who is aware of his own guilt, tries to leverage his wealth and connections to help Maslova. While using all formal and informal means to ease Maslova's fate, he realizes that the bureaucrats he interacts with have numbed themselves to the reality of what they are doing; they follow the letter of the law, but are unwilling to acknowledge the arbitrary and unjust consequences of their actions and to make the effort needed to ensure that true justice prevails.

Tolstoy was not only critical of judges and juries, but also of legal attorneys, who first appeared in Russian courts when adversarial procedure was introduced by the judicial reform of 1864. Maslova's dressed-up, self-confident, expensive, and absolutely useless advocate Fanarin in Resurrection demonstrates the failure of liberal procedures of fair process. Tolstoy depicted the attorney's manipulation of the legal code as a com-mercial enterprise that enabled parvenus to seek power through peoples' suffering. In the novel, both officials playing power games with each other, and legal attorneys seeking commercial success, are simply parasites, exploiting the unfair and useless system of so-called justice.

Through talking with prisoners during his visits to the jail, Nekhliudov comes to understand the senselessness of the law, which potentially makes everything a crime.

> A group of stone-masons had been ordered back to their homes and were now being kept in prison because they had no passports, yet they had passports which were only a fortnight overdue ... The same thing had happened every year; they had many times omitted to renew their passports till they were overdue, and nobody had ever said anything; but this year they had been taken up and were being kept in prison the second month, as if they were criminals ... Nekhludoff listened, but hardly understood what the good-looking old man was saying, because his attention was riveted to a large, dark-grey, many-legged louse that was creeping along the good-looking man's cheek. (32:485)[4]

Looking at this louse, seeing what happens after "justice is done," Nekhliudov realizes that because of the clean hands of the civil servants, healthy, hard-working people were found guilty of breaking a nonsense regulation and now have to suffer from parasites. The laws of the state bring suffering and moral decay to all those who are involved in "justice." Tolstoy's novel pushed readers toward a moral resurrection: an awakening from the moral stupor in which the state operates.

Tolstoy's critics – who viewed Nekhliudov as Tolstoy's alter ego – claimed that Tolstoy, driven by enormous pride, was questioning the laws of the Tsar and the Church in order to become a new Russian sovereign. Indeed, many publicists in late imperial Russia juxtaposed Leo Tolstoy and Nikolai Romanov in terms of the authority they each held. Tolstoy's moral authority as a writer and public intellectual seemed particularly threatening because of his connection with the peasants, which he had fostered since his early years in Yasnaya Polyana.

According to Russia's legal system that Tolstoy first began criticizing in his student days (reading Catherine's "Instruction"), Russian rule was based on paternalistic authority, rather than a social contract; care for the Russian people was the only sacred duty of the sovereign. However, Tolstoy used his writing to demonstrate that prisons were not there for the Tsar to protect "good people" from "bad ones," but to reinforce the worst aspects of human nature. In Tolstoy's discussions with peasant children, "law" and "crime" were irrelevant, useless categories. He illustrated this idea in a parable that he put in a reading book for children:

> One poor man came to the rich man and begged for alms. The rich man gave nothing and said: "Get out!" But the poor man didn't leave. Then the rich man got angry, lifted a stone and threw it at the poor man. The poor

man lifted the stone, put it under his shirt and said: "I will keep this stone and throw it at him." And the time had come. The rich man did a bad thing [and was punished] – everything he had was taken from him, and he was taken to prison. When they took him to prison, the poor man came up to him, took out the stone from under his shirt and hesitated; then he thought about it, threw the stone down and said: "I carried the stone in vain for so long: when he was rich and strong I was afraid of him; and now I pity him."[5]

Tolstoy criticized the laws of the Russian Empire as a useless and heavy stone that people had to carry in vain in order to punish injustice. However, awakened, enlightened people of every social stratum, in Tolstoy's view, could realize that they did not need this heavy burden of the state to protect them from each other. Also, no social contract would be needed when peace and love were obtained here and now by following universal instincts of natural love and goodness. This powerful message made Tolstoy's teaching a dangerous political force not only against the tsarist state, but against the very authority of the law.

Notes

1 S.A. Tolstaya, Dnevniki Sofii Andreevny Tolstoi (1897–1909), ed. S.L. Tolstoy (Moscow: Koop. izd. "Sever," 1932), 242.
2 Ibid.
3 Quoted in Boris Eikhenbaum, Molodoi Tolstoy (Petrograd, Berlin: Izd. Z. I. Grzhebina 1922), 17.
4 Leo Tolstoy, Resurrection, trans. Louis Maude (electronic publication of Pennsylvania State University, 2000), 1945.
5 Quoted in A. Zorin, Zhizn Lva Tolstogo: Opyt prochtenia (Moscow: Novoe literaturnoe obozrenie, 2020), 45.

CHAPTER 10

Politics

G. M. Hamburg

Tolstoy was born into an empire dominated by three interlocking institutions: autocracy, army, and forced labor.

The title "autocrat" originally meant "sovereign of an independent state," but, in the late sixteenth century, it took on a broader domestic significance, implying the ruler's unlimited authority. In 1832, the law code defined the Russian Emperor as an "autocratic and unlimited monarch," and specified: "Submission to his sovereign authority is required not only out of fear, but because God Himself demands it as a matter of conscience." Nineteenth-century jurists debated whether the autocrat stood above the law, or whether the law, once propounded, required the crown's adherence.[1] Nevertheless, the autocracy's existence made the Russian Empire politically distinctive. Under Alexander I (1801–25) and Nicholas I (1825–55), the government was a quasi-despotism. A shrewd biographer of Nicholas I has described his government as "a ruthless tutelary regime."[2]

In Tolstoy's time, the civilian bureaucracy experienced explosive growth. From 1796 to 1847, the number of government officials quadrupled, with most of the growth occurring in two ministries (internal affairs and justice) centrally involved in the administration of the serf system. From 1853 to 1903, the state bureaucracy increased numerically fivefold. Throughout the nineteenth century, the growth in the bureaucracy far outstripped population growth.[3] This meant that the government's reach into local life expanded, and its per capita weight became more onerous for taxpayers.

During Tolstoy's time, the size and significance of the Russian armed forces also changed dramatically. In 1762, when Catherine II came to the throne, there were less than 300,000 troops in the Russian army. By the Crimean War of 1853–6, there were a million men under arms. In 1914, the standing army numbered 1.3 million troops; the war mobilization called roughly 5.3 million men to the colors.[4] Again, even accounting for population growth, the army's domestic importance and the economic burden it placed on the populace dwarfed its earlier role.

Imperial Russia's civilian and military leadership disproportionately consisted of hereditary nobles of Orthodox faith and of Great Russian ethnicity. In 1853, among the top three ranks in the bureaucracy, approximately three-quarters of high-ranking officials owned serfs. Among them, forty-eight owned one thousand souls or more. In the post-serfdom era, the hereditary nobility of Orthodox faith and Great Russian ethnicity continued to dominate elite officialdom. In 1903, in the State Council, committee of ministers, and Ruling Senate, most members were landowners, some large landowners.[5]

Most senior officers during the era of serfdom were nobles. Less than 30 percent of senior officers owned serfs, and the majority of them held under a hundred souls. However, members of the Imperial Guards tended to be wealthier, so several of them possessed 500 or more souls.[6] The closer to the Emperor, the more likely a senior officer was to own serfs. In the post-serfdom era, upper officers still had an elite profile. In 1912, a minority of senior officers were landowners, but among generals one in seven was a landowner.[7]

We should not imagine that all serf-owning officials and officers were uniformly conservative; after all, the Decembrist movement included critics of serfdom, advocates of constitutional monarchy, and republicans. However, as a general rule, civilian and military officials upheld the pillars of the established social order. In moments of social difficulty, such as the Pugachev uprising of 1773–4, the army suppressed the rebels and preserved the serf system. In 1831, just three years after Tolstoy's birth, the government sent an army detachment to put down a rebellion at a military settlement in Novgorod province; after firing on the crowd, troops arrested hundreds of people and tried them at a military tribunal. In April 1861, a few weeks after promulgation of the emancipation decree, the government sent troops to Kazan province to suppress the peasant movement led by Anton Petrov. On this occasion, General Anton Stepanovich Apraksin ordered troops to fire on disobedient peasants: ninety-one were killed and eighty-seven wounded by this salvo. During the revolution of 1904–7, the government routinely employed the army to suppress civil disorders. Prime minister Pyotr Arkadevich Stolypin's reliance on military field tribunals to execute revolutionaries showed how effective, and how brutal, the domestic use of military forces could be.

Before 1861, civilian officials and army officers collaborated in maintaining Russia's system of forced labor. Most common people in Russia tilled the land. Over half worked under the supervision of government officials or of the royal family, the remainder under private owners, who treated them de facto as chattel slaves. Over the eighteenth century, the government expanded serf-owners' prerogatives to discipline their peasants. They could impose monetary fines; withhold food; confiscate serfs' property; punish them by beating with rods, staffs, whips, or the knout; consign them to a diet of bread and water; fasten chains on their legs; force them to do disagreeable work; shave half their hair; shave their beards; ban their travel beyond estate boundaries or exile them to a distant estate. After 1760, lords could send their serfs to settlements in Siberia.[8] Most of these eighteenth-century methods of discipline persisted in the nineteenth century, even though imperial laws moderated or limited their application. Serf-owners acted as the government's instruments for keeping peasants in line, just as nobles relied on government to maintain the existing order.

Paradoxically, until 1861, the army staffed infantry regiments with serf soldiers. Under Catherine II's 1793 decree, peasant recruits were conscripted for twenty-five-year terms – akin to a life-term. The government's recruitment formula – originally set at 1 in 500 peasant males per year – varied according to need, with the ratio of recruits increasing as needed over the first half of the nineteenth century.

The social contradiction of this autocratic-military-serf system was clear to everyone, from village to Petersburg high society. Russia's great-power status depended on the fighting capacity of its serf army; the existence of the Empire's forced labor system required serf infantry to suppress social disorders. Although the 1861 peasant emancipation sundered the legal nexus between lords and peasants, it did not immediately terminate serf property arrangements: for nine years, serfs continued to be bound to their masters' land under the emancipation's so-called temporary obligation provision. Even after peasants received allotment parcels, they had to make redemption payments to compensate the treasury. Transformation of the serf army into a universal conscription army did not occur until after 1874, when war minister Dmitry Alekseevich Miliutin's army reform was promulgated. Thus, Tolstoy grew to maturity observing the dichotomy between social privilege and forced labor.

The autocracy severely limited the possibility for anyone other than high officials or senior army officers to participate in political decision-making; indeed, it restricted political inputs to a small circle around the Emperor. Nobles could meet in provincial assemblies but normally could not debate issues of national import. On July 14 and 15, 1812, the Moscow nobility was invited to raise money to resist the French invasion, but assembly members did not know whether they had the right to ask the Emperor about French troop movements and the Russian army's response. On March 30, 1856, Alexander II (1855–81) spoke to the Moscow nobility about rumors he intended to abolish serfdom. He asked those present to "think about how to carry out such a deed," but provided no rules for their deliberation. Only late in August 1859 did he countenance an ad hoc framework for the nobility to discuss their proposals for serfdom's abolition. Later, the zemstvo reform of 1864 created an all-estate body for deliberation concerning local needs, but the government almost invariably rebuffed attempts by the zemstvos to coordinate their activities across provincial lines and it blocked a national zemstvo "congress" to address broader issues.

The public responded to these restrictions in various ways. For example, critics of the existing order organized informal groups to deliberate on the Empire's needs, and sometimes they established secret societies to do so. The Guards' rebellions of March 1801 and December 1825 were striking examples of the ambitions of secret societies in the serf era. After 1861, students at Russian universities formed unofficial groups to raise money for scholarships, but they also set up underground circles to disseminate criticism of the government or to take action against it. From the emancipation through the revolution of 1904–7, these circles became a political factor with which the government had to contend. It should be said that intellectuals sometimes distinguished their legal and illegal activities, by dividing themselves into concentric circles: an umbrella organization operating legally, and smaller revolutionary cells clandestinely. Examples of such organizations were the Decembrists' Union of Welfare, the Petrashevsky circle of the late 1840s (of which Dostoevsky was a member), and populist groups of the 1860s and 1870s.

The public also dealt with restrictions from above by addressing the "eternal questions" rather than speaking directly about political matters. The "eternal" or "vexed" questions were an inheritance from the Russian Enlightenment, which tended to frame important issues in religious or ethical terms, and which also frequently conflated moral and political inquiry.[9] In the nineteenth century, the discourse over moral issues gave a metaphysical dimension to Russian thought, while simultaneously hinting at contemporary political problems and at their answers. Because it was licit for Russian writers to probe the eternal questions, and because Russian writers became adept at Aesopian language, literature became the venue that did much to shape critical public attitudes toward the established order.

The "Great Reforms" transformed Russian life in many respects, not the least of which was partially dismantling Nicholas I's tutelary regime and creating possibilities for more public involvement in politics, mainly through the self-governing institutions (the zemstvos and urban assemblies) but also through free publication of scholarship, a more relaxed censorship regime and thus a freer press, and public access to trials (see Chapter 6). However, the reforms did not satisfy everyone. They gave rise to a political polarization that persisted to the end of the old regime.

On the one hand, aristocratic opposition to peasant emancipation with land surfaced in 1859 in the provincial noble committees. Later, after the emancipation's promulgation, government officials such as Pyotr Alexandrovich Valuev and Pyotr Andreevich Shuvalov sought to support noble landowners by creating mechanisms at the national level for them to discuss legislation affecting rural Russia.[10]

On the other hand, the nascent Russian left objected to the "Great Reforms" because they had not constructed a just society. Populists such as Nikolai Gavrilovich Chernyshevsky advocated material and gender equality, to be implemented through peasant communes or workers' associations. Later populists, like Pyotr Lavrovich Lavrov and Nikolai Konstantinovich Mikhailovsky, championed collaborations between intellectuals and toilers. Mikhailovsky wanted the future society to foster a diversified division of labor. The Russian Marxists, who followed the populists' objections to capitalism, imagined freedom principally as overcoming human dependence on nature. This was the "leap to the kingdom of freedom" that Marx and Engels had anticipated.

As early as 1866, when Dmitry Vladimirovich Karakozov attempt to assassinate Alexander II, a portion of the Russian left embraced terrorism as a means to destabilize the government. However, the historian Claudia Verhoeven has suggested that terrorism "is not simply a strategy, not a means toward this or that political end, but rather a paradigmatic way of becoming a modern political subject."[11] If she is right, Russian terrorists not only threatened the status quo, but introduced the regime to a new, "modern" political landscape.

Of course, not all of the left endorsed terrorism. The "going to the people" of 1874–5, in which as many as 3,000 young people went to the countryside to raise peasants' social consciousness, eschewed violence. Its spectacular failure – the arrests of roughly 1,600 young people and their joint trials in 1877 – persuaded survivors to turn back to terrorism: hence, the establishment in 1879 of the "The People's Will" and its systematic attempt to hunt down and kill the Tsar.[12]

The government resolutely fought the terrorists by imposing martial law in several revolutionary hotspots, and, after the February 1880 bombing of the Winter Palace, by appointing General Mikhail Tarielovich Loris-Melikov to serve as a "vice-emperor." Melikov's program combined police measures, reforms favoring the peasantry, further moderation of censorship rules, and a remarkable plan to add to the Imperial State Council three or four hundred elected public figures to discuss necessary changes in rural Russia. The plan was not a constitution, but perhaps a step toward one.[13]

The assassination of Alexander II made continuation of Loris-Melikov's program "unthinkable."[14] In April 1881, Alexander III (1881–94) signed a manifesto declaring: "The voice of God directs us intrepidly to conduct the business of government in conformity with the Divine design, with faith in the strength and truth of autocratic authority, which we pledge to uphold and preserve for the people's welfare against serious infringements on it."[15] In August 1881, the "Statute on Intensified Security" imposed martial law in most of Russia.

These two measures set the stage for religious persecutions, political repression, and the so-called counter-reforms of the 1880s and early 1890s. Religious discrimination occurred in the Baltic provinces, where Lutheran ministers became the government's targets; in the Pale of Settlement, where the government introduced new restrictions on Jewish settlers; in Moscow, from which the local authorities expelled 20,000 Jewish craftsmen in 1891–2; but also elsewhere in the country.[16] Repressions took the form of denunciations of "suspicious individuals" and their administrative exile, attempts to control and to intimidate the press, the closure of various journals, and the banning of plays that criticized the government. The censors blocked Tolstoy's religious tract *What Do I Believe?* Other works – *The Kreutzer Sonata* was an example – were at first banned, before the government relented.[17] The government carefully monitored Tolstoy's writing and even sent agents to watch him at Yasnaya Polyana.

The "counter-reforms" strove to fortify the nobility. The land captains, created in July 1889 from the landed nobility, had the duty to fine and arrest peasants for perceived disciplinary violations. They acted as judges and juries in petty affairs, thus returning to the nobility a measure of the seigneurial authority they had enjoyed in the serf era. The zemstvo "counter-reform" of 1890 decreased the peasants' influence and increased the nobility's electoral weight in zemstvo assemblies.[18] In 1895, when liberal nobles objected to these measures in the hope that Nicholas II (1894–1917) would alter the government's conservative direction, he pledged instead: "I shall firmly and undeviatingly preserve the principle of autocracy, just as my unforgettable father did."[19]

Unfortunately for Nicholas II, the government did not entirely control the Russian economy, which developed in a capitalist direction and subjected workers to the strains of life in a market society. Nor was the government able to block the formation of liberal political organizations, or even the emergence of radical leftist parties. By 1905, Russia was divided into two camps – the defenders of the old order and advocates of a new one – with neither able to achieve a decisive political advantage.[20] The manifesto of October 17 promised free elections to a State Duma in a vain attempt to end revolutionary violence. Until the end of Tolstoy's life and beyond, therefore, Russian political life remained turbulent, violent, and uncertain.

Tolstoy's early writings probed "eternal questions," such as God's existence and whether it is possible to live a moral life. He also raised complex ethical questions, such as justifications for killing in warfare. In 1857, however, he witnessed an execution of a criminal in Paris. He found the scene repellent, because of the "elegant machine that, in an instant, murdered a strong, lively, healthy human being," and because of the "disgusting crowd." On the spot, he recorded a categorical political judgment: "Human laws are nonsense … Political laws are a terrible lie … I shall never in any place serve *any* government" (60:167–8). Thus for Tolstoy by the late 1850s, the "eternal questions" were opening out into politics.

In early 1861, Tolstoy founded a school for peasant children at his estate. He criticized other landowners for not taking similar concrete actions to help the peasantry (60:380, 477–9). He also applied for the post of peace arbitrator (60:395), which carried the authority to mediate land disputes between serfs and lords as the emancipation proceeded. Meanwhile, he distanced himself from political debates. To his friend Vasily Petrovich Botkin, he wrote: "In Petersburg, Moscow, and Tula there are elections [to noble assemblies] – that is your parliament; but all that, I confess, interests me little. Until there is more equality in education, there cannot be a better political system" (60:414).

After news of the Tsar's murder reached Tolstoy in March 1881, he wrote a letter to Alexander III appealing for mercy toward the assassins (63:44–52). In it, Tolstoy argued the Tsar's duty as a Christian was to avoid vengeance, to "resist not evil" (63:46). Tolstoy maintained that neither conservative measures ("severity, executions, exiles, the police, tightened censorship") nor liberal palliatives ("freedom, moderate penalties, representation, a constitution, assembly of the land") could stop determined assassins (63:48). Applying the "law of God" by pardoning the sinners, therefore constituted the wise path. The Christian "solution" to the current problem would have to be accompanied by recognition that the terrorists are not bandits, "but rather people who hate the existing system ... and have in mind bases for a better future order." The idealism could only be answered by another ideal – the law of love (63:52). Although Tolstoy wrote from a religious perspective, his letter made two political points: capital punishment is counterproductive; and only Christian love can protect the Russian monarch in the future.[21]

After 1881, Tolstoy's Christian anarchism responded to his insistent probing of the "eternal questions," to his personal existential agony of the late 1870s, but also to the difficult political situation of the Russian Empire. His spiritual vision was based on Christ's teaching of "love, humility, self-abnegation, self-sacrifice, and returning good for evil" (23:306). He took to heart Christ's dictum in Matthew 5:39: "It is said to you, 'an eye for an eye, a tooth for a tooth.' But I say to you: resist not evil" (23:310–12). He interpreted non-resistance as serving the Gospel, not state institutions. In *The Kingdom of God Is Within You*, Tolstoy maintained: "Government is the application to human beings of the rope, of the chain that binds them or leads them, of the knout that beats them, or of the knife and axe that sever their limbs, nose, ears or head – the application of these instruments or the threat of them" (28:131). This formula made clear Tolstoy's visceral opposition to forced labor, to systems of social subordination and class rule. No political mechanism, he believed, could curb governmental violence or its manifest abuses of the people. The only way to undercut wicked state authority, he thought, was to refuse allegiance to the government, for this act "undermines the government's authority and furthers the people's liberation" (28:176). In the end, Tolstoy proposed that Russians choose "the law of violence" or "the law of love" (37:149–221).

Tolstoy's last great fictional works tried to highlight this choice. *Resurrection* was an exposé of the Empire's judicial and penal system, of the Siberian hard labor system, but also of the harm done by religious persecutions. The hero Nekhliudov's resolution, "Seek the Kingdom of God and His justice," was meant as an alternative to the law of violence. *Hadji Murat* dramatized the costs of religious warfare and of the collision between what Tolstoy called "two poles of governmental absolutism – the Asiatic and the European."[22] At the novel's end, the ritual display of Hadji Murat's head as war trophy provoked from the novella's moral conscience, Marya Dmitrievna, the verdict: "War! Butchers! That's all you are!" (35:110).

Notes

1 Nikolai Mikhailovich Korkunov, *Russkoe gosudarstvennoe pravo. Tom 1. Vvedenie i obshchaia chast'* (St. Petersburg: Tipografiia M. M. Stasiulevicha, 1893), 158–62.
2 Mikhail Aleksandrovich Polievktov, *Nikolai I. Biografiia i obzor tsarstvovaniia* (Moscow: Mir knigi, 2008), 181–4, *passim*. Polievktov completed his book in 1916; it appeared in 1917.
3 Petr Andreevich Zaionchkovskii, *Pravitel'stvennyi apparat samoderzhavnoi Rossii v XIX v.* (Moscow: Mysl', 1978), 66–7, 221.
4 Zaionchkovskii, "Ofitserskii korpus russkoi armii pered Pervoi mirovoi voinoi," *Voprosy istorii* 4 (1981), 21–9.
5 Zaionchkovskii, *Pravitel'stvennyi apparat samoderzhavnoi Rossii*, 91–2, 200–6.
6 Dmitrii Georgievich Tseloruongo, "Formuliarnye spiski ofitserskogo korpusa russkoi armii epokhi Otechestvennoi voiny 1812 goda," in A.G. Tartakovskii (ed.), *Issledovaniia po istochnikovedeniiu istorii SSSR do oktiabr'skogo perioda. Sbornik statei* (Moscow: Institut istorii, SSSR, 1990), 115–31 (at 121–3).
7 Zaionchkovskii, "Ofitserskii korpus russkoi armii," 26–7.
8 Vasilii Ivanovich Semevskii, *Krest'iane v tsarstvovanie Imperatritsy Ekateriny II. Tom pervyi* (St. Petersburg: Tipografiia M.M. Stasiulevicha, 1903), xvii–xviii, 178–237.
9 On the conflation of political and moral questions in eighteenth-century Russia, see G.M. Hamburg, *Russia's Path toward Enlightenment: Faith, Politics, and Reason, 1500–1801* (New Haven, CT: Yale University Press, 2016), 742–3.
10 Igor' Anatol'evich Khristoforov, *"Aristokraticheskaia" oppozitsiia velikim reformam: konets 1850 – seredina 1870-kh gg.* (Moscow: Russkoi slovo, 2002), 168–9, 290–1.
11 Claudia Verhoeven, *The Odd Man Karakozov: Imperial Russia, Modernity, and the Birth of Terrorism* (Ithaca, NY: Cornell University Press, 2009), 4.
12 On the "going to the people," see Boris Samuilovich Itenberg, *Dvizhenie revoliutsionnogo narodnichestva. Narodnicheshkie kruzhki i "khozhdenie v narod" v 70-kh godakh XIX v.* (Moscow: Nauka, 1965), esp. 373–4, 385–96; on "The People's Will," Stepan Stepanovich Volk, *Narodnaia volia, 1879–1882* (Moscow: Nauka, 1966).
13 Andrei Valentinovich Mamonov, "Graf M.T. Loris-Melikov: k kharakteristike vzgliadov i gosudarstvennoi deiatel'nosti," *Otechestvennaia istoriia* 5 (2001), 32–53, *passim*.

14 Russkii patriot [Boris Nikolaevich Chicherin], *Rossiia nakanune dvadtsatago stoletiia,* 3-e izdanie (Berlin: Izdanie Gugo Shteinitsa, 1901), 31.

15 *Polnoe sobranie zakonov. Sobranie tret'e. Tom 1* (St. Petersburg, 1885), no. 118, 53–4, here 54.

16 Zaionchkovskii, *Rossiiskoe samoderzhavie v kontse XIX stoletiia. (Politicheskaia reaktsiia 80-kh – nachala 90-kh godov),* (Moscow: Izdatel' "Mysl'", 1970), 122–237.

17 Zaionchkovskii, *Rossiiskoe samoderzhavie,* 161, 280–1, 299–302, *passim.*

18 Nikolai Alekseevich Troitskii, *Rossiia v XIX veke: Kurs leksii* (Moscow: Vysshaia shkola, 1997), 320–1.

19 Quoted in Sergei Sergeevich Ol'denburg, *Tsarstvovanie Imperatora Nikolaia II. Tom 1* (Belgrad: Izdanie Obshchestva Rasprostraneniia Natsional'noi i Patrioticheskoi Literatury, 1939), 39.

20 Abraham Ascher, *The Revolution of 1905: Russia in Disarray* (Stanford University Press, 1988), 11–12.

21 Ekaterina Vladimirovna Surovtseva, "Pis'mo L N. Tolstogo Aleksandru III o pervomartovtsakh v kontekste obshchestvennoi zhizni Rossii," *Molodoi uchenyi* 179:45 (noiabr' 2017), 257–63.

22 Sergei Nikolaevich Shul'gin, "Iz vospominanii o gr. L. N. Tolstom," in *L.N. Tolstoi v vospominaniiakh sovremennikov v dvukh tomakh* (Moscow: Gosudarstvennoe Izdatel'stvo khudozhestvennoi literarury, 1955), Tom 1, 162–3.

CHAPTER II

War and the Military

Donna Tussing Orwin

As a student of Rousseau's *Second Discourse* (1755) and *The Profession of Faith of the Savoyard Vicar* (1765), Tolstoy regarded war as an aberration, writing in a draft of his very first war story, "The Raid" (1852), that "Only the persistence of this unnatural phenomenon makes it natural, and the feeling of self-preservation – just" (3:234).[1] So if he so hated war, why did he join the army and go on to write a work like *War and Peace*, which, if it does not glorify war, does not simply attack it either? This chapter provides an overview of how the military operated in Russia during Tolstoy's lifetime and explores the background to his complex attitude.

Tolstoy came from military aristocracy, and he was very proud of his heritage (see Chapter 3). His earliest surviving writing – a school notebook dated 1835 – is signed with the initials for Gr. L.N. Tolstoy (Count Lev Nikolaevich Tolstoy) by its six- or seven-year-old author (90:93). His branch of the Tolstoys traced themselves back to a *voivode* (an administrator and military commander of a territory) serving under Ivan the Terrible in the sixteenth century. The Volkonskys from his mother's side had a storied military history dating back at least to the thirteenth century. His maternal grandfather, Prince S.N. Volkonsky, served as a soldier and diplomat under Catherine II and her son Paul. In 1812, at the age of seventeen, over his parents' objections, Tolstoy's father Nikolai Ilyich Tolstoy had enlisted in the army. He fought in the European campaign against Napoleon, who had already been expelled from Russia. Having chased Napoleon all the way to Paris, the generation of Tolstoy's father imbibed liberal ideas. For some of them, these led to the Decembrist Revolt of 1825 in the interregnum after the death of Tsar Alexander I. Tolstoy's father, though politically conservative, had known many Decembrists and told his son about them. Sorry to have missed this seminal moment in Russian history, Tolstoy set out to imagine its underpinnings in what became *War and Peace* but was originally called *The Decembrists*.

Napoleon's stunning success in wars against Europe's traditional regimes forced them to rethink both their military strategy and their politics. France's enemies, including Russia, were impressed by its ability after the Revolution to mobilize the entire society for war. Other regimes, Russia among them, adopted nationalism to unite their people for their own purposes. Eventually Russia's national myth, propagated nowhere more effectively than in *War and Peace*, became that the *narod*, the people in aggregate, not generals and tsars, won wars.

One answer to why Tolstoy joined the army is that the very horror of war, once fully appreciated, tests character in a way that no other experience can do. The young Tolstoy wanted to prove himself as brave and honorable a soldier as his ancestors had been. There was also an issue of class honor: the officer corps at the time Tolstoy enlisted was made up almost entirely of gentry, who, although after a decree from Peter III in 1762 were not required to serve in the military, considered it their duty to do so. In 1852, he enlisted in the Caucasus, where he had traveled with his older brother Nikolai, who was serving there. He had stepped into the long war in the North Caucasus against Muslim mountain-dwellers that began in the early nineteenth century and ended in the east with the capture in 1959 of the charaismatic Sufi Iman Shamil. (Fighting flared up in the west, but ended in 1864.) While in the Caucasus, Tolstoy paid no attention to the imperial politics behind the war. His writings there focus instead on the war experience itself. The most important of them, *The Cossacks* (begun in 1853, pub. 1863), explores Cossack culture, itself influenced by that of the hill tribes. The late unfinished masterpiece *Hadji Murat* (1896–1904, pub. 1911) expands into a comprehensive vision of the war from the differing viewpoints of participants on both sides of it.

Tolstoy was a junior artillery officer, commended more than once for bravery, and he wavered between retirement and a military career. When the Crimean War (1853–6) began, he requested a transfer to it. He and many of his comrades believed the war needed fighting because Russia was again under invasion. The political reality was more complex. As in the Caucasus, Russia's goal was imperialist expansion, this time at the expense of a declining Ottoman Empire. One justification for the war was Russia's role as protector of Russian Orthodox populations within the Empire – hence it began hostilities in what is now Romania – but it was also prompted by the long-term Russian desire to control the Turkish Straits, the only passage between the Black and the Mediterranean Seas.[2] The invasion of Crimea that gave the war its name was a part of a larger strategy by Russia's rivals in which the British, the French, and, at the end of 1854, even Russia's erstwhile ally Austria joined together to counter Russian ambitions.

The war exposed Russian military weaknesses. Russia was sparsely populated and poor. Surrounded on all sides by potential enemies, it had expanded partly in order to create buffer zones against these. In doing so, however, it had created untrustworthy border regions, as well as an enormous landmass that needed defending in many places very far from one another. This required it to maintain a huge army – around 1 million men when the Crimean War began, to which another million were added to fight it – while being unable to collect large numbers in any hot spot; furthermore, at the time of the war it had almost no railroads to transport troops and supplies. Soldiers (not officers) were peasant serfs sent for twenty-five-year terms by their owners in response to levies from the government. It would have been politically dangerous to train them and send them back to their villages once they knew how to use weapons and fight; therefore Russia could not create a system of reserves to be called up during emergencies.[3] A conscript army serving essentially for life did produce dedicated, skilled soldiers for whom the army became a substitute for family, but they were not backed up by essential services. The country lagged behind its other European rivals in the industrialization needed to produce up-to-date weapons and other war supplies. Ironically, the failure to address such problems was due partly to the Russian victory over Napoleon. Having played a major role in his downfall, Russia emerged as the dominant military power in Europe, and Nicholas I, who succeeded to the throne in 1825, chose to rest on his laurels. It was not that he neglected the army; on the contrary, in the tradition of other Romanov tsars he was an autocrat obsessed with military order. His emphasis, however, was more on parades, medals, and discipline than on military reform. So when he provoked the Turks by insisting that they recognize the rights of Orthodox Christians in their empire, he was not ready for war.

During Tolstoy's years in the military, he wanted to improve, not condemn it. When he arrived in the Crimean War theater (first in what is modern-day Romania), he joined a reform-minded group of junior officers. The idea of his three *Sevastopol Sketches*, written after he was transferred, at his request, to Crimea, grew out of material originally destined for a proposal by this group, turned down by the Tsar, for a journal intended for soldiers. The second and third sketches (1855–6) hint at problems with the army – corruption and supply issues – that censorship would not allow him to make clear. Like *War and Peace*, which they anticipate in this regard, the sketches denigrate ambitious adjutants and praise the front-line soldiers and officers who held out against the enemy siege much longer than expected. A plan mentioned in Tolstoy's diary at the time even called for rifled artillery (January 23, 1855; 47:35, 275). (This was one of those equipment failures mentioned above. The fact that Russia was still using smoothbore weapons, inferior in both accuracy and range to rifled ones, contributed to its defeat in the war, and rifles were introduced in 1860.) Just after the death of Nicholas I in 1855, he submitted a plan for general improvements to the army (March 4, 1855; 47:37, 278). It was not accepted and does not survive, but we can speculate on what it might have contained from drafts of an unfinished work "A note on the negative sides of the Russian soldier and officer" (4:285–94). It divides soldiers into the oppressed, the oppressors (who have graduated from the oppressed to this status), and the "desperados." Officers, "with rare exceptions," are "mercenaries," "robbers," and "immoral ignoramuses." Tolstoy's suggestions for reform included more money for soldiers, more emphasis on education, merit as the principle for promotion, an end to the culture of oppression, and a clampdown on corruption.

In later works like "Nikolai the Stick" (1884–97), "For Shame" (1895), *Father Sergius* (1890s), and a chapter of *Hadji Murat* written in 1903, Tolstoy denounces military culture under Nicholas. This dark side of his experience is also expressed in an introduction he wrote in 1889 to memoirs, first published and read by him in 1857, of another artillery officer in the war. In his introduction Tolstoy revisits Sevastopol from the point of view of a naïve officer, sent to the front directly from school, horrified by the realities of war, surviving them, and not able or willing to express his real thoughts because no one else does so. The republished memoirs came out in 1889 without Tolstoy's introduction, which was published only in 1902 under the title "Against War" (27:520–29, 735–6).

Crushing defeat in the Crimean War and the succession to the throne of Alexander II led to reforms, the most significant of which was the emancipation of the serfs in 1861 (see Chapter 6). Military reform was overseen by minister of war D.A. Miliutin, with whom Tolstoy was acquainted (59:33, 330–1). Miliutin advocated for universal conscription rather than conscripting only peasants. Introduced only in 1874, it required every male individual to serve six years of active duty in the military followed by nine years in the reserves.[4] Russian elites had opposed this change, and it only became possible after the Franco-Prussian War of 1870–1. Germany's decisive victory in it altered the balance of power in Europe, and made the Prussian militarist model of a mandatory draft irresistible even to old-fashioned Russia. In 1871, when Tolstoy first heard of the "Prussian" model, he opposed it because it would replace "the type of the traditional Russian soldier who had conferred so much glory on Russian arms" and was responsible for the "defense, glorious throughout the centuries, of Sevastopol."[5] Here the soldier speaks, the one who in 1855 called for the foundation of a new religion, based on the original teachings of Christ, in the very same diary entry that mentions his plan for army reform.

Miliutin's reforms were tested (with uneven results) in the Russo-Turkish War. Starting in 1875, Slavic peoples in the Balkans rebelled against Turkish rule, and in 1877, Russia went to war in their defense. The war was broadly popular, but, in *Anna Karenina*, which he was completing at the time, Tolstoy came out against it. In the epilogue, Levin, his spokesman in this regard, declares that Russians have no reason to defend Serbians and Montenegrians just because they are Slavs, and that wars are so dreadful that only governments – not individuals, Christians who must not kill – can or may have to start them, while the people renounce their personal will in such matters (Pt. 8, Ch. 15).

Although he was anti-nationalist, Tolstoy was not simply anti-war in *Anna Karenina*. Central Asia, the site of imperialist expansion in the 1870s, is also mentioned in the novel without implicit criticism as the place where Vronsky's friend Prince Serpukhovskoi has served and advanced his career (Pt. 3, Chs. 20–1). Not long after he had completed the novel, however, Tolstoy wrote an article called "Church and State" (ca. 1879; 23:475–83, 566), which decouples Christianity from government and its crimes, including war. In his tract *What I Believe* (1882–4; 23:304–465), he first presented non-resistance, which included conscientious objection to military service, as a fundamental tenet of Christianity. From this time forward, he never again defended armies, though at moments he reported his own patriotic impulses.

Tolstoy's change of heart, though fundamentally based on religion, had political reasons as well. He considered Germany's victory in the Franco-Prussian War the beginning of the militarism of the rest of the century ("Patriotism and Government," 1900; esp. Ch. 4). As a result of it, enmity between France and Germany simmered for decades afterwards, leading eventually to World War I. Military alliances amongst European countries kept shifting in ways it is hard to follow. Russia's underlying concern during the whole period was Germany. First, in 1873, Russia joined the Three Emperors League with Germany and Austria-Hungary. While mistrusting both its partners, it saw limited cooperation with them as a way to avoid unwinnable conflicts. The League lasted, with interruptions, until 1887. The Triple Alliance of Germany, Austria-Hungary, and Italy began in 1882 and was renewed off and on until 1915. After the end of the Three Emperors League, Russia joined an isolated France in the Franco-Russian Alliance (1891–1917) to counter the Triple one. (There are other twists and turns in this complicated story.) Tolstoy's article "Christianity and Patriotism" (1893–4; 39:27–80) depicts with devastating irony a celebration of the Franco-Russian Alliance, attacks militarism, and calls for draft resistance. Imperialist powers jostled for influence in Asia, Africa, and the Americas. (For Russia, this led eventually to the disastrous Russo-Japanese War of 1904–5, in the far east.) At home, after the assassination of Alexander II in 1881, a form of martial law, lasting until 1917, was imposed that curtailed the rights of peasants, and also of minorities. Pogroms began against the Jews, while brutal corporal punishment persisted in the military and society at large.[6]

Tolstoy responded to contemporary suggestions of how to manage the international political situation with eloquent rage. He denounced as hypocritical the convening (by Nicholas II) of the Hague Convention in 1899 to establish laws of war; since it was followed by more imperial conflict, it was also unsuccessful ("Patriotism and Government," 90:425–44, esp. Ch. 5). Nor were international tribunals and courts the way forward ("Carthago Delenda Est," 1898; 39:197–205). Instead Tolstoy proposed another solution. "Two Wars" (1898; 31:97–101) contrasts the Spanish-American War with refusal to serve in the army by the Russian Doukhobors (for the Doukhobors and pacifism, see Chapter 29). The first was old-style pagan war, while the other represented a new holy war to rid the world of militarism and conflict altogether. The draft resister is the heroic warrior of the new army. The article "The Beginning of the End" tells the story of a Dutchman, called up to the National Guard, who refuses to serve (1896; 31:78–86). The Dutchman's reasons for this were not religious. Instead he declared that killing in war was murder pure and simple, and he could not agree to this. Thus, as Tolstoy presents it in his article, Christ's injunction "Thou shalt not kill" is a universal moral law, applying to all races and religions. He argues here and elsewhere that warriors like this one will, by their example, shift human consciousness to the point where tens of thousands of self-identified Christians, who now obediently go to war, will refuse to do so.[7] Tolstoy equates Christianity with reason, and reason with virtue. Hence he decried the outbreak of the

Russo-Japanese War in 1904 with an article entitled "Bethink Yourselves!" (*Odumaites'!* 36:100–48).

Strikingly, Tolstoy the pacifist uses the language of war to articulate his solution, thus exemplifying that complex attitude we noted at the beginning of this essay. It is as if he separates the good side of the warrior – honor and courage – from the dark one. In his *Reminiscences* (1903–6), Tolstoy writes that he admired the "freedom," the distaste for government service, especially under Nicholas I, and the "personal dignity" of his father and his father's generation (34:356–7). By the 1890s, the officer corps had declined significantly in prestige.[8] One way to understand the role Tolstoy assumed in Russia in his later life, is that of a Decembrist warrior advocating for a just society. Therefore it is no accident that "For Shame," directed against corporal punishment, was entitled "The Decembrists and Us" until its final draft (1895; 31:278)[9] and featured S.I. Apostol-Muravyov (executed for his role in the uprising) as "one of the best people of his own, and of any time," who forbade corporal punishment in his regiment (31:72).The weapons of the warrior for peace are words and reason or, as Tolstoy expressed it in "Two Wars," "gentle reasonableness and patient firmness" (31:99). In his later life, he became a warrior of this sort, one who, even as he rejected war, fought for the good and, like his father and the eponymous protagonist of his late work *Hadji Murat*, put "personal dignity," true honor, above all else.

Notes

1 See Donna Tussing Orwin, *Tolstoy's Art and Thought* (Princeton University Press, 1993), 43, 52–3.

2 For a cogent summary of reasons, see Nicholas Riasanovsky and Mark D. Steinberg, *A History of Russia,* 7th edn (Oxford University Press, 2005), 313–16.

3 A small reserve was created under Nicholas I in 1834 by allowing some men with good service records to return home after their fifteenth year, but it did not solve the problem mentioned here. See John Shelton Curtiss, "The Army of Nicholas I: Its Role and Character," *American Historical Review* 63:4 (July 1958), 880–9 (at 883).

4 David R. Stone, *A Military History of Russia from Ivan the Terrible to the War in Chechnya* (Westport, CT: Praeger Security International, 2006), 129.

5 See letter to S.S. Urusov, April–May 1871 (61:254).

6 On Tolstoy's attitude toward Jews and his response to the pogroms, see Harold K. Schefski, "Tolstoi and the Jews," *Russian Review* 41:1 (January 1982), 1–10.

7 See, for instance, chap. 14 of "Christianity and Patriotism."

8 William C. Fuller, Jr., "The Imperial Army," in Dominic Lieven (ed.), *The Cambridge History of Russia*, vol. 11: *Imperial Russia, 1689–1917* (Cambridge University Press, 2008), 546–7.

9 Tolstoy changed the title because he knew the censor would not accept the original one.

CHAPTER 12

Tolstoyans

Charlotte Alston

In the 1891 colony census, one individual in Victoria, Australia, self-identified as a member of the "Tolstoian church."[1] The idea of a Tolstoyan church is something of a contradiction in terms, as the Christian anarchist movement inspired by Tolstoy, which gained ground across the Russian Empire but also internationally from the 1880s, was grounded in a rejection of all forms of organization and coercion, and based on the individual following his or her own conscience, reason, and relationship with God. Nevertheless, from the 1890s onward there were a growing number of people who identified themselves as fellow thinkers, if not followers, of Tolstoy. Individuals disillusioned with the society they lived in were inspired by the tracts and short stories Tolstoy wrote in the decades before his death, and they set up their own societies, newspapers, and experiments in communal living. The solitary self-declared member of Victoria's 'Tolstoian Church' was aware of belonging to a movement with international reach and momentum, sustained by periodicals, correspondence, and the exchange of literature and visits. As one English follower wrote to Tolstoy in 1895, "I know not how it may be in Russia, but here the light is spreading from mountain peak to valley with exhilarating speed. You have disciples everywhere."[2] This chapter explores some of the key features of the Tolstoyan movement, and the ways these manifested themselves in different time periods and geographical contexts.

Tolstoy had a complicated relationship with the movement that took his name. He was always delighted to discover groups and individuals who shared his beliefs and were working along the same lines, and he played an active role in putting sympathizers in touch with each other and with local centers of Tolstoyan activity.[3] On the other hand, he was uncomfortable with the idea that there were "followers" who were inspired by his "teaching."[4] Most Tolstoyans shared his view. Although they accepted the label "Tolstoyan" as a shorthand, a way of acknowledging their common concerns and beliefs, they rejected the idea of a movement: both

93

because they emphasized their own independence of thought – Vladimir Chertkov, Tolstoy's closest associate, described the Tolstoyans as "companions of Tolstoy," and people "who share Tolstoy's views" rather than followers – and because they felt the label was a distraction, which allowed their serious consideration of Christ's commandments to be marginalized.[5] Nor were Tolstoyans uncritical followers. They put their independence of thought into action, happily critiquing key elements of Tolstoy's work, from his attitude to chastity through to the central principle of non-resistance.[6] One thing that did unite Tolstoyans was the profound impact of their first reading of Tolstoy's works, which in many cases completely changed the course of their lives. Readers described the revelation brought about when "one's inner consciousness instantly affirms a new truth presented to one"; and a waking from somnambulism through a shock that could "open our eyes to the disagreement between our confessed morals and our actual mode of living."[7] Tales of Tolstoyan conversion, written by businessmen, lawyers, soldiers, shopkeepers, or aristocrats, occupied an important place within the movement, providing copy for Tolstoyan newspapers and inspirational examples for others to draw on.

Tolstoy asked his readers to be honest with themselves and others, to follow their own conscience, and not to carry on behaving in ways that conventional society demanded. While his emphasis was on individual thought and action, putting Tolstoy's ideas into practice brought an imperative to connect with others, to organize, and to demonstrate how to live the right life. In the 1890s, aspiring Tolstoyans wrote to Tolstoy, explained their change of views, asked him questions, and in some cases sent their own publications. Tolstoy actively put such individuals and groups in touch with each other, and with their nearest centers of activity. The pilgrimage to Tolstoy's estate at Yasnaya Polyana was a wider phenomenon in which many writers and journalists engaged, but was also important for committed Tolstoyans anxious to talk with Tolstoy in person. Leading members of the Russian Tolstoyan movement, including Vladimir Chertkov, Evgeny Popov, and Ivan Gorbunov-Posadov, also played a part in greeting, hosting, and corresponding with their counterparts in other countries, and in providing material for publishing projects.[8] While some felt that proselytizing was problematic and amounted to a kind of verbal or written force that should be rejected on principle, talking to, and about, other centers of activity gave the Tolstoyan movement a sense of reach and momentum.

Efforts to get back to the land and live self-sufficiently in agricultural communities were central to the Tolstoyan movement and are one of the principal ways the movement is remembered. The proliferation of such enterprises across the Russian Empire in the 1880s and 1890s certainly alarmed the tsarist authorities at the time. There were settlements for example at Sochi, on the Black Sea; Dugino, in Tver; Shevelevo, in Smolensk; and Pavlovka, in Kharkov province. Many of these communities inspired smaller satellite groups of sympathizers in their vicinity.[9] The idea of separating oneself from society did not go uncontested, however. Tolstoy understood that the imperative to live in communities of like-minded people stemmed from the "painful" contradictions that sincere Tolstoyans recognized between their surroundings and their convictions, but he feared that isolating oneself from unchristian society would not resolve this contradiction.[10] The founders of Tolstoyan colonies (whether in Russia, Europe, or farther afield) were themselves well versed in debates about the merits of separation from society, and in most cases had grander aspirations; they wanted to place themselves "right in the midst of life" and to act as examples that would lead others to follow them.[11]

Just as important as these experimental communities, however, were efforts to publish and disseminate Tolstoy's works, to connect with other sympathetic groups and individuals, and to demonstrate the ways in which the right life could be lived within established society. The Moscow Vegetarian Society was a regular meeting place for Tolstoyans, its walls decorated with portraits of Tolstoy and its mission statement going beyond diet to advocate "the establishment of love and peace among all living creatures."[12] The Tolstoyan publishing house Posrednik (The Intermediary), run by the successful commercial publisher Ivan Sytin with editorial oversight from Vladimir Chertkov and later Ivan Gorbunov-Posadov, published and disseminated a wide range of books representing aspects of Tolstoy's worldview. These included short stories and tracts by Tolstoy himself, but also works on anti-militarism (Vsevelod Garshin's *Four Days on the Field of Battle*, 1886), vegetarianism (A.N. Beketov's *Man's Diet in Its Present and Future*, 1893), and the evils of money, property, and power (P.V. Zasodimsky's *Black Crows*, 1892).[13] In Britain, Switzerland, and the Netherlands, publishing houses set up by homegrown Tolstoyans or Russian émigrés operated similarly heterogeneous publishing policies.[14]

For Tolstoy, the most important indicator of the advance of true Christian thought was the increasing incidence of conscientious objection to compulsory military service. This occurred both amongst non-resistant sects (the famous burning of arms by the Doukhobors in the Caucasus in 1895, discussed in Chapter 29), but also in the case of individuals who had read Tolstoy or other sympathetic writers. Conscientious objectors occupied a special status in the Tolstoyan movement at large, as individuals who had made the ultimate principled stand against militarism and the state. Tolstoyans published the letters of Pyotr Olkhovik, a twenty-one-year-old peasant from Kharkov who refused to enlist in the imperial army, in Russian, English, French, and Dutch editions. Accounts of the cases of Evdokim Drozhzhin in Russia, Johannes van der Veer in the Netherlands, and Albert Škarvan and František Sedlák in Austria-Hungary also circulated internationally. Activism by and on behalf of conscientious objectors became an important feature of the Tolstoyan movement during and after the First World War, as the experience of war won new converts; collective appeals calling on Russians not to participate in the conflict resulted in the imprisonment of senior Tolstoyans.[15] After the February revolution in 1917 Vladimir Chertkov successfully campaigned for legal status for conscientious objectors in Russia.[16]

While Tolstoy provided uncompromising answers to the questions that faced his followers about how they should live, following the tenets of his philosophy also raised more questions. Did the good work of disseminating Tolstoy's works justify the use of some traditional commercial methods in publishing? Posrednik was in no small measure a success because of the experience and networks brought to the publishing house by Ivan Sytin, but Tolstoyans who disapproved of the commercial side of his publishing business gradually cut him out of Posrednik's operations.[17] Arthur Fifield, the manager of the English publishing house The Free Age Press, also struggled to steer the course between managing an ethical business and a successful one.[18] Tolstoyan communities, wherever they were located, embraced a broad range of views and practices, from fruitarianism and hand-farming to nudism and free unions. Members broadly sought to respect each other's views. But getting these enterprises onto a self-sufficient footing required organization, while a commitment to non-resistance required that there be no organization. External threats – whether physical attacks, as at Blaricum in the Netherlands, the theft of property, or threats to the ownership of communal land – forced commune members to face the ultimate tests to their commitment to non-resistance.[19]

The impact of Tolstoy's ideas followed sometimes unpredictable chronological patterns, influenced by the translation and circulation of his work, and by the particular contexts in which it was read. In Western Europe, translation of Tolstoy's later work was driven by wider enthusiasm in the 1880s for the Russian novel. In China, Tolstoy became an inspiration for utopian intellectuals in the wake of the May Fourth Movement in 1919; they revered him as a philosopher who put his ideals into practice and reached out to the peasant masses.[20] In South Africa, Gandhi and Hermann Kallenbach drew on Tolstoy's ideas in the context of the *satyagraha* campaign of the 1910s (see Chapter 32).[21] While the contexts differed, the forms of activism remained recognizable. In Bulgaria, numerous publishing houses and periodicals were active from the early 1900s through until the 1930s, engaging with issues ranging from peace to diet, and reporting news from sympathetic movements from Estonia to Britain. [22] Bulgarian Tolstoyans founded agricultural colonies, including one named Yasna Polyana, after Tolstoy's estate.[23] In both Finland and Japan, Tolstoy's ideas were enthusiastically spread through lectures, periodicals, and correspondence networks.[24]

In Russia, the Tolstoyan movement was reinvigorated in the revolutionary years 1917–21, as communal enterprises of all kinds developed. Elders of the Tolstoyan movement circulated around communities established by a new younger generation, including the New Jerusalem, Life and Labour, and Beryozki communities in the vicinity of Moscow, as well as communities in Samara, Smolensk, Vladimir, Poltava, Kaluga, the Crimea, and Alma-Ata.[25] The Russian movement did not decline but was forcibly suppressed in the late 1920s as a result of Stalin's drive to collectivize agriculture across the Soviet Union. Tolstoyan communities were first relocated to Siberia, and eventually liquidated completely.

The late 1960s and early 1970s saw a revival of Tolstoyan activism and the beginnings of scholarly interest in the Tolstoyan movement. Dissident Soviet journalist Mark Popovsky collected correspondence and autobiographical accounts from surviving Tolstoyans who had preserved archival remnants of the movement.[26] A rediscovery of Tolstoy was a distinct strand in the Soviet hippie movement of the 1970s, as individuals read, wrote, and circulated samizdat (self-published) texts on or by Tolstoy, and on themes relating to non-resistance.[27] In Canada, pacifist scholar Peter Brock recovered and published memoirs and accounts of Slovak and Russian Tolstoyism.[28] In 1968 Charles Planck, inspired by Tolstoy's emphasis on personal revolution and on questioning how to live, established Tolstoy College within the State University of New York. Members of the college took Tolstoy's anarchism and pacifism as starting points, but these ideas intersected with their experience of anti-Vietnam-war activism and the gay liberation movement: working with Vietnam veterans and the gay community, they opposed compulsory heteromasculinity as a form of coercion.[29]

Whether in the 1890s, 1920s, or 1970s, Tolstoy's ideas were adopted and interpreted in many different geographical, social, and political contexts. They were meaningful for a range of people struggling with questions about how to live the right life in a modern society that seemed at odds with their principles. A reading of Tolstoy's late works and identification with his views fueled their activism and the bonds between them, but Tolstoyans were almost always critical individuals who interpreted, debated, and critiqued ideas. While some later rejected Tolstoyism outright, others lived (and still live) quietly according to Tolstoyan principles.[30] Despite their different geographical contexts and time periods, Tolstoyans felt themselves to be part of a connected movement.

Notes

1 Henry Heylyn Hayter, *General Report on the Census of Victoria, 1891* (Melbourne: R.S. Brain, 1893), 72.
2 John Morrison Davidson to Tolstoy, June 25, 1895, Gosudarstvennyi muzei L.N. Tolstogo (GMT) TS231/19.
3 Tolstoy to Dmitri Khilkov, March 12, 1895, in R.F. Christian (ed.), *Tolstoy's Letters*, vol. ii: *1880–1910* (London: Athlone Press, 1978), 515–16.
4 Leo Tolstoy, *What Is Religion, and Other New Articles and Letters* (New York: Thomas Crowell, 1902), 144–5.
5 Vladimir Chertkov, "If Tolstoy were Tsar," *Brotherhood* 5:6 (October 1897), 63; Lodewijk van Mierop, "Geen Tolstoyaan maar Christien," *Vrede* 2:15 (May 15, 1899), 109.
6 E.V. Agarin, "L.N. Tolstoi i Tolstovstvo v kritike posledovatelei," *Sums'kii istoriko-archivnii zhurnal* 23 (2014), 18–29.
7 Isabella Fyvie Mayo to Vladimir Chertkov, July 13, 1905, RGALI f. 522, op. 2, ed. khr. 613; Frederick van Eeden, *Happy Humanity* (New York: Doubleday, Page, 1912), 89.
8 John Kenworthy to Vladimir Chertkov, August 31, 1896, and September 26, 1896, RGALI f. 552, op. 2, ed. khr. 415.
9 Irina Gordeeva, "Kommunitarnoe dvizhenie v Rossii v poslednei chetverti XIX v," Ph.D. thesis, Russian State University for the Humanities (2000), 157–206; Efim Agarin, *Trudami ruk svoix: tolstovskie zemledel'cheskie kolonii v dorevolotsionnoi Rossii* (Moscow: Common Place, 2019).
10 Tolstoy to George Gibson, March 11/23, 1898, in Natalia Velikanova and Robert Whittaker (eds.), *Tolstoi i SShA* (Moscow: IMLI RAN, 2004), 760–1.
11 Boris Mazurin, "The Life and Labour Commune," in William Edgerton (ed.), *Memoirs of Peasant Tolstoyans in Soviet Russia* (Bloomington and Indianapolis: Indiana University Press, 1993), 40; George Gibson to Tolstoy, April 21, 1898, GMT, BL216/78.

12 Ronald D. LeBlanc, *Vegetarianism in Russia: The Tolstoy(an) Legacy*, Carl Beck Papers 1507 (University of Pittsburgh, 2001).

13 Robert Otto, *Publishing for the People: The Firm Posrednik 1885–1905* (New York: Garland, 1988), 134–43.

14 Antonella Salomoni, "Emigranty-tolstovtsy mezhdu khristianstvom i anarkhizmom (1898–1905 gg.)" in Iu. Sherrer and B. Anan'ich (eds.), *Russkaia emigratsiia do 1917 goda – laboritoriia liberal'noi i revoliutsionnoi mysli* (St. Petersburg: Evropaiskii Dom, 1997), 112–27.

15 Joshua Sanborn, *Drafting the Russian Nation: Military Conscription, Total War and Mass Politics 1905–1925* (DeKalb: Northern Illinois University Press, 2003), 186–7; Edgerton, *Memoirs of Peasant Tolstoyans*, 123–8, 184–209.

16 Alexei Zverev and Bruno Coppetiers, "V.D. Bonch-Bruevich and the Doukhobors: On the Conscientious Objection Policies of the Bolsheviks," *Canadian Ethnic Studies* 27:3 (1995), 189–92.

17 Otto, *Publishing for the People*, 74.

18 Arthur Fifield to Vladimir Chertkov, December 13, 1900, RGALI f. 552, op. 2, ed. khr. 967.

19 Accounts of these challenges can be found in André de Raaij, "A Dead Seed Bearing Much Fruit: The Dutch Christian Anarchist Movement of the International Fraternity," in Alexandre Christoyannopoulos (ed.), *Religious Anarchism: New Perspectives* (Newcastle-upon-Tyne: Cambridge Scholars, 2009), 76–7; Nellie Shaw, *Whiteway: A Colony on the Cotswolds* (London: C.W. Daniel, 1935), 68–9, 115–19; and Ralph Albertson, "The Christian Commonwealth in Georgia," *Georgia Historical Quarterly* 29:3 (1945), 140–1.

20 Shakhar Rahav, "Scale of Change: The Small Group in Chinese Politics 1919–1921," *Asian Studies Review* 43:4 (2019), 677–8.

21 Surendra Bhana, "The Tolstoy Farm: Gandhi's Experiment in 'Cooperative Commonwealth,'" *South African Historical Journal* 7 (1975), 88–100.

22 William Edgerton, "The Social Influence of Lev Tolstoj in Bulgaria," in Jane Gary Harris (ed.), *American Contributions to the Tenth International Congress of Slavists* (Columbus, OH: Slavica, 1988), 123–38.

23 Mary Neuberger, "Notes from the Field: Bulgaria's Tolstoyan Vegetarians," https://notevenpast.org/notes-from-the-field-bulgarias-tolstoyan-vegetarians (accessed October 1, 2020).

24 Armo Nokkala, *Tolstoilaisuus Suomessa* (Helsinki: Kustannusosakeyhtiö Tammi, 1958), 428; Claus M. Fischer, *Lev N Tolstoj in Japan* (Wiesbaden: Otto Harrassowitz, 1969), 89–140.

25 Richard Stites, *Revolutionary Dreams: Utopian Vision and Experimental Life in the Russian Revolution* (Oxford University Press, 1991), 209–10; Edgerton, *Memoirs of Peasant Tolstoyans*.

26 Mark Popovskii, *Russkie muzhiki rasskazyvaiut: posledovateli L. N. Tolstogo v Sovetskom Soiuze 1918–1977* (London: Overseas Publications Interchange, 1983); Arsenii Roginskii, *Vospominaniia krest'ian-tolstovtsev 1910–1930-e gody* (Moscow: Kniga, 1989).

27 Irina Gordeeva, "Tolstoyism in the Late-Socialist Cultural Underground: Soviet Youth in Search of Religion, Individual Autonomy and Nonviolence in the 1970s–1980s," *Open Theology* 3 (2017), 494–515.
28 Peter Brock, "Tolstoyism and the Hungarian Peasant," *Slavonic and East European Review* 58:3 (July 1980), 345–69; *Life in an Austro-Hungarian Military Prison: The Slovak Tolstoyan Albert Škarvan's Story* (Syracuse University Press, 2002); Peter Brock and John Keep (eds.), *Life in a Penal Battalion of the Russian Army: The Tolstoyan N.K. Izumchenko's Story* (Syracuse University Press, 2001).
29 Jennifer Wilson, "'I'm Not a Man. I Don't Want to Destroy You': Tolstoy College and LGBTQ Studies in the Vietnam War Era," *Journal of Social History* 52:4 (2019), 1355–76.
30 See Charlotte Alston, *Tolstoy and His Disciples: The History of a Radical International Movement* (London: I.B. Tauris, 2014), 198–229.

CHAPTER 13

Clothing

Daniel Green

Over the course of his life, Tolstoy wore all the types of clothing expected of a nobleman: uniforms, fashionable dress, and the more relaxed attire common in the countryside. Yet the most iconic image of Tolstoy is the one he cultivated during the last three decades of his life: bearded and wearing peasant-style clothes. This is the image that appears in Repin's portraits and the one that was sent around the world in photographs and film. This chapter outlines the dress norms of Tolstoy's time and shows how the author used his body as a canvas for his religious and political ideas. It also explores the impact this process of self-fashioning had on his family and on Russian society.

Dress Culture in Imperial Russia

In nineteenth-century Russia nobles and peasants lived in different cultural worlds; to understand this divide, we need to go back to the early eighteenth century. As part of his program of modernization, Peter the Great imported not only technologies and ideas from the West, but also cultural practices. His vestimentary decrees changed the appearance of many of his subjects. In 1701 he instructed Moscow residents and visitors to adopt "German dress" and from 1705 he obliged men to shave their beards. These requirements, however, applied only to a small proportion of society; the clergy were exempt, as were the peasants, who comprised the vast majority of the population. The result was two distinct cultural systems: one rooted in Russian folk culture and the other Europeanized and under the control of the imperial court.

One context in which these cultural systems overlapped was the masquerade, a festive carnivalesque event in which the usual social hierarchies did not apply. It provided the opportunity to dress as an other: nobles could become peasants and vice versa, and men and women could wear each other's attire. It was through the masquerade that noblewomen began their return to traditional Russian clothing. In the 1770s, German-born Catherine the Great introduced the *sarafan* (a long, sleeveless dress) and *kokoshnik* (a decorative headdress) to the court, initially as part of a masquerade costume symbolizing Russianness. The costume stuck and became known as "Russian dress" (*russkoe plat'e*). It became the standard dress for women at court and even the official uniform for female courtiers from 1834.

In contrast, noblemen were expected to conform to European clothing norms and were censured when they did not. As a result, wearing traditional Russian clothes in society became a means of protest, albeit one with complex symbolism. For example, in 1825 Nikolai Bestuzhev dissuaded his co-conspirator Kondraty Ryleev from wearing a traditional Russian caftan to the Decembrist uprising (when, in a failed coup, officers led their troops onto Senate Square in St. Petersburg and refused to swear allegiance to Nicholas I after the death of his brother Alexander I); Bestuzhev called Ryleev's dressing-up a "masquerade" and argued that his intention – to show the connection between soldiers and peasants – would not be understood.[1] In the 1840s, many Slavophiles (nobles who sought to reconnect with the culture of an imagined Russian past) adopted forms of traditional dress despite considerable opposition. Critics of the Slavophile writer Konstantin Aksakov, who wore articles of historical clothing, made fun of this choice and argued that it was ridiculous for him to claim to represent a national identity in clothes no one else in the nation wore.[2] In the second half of the nineteenth century, when radicals of various stripes used clothing to advance their ideologies, they faced the same challenge: how could they ensure that the symbolism of their dress was taken seriously and not interpreted as a form of masquerade? This situation was made more complex by large-scale social changes such as the abolition of serfdom, which weakened the cultural distinctions between the peasantry and the nobility. Toward the end of the century, peasants began wearing the same Europeanized clothes as inhabitants of towns and cities, while stylized folk clothing known as "town costume" became fashionable in cities.

Tolstoy as a Young Man

In the world Tolstoy was born into, the nobility served the state, which exercised control over what they wore through uniform dress regulations. This allowed a person's role and rank to be identified at a glance. In social settings, nobles had some leeway in their clothing choices, but were

Figure 2   "The Brothers Tolstoy." ITAR-TASS News Agency / Alamy Stock Photo.

nonetheless encouraged to follow fashion and admonished if they deviated from certain norms. Men typically wore tailcoats, while women wore gowns. However, women were less constrained by the divide between European and Russian dress and could wear elements of traditional Russian clothing in society; in the countryside, they were even encouraged to do so.[3]

As a young man, Tolstoy dressed at the height of fashion. He frequented Russia's best tailors, including E.F. Sharmer, who would later provide clothes for the materialistic hero of *The Death of Ivan Ilyich* (1886). Tolstoy also wore a number of uniforms, starting when he was a student at Kazan University and ending when he resigned his lieutenant's commission in the army in 1856. In a photograph from 1854, Tolstoy and his three brothers appear in a mix of uniform and fashionable dress. Lev Tolstoy is on the left in the Caucasian jacket of an ensign, while his brothers Dmitry, Nikolai, and Sergei are in tailcoats. This picture (which is often reproduced in mirror image because Lev Tolstoy is wearing his sword belt over his left rather than his right shoulder) shows the types of clothing worn in society by noblemen in the 1850s.

When he was at Yasnaya Polyana, Tolstoy started wearing a dressing gown (*khalat*), an item of clothing worn domestically, when its wearer had no service or social obligations. It also carried associations with creativity and freedom of thought, which aligned with his burgeoning career as a writer and thinker. Later, Sofia Tolstaya suggested that her husband's interest in philosophy was linked to the dressing gown: "After returning to Yasnaya Polyana, he fancied himself a Diogenes. He sewed himself a long dressing gown from some coarse material and never took it off. He led a more austere lifestyle and studied the philosophers."[4] Tolstoy was using his clothes to act on two Diogenean impulses: to better understand the world and to live more simply.

Tolstoy soon became interested in peasant life and education, something that required him to leave the house and go outside to work. For this, he needed to change out of his dressing gown. Although European clothing was the norm for noblemen on country estates, peasant clothes were more practical for physical labor. Noblemen would often wear a *tulup* (a warm coat, usually made of sheepskin, with a fur layer on the inside) or its shorter equivalent, the *polushubok*, in winter. Throughout his life, Tolstoy vacillated between a focus on his writerly endeavors, for which he wore a dressing gown, and an all-consuming engagement with outdoor labor, symbolized by the *tulup* or *polushubok*. The contrast between these kinds of clothing and the types of lives they are associated with is drawn sharply in *Anna Karenina* (1875–8), which opens with Stiva Oblonsky waking and putting on his luxurious dressing gown and slippers. Here, the dressing gown symbolizes an unproductive and idle existence, something that Tolstoy struggled to avoid in his own life. Later in the novel Levin works alongside his peasants clad in a *tulup* and recounts a train journey in which he was almost ejected from the carriage because he was wearing a *polushubok*. Levin makes an even clearer switch from noble to peasant dress when he rejects his fur coat (*shuba*) in favor of a *poddevka* (a type of caftan); earlier, he had worried about the lowly company his brother kept when he observed one of Nikolai's companions wearing the same article of clothing (18:161/Pt. 2, Ch. 13; 18:92/Pt. 1, Ch. 24). Similarly, Tolstoy indicates a deficiency in his female characters' value systems when he shows them enjoying elegant clothes. He relied on his wife to ensure he was accurately reproducing this world of high-society female fashion. Sofia Tolstaya often edited his descriptions of women's clothing and was sometimes asked to come up with entire outfits for his female characters.[5]

Tolstoy's Turn to "Simple" Dress

Tolstoy was simultaneously drawn to and repulsed by the dressing gown, but increasingly attracted to the peasant-style clothes with which he is most associated. He used both types of clothing to signal his disdain for excessive interest in dress, but in doing so paradoxically drew attention to his own dress choices.

Tolstoy's rejection of fashionable dress was connected to his admiration for Rousseau and the idea of turning away from civilization. He came to see a dichotomy between a way of life that conformed to social conventions and one that followed Christ's teachings. He once told his wife: "nobody has their own thoughts – the question is only whether to follow those of Christ or Mme Minangois [a fashionable dressmaker]" (14:50).

Vanity was something Tolstoy struggled with a great deal. Though he was obsessed with his appearance (from childhood he was consumed by the idea that he was ugly), he believed that it was sinful to focus too much on one's clothes. In "Christian Teaching," written 1894–6, he warns that when clothing serves more than a protective function, it becomes a source of lust (39:133). Tolstoy also valued the labor invested in the manufacture and cleaning of clothes. He believed a person needs to do this work themselves in order to combat the sin of idleness (39:175). In an attempt to tame his own sinful nature, Tolstoy not only changed the way he dressed, but also began to make clothing himself. He makes numerous references to sewing boots in his diary starting in 1884. In 1891 he records:

> Work, any work (such as on boots) gives people the chance to step out of themselves and into their work. Godly work in particular. Any work (including making boots) is God's affair and if you do not engage in it you will not enter the Promised Land. That's the very self-abandonment of work. (52:53)

Tolstoy's radical clothing choices can be traced back to the early 1860s, when he started sporting the beard that became an integral part of his image. That same decade, he also began wearing clothes with a peasant silhouette on his estate, though he still wore European clothing in town. His preference was to go to expensive tailors, whom he argued produced higher-quality items, which lasted longer.[6] According to his son Sergei, it was not until the early 1880s that Tolstoy started wearing his countryside dress in Moscow.[7] The key item in his wardrobe was the long, loose shirt. Though this type of clothing shared some similarities with the artist's smock, it was primarily associated with the peasant shirt.

Peasant shirts were usually made of undyed homespun cloth, baggier than those worn by nobles, and not tucked in at the waist. They were worn as an outer layer, without any need for a jacket to make the costume complete. Most, known as *kosovorotki*, had their buttons slightly to one side. Tolstoy's shirts were also loose and worn as outerwear, but they differed from peasant clothes in that they were often dyed, made of luxurious materials, and buttoned in the middle. Other elements that distinguished Tolstoy's shirts were their mother-of-pearl buttons and large pockets. One also had a useful innovation for a writer: a pocket for a pencil. The Leo Tolstoy Museum-Estate has five extant examples of Tolstoy's shirts in silk, linen, flannel, and wool.[8] Some were made at Yasnaya Polyana, while others were ordered from expensive tailors. Contrary to Repin's paintings of 1891 and 1901, Tolstoy did not usually go barefoot, nor did he often wear peasant bast shoes (*lapti*); he preferred boots made of leather (*sapogi*) or felt (*valenki*). At home he wore *ichigi*, Caucasian leather boots with a soft sole.

Effects on the Tolstoy Family

In his turn to a simpler life, Tolstoy saw himself as providing a model for his family. In 1884 he wrote:

> This year, I have been living in the countryside in a new way . . . I go to bed and get up early, don't write, but work a lot, at times on my boots, at times at mowing. I spent all last week working in the fields mowing. And I am happy to see (or so it seems to me) that something is happening in my family: they don't judge me and are themselves ashamed. (85:69)

In fact, Tolstoy's family had mixed reactions to his new lifestyle. The household was used to the idea of nobles wearing peasant clothes, but only as part of a masquerade. Sofia Tolstaya recalls that the children found their father's example difficult to imitate. Maria tried to live by her father's precepts but found austere living hard, while Tatiana was attracted by his teachings, but also enjoyed the trappings of society.[9] Meanwhile, their brothers, Andrei and Mikhail, took great delight in their lycée uniforms.[10] Sofia Tolstaya also had reason to be wary of her husband's interest in peasants. On the eve of their marriage, he had shared his diaries with her, detailing his intimate relations with women, including a married serf, Aksinya Bazykina, who still lived on the estate. Sofia Tolstaya sewed herself a peasant costume in order to spy on them and ensure that their relationship did not continue.[11]

Figure 3   Ilya Repin, *Leo Tolstoy Barefoot* (1901). State Russian Museum, St. Petersburg /
Bridgeman Images.

There were other things that Sofia Tolstaya found difficult at Yasnaya Polyana. Life there was spartan and she was particularly frustrated by her husband's changeable attitude to luxury:

> It was impossible to keep track of all his changes in opinions, moods, and desires.
>
> At one time he would strive for simplicity, drive me round in carts, and insist on coarse linens for our first son. Another time he would make me promise that I would travel first class, rather than second as I wished, and bring me back from Moscow bonnets and clothes from Mme Minangoy [Minangois], the most expensive dressmaker then in Moscow, and gilded shoes from Pinet. At one time the children would be looked after by a grubby Russian nanny, at another an Englishwoman was sent for from abroad; and so it was with everything.[12]

When Tolstoy took on more manual labor, he increased rather than decreased Sofia Tolstaya's workload, as many of the household servants were sent away. She was not alone in regretting his neglect of his writing desk. Tolstoy's editor and follower, Vladimir Chertkov, entreated him:

> Your stories, L[ev] N[ikolaevich], are needed now more than ever ... Write something small for pictures, or something longer for books, write something unprintable. Only write. These are the kind of boots that we and all the people need and which we ask of you because you alone can sew them. And most importantly, they're not boots, but bread, our daily bread ... (85:382)

Although Tolstoy's behavior made things difficult at home, he was an inspiration to many others.

Impact and Legacy

Tolstoy not only had a reading public eager for him to write more fiction, but also followers, *tolstovtsy*, who sought to emulate his spiritual lifestyle (see Chapter 12). In the mid 1880s they adopted blue or white loose shirts in imitation of portraits of Tolstoy by Kramskoi and Repin (see Figures 3, 10, and 11).[13] They were one of several radical groups in the second half of the century that adopted a style of dress at odds with their class identity. In the 1870s the *narodniki*, members of an agrarian socialist movement, also adopted peasant dress. While there were significant differences between Tolstoy's views and those of the *narodniki*, they had in common an interest in peasant ways of life, including dress and a focus on labor. They organized carpenters, tailors, and boot-makers into cooperatives and learned trades to pass as peasant artisans. In 1874 thousands went into the countryside dressed as peasants to preach revolution. The peasants were nonplussed and the radicals were arrested. A decade later Tolstoy was also perceived by the peasants as someone separate from their world. Repin records that local peasants would doff their hats and bow to Tolstoy, while those from elsewhere regarded his peasant-style dress with irony and puzzled smiles.[14]

In the last decades of the imperial era elements of traditional male Russian clothing had become a part of uniform dress, including *kosovorotki* and high Russian boots.[15] Yet traditional clothing worn in society remained a symbol of oppositional thought. In the 1900s *tolstovtsy* wore dark blue and black *kosovorotki* while social democrats and revolutionaries wore them in dark blue and red.[16] By the end of the 1910s peasant-style shirts had become known as *tolstovki* after their most famous adopter. They remained popular until the 1930s as an example of "democratic" dress.[17]

Tolstoy began his journey away from fashionable Europeanized dress in the 1860s. By the time he died in 1910 he had become a global phenomenon, challenging the world to reject "civilized" behaviors through his writing and his example. His adoption of peasant-style clothing epitomizes his attempt to find a way of life that conformed to Christian teaching. That his clothes, although similar in appearance, differed from those of the peasants reflects the difficulty of this struggle. His clothing was the clearest outward symbol of his views and of his complex relationship with society and his family. It was a symbol he shaped skillfully, but that went on to take on new meanings outside of his control.

Notes

1 Nikolai Bestuzhev, *Vospominaniia Bestuzhevykh* (Moscow and Leningrad: Akademiia nauk SSSR, 1951), 36.
2 A.I. Gertsen, *Byloe i dumy*, 3 vols. (Moscow and Leningrad: Gosdarstvennoe izdatel'stvo, 1931), vol. 1, 441.
3 Christine Ruane, *The Empire's New Clothes: A History of the Russian Fashion Industry 1700–1917* (New Haven, CT: Yale University Press, 2009), 154.
4 S.A. Tolstaia, "Materialy k biografii L. N. Tolstogo i svedeniia o semeistve Tolstykh i preimushchestvenno gr. L'va Nikolaevicha Tolstogo," in S.A. Makashin (ed.), *L.N. Tolstoi v vospominaniiakh sovremennikov*, 2 vols. (Moscow: Khudozhestvennaia literatura, 1978), vol. 1, 35.
5 Andrew Donskov, "Editor's Introduction," in *Tolstoy and Tolstaya: A Portrait of a Life in Letters* (University of Ottawa Press, 2017), lii.

6 S.A. Tolstaia, *Moia Zhizn'*, 2 vols. (Moscow: Kuchkovo pole, 2011), vol. 1, 260.

7 S.L. Tolstoi, *Ocherki bylogo* (Tula: Priokskoe knizhnoe izdatel'stvo, 1975), 130.

8 I am grateful to Galina Alexeeva and Nadezhda Pereverzeva for providing information about the shirts in the Leo Tolstoy Museum-Estate collection.

9 Tolstaia, *Moia Zhizn'*, vol. 1, 388.

10 Ibid., vol. II, 355, 366–7.

11 Ibid., vol. I, 85.

12 Ibid., vol. I, 76.

13 R.M. Kirsanova, *Kostium v russkoi khudozhestvennoi kul'ture 18 – pervoi poloviny 20 vv.* (Moscow: Bol'shaia rossiiskaia entsiklopediia, 1995), 276.

14 I.E. Repin, "Iz moikh obshchenii s L. N. Tolstym," in Makashin (ed.), *L.N. Tolstoi v vospominaniiakh sovremennikov*, vol. 1, 484.

15 Il'ia Gerasimov (ed.), *Novaia imperskaia istoriia Severnoi Evrazii*, 2 vols. (Kazan: Ab Imperio, 2017), vol. II, 272–3.

16 Ol'ga Khoroshilova, *Kostium i moda Rossisskoi imperii epokha Nikolaia II* (Moscow: Eterna, 2012), 260.

17 Kirsanova, *Kostium v russkoi khudozhestvennoi kul'ture 18*, 276–8.

CHAPTER 14

The "Woman Question"

Anne Lounsbery

In the second half of the nineteenth century, few social problems were deemed more urgent in Russia than those of sexuality and female emancipation: indeed the issues referred to collectively as the "Woman Question" (*Zhenskii vopros*) were seen as inseparable from the most fundamental decisions regarding how society was to be organized. A series of questions about women's social roles (were women to be emancipated or not, maternal or not, educated or not?) were tied to thorny economic, religious, legal, and political issues at a time when institutions were "modernizing" (or Westernizing) with disorienting speed. Especially as the state worked to implement vast legal and social changes (Alexander II's "Great Reforms" described in Chapter 6) aimed at restructuring many sectors of Russian society, Tolstoy was not alone in raising questions about the traditional family's ability to sustain itself in modernity. Both canonical and less canonical works by his contemporaries implied similar reservations, with some looking ahead to various brave new worlds in which all such problems would be resolved. But even by the standards of an era preoccupied with the Woman Question, Tolstoy's intense focus on questions of sex and gender is remarkable.

Women's roles in Russian novels were conditioned by laws and social mores that often differed sharply from those elsewhere. In France, for example, the 1804 Napoleonic Code put men in control of virtually all property, whereas in Russia as early as the eighteenth century, married women enjoyed the right to own and manage their own property. Yet despite their legal rights, Russian women had traditionally lived under strict and even tyrannical patriarchal control, with husbands and fathers exercising enormous power over wives and children. Since the patriarch's power within the family mirrored that of the autocrat at the level of the state (and that of serf-owners over their human property), it is not surprising that reform-minded Russians tended to favor the more or less radical revision of "traditional family values" (see Chapter 15). In fact, progress itself could be associated with change in family structure, including the emancipation of women within, beyond, and even from the family, an institution that some judged to be irredeemably backward.

Direct impetus for the Woman Question's emergence can be traced to anguished soul-searching and loosened censorship following the Crimean War and the death of Nicholas I (1855). Women's issues had been publicly raised in earlier decades (for example, in debates about women's education and in discussions of George Sand, whose scandalous novels questioned the possibility of sexual and emotional satisfaction within the traditional family). But the first systematic treatment of the Woman Question as a social issue came only after 1858, when poet-publicist M.L. Mikhailov began publishing a series of articles (mostly in *The Contemporary*) arguing for women's rights. Refuting well-known anti-feminist French writers Jules Michelet and Pierre-Joseph Proudhon (who claimed women were biologically and intellectually inferior), Mikhailov argued that women – like blacks in America, he noted – had simply not been given opportunities for development. In 1860 he published a Russian translation of Harriet Taylor Mill's and John Stuart Mill's 1851 essay "The Enfranchisement of Women": and while the issue of enfranchisement had no relevance in Russia, the Mills' argument proved important in that it linked "women's emancipation to the whole tendency of extending rights and abolishing the old privileged monopolies of monarchy, aristocracy, and church."[1] In the ensuing decades – that is, throughout most of Tolstoy's adult life – Russian thinkers across the political spectrum were developing these links, debating issues ranging from prostitution and birth control to female peasant labor and socialist sewing collectives. The left in particular emphasized the extent to which women's liberation depended on thoroughgoing social transformation, and even on revolution.

Thus while English novels often looked, implicitly or explicitly, toward an idealized traditional family that was thought to be under threat, Russian novels not infrequently did the opposite.[2] In Nadezhda Khvoshchinskaya's 1861 novella *The Boarding School Girl*, for instance, family life is matter-of-factly equated with institutionalized violence (beatings, coercion). The young provincial heroine asks herself, "What kind of life is this? What's housework – swearing, nonsense, racket all day! . . . it's impossible to live this way."[3] The narrative concludes with her escape from impending marriage: she runs off to Petersburg to become economically self-sufficient (as a translator and copyist), thus joining what the text represents as modernity – an escape that in this case requires an emphatic rejection of all sexual relationships. Chernyshevsky's extraordinarily influential *What Is to Be Done?* (1863) reveals a similar interest in the liberatory potential of alternative domestic arrangements, but without the rejection of conjugal love: instead, by linking his heroine's political awakening to her sexual emancipation, Chernyshevsky (building on Sand) offers readers both a how-to manual for revolution and a story of happy bigamous domesticity. Dostoevsky – who famously declared that "the contemporary Russian family is becoming more and more an *accidental* family"[4] – found Tolstoy's treatment of family life to be out of step with the times: he claimed that "gentry literature" (*pomeshchich'e slovo*, literally "the land-owner's word") had already "said everything it had to say (superbly in the case of Lev Tolstoy)."[5] But in fact Tolstoy's writings repeatedly addressed the most urgent contemporary issues, foremost among them the Woman Question, and his ideological evolution, as we will see, was toward increasing radicalism.

As early as his first novel *Family Happiness* (1859), the story of what starts out as a love match between a very young woman and an older man, Tolstoy was thinking about how mythologies of romantic love and the institution of marriage could deform women's lives. *Family Happiness* ends by suggesting that perhaps the best a married woman can hope for is that some attenuated version of conjugal contentment can be achieved – that is, after the possibility of happiness has been renounced and emotional resources have been redirected to the next generation. In a word, the text espouses what today's theorists term "reproductive futurism."[6] *War and Peace*, too, privileges reproduction and future generations above all, a move that obviously requires a significant investment in the heterosexual family ideal. In *War and Peace* an emphatically traditional vision of family life and gender roles helps make possible a certain vision of the Russian nation as a whole, united by blood ties and necessary sacrifice in a story of national survival. Such an emphasis on generational continuity can help naturalize not just gender roles but even institutions like serfdom, which can be construed as a family relation rather than a relation of power (as we see in Tolstoy's early novella *Childhood*, 1852).

Anna Karenina (1875–8) is in large part a cautionary tale about the consequences of unbinding people (especially women) from the family responsibilities that in turn bind all of society together. As an adultery novel, it places the Woman Question in clear relationship to all the other questions facing Russia during the Great Reforms – legal, religious, economic, social – thereby highlighting the fragility not only of marriage, but of other institutions that structure people's lives: calling marriage into doubt calls *everything* into doubt.[7]

Adultery novels mediate between subjectivity and social constraint by focusing on marriage as the institution where the personal and the political merge most powerfully, where authenticity (which is supposed to be experienced as something personal) and authority (which is supposed to be experienced as something external) are meant to come together. In *Anna Karenina* a somewhat baffling plot element highlights the tensions generated by such expectations: why exactly does Anna decline Karenin's early offer of divorce, and why does Karenin change his mind later when Anna says she wants a divorce? While the text suggests certain motivations that might lie behind both refusals, and while both characters offer their own somewhat garbled reasons for what they do, these explanations are neither conclusive nor sensible. The passages where divorce is discussed are confusing, sometimes contradictory.[8] Even though Anna's dissolute brother assures her that "divorce would completely solve [*razviazyvaet*, literally "untie"] everything" (18:449/Pt. 4, Ch. 21), the text overall seems to imply that divorce offers no real solution: it simply lacks the power to untie the bonds that tie a woman to her husband.

Tolstoy's preoccupation with sexuality, marriage, and women's proper role never diminished. Indeed, in his last decades such concerns become central to his ideas about the entire social order.[9] For late Tolstoy, who advocates (but does not practice) sexual abstinence, what is wrong – very wrong – about sex and marriage cannot be separated from what is wrong with virtually all other social institutions, from the police and the Orthodox Church to the fine arts and the market economy: all are based on coercion and violence. Such subversive ideas find expression in the infamous novella *The Kreutzer Sonata*, which was the subject of intense debate and scandal across the political spectrum. Beginning in 1889, *The Kreutzer Sonata* circulated widely but mostly in illegal form: the authorities did not permit its publication as a separate (i.e. affordable) edition, although Sofia Andreevna Tolstaya was granted permission to include it in the eighth edition of her husband's Collected Works after she personally petitioned the Tsar.[10]

The novella tells the story of an upper-class man who has murdered the wife he suspects has been unfaithful, though the question of her infidelity (did she or didn't she?) is never resolved. Virtually the entire text is taken up by the words of the murderer Pozdnyshev, who narrates the story of his life and crime to an unnamed interlocutor. Their conversation is quite explicitly set up by and as a dialogue on the Woman Question: the text opens in a train compartment, where a group of passengers representing different social and moral positions (a "progressive" woman, an old patriarchal merchant, etc.) discuss what is to be done about divorce, adultery, courtship, and romantic love inside and outside of marriage. The epigraph is our first signal that the novella's view of what constitutes "adultery" will be expansive: "But I say unto you, that every one that looketh on a woman to lust after her hath committed adultery with her already in his heart" (Matthew 5:28).

And indeed Pozdnyshev ends by asserting that all sexual relations are in effect adulterous, because they cannot be separated from the coercion, injustice, and violence characterizing relations between men and women generally. Thus under current social arrangements, man is "a depraved slave owner" and woman is "an abject and depraved slave," barred from achieving fully human status because she is "an instrument of enjoyment" (27:24–5). Garden-variety misogynistic tropes are right on the surface in *The Kreutzer Sonata*, and readers have never found it difficult to trace their roots to Tolstoy's own biography. "Women, like tsaritsas, hold nine-tenths of the human race in a state of slavery and hard labor," says Pozdnyshev, "simply because they have been deprived of equal rights with men. And so they avenge themselves by acting on our sensuality . . . [making of themselves] a weapon to act upon our sensuality . . . I see in it something that's outright dangerous to people, something against the law; I feel like calling a policeman, appealing for protection from danger" (27:25).

But if we read passages like these as *nothing more than* misogyny, we will fail to see how tightly they are bound to Tolstoy's critiques of other social institutions, including the state writ large. The power imbalance and violence of gender relations mirror the power imbalance and violence between people and the state: hence "the internal ideological relatedness between [Tolstoy's calls for] abstinence and his pacifism."[11] In other words, what is wrong with marriage lies not in sex but in the fact that marriage, like all institutions, perpetuates and justifies power imbalances and violence. What would initially seem to be a jarring parallel between marriage and armies therefore makes sense. This is the logic that underlies the call for total abstinence, even, Tolstoy declares, if it leads to the extinction of humanity: only abstinence can free people, especially women, from the objectification and "slavery" (a recurring word in *The Kreutzer Sonata*) that go along with sex. For late Tolstoy, to be free and good would be to cast off the yoke of sexual desire and reproduction, which would mean creating new forms of sociality premised neither on blood ties nor on sexual and economic exploitation.[12] As extreme as such propositions

sound, they share common ground with ideas that were being put forth by
Tolstoy's contemporaries – not a few of whom were calling for the
abolition of traditional family structures – as well as with modern-day
feminists' and queer theorists' critiques of the family and reproductive
futurism.[13]

The Kreutzer Sonata analyzes sex not only in relation to state power, but
also in relation to what we would today call consumer capitalism.
According to Pozdnyshev, woman is "a slave *in the marketplace*," and
modern courtship consists of too many choices among too many indul-
gences up for sale: maidens display their physical charms ("Choose me, not
her! Look at *my* shoulders!") while "men walk about as if at a bazaar,
making their selections" (27:23–4, emphasis mine). Indeed in *The Kreutzer
Sonata* the life of the rich seems to be characterized above all by a profusion
of choices among various pleasures, all of which are linked to sexual
profligacy (should I enjoy this culinary delicacy or that one? this woman
or that one?). One of these pleasures, as Pozdnyshev suggests, is art: "we all
know how a man looks at a woman – 'wine, women and song,' as the poets
say. Look at all poetry, all painting and sculpture, starting with love lyrics
and those naked Venuses and Phrynes" (27:36).

The art–sex parallel is at the center of another text Tolstoy wrote around
this time, *What Is Art?* (1897–8) – a moralizing and rather tortured tract
concerning art's role in modern society. Just as *The Kreutzer Sonata* ends
by condemning all sex, so *What Is Art?* ends by condemning virtually all
art. And the terms of the indictments are strikingly similar: Tolstoy
attributes both sexual profligacy and artistic production to the *excesses*
made possible by modern life – a link that explains both texts' preoccupation with the mass production made possible by capitalism. *The Kreutzer
Sonata*'s Pozdnyshev says, for example, "Go to any big city and walk
around the stores. There are millions of them, and it's impossible to
estimate the amount of human labor they represent." All this, he claims,
is aimed at satisfying women's demands, which grow out of the demands
placed on *them* by the sexual marketplace: "Count the factories. The great
majority of them make useless ornaments … for women. Millions of
people, generations of slaves, all perishing of hard labor in factories just
to satisfy women's whims" (27:25). *What Is Art?* employs arguments and
rhetorical techniques akin to Pozdnyshev's, associating art with shameless
behavior (naked ballerinas, etc.) and inundating us with numbers and
lists to convey a sense of surfeit. Long passages estimate the labor
hours devoted to creating works of art ("there are 30,000 artist-painters

in Paris alone"; "if not millions, then at least hundreds of thousands [of books] are typeset and printed … millions and millions of working days are spent," 30:158, 119).

The results of modernity's excesses, for both sex and art, are (1) exploitation and (2) the corruption of elites' tastes and desires. According to Tolstoy, in the case of art, these tastes have been "refined" to the point that sophisticates prefer works that are at worst iniquitous (like adultery novels) and at best meaningless (like Symbolist poetry). In the case of sex, so assiduously has the modern marketplace catered to men's desires that they find it normal to organize their lives around satisfying such desires, regardless of the consequences for other people – for instance, leaving women no choice but to sell themselves. The striking radicalism of these positions makes it clear that thinking about the Woman Question led Tolstoy to interrogate the very foundations of the social order.

Notes

1 This paragraph draws on Richard Stites, *The Women's Liberation Movement in Russia: Feminism, Nihilism, and Bolshevism, 1860–1930* (Princeton University Press, 1978), 29–63; quote is from 44.
2 Anna A. Berman, "The Family Novel (and Its Curious Disappearance)," *Comparative Literature* 72:1 (2020), 1–18 (at 1).
3 Nadezhda Khvoshchinskaya, *The Boarding School Girl*, trans., intro. and annotated by Karen Rosneck (Evanston, IL: Northwestern University Press, 2000), 103–4.
4 F.M. Dostoevskii, *Sobranie sochinenii v 15 tomakh* (Leningrad/St. Petersburg: Nauka, 1988–96), vol. XIV, 202–3, emphasis in the original.
5 Ibid., vol. XV, 490.
6 Lee Edelman, *No Future: Queer Theory and the Death Drive* (Durham, NC: Duke University Press, 2004).
7 See Tony Tanner, Introduction to *Adultery in the Novel* (Baltimore, MD: Johns Hopkins University Press, 1979).
8 See for example *Anna Karenina*, III:13, IV:4, 5, 12, 17, 21–3, V:8, 28, VI:21–4, 32, VII:9, 17–19, 25.
9 Ani Kokobobo, "A Sexual Theory of the State – Pacifism, Abstinence, and the Late Tolstoy as Gender Theorist" (forthcoming paper cited by author's permission).
10 On the text's composition, circulation, censorship, and reception, see Peter Ulf Møller, *Postlude to The Kreutzer Sonata: Tolstoj and the Debate on Sexual Morality in Russian Literature in the 1890s* (Leiden: Brill, 1998).
11 Kokobobo, "Sexual Theory of the State."

12 Tolstoy's last novel, *Resurrection* (1899), would also draw attention to the links between sexual exploitation, social institutions, and economic structures, even envisioning a world where all might live as brothers and sisters pursuing the common good.

13 On Tolstoy's contemporaries, see Stites, *Women's Liberation Movement in Russia*, esp. 258–69. On queer theory, see Kokobobo, "Sexual Theory of the State."

CHAPTER 15

The Family

Anna A. Berman

The Russian family in 1910 – the year Tolstoy died – was quite a different institution than it had been at his birth in 1828. As Russia went through an age of great reforms, relations between spouses, parents and children, siblings, and extended kin all evolved to match their changing society and its ideals. Tolstoy was, of course, well aware of debates about the state of the Russian family that raged at mid-century, but the evolution of his own thought did not run in tandem with them. Instead, his critique of the family talked past that of many of his contemporaries to focus on the moral issues closest to his heart.

The Russian Family in Flux

Tolstoy was born into a traditional gentry family in a period of relative stability for the Russian family ideal. For centuries, the family had been a conservative institution defined by a rigid patriarchal structure reinforced by both Church and custom. As laid out in the *Domostroi*, a sixteenth-century domestic manual, the husband was head of the house, and his wife should obey his every command. Children were to be taught "with the rod." In the early eighteenth century, Peter the Great began attempts to reform the family as part of his broader modernizing agenda. Seeing the Russian nobility as coarse and ignorant (in comparison with European aristocrats), he tried to instill Western, enlightened values through taking over the education of their sons. Pushing Russia beyond the *Domostroi* model, Peter brought women out of the *terem* (space of female seclusion) and gave young people more control over whom they married.

Russia's patriarchal family model proved resilient, however. The first official code of laws (1833) enshrined this conservatism, leaving virtually all power in the hands of fathers and husbands.[1] A wave of George Sandism in the 1830s to 1850s that valorized women's freedom in love changed the family values of a small circle of intellectuals, but did not topple the existing order. Likening family life to the root that sustains the tree of the State, Metropolitan Filaret proclaimed in 1837 that in order for the State to be strong and to produce the fruits of societal well-being, family life must be "strong in blessed spousal love, sanctified parental power, children's respect and obedience," and that following from this respect for parents would be born and grow reverence for the Sovereign.[2] The family was the model in microcosm for the State.

In Tolstoy's early years, he largely accepted this idealized conception of the patriarchal family. Works like *Childhood* (1852, set in the 1830s) and *War and Peace* (1865–9, set in 1805–20) were not blind to the dangers of all-powerful fathers; there are hints of the father's profligacy in *Childhood* and Prince Bolkonsky tyrannizes over his daughter in *War and Peace*. Yet on the whole, Tolstoy depicted gentry nests filled with loving family relations. Dostoevsky would dismissively call them *"no more than historical portraits of the distant past."*[3] And he was right that the family had ceased to be a stable institution by the 1860s.

Based on serfdom and presuming a powerless, oppressed status for women and children, the gentry family became increasingly difficult to idealize in the pre-reform era. By the time Tolstoy married and began to found his own family in 1862, ideas about what the Russian family should be were in flux. As jurists struggled to rewrite imperial family law as part of Alexander II's Great Reforms, writers and thinkers from across the political spectrum jumped into the debate. With characteristic urgency, Nikolai Dobroliubov (1858) called "the question of so-called *family morality* ... one of the most important social questions of our time" and Mikhail Mikhailov – an advocate of women's rights – claimed in 1860: "The complete rebuilding of society is impossible without remaking its basis, the family."[4]

The status of women was central to these debates (see Chapter 14). One side of the critique of the family focused on the failures of women's education to prepare them for their true calling as mothers. For example, an 1864 article in the *Journal for Parents and Teachers* (*Zhurnal dlia roditelei i nastavnikov*) complained that girls who from age twelve "had been accustomed to play at being ladies, greedily follow all fashions, day after day attend evenings and balls and always be surrounded by a crowd of admirers" were spoiled for their future roles and incapable of experiencing true maternal happiness.[5] Such critics saw the decorative function girls were trained to fill as damaging to Russian society because it left them ill-equipped to manage a household or to educate their own children. Tolstoy agreed with such critiques. He lauds Natasha Rostova's total disregard for her appearance, and her replacement of singing and other allurements with joy at her children's diapers at the end of *War and Peace*. Her model stands in stark contrast to the *Journal of Parents and Teachers* description of women who feel out of place in the nursery, where the happy cries of their children upset their nerves, and where their crinoline dresses do not allow them to get close enough to their children to play ... a description that finds echoes in Anna Karenina's experiences as an elaborately dressed mistress and failing mother on Vronsky's estate.

The other side of the critique of women's roles in the family focused on their lack of rights. An unsigned article in *The Voice* (1871) opened with the frequently heard claim:

> No matter how much we try to prove the excellence of our laws about marriage; no matter how much we shield ourselves with the obviousness of arguments that these laws are strengthened in the form of those church definitions, which follow directly from the essence of the sacrament itself; finally, no matter how much we point to the patriarchal nature of our daily life [*byt*], in which supposedly all internal relations between family members rest on moral sources – real life, as we see, is far from reflecting this instruction.[6]

There followed a typical list of family cruelties brought to public attention in recent court cases. As Russian law stood, women were required to live with their husbands who had the legal right to rape and beat them. Although married women retained the rights to their property, if they fled to their own estate to avoid abuse, they could be compelled to return. And there were many cases of husbands mortgaging or selling their wives' estates without their permission or knowledge.[7] The only way for a girl to escape a tyrannical father was through marriage (which required parental consent), but this just left her under the control of a potential new tyrant.

To combat this sad state of affairs, radicals began promoting a complete remake of the Russian family. The idea of a "fictitious marriage" to a "brother" whose explicit aim was to free the woman from her parental home was popularized by Chernyshevsky in his wildly influential *What Is to Be Done?* (1863). Vera Pavlovna escapes from a stifling home through an unconsummated marriage to her brother's enlightened tutor, Lopukhov, and the two cohabitate as equals while each pursues meaningful work to better society. When Vera falls in love with Lopukhov's best friend, he frees her to follow her heart by faking his own death and disappearing (ultimately to return and remarry, settling in a bigamous quartet with his former wife and friend). We see echoes of George Sand's influence in the valorization of women's freedom in love. Tolstoy held Chernyshevsky and his ideas about love triangles in contempt, polemicizing with them in *Anna Karenina* (1875–8), when the heroine dreams of having two husbands. Anna – living in Tolstoy's more traditional (and realistic) world – would have to face excruciating social censure, as well as lose her son, for giving her heart outside of marriage.

The same year Tolstoy began publishing *Anna Karenina*, another novella appeared in which a married woman had an affair with a man she met at a train station, this one exploring a more liberal response to the problem. In Fyodor Stulli's *Twice Married* (1875), instead of the heroine being destroyed by having overstepped societal norms, her elderly husband agrees to accept the child of her affair as his own on the condition that her lover marry her after his death. Before going ahead with the second marriage, the heroine reads books to become enlightened and independent and when she re-enters wedlock it is on more equal footing with her husband. Many writers and critics would push for this new, more egalitarian model of affective marriage, where the Russian family was bound by mutual love and support, not blind obedience.

Tolstoy's Evolving Family Ideal

Tolstoy was fully cognizant of the way critics were rethinking the family, but his own thought was moving in a different direction. In the broadest terms, Tolstoy's evolution went from an idealization of the traditional patriarchal family (through the 1860s), to an acknowledgement of its flaws (1870s), to a rejection of the family as an ultimate life goal (1880s onward). Much as in the epilogue to *War and Peace* "conversations and discussions about women's rights, about the relations between spouses, about their freedom and rights" did not interest Natasha Rostova and were incomprehensible to her, Tolstoy through the 1860s held motherhood to be women's highest calling and saw no need for structural reforms.[8] Happy in his own family life, he believed in the model he had inherited.

In the 1870s, Tolstoy's views became more sombre. *Anna Karenina* begins with family rupture ("All was confusion in the Oblonskys' house") and addresses contemporary debates head-on. At the Oblonskys' dinner party, it is the men who do the talking about women's roles and rights, just as it was men who wrote most of the articles in the press. Tolstoy does not shy away from the complexities of the topic and offers no clear answers. He rejected both sides of the contemporary debates, horrified at the abuse of defenseless women, while also scoffing at naïve George Sandian visions of free love. Dolly chooses to stay with her unfaithful husband and watches helplessly as he squanders away both his and her own property, leaving their children with an ever-shrinking inheritance. Anna follows her heart but cannot find happiness in the role of a mistress who has given up her son and her place in the social world. Kitty is the happiest of the lot, but her husband is still full of suicidal thoughts that he does not share with her. The one thing that is clear and consistent is the need for belonging to an extended kinship network; siblings provide one another with support from the first to last chapter of the novel (just as they were a crucial support in Tolstoy's own life). In other words, Tolstoy was conflicted about the marital ideal, but not about lateral, asexual kinship bonds. These would come to be the only kind he truly valued.

As Tolstoy clarified his new ideas about the meaning and purpose of the family in the 1880s, he put forward a vision that seemed out of touch with contemporary reality or with the practicalities of daily life. This new vision left no place for sexual love and was based on impersonal service to a higher cause. In 1887, he wrote to his second son, Ilya Lvovich, who was contemplating marriage: "This is what I think: to marry in order to enjoy oneself more will never work. To put marriage – union with the person you love – as your main aim, replacing everything else, is a big mistake. And it's obvious when you think about it. The aim is marriage. Well, you get married, and then what?"[9] The gentry nest that had been an end goal for Tolstoy in the 1850s to 1860s was no longer an ultimate purpose. In the letter to Ilya, Tolstoy explained:

> Marriage and the birth of children offer so many joyful things to look forward to that it seems that these things actually constitute life itself, but this is a dangerous delusion. If parents live and produce children without having any aim in life, they only put off the question of the aim of life and the punishment to which people are subjected when they live without knowing why – they only put it off, but they can't avoid it, because they will have to bring up and guide children and there will be nothing to guide them by.[10]

Husband and wife should only unite, Tolstoy made clear, if they had a shared goal and wanted to move forward together in attaining it.

By this new logic, a marriage entered into for the wrong reasons (i.e. lust or desire for personal pleasure) could only be a hindrance on life's true path. As Tolstoy wrote in his "Afterward to the *Kreutzer Sonata*" (1890):

"We must understand that no aim worthy of a man, whether it be the service of humanity, of the fatherland, of Science or Art – let alone that of God – can be attained by means of coupling with the object of one's love, whether within or outside marriage. On the contrary . . . falling in love and sexual intercourse invariably make it more difficult for a man to achieve any worthwhile goal."[11] Family, in this new estimation, is a fallback for people not strong enough to engage in true service to God: "The Christian ideal is love for God and one's neighbour, together with self-renunciation in order to serve God and one's neighbour. Sexual love and marriage are a service of self, and so at the very least an obstacle to the service of God and other people; from a Christian point of view they are a falling away, a sin."[12] And if people fall, if they succumb to love and marry, then "Through the children that are its consequence, this marriage restricts the man and woman to a new, more limited form of service to God and other people. Before marriage they could be of direct service to God and other people in the most varied ways; marriage limits their possible activities, requiring that they should rear and feed the children who will be of service to God in future."[13]

This critique of marriage and the family disregards the issue of sexual difference. Gone is the idealization of motherhood; men and women must fulfill the same purpose of serving God. Tolstoy talks past all the contemporary debates about marital relations and spouses' rights and responsibilities. There is only one true responsibility: to follow one's conscience (the kingdom of God is *within*) and to selflessly serve. Human laws are below consideration when one is concerned with God's law. In framing the issue this way, Tolstoy ignores all the quotidian realities of actually belonging to a real family made of real people. His abstract talk of living for the soul infuriated his wife, Sofia Andreevna, who was left to handle all the tasks of managing a household and overseeing a large family (whatever Tolstoy might write, children do need regular meals, clothes, and lessons, and money is needed to provide these things).

As Tolstoy's lived experience of family disintegrated, with increasing tensions between him and Sofia Andreevna, a shared cause like he advocated in his letter to Ilya Lvovich brought a period of restored unity. From September 1891 to June 1893 the Tolstoy family became deeply involved in famine relief in the Tula, Riazan, and Orlov provinces. They worked together to raise money and set up soup kitchens that ultimately fed thousands of peasants. Watching his family come together around this cause, Tolstoy was happy. But the famine passed, and with it this respite of family harmony. Tolstoy returned to his abstract ideal of a desexed brotherhood of egoless individuals coming together in the unity of the whole human family. And meanwhile, he failed to live lovingly with the real people who were his next of kin.

Notes

1 See William G. Wagner, *Marriage, Property, and Law in Late Imperial Russia* (Oxford: Clarendon Press, 1994), 62.

2 Filaret, *Slovo i rechi, Tom IV 1836–1848* (Moscow: Tipografiia A.I. Mamontova, 1882), 76.

3 Dostoevsky, *Polnoe sobranie sochinenii v tridtsati tomakh* (Leningrad: Izdatel'stvo "Nauka," 1972–90), vol. xxv, 173.

4 Quoted in Todd, *Literature and Society in Imperial Russia, 1800–1914* (Stanford University Press, 1978), 256; M.L. Mikhailov, *Zhenshchiny, ikh vospitanie i znachenie v sem'e i obshchestve* (St. Petersburg: izdanie P. K. Kartavova, 1903), 3.

5 S.N., "Ob oshibkah i neobkhodimykh kachestvakh materi," *Zhurnal dlya roditelei i nastavnikov* 1:3 (1864), 40.

6 "Nashi zakony o brake," *Golos* 158 (1871).

7 Barbara Alpern Engel, *Women in Russia, 1700–2000* (Cambridge University Press, 2004), 36.

8 *War and Peace*, Epilogue 1, Ch. x (12:267–8).

9 Translation from *Tolstoy's Letters*, ed. R.F. Christian (New York: Scribner Press, 1987), 433.

10 Ibid., 434.

11 "An Afterward to 'The Kreutzer Sonata'" in *The Lion and the Honeycomb: The Religious Writings of Tolstoy*, ed. A.N. Wilson, trans. Robert Chandler (San Francisco: Harper & Row, 1987), 66–7.

12 Ibid., 71.

13 Ibid., 75.

PART III

Literature, the Arts, and Intellectual Life

CHAPTER 16

Tolstoy's Oeuvre

Chloë Kitzinger

Leo Tolstoy's oeuvre sprawls across the boundaries of genres, styles, and centuries. Tolstoy first experimented with fiction in his diary at age twenty-two ("A History of Yesterday," March 1851), and he was drafting a denunciation of capital punishment in late October 1910, days before his death. These fragments bookend a vast corpus, which encompasses three major novels (*War and Peace*, *Anna Karenina*, and *Resurrection*); short stories that revised the basic terms of their genre on the eve of literary modernism; and religious, philosophical, and political tracts that inspired followers throughout Russia and around the world. Across these many forms, Tolstoy explored a persistent set of questions about self, other, and God. This chapter sketches the shape of Tolstoy's oeuvre, focusing on one or two works from each decade of his career.

Tolstoy's career began with his novella *Childhood* (*Detstvo*), published in the journal *The Contemporary* in September 1852. In "A History of Yesterday," Tolstoy had set out to narrate the "soul-side" of the events of a single day. But he foresaw, and discovered in practice, that "there would not be enough ink in the world to write" such a book or "typographers to print it" (1:279). *Childhood* avoids this impasse by foregrounding what Tolstoy's contemporary Nikolai Chernyshevsky called "the psychic process ... the dialectic of the soul."[1] Instead of trying to give a complete accounting of one day's impressions, Tolstoy moves from one episode to another through the "window" of his narrator-hero Nikolenka's perceptions[2] – from his indignation at being woken by his tutor swatting flies over his bed, to the erotic tenderness he feels for his childhood companion Katenka when her dress slips down her shoulder. He thus creates a synthetic image of inner life, through which the novella sets out to represent childhood itself.

This generalizing ambition was crucial to Tolstoy, who envisioned *Childhood* as the first part of a novel that he called "The Four Epochs of Development." Although Nikolenka's life shares many details with

Tolstoy's, *Childhood* is equally shaped by a set of literary models, from Rousseau and Rodolphe Töpffer to Sterne and Dickens. The result is a hybrid text in the mode of "pseudo-autobiography,"[3] whose episodic narrative overlays a clear poetic structure: the novella begins with a morning scene in which Nikolenka pretends to have had a dream about his mother's death, and it ends with her death in actuality. In its genre as well as its plot, *Childhood* inaugurates two questions that hang over the rest of Tolstoy's career: what are the dangers of fiction? and what unique power does it hold to capture the nature of reality?[4]

At the time when Tolstoy wrote *Childhood*, the Russian literary scene was in transition. It was dominated by "thick journals" like *The Contemporary*: monthly subscription volumes which included works of fiction, poetry, memoir, history, science, literary criticism, and more. The formidable critic Vissarion Belinsky, who had presided over the 1840s debuts of Dostoevsky, Turgenev, and Goncharov, died in 1848, and the journals were eager for new voices. *Childhood* gained Tolstoy entrance into *The Contemporary*'s inner circle, and his 1855 *Sevastopol Stories*, sent from the front lines of the Crimean War, brought wider fame. He returned to St. Petersburg prepared to trade his military career for that of a professional writer.

However, Tolstoy soon grew disenchanted with the professional enter-prise of literature, amid intensifying debates between the "aesthetic" writers and critics, and the radicals who spoke for the social utility of realist literature as a mirror of real life. In 1859, Tolstoy renounced his recently published novella *Family Happiness* and declared his departure from literature – the first of several crises punctuating his career. He threw himself into managing the peasant schools he had founded around his family estate, and began a pedagogy journal (*Yasnaya Polyana*, 1862) for which he wrote many of the articles himself. One was the Rousseauian manifesto "Who should learn to write from whom, the peasant children from us or we from the peasant children?," whose title captures Tolstoy's misgivings. But by the time it was printed, he was already gravitating back toward literature. To defray a gambling debt, he published *The Cossacks* (1863), a novella begun ten years earlier, which gives definitive voice to the same tension between spontaneous "nature" and self-reflective "civiliza-tion" that structures his pedagogical article. Soon afterwards, he began work on *War and Peace* (*Voina i mir*, 1865–9).

In an 1868 article, Tolstoy wrote: "What is *War and Peace*? It is not a novel, still less an epic poem, still less a historical chronicle. *War and Peace* is that which its author wanted and was able to express, in the form in which it expressed itself" (16:6). It is no wonder that he resisted assigning his book to a single genre. *War and Peace* follows two fictional families from Russia's entry into the Napoleonic Wars in 1805 through Napoleon's invasion of Russia in 1812. As in *Childhood*, but on a grand scale, the characters offer windows into an electrifying range of experiences, from falling in love at a ball to falling asleep on the eve of battle; from what it is like to hunt wolves in the autumn to what it is like to die. However, Tolstoy increasingly strays from his network of fictional characters to portray the mass experience of historical events – the fires that broke out after Napoleon's occupation of Moscow, or the French army's retreat during the winter of 1812. And he digresses still further to analyze the contradiction between these *modes* of experience: the sense of freedom and agency that we have as individuals, and the fact (as he argues) that history unfolds according to impersonal, deterministic laws. Even as *War and Peace* immerses its reader in an instantly recognizable model of life in the world, it suggests that human narrative and perception distort the real conditions governing our actions.[5]

War and Peace appeared toward the end of the decade in which the Russian novel had come into its own, with Goncharov's *Oblomov* (1859), Turgenev's *Fathers and Children* (1862), and Chernyshevsky's *What Is to Be Done?* (1863) among others. Its first parts appeared in *The Russian Herald* simultaneously with installments of Dostoevsky's *Crime and Punishment* (1866). Where Turgenev, Chernyshevsky, and Dostoevsky all centered their works on the contemporary figure of the radical or "nihilist," Tolstoy turned to the outmoded romantic genre of historical fiction. But *War and Peace*'s historical setting does not sever it from its moment. Tolstoy first conceived it as a novel about a Decembrist returning from exile in 1856, now grown beyond his revolutionary "missteps and misfortunes" (13:54). With the turn back to 1812, Tolstoy's skepticism about progressivism and radical politics was transposed to the very possibility of intentional historical action, and eventually, to the existence of free will itself.[6]

Soon after *War and Peace* had completed publication in 1869, Tolstoy again turned away from artistic literature to produce a series of reading primers (1872–5). At the same time, he continued to grapple with the questions *War and Peace* had raised about history and human action. He tried, and failed, to take them up in a new historical novel set in the time of Peter the Great. Unable to unlock these questions on the ground of history, he instead began a novel of private and family life, *Anna Karenina* (1875–8).

Anna Karenina begins with a biblical epigraph ("Vengeance is mine, I will repay," Romans 12:19) that Tolstoy probably found in Arthur Schopenhauer's *The World as Will and Representation* (1819/1844).[7] He began reading Schopenhauer as he was writing the epilogue to *War and Peace*, and his ongoing struggle with Schopenhauerian pessimism hangs over *Anna Karenina*. (For more on Tolstoy and Schopenhauer, see Chapter 21.) The novel tells two stories: Anna's adulterous affair with Count Alexei Vronsky, and Konstantin Levin's courtship of and marriage to Princess Kitty Shcherbatskaya. Where Anna and Vronsky's attraction to one another embroils them in a destructive cycle of physical desire, Kitty and Levin's marriage suggests the possibility of a communion beyond the limits of the embodied mortal self. These models of love develop in tandem throughout the narrative. A worldview that affirms the unity among people, founded on belief in God and the immortal soul, competes with a vision of people as divided from one another by the appetites of their individual bodies. The novel ends hopefully, with Levin's embrace of a religious faith that saves him from despair. But the vividly tragic ending of Anna's plot lingers side by side with Levin's schematic conversion, raising the specter of a "world as will" whose true nature lies in violent, fruitless struggle.

Unlike *War and Peace*, which refracted contemporary debates through the lenses of history and an authoritative narrator, *Anna Karenina* depicts its own moment through its characters' perspectives, a destabilizing relativity of perception. The narrator rarely speaks in his own voice. However, the figure of Levin becomes increasingly autobiographical – preoccupied, as Tolstoy himself was, with the problem of articulating the meaning of life in the face of inevitable physical death. As Anna is sealed into her tragic plot, Levin reaches for a way of being that could anchor the everyday. The novel thus reflects Tolstoy's disillusionment not only with the modernizing world it describes, but also with the modern enterprise of literary fiction. Even as he grudgingly finished *Anna Karenina*, his heart lay in the work of discovering and defining his faith, in more precise words than his character Levin feels the need to formulate. By late 1879, he had begun work on the text later known as *Confession* (*Ispoved'*, 1882).

Confession marks the most dramatic of Tolstoy's crises: a turn in his self-identity from literary writer to moral and religious teacher, which coincided with the twilight of Russian realism itself. Like *Childhood*, *Confession* occupies a hybrid first-person genre, a conversion narrative that draws upon (and resacralizes) the secular tradition of autobiography inaugurated by Rousseau.[8] The protagonist ("I"), a privileged landowner and writer, falls into despair about the nature and purpose of his life. Tempted by suicide, he finds his only solace in reflecting on the working people and peasants. He realizes that "faith is the force of life": that which enables the people to go on living rather than destroying themselves (23:35). However, he cannot find any institutional religion that will honor this truth without asking him to believe something contrary to his own reason. His path to faith thus ends with a call to rethink the entire edifice of Christianity.

Confession paved the way for a range of works – most banned from official publication in Russia – in which Tolstoy pursued this mammoth task over the next thirty years. These include his iconoclastic *Critique of Dogmatic Theology* (1879–80); his rewriting of the Four Gospels, from which he tried to remove all traces of contradiction, mystification, and miracle (1880–1); and his credo *What Do I Believe?* (1883–4), founded on a literal interpretation of Christ's Sermon on the Mount, particularly the tenets "Love your enemies" and "Resist not evil." Tolstoy developed his ideas of universal love and non-resistance to evil by violence in later works, including the philosophical meditation *On Life* (1888), the anarchistic tract *The Kingdom of God Is Within You* (1893), and the aesthetic treatise *What Is Art?* (1898).

Tolstoy's Christianity had far-reaching practical and political implications, among them pacifism, an absolute opposition to corporal and capital punishment, and the advocacy of vegetarianism, manual labor, and celibacy. He wrote to explore and expound these principles, but he was no longer bound by the confines of artistic literature. His voluminous post-conversion corpus includes tracts, public letters, and articles; fables and parables "for the people" (*narodnye rasskazy*); celebrated short stories and novellas (including many published after his death); and the novel *Resurrection* (*Voskresenie*, 1899), which traces the intertwined spiritual regenerations of Prince Dmitry Nekhliudov and his family's former servant Katerina Maslova, whom he seduced as a young girl. Lavishing his gift for evocative physical detail on descriptions of famines, executions, prisons, and slaughterhouses, in his plots and characters Tolstoy now reached for the universality of the "emblematic."[9] Two examples will speak for the whole.

The sustained stream-of-consciousness narrative leading up to Anna Karenina's death had already brought Tolstoy to the shores of literary modernism. Despite his denunciation of modernist aesthetics in *What Is Art?*, his late fiction is equally experimental. His belief in a mode of life that transcends the individual mortal body disrupts the particularity and stable concreteness on which literary realism is built. In this regard, *The Death of*

Ivan Ilyich (*Smert' Ivana Il'icha*, 1886) serves as a manifesto. We first meet Ivan Ilyich as a corpse, and the narrative presents the details of the life history that has condemned him. His illness begins from a fall as he is hanging the curtains in a new apartment. As the disease takes hold, more and more of his *biographical* trappings fall away – profession, friends, married and family life – until he is left, in agony, to face the unembellished fact of his death. His anguish ends only when he sees that he is dying because he has not lived in the right way. In this new state, he feels sudden compassion for his son and wife, and with this release from egotism comes the realization that "death is no more": the story's protagonist is no longer identical with the Ivan Ilyich whose biography we have heard, the Ivan Ilyich who dies. At the end of the narrative, chronology itself breaks down as the protagonist moves beyond the awareness of time. Rather than using the story to build a realist character and plot, Tolstoy has used it to dismantle them. Many of his late stories enact a similar fragmentation – not for its own sake, but in pursuit of a glimpse of life beyond space, time, and embodied self.

Tolstoy's narrative art takes a different form in the polemical passages of his writing. Here, realist poetics serve a rhetorical purpose as he commandeers the reader's sensuous imagination. A surpassing example of this strategy comes in "The First Step" (*Pervaia stupen'*, 1892), Tolstoy's article on the moral imperative of abstinence, beginning with vegetarianism. The climax of the article is Tolstoy's description of his visit to a slaughterhouse. Starting with the "heavy, repulsive, putrid smell of carpenter's glue" that hangs in the entryway, he carries the reader through the stages of an ox's slaughter (29:79). As the ox is stabbed, then bled, then skinned and dismembered, Tolstoy repeats its struggles in refrain ("the ox's legs struggled"; "the ox continued to struggle"), until at last it is "crucified" on a winch and falls still (29:81–2). Tolstoy watches three more slaughters, changing his position to see how the butchers force the oxen into the pen by twisting their tails. Then he describes the killing of a bull, then a ram. Evocative details relentlessly repeat – the smell of the blood, the twitching of dying animals – until Tolstoy ends the scene to resume his case: the first step to a good life is abstention, beginning with meat because it is produced by "murder," whose only motivation is greed. The saturation of detail becomes a weapon to overwhelm the resisting reader: not to build a fictional world, but to remake the world in which the article is read.

Tolstoy wrote without pause until the end of his life in 1910, at the age of eighty-two. He lived to decry the Russo-Japanese War and the 1905 revolution; to know Chekhov and Gorky and to correspond with Gandhi, among scores of others around the world. As he had explored the facets of life and faith across genres, he now explored death – a prospect he greeted joyfully, as the threshold of a new form of existence. He recorded his progress toward death in his diaries, and again reimagined death in fiction. His great historical novella *Hadji Murat* (1896–1904, pub. 1912) ends with a stage-by-stage slaughter recalling the one described in "The First Step," but now transfigured by a human consciousness. As he dies, Hadji Murat is flooded with memories, but they evoke no feeling in him: "not pity, not malice, no desire at all." His body moves by inertia, rising as if from the dead to confront his enemies, and he feels the deathblow and wonders why they have done it. "This was his last consciousness of a connection with his body. He felt nothing more, and his enemies trampled and hacked at what no longer had anything in common with him" (35:116). Tolstoy, too, anticipated the day when his mortal body would no longer have anything in common with him. He invented a genre that rehearsed this transformation: the "circle of reading," a series of daily almanacs in which excerpts from dozens of thinkers and texts intermingled with his own writings, often unsigned (*Krug chteniia*, 1906–8; *Na kazhdyi den'*, 1909–10). Here, at the last, Tolstoy's unclassifiable oeuvre dissolves into the course of human thought.

Notes

1 N.G. Chernyshevskii, "*Detstvo* i *Otrochestvo*: Sochinenie grafa L.N. Tolstogo," in V.Ia. Kirpotin (ed.), *Polnoe sobranie sochinenii*, 15 vols. (Moscow: Gosizdat. Khudozhestvennoi literatury, 1947), vol. iii, 423.

2 B.M. Eikhenbaum, *Molodoi Tolstoi* (Munich: Wilhelm Fink Verlag, 1968), 72.

3 Andrew Baruch Wachtel, *The Battle for Childhood: Creation of a Russian Myth* (Stanford University Press, 1990), 15ff.

4 Robin Feuer Miller, "The Creative Impulse in *Childhood*: The Dangerous Beauty of Games, Lies, Betrayal, and Art," in Elizabeth Cheresh Allen (ed.), *Before They Were Titans* (Boston: Academic Studies Press, 2015), 166.

5 Gary Saul Morson, *Hidden in Plain View: Narrative and Creative Potentials in 'War and Peace'* (Stanford University Press, 1987), 130–89.

6 Kathryn Feuer, *Tolstoy and the Genesis of War and Peace* (Ithaca, NY: Cornell University Press, 1996), 194–206.

7 B.M. Eikhenbaum, *Lev Tolstoi, Semidesiatye gody* (Leningrad: Khudozhestvennaia literatura, 1974), 170–1.

8 Irina Paperno, "*Who, What Am I?*": *Tolstoy Struggles to Narrate the Self* (Ithaca, NY: Cornell University Press, 2014), 60–78.

9 Richard Gustafson, *Leo Tolstoy: Resident and Stranger* (Princeton University Press, 1986), 202.

CHAPTER 17

Peasant Schools and Education

Daniel Moulin-Stożek

Tolstoy occupies an important but often overlooked place in the development of educational thought, situated between the German pedagogical revolution of the eighteenth century and the proliferation of alternative education movements in the twentieth. Although initially inspired by the philosophy of Jean-Jacques Rousseau (1712–78), Tolstoy's educational experiments heralded a novel turn by rejecting educational theory as a foundation for the curriculum altogether. Instead, Tolstoy set out to facilitate the creation of the peasants' own approach to schooling through dialogue with his pupils. This radical method has a close relationship with the development of Tolstoy's literature and philosophy. Tolstoy's work in peasant schools therefore serves as an entry-point into his world, through which we can comprehend the unity and growth of his whole moral, artistic, and educational vision.

Tolstoy's engagement with education can be split into three main phases of activity. The first occurs between 1857 and 1862, prior to the writing of *War and Peace*, when Tolstoy set up his first schools for peasant children at Yasnaya Polyana. The second period takes place a decade later, prior to the publication of *Anna Karenina*, when Tolstoy reopened his school and published the *Azbuka* (*ABC Book*) – a primer for learning to read. A third and final phase of educational thinking – evident in a range of essays, letters, aphorisms, and fables – spans the years after his spiritual crisis of the late 1870s to his death.

Tolstoy founded his peasant schools in the run-up to the emancipation decree of 1861. The preparations for the freeing of the serfs had led to a nationwide consideration of public education to which Tolstoy sought to contribute. Thoroughly engaged with contemporary European educational theory, he read deeply and took a pedagogical tour of England, France, and Germany in 1860–1, visiting schools and meeting educators. Based on these experiences, Tolstoy attempted to influence the national debate in Russia through creating his own educational journal, *Yasnaya Polyana* (published monthly between February 1862 and March 1863). In the journal Tolstoy detailed the experiments of his pedagogical laboratory (*pedagogicheskaia laboratoriia*, 8:16) – a concept he borrowed from contemporary German pedagogy. Tolstoy reasoned that true freedom would involve the peasants in determining the Russian schooling system. Thus, Tolstoy's experiment was not just aimed at individual peasant children's freedom in the classroom; it was also an experiment in ascertaining and understanding the lives, aspirations, and will of the peasants in general.

Rousseau's ideal of children's natural goodness was a starting point for Tolstoy's pedagogy. However, Tolstoy explicitly rejected the application of European philosophy, particularly that of Rousseau's fictional *Émile* (1762), as a solution to the problem of public education in Russia. On a strictly scientific basis, Tolstoy argued that educational practice should follow 'what works' rather than a made-up theory, such as that offered by Rousseau, Immanuel Kant (1724–1804), Johann Pestalozzi (1746–1827), Friedrich Froebel (1782–1852), or any other pedagogue. This argument already appeared in the naturalistic turn in German pedagogy in the generation after Kant, but Tolstoy added an astute and ground-breaking observation: that applying any philosophy of education risked marginalizing learners. Every child is unique and should learn in the manner that suits them best, Tolstoy reflected. And why should something as personal, immediate, and free as learning be prescribed by a theorist far removed from the experience of Russian peasant children? Tolstoy thus anticipated concepts of "epistemic violence" and "epistemic justice" used by decolonial educationists a century later.

Tolstoy's criticism of contemporary approaches to schooling in the *Yasnaya Polyana* journal is more than concern about the stupefying lessons, corporal punishment, and restricted bodily movement that he had observed in schools in Russia and abroad. He believed imposing alien forms of knowledge upon an unempowered population was an act of violence. Precursory to the early pragmatists and constructivists of the next generation, most notably the American philosopher John Dewey (1859–1952), Tolstoy identified the need for learners to be involved in the process of constructing knowledge. This not only improved engagement, but was also a matter of justice for Tolstoy. He was the first educationist to grasp the close relationship between knowledge and pedagogy on the one hand, and violence and injustice on the other – an association which, following Foucault and other post-structuralists, has subsequently become a key concern of critical and indigenous pedagogies. On this matter Tolstoy was indignant. To instigate a top-down curriculum based on the theories of the upper classes only resulted in schools that "violated the spirit of the children" (*nasilovanii dukha uchenikov*, 8:140).

Tolstoy claimed that any predetermined educational theory would disenfranchise the people from a say in their own education and would impose a particular and artificial worldview on the peasantry. The use of European phonetic methods in teaching the Russian alphabet, Tolstoy argued, divorced the peasantry from the equally effective practice of learning traditional Slavonic prayers by heart. This example shows both the conservative and radical elements of Tolstoy's position. For while Tolstoy sought to address the need for educational reforms based on the individual rights claimed by the *philosophes* of the European Enlightenment, he also identified a tension in the application of such ideas and the true freedom of the peasantry. It would not do to replace traditional methods of recitation of the psalter with the phonetic method, or Bible stories with secular fairy tales on account of a so-called expert's predilection or theory. What was needed was the peasants' own engagement with the development of a Russian system of education firmly located in the peasantry's own experiences and needs.

It is ironic that Tolstoy was led to reject philosophy as a foundation for pedagogy, as it was a philosophical novel that first inspired him to engage with the problems of education: Berthold Auerbach's *Neues Leben* (1851). In 1861, Auerbach (1812–82), a Jewish-German writer now best known for documenting the folktales of southern Germany, was made uneasy by the arrival of a strange-looking man at his home in Berlin. He was concerned that the visitor, calling himself 'Count Eugen' (the name of *Neues Leben*'s protagonist), had arrived from Russia to sue for libel on account of his likeness to Auerbach's hero. However, the visitor was not actually a Count Eugen preparing for litigation, but an enthusiastic Count Lev Tolstoy, who, after reading *Neues Leben*, had been inspired to imitate Auerbach's hero and take up the cause of public education in Russia.

Tolstoy's meeting with Auerbach was the highlight of his pedagogical tour of Europe. Understanding why Tolstoy loved Auerbach's novel provides some useful background to the development of Tolstoy's educational thought. In *Neues Leben*, Count Eugen, a refugee of the 1848 revolution, swaps his identity with a teacher he meets by chance and goes to America, taking advice from the teacher on education. This advice is radically dismissive of pedagogical theory. Rather, Eugen is taught that each teacher's method should be developed together with the children according to their needs. Prophetic of Tolstoy's later life, Count Eugen renounces his aristocratic title, marries, and founds a school for peasants where there are no social divisions between educator and educated, and in which Eugen furthers his own moral development by learning from the children.

Neues Leben describes pedagogical methods strikingly akin to those Tolstoy tested and described in the *Yasnaya Polyana* journal – most notably the assertion that there is no static method or theory that may help an instructor learn to teach, or a pupil learn to learn. In both Auerbach's fictional and Tolstoy's real schools, pupils directed their own learning. Teachers were to be educated by the process of engaging with pupils. Pupils were encouraged to use the vernacular as a means of their own empowerment, particularly the texts of the Gospels (which at Yasnaya Polyana, Tolstoy translated for them from the Old Slavonic). These principles aimed to further the ultimate purpose of education shared by Tolstoy and Auerbach's fictional Eugen: the cultivation of faith. However, for Eugen, faith was not belief in any given catechism, but rather a kind of personal piety. As such, genuine faith could not be "taught." In the *Bildung* tradition, it is the natural conclusion of a child's free development, a consequence of authentic experience and self-realization. This approach to religion is perhaps unsurprising in a novel written in the wake of the European Enlightenment by a German-Jewish philosopher, but it was also endorsed by Tolstoy in this early period as a way of understanding the lived religion and moral worldview of the Russian peasantry.

Throughout this earlier period, Tolstoy absorbed German Protestant theology, reading Martin Luther (1483–1546), Johann Fichte (1762–1814), and Friedrich Schleiermacher (1768–1834) for pedagogical purposes. This was a precursor to his later engagement with religious ethics. Tolstoy first identified what he would go on to conceptualize as "ethical consciousness" in his later moral philosophy, in the negative terms of its obstruction by contemporary schools. These, he claimed, stifled children's "moral development" (*nravstvennoe razvitie*, 8:13). In Russia, Tolstoy surmised, there was a chance to avoid the pernicious immoral effects of a national education system such as he had seen in modern Germany, if only an alternative method could be developed and advocated that would harness and cultivate the innate goodness of the Russian peasants. Tolstoy's solution was to teach with the goal of making students equal to their teachers and teachers equal to their pupils.

Applying this principle led Tolstoy to develop an innovative approach in the classroom which inspired later progressive and alternative educators. According to Tolstoy, the purpose of education was not just the learning of certain facts, but a holistic process of self-realization, of engaging with questions of life's ultimate purpose. This dynamic process could never be asserted top-down, nor based on the philosophy or creed of the ruling class; it must be learnt for itself, from life itself, arising in a dynamic and authentic relationship between educator and educated. The importance of such intrinsic moral motivation would later become a key principle of the work of the famous American educational psychologist Lawrence Kohlberg (1927–87), who also sought to make schools communities of justice by understanding the processes by which children develop moral awareness. The importance of relationship, on the other hand, anticipates the educational thought of Martin Buber (1878–1965).

After writing *War and Peace*, from 1872 to 1875 Tolstoy returned to the problem of public education. Based on renewed experiments at Yasnaya Polyana, he created and tested his primer for learning Russian, the *Azbuka*. Its publication in 1872 brought Tolstoy into conflict with leading educationists in Moscow and led to a trial of Tolstoy's methods versus the prevailing phonetic methods. The resulting negative verdict of the trial committee led Tolstoy to publish a *New Azbuka* in 1875, preceded by an essay restating his general views on public education following the same line of argument as in the *Yasnaya Polyana* journal a decade earlier.

Developed from his earlier experiences while teaching, Tolstoy's approach to textbooks prefigured his later moral essays and fables. In addition to introducing the rudiments of language, they were designed to promote moral understanding through very short narratives. While attendant to the lived moral realities of the peasantry and inclusive of things familiar to them, Tolstoy's textbooks also included fables adapted from other cultures, such as India, China, and America, that supported the same moral principles as the Russian stories. This intercultural approach anticipated the contemporary movement toward "global citizenship education," which seeks to cultivate positive attitudes to cultural difference and international cooperation.

Tolstoy's final phase of educational activity – following his spiritual conversion of the late 1870s – is the one most often overlooked by educationists. Yet, in this period, Tolstoy's writings reached the natural conclusions of his previous educational endeavors, reflecting a maturation of the moral and spiritual insights he made when teaching in the peasant schools. Concepts of good and bad education play a key role in Tolstoy's system of philosophy and ethics presented in essays and tracts such as *On Life* (1887) and "Religion and Morality" (1894), and fables such as "The Restoration of Hell" (1903). Building on his critique of contemporary schooling, he declared both science and organized religion to be false teachings – the root cause of violence, exploitation, and oppression in society more generally. In order to counter these ills, authentic education was essential. Fortunately, according to Tolstoy, the universal laws of nonviolence and love are self-evident. An education based on free principles but guided by ethical teachings would naturally increase learners' moral consciousnesses, building a better world.

A corollary of this educational vision was Tolstoy's compilation of wise thoughts and sayings designed for daily reading, published from 1904 onwards. These "Calendars" or "Cycles of Reading" contained several aphorisms for each day, each espousing a moral principle by a famous contemporary or ancient thinker. Among the thinkers Tolstoy selected were the Unitarian ministers William E. Channing (1780–1842) and James Martineau (1805–1900). Their words appear alongside those of the Hebrew prophets and Stoic philosophers; Buddha, Krishna, and Confucius; Christ, St, John, and Mohammed; Kant and Rousseau; and the religious leaders Báb (1819–50, a central figure in the Baha'i Faith) and Swami Vivekananda (1863–1902, a Hindu monk), among others. Tolstoy also included his own self-attributed aphorisms liberally. The point of this exercise was to show the simplicity (and similarity) of the right way to live across time and cultures. Condensed in a handy and clearly worded synthesis, the "Cycles of Reading" were intended to make such a moral education accessible to all who could, or were beginning to, read.

Through pamphlets and tracts published abroad, Tolstoy's universalist philosophy exerted global influence among radical religious movements. Made known by translators and biographers such as Aylmer Maude (1858–1938) and Ernest Crosby (1856–1907), Tolstoy's educational ideas were readily absorbed by a variety of progressive and fringe groups. For example, the Nobel prize-winning activist and educator Jane Addams (1860–1935) developed educational programmes at the Hull House Settlement in Chicago under the influence of Tolstoyan principles. Hull House – an urban centre for social care, education, and reform – benefited from the money Tolstoy raised through the publication of his last novel, *Resurrection* (1899). Indicative of the network of progressive reformers inspired by Tolstoy, the famous American educationist John Dewey served on its board.

Tolstoy believed the wisest thoughts of religious and ethical figures throughout time and human culture could be easily comprehended by a child or adult, aristocrat or laborer. However, because for Tolstoy simplicity was an important part of wisdom, it followed that those who had been most corrupted – the adults and the rich – found these truths the most challenging. In this emphasis on the deceptive simplicity of moral development, we see an important overlap between Tolstoy's art and his views of education, and the paradox they both share. For Tolstoy's very denial of philosophy in ethics and of theory in education owe a profound debt to philosophy and theory. Tolstoy offered a solution to this paradox that avoided reductionism, yet was coherent with his desire to establish simple, ethical, foundational criteria by which to teach. He could only accept pedagogical principles corroborated by experience and those that were germane to the most immediate and pressing needs of learners themselves. To presuppose any pedagogy, he believed, would not do justice to the learner. This distinctive approach to education has an epistemological humility at its crux – albeit one that is so fervent it became arrogant in its missionary zeal.

Tolstoy's experiences teaching in the early 1860s were decisive in determining the trajectory of his thought. The impact of the peasant school on his literary aesthetics is self-evinced by the candidly titled early essay "Should we teach the peasant children to write, or should they teach us?" (1862). Tolstoy wondered at the literary creations of his students, claiming that they, as children, are closer in sensitivity to the ideals of goodness, truth, and beauty and therefore need nothing more than prompts to begin writing great literature. Tolstoy succinctly expressed the same principle, expanded to the domain of ethics, in later moral fables like "Little girls wiser than men" (1885). As the flood waters melt in a village, it is two peasant girls who stop a fray between adults by virtue of their natural moral intuition.

Following Rousseau, Tolstoy maintained that because adults do wrong as a result of a corrupt society, it follows that children, as yet undefiled by the ways of the world, are adults' best moral educators. On such a premise Tolstoy formed a group of peasant children to review the teachings of Jesus and produce an abridged account of Jesus' life ("The Teaching of Jesus," 1908). This late work illustrates the consistency of Tolstoy's lifelong educational beliefs. It also raises the same criticisms that can be levied at the *Yasnaya Polyana* journal. Tolstoy's voice predominates in his writings about children, not the children's. Thus, Tolstoy's free and emancipatory approach can be brought into question. Tolstoy's class of peasant children supposedly presented a Jesus who is the teacher of Tolstoy's own ethical beliefs. He, like Tolstoy, is a gifted pedagogue who ushered in God's kingdom – not by the resurrection, the institution of the Church and its sacraments, or in any way by the miraculous – but by the changing of hearts through the power of story. This text, representative of Tolstoy's whole philosophy, thus presents a discernible and radical link between the Enlightenment critique of religion, nineteenth-century literature, and the making of modern education as a project of the social gospel in the early twentieth century.

Although Tolstoy largely failed to apply his concerns about unequal power relations and epistemic violence to his own educational practice, his work in peasant schools was truly ahead of its time, nonetheless. Only recently have educational movements become concerned with epistemic justice, pupil voice, and global citizenship. In all his educational work, Tolstoy drew on the world's cultures yet sought to engage with the lived experience of the individual child. He envisioned a free system of schooling which was in epistemological, cultural, and linguistic sympathy with its learners, and that at the same time fostered an outward love based on the hope of a universal ethics.

CHAPTER 18

Russian Philosophy

Randall A. Poole

Russian idealism is the most precious legacy of Russian philosophy. Idealism has been understood in very different ways in the history of philosophy, but its central modern meaning, following Kant, is that reason has the power to determine the will by its own ideals, and that this power (self-determination) refutes materialism or determinism in the ordinary sense of the term. Russian idealism developed in two phases: in the second quarter of the nineteenth century, and after 1880. A pivotal point between them was Tolstoy's religious conversion, completed in 1879, when he arrived at what might be called his "idealist conception of faith." This conception, laid out in *A Confession* (1882), was a powerful stimulus to the further development of Russian philosophy, which culminated in the so-called Russian religious-philosophical renaissance of the early twentieth century. The idealism of this later period is often called "Russian neo-idealism," to indicate that it was a revival of classic German idealism, especially Kant, and of the earlier cycle of Russian idealism (which owed more to Schelling and Hegel). Tolstoy's account of how his efforts at moral self-perfection brought him to faith helped to give Russian neo-idealism its characteristic Kantian direction, grounding it in human nature (that is, in reason, free will, and morality). The present chapter focuses first on Russian philosophy after 1880, when Tolstoy's influence was greatest, then turns to developments earlier in the century.

Tolstoy's religious conversion was a gradual process that occurred as he gained a deeper understanding of the meaning of his virtually lifelong idealism. In *A Confession*, he recounts that by the age of sixteen he had lost his childhood faith in Orthodox Christianity, though perhaps not in God altogether. He devoted himself to self-perfection, which became his "only real faith."[1] He was keenly aware that the task of self-perfection involved the positing and pursuit of ideals. As early as 1847 he had acquired, as he later wrote in *Boyhood*, "an ecstatic worship of the ideal of virtue, and the conviction that a man's destiny is continually to perfect himself."[2]

At this stage his idealism was practical and "lived"; he had not yet begun seriously to examine its philosophical underpinnings or implications. Like most educated people of his time, Tolstoy also acquired a belief in progress as a general historical law, which gradually subsumed his striving for self-perfection. He wrote that he would have formulated this belief as follows: "'Everything is evolving and I am evolving; and the reason why I am evolving together with all the rest will one day be known to me.'"[3]

Tolstoy's conversion followed from the spiritual crisis that he experienced in the mid 1870s. Did life have any meaning that suffering and death did not destroy? After intense searching and struggle, he recognized that life can have no meaning apart from the Infinite (the Absolute or God), and that only faith can "give an infinite meaning to the finite existence of man, a meaning that is not destroyed by suffering, deprivation or death."[4] But what are the grounds for faith in the Infinite? Tolstoy found them in the ideals that had driven his earlier efforts at perfectibility. "I returned," he writes, "to the idea that the single most important aim of my life is to improve myself," that is, to live according to the will of God.[5] Tolstoy's conversion came about with his realization that he could "find the manifestation" of God's will in his own self-conscious striving for moral perfection, or in what he simply calls "life." He discovered that faith comes from within the human person, most poignantly in acts of self-determination. The ideals of reason (such as truth and the moral law) that make self-determination possible are infinite or absolute by their very nature. As Tolstoy now understood, they and the freedom to act on them entail a higher divine reality to which we are connected and called. This was his idealist conception of faith. It had much in common with Kant's moral theology.[6]

Tolstoy's account of his conversion, and more generally of the inner dynamics of faith, was immensely influential. It formed part of a constellation of sources and events that from this time forward spurred the development of Russian idealism and religious philosophy. Others included the publication of Dostoevsky's *Brothers Karamazov* (1879–80) and Boris Chicherin's *Science and Religion* (1879) (he sent two copies to Tolstoy). In 1878 Vladimir Solovyov (1853–1900) delivered his famous *Lectures on Divine Humanity* (*Bogochelovechestvo*) to audiences of nearly a thousand in St. Petersburg (Tolstoy attended one of them). With other philosophical idealists, Solovyov assumed leadership of the Moscow Psychological Society, a learned society founded in 1885 that became the first and most important center of Russian philosophy in the three decades before the revolution. In 1889 the society began publication of Russia's first regular, professional journal of philosophy, *Questions of Philosophy and Psychology*. The journal was issued five times a year until 1918.

Tolstoy had never courted the attention of specialists or professionals. But in 1885 Nikolai Grot (1852–99), a philosophy professor at Moscow University, sent Tolstoy, by way of self-introduction, one of his own essays with the dedication, "to the deeply respected author of *A Confession*."[7] Grot began his philosophical career as a positivist but by 1885 he was moving toward idealism, and Tolstoy's moral and religious ideas were a factor in the shift. Grot and Tolstoy immediately struck up a friendship. (Tolstoy was also friends with the philosophers Nikolai Strakhov, 1828–96, and Boris Chicherin, 1828–1904.) Through Grot, Tolstoy became involved in the Moscow Psychological Society and published three articles in *Questions of Philosophy and Psychology*, including *What Is Art?* In his lead editorial in the inaugural issue of the journal, Grot singled out Tolstoy, "with his new teaching of life and of the moral tasks of man," for his exceptional role in raising public interest in philosophy. "It may be," he suggests, "that no specialist has so strongly promoted the awakening of the philosophical spirit in Russian society as much as Count L.N. Tolstoy has indirectly done."[8]

Tolstoy's association with the Psychological Society helped him to complete his major philosophical tract, *On Life*, which is generally regarded as the best exposition of his metaphysics. He read a synopsis of the work at a Psychological Society meeting in March 1887.[9] Its publication banned in Russia, it appeared in Paris in March 1889, in a French translation done by Tolstoy's wife. The first full Russian edition appeared in 1891 in Switzerland. In *On Life* Tolstoy, heavily influenced by Schopenhauer, advanced an impersonalistic metaphysical spiritualism (a form of pantheism). According to him, the only substantial reality is "reasonable consciousness" (*razumnoe soznanie*), which is God or divine logos (*razum*). Tolstoy also defines this reality as divine love, or simply "true life."[10] Our task is to liberate this higher divine self by subjecting our lower animal self ("animal personality") to reason, which is also the law of love.[11] Since the liberated self is God, it is not clear what value the human (as opposed to the divine) actually has. This was a paradoxical conclusion compared to *A Confession*, where Tolstoy's Kantian approach to morality rests on and affirms the value of embodied personhood. In general, Grot and other Russian idealists were highly critical of *On Life*, precisely because of its philosophical impersonalism, devaluation of the human, and resulting nihilism.[12]

Despite this criticism, Russian philosophers took seriously Tolstoy's idealist approach to faith. In 1902 the Psychological Society published the anthology *Problems of Idealism*.[13] The appearance of the volume marked the conversion from Marxism to idealism of four contributors who ever after would be among the most famous names in Russian philosophy: Pyotr Struve (1870–1944), Nikolai Berdiaev (1874–1948), Sergei Bulgakov (1871–1944), and Semyon Frank (1877–1950). In their chapters they explained how their turn to idealism resulted from their clearer understanding of the nature of moral experience, in particular the authenticity of moral ideals and the freedom to act on them. In *Problems of Idealism* their philosophical formulation of moral experience was called "ethical idealism," but it harbored an idealist conception of faith patterned after Tolstoy's conversion experience.

Their debt to Tolstoy is quite explicit in their subsequent writings. In the 1912 collection *On Lev Tolstoy's Religion*, Bulgakov lauded Tolstoy for showing that religious consciousness, because it comes from the inner work of self-determination, is by its nature an individual achievement.[14] Five years later, in his classic work of religious thought, *Unfading Light: Contemplations and Speculations*, he adopted Tolstoy's insight as his own, writing that "religion is a *personal* work in the highest degree and thus it is a continual, creative work."[15] Semyon Frank, in his 1908 article "Lev Tolstoy and the Russian Intelligentsia," also extolls the virtues of individualism, considering it "the premise and inner condition of the religious-metaphysical worldview." By individualism he means not personal eccentricity but self-perfection, "spiritual work" on oneself, and "the constant work of self-knowledge and self-deepening." And as an example of how the religious-metaphysical worldview emerges from individualism – understood in the idealist sense of individual self-determination and perfectibility according to infinite ideals – Frank commends to the reader *A Confession*.[16]

It is clear that Russian neo-idealism could support a robust personalism: the defense of personhood (*lichnost*), the idea that human beings are persons or ends-in-themselves, each having an intrinsic and absolute worth. In fact, ever since the Slavophiles, personalism had been a deep feature of the Russian religious-philosophical tradition. It held that human beings, through their ideals and the freedom to act on them, could transcend the natural world, aspire toward the Absolute, and affirm their personhood.

Thus far this chapter has focused on Russian philosophy in the period after 1880, when Tolstoy most influenced its development. In

1880 Tolstoy turned fifty-two. He had lived through much of the preceding course of nineteenth-century Russian philosophy. In 1869 Nikolai Strakhov wrote that Tolstoy was a realist preoccupied with the theme of human dignity.[17] What could Tolstoy have learned from Russian philosophy about that theme and its relation to the two other philosophical problems that most preoccupied him, the meaning of progress and the foundations of faith?

Tolstoy was born three years after the Decembrist rebellion of 1825. By then the intellectual climate in Russia had shifted from the political interests of the Decembrists to speculative philosophy, by way of post-Kantian German idealism and Romanticism. Schelling first captured the Russian imagination, in the 1820s, followed by Hegel in the 1830s. Both had a profound impact on Russian thought, in particular on the famous Slavophile–Westernizer controversy of the 1840s. While the Russian Schellingians (soon to include the Slavophiles) and Russian Hegelians (the future Westernizers) agreed on the importance of defending human dignity, they had quite different understandings of human freedom, personhood, and historical progress. The Schellingians took a religious approach. They understood free will within a theological anthropology based on the idea that human beings are created in the image and likeness of God (Genesis 1:26). Individual perfectibility and historical progress toward the good were possible, but depended on aligning the human will to the will of God, as discerned by conscience and reason – aided by revelation, tradition, and community (not least of all the Church).

Russian Hegelians initially adopted a deterministic philosophy of history, according to which historical progress was being realized by the Absolute. Human beings were instruments of that process, consciously or not. Nikolai Stankevich (1813–40), who was one of Tolstoy's intellectual heroes, used the term *razumenie* to describe the Reason that unfolds of its own accord in history.[18] In the second half of the 1830s, Hegelianism was largely interpreted as a philosophy of "reconciliation with reality," but by the early 1840s this conservative historicist approach gave way to a Left-Hegelian "philosophy of action," which resulted in the affirmation of individual freedom, responsibility, and dignity. The emphasis shifted from the self-realization of the Absolute in history, which implied the individual's reconciliation before historical necessity, to the self-realization of the individual through active participation in history. In general, the shift meant the abandonment of metaphysics (at least in the form of Hegelian absolute idealism) and a certain tendency toward materialism and atheism, which obviously posed its own type of threat to human freedom and dignity.

The Russian reception of Schelling and German Romanticism, on the one hand, and of Hegelianism, on the other, formed the two philosophical poles of the debate between the Slavophiles and Westernizers. The ferment began in 1836, when Pyotr Chaadaev (1794–1856) published the first of eight *Philosophical Letters* (written between 1828 and 1830) in the Russian journal *Teleskop*. The letter asserted that because Russia derived its Christianity from "miserable, despised Byzantium," it was closed off from universal historical development and had "contributed nothing to the progress of the human spirit." The Slavophiles responded to this explosive charge by arguing that Russia's distinctive path of historical development, outside the classical legacy of the West, actually was a blessing: it enabled the country to avoid the rationalistic, formalistic, and antagonistic principles of Roman law and civilization. Instead, pre-Petrine Russia cultivated its own distinctive virtues – moral, spiritual, and communal ones that were held to be embodied in the village commune and in the Orthodox Church.

The Westernizers were united by a general belief that Russia should develop along Western, European lines, which for them embodied the idea of progress. They formed a broad camp spanning a range of political views from radical (Mikhail Bakunin, 1814–76) to liberal (Timofei Granovsky, 1813–55, Konstantin Kavelin, 1818–85, and Boris Chicherin). Vissarion Belinsky (1811–48) and Alexander Herzen (1812–70) occupied an intermediate position. Like Bakunin, they were Russian Left Hegelians. Belinsky, a literary critic and the most visible figure among the Westernizers, was one of the founding members of the Russian intelligentsia. Alexander Herzen, the founder of "Russian socialism," ranks among the most famous Russian thinkers. Tolstoy enjoyed a friendship and correspondence with him.

Tolstoy cannot easily be classified as either a Westernizer or a Slavophile. In the 1860s he rejected the idea of social and historical progress, the defining criterion of Westernism. Instead, he focused on moral self-perfection and, after his conversion, on religious consciousness. This shift aligned him more closely with the Slavophiles.

Slavophile religious thought was developed in the 1850s by Ivan Kireevsky (1806–56) and Alexei Khomiakov (1804–60), partly in response to the materialism and atheism of the Left Hegelians. Their main concepts were faithful or believing reason, integral personhood, and *sobornost'* (catholicity or conciliarity). In 1856 Kireevsky published a landmark essay on the compatibility of faith and reason, or "believing reason," which achieves the wholeness of mind, spirit, and soul – integral personhood – necessary to apprehend reality in its noumenal depths.[19] In certain respects this anticipated Tolstoy's concept of "reasonable consciousness," rooted in and aspiring toward divine reason. As for Khomiakov's influence on Tolstoy: in *Anna Karenina*, Levin reads the second volume of Khomiakov's theological writings, and "in spite of its polemical, polished, and witty style, which at first repelled him, he was struck by its teaching about the Church. He was struck by the thought that it was not given to isolated man to attain divine truth, but that it is given to a community united by love – the Church."[20] Levin precisely formulated the very essence of Khomiakov's concept of *sobornost'*.

By the time of Khomiakov's death in 1860, Russian thought had entered a new stage. Thinkers such as Nikolai Chernyshevsky (1828–89), Nikolai Dobroliubov (1836–61), and Dmitry Pisarev (1840–68) advanced various combinations of materialism, scientism, util-itarianism, and "rational egoism." Their outlook, frequently referred to as "nihilism," was notoriously embodied by Bazarov, the hero of Ivan Turgenev's novel *Fathers and Children*. But already by the 1870s, there was a reaction against "objectivist," deterministic theories of progress. This shift took place with the elaboration of Russian populism, the main revolutionary movement of the seventies. In his influential essay cycle *Historical Letters* (1868–9), Pyotr Lavrov (1823–1900) argued that pro-gress was not a necessary historical law but rather a moral task to be accomplished by "critically thinking individuals" inspired by ideals such as justice and human dignity. The stage was set for the new wave of philosophical idealism that broke upon the Russian intellectual landscape by 1880. Russian philosophy was entering its great age, inspired in no small measure by the idealism that Tolstoy had long lived and that had brought him to faith.

Notes

1 Leo Tolstoy, *A Confession and Other Religious Writings*, trans. Jane Kentish (London: Penguin, 1987), 21.
2 Aylmer Maude, *The Life of Tolstoy*, 2 vols. (Oxford University Press, 1987), vol. 1, 41, quoting (without clear indication) the conclusion of *Boyhood* (translation modified).
3 Tolstoy, *A Confession and Other Religious Writings*, 26–7.
4 Ibid., 54.
5 Ibid., 65–6.

6 See Randall A. Poole, "'Russia's First Modern Man': Tolstoy, Kant, and Russian Religious Thought," *Tolstoy Studies Journal* 22 (2010), 99–117, a review essay of Inessa Medzhibovskaya, *Tolstoy and the Religious Culture of His Time: A Biography of a Long Conversion, 1845–1887* (Lanham, MD: Lexington Books/Rowman & Littlefield, 2008).

7 Medzhibovskaya, *Tolstoy and the Religious Culture of His Time*, 276.

8 N. Ia. Grot, "O zadachakh zhurnala," *Voprosy filosofii i psikhologii* 1, kn. 1 (1889), xiii–xiv.

9 Tolstoy's presentation and related materials are included as an appendix to Inessa Medzhibovskaya, *Tolstoy's On Life: From the Archival History of Russian Philosophy* (DeLand, FL and Toronto: The Tolstoy Society of North America and *Tolstoy Studies Journal*, 2019), 343–400.

10 Leo Tolstoy, *On Life: A Critical Edition*, ed. Inessa Medzhibovskaya, trans. Michael Denner and Inessa Medzhibovskaya (Evanston, IL: Northwestern University Press, 2019), chaps. 9–10, 14.

11 Ibid., ch. 22–33. Years later Tolstoy succinctly formulated his doctrine in his essay *The Law of Love and the Law of Violence* (1908). There he claims that Christian teaching acknowledges love to be "metaphysically the origin of everything" and "the essence of human life." Tolstoy, *A Confession and Other Religious Writings*, 172–3.

12 James P. Scanlan, "Tolstoy among the Philosophers: His Book *On Life* and Its Critical Reception," *Tolstoy Studies Journal* 18 (2006), 52–69; Randall A. Poole, "Tolstoy and Russian Idealism," in Inessa Medzhibovskaya (ed.), *A Critical Guide to Tolstoy's On Life: Interpretive Essays* (DeLand, FL and Toronto: The Tolstoy Society of North America and *Tolstoy Studies Journal*, 2019), 33–5, 47–54.

13 Randall A. Poole (ed. and trans.), *Problems of Idealism: Essays in Russian Social Philosophy* (New Haven, CT: Yale University Press, 2003).

14 *O religii L'va Tolstogo* (Moscow: Put', 1912; Paris: YMCA Press, 1978). For details, see Poole, "Tolstoy and Russian Idealism," 40–2.

15 Sergius Bulgakov, *Unfading Light: Contemplations and Speculations*, trans., ed., and intro. Thomas Allan Smith (Grand Rapids, MI: Wm B. Eerdmans, 2012), 30.

16 S.L. Frank, "Lev Tolstoi i russkaia intelligentsiia," in Frank, *Russkoe mirovozzrenie* (St. Petersburg: Nauka, 1996), 443–4. See also Poole, "Tolstoy and Russian Idealism," 42–4.

17 Donna Tussing Orwin, *Tolstoy's Art and Thought, 1847–1880* (Princeton University Press, 1993), 6.

18 Medzhibovskaya has argued that in 1879 Tolstoy realized that *razumenie* is internal to the subject, not external to it. He now understood that *razumenie* is the inner recognition of divine reason (*razum*, logos), and that this is what makes possible true self-determination. She regards this discovery as the pivotal point of Tolstoy's conversion. See Medzhibovskaya, *Tolstoy and the Religious Culture of His Time*, 201–2.

19 Ivan Kireevsky, "On the Necessity and Possibility of New Principles in Philosophy," in Robert Bird and Boris Jakim (eds. and trans.), *On Spiritual Unity: A Slavophile Reader* (Hudson, NY: Lindisfarne, 1998), 233–73.

20 But after reading some Church history, he became disenchanted with Khomiakov's teaching about the Church; "and that edifice crumbled to dust just as the philosophical structures had done." *Anna Karenina*, trans. Louise and Aylmer Maude (Oxford University Press, 1918), Pt. VIII, ch. 9.

CHAPTER 19

The Russian Literary Scene

Ilya Vinitsky

In the beginning of the twentieth century, Tolstoy, who had always been an ardent critic of any cult of historical personality – be it Napoleon, Shakespeare, or Beethoven – was constantly referred to in Russian journals as a superhuman giant, a godhead, a colossus, a valiant knight (*bogatyr*), or even a lighthouse at night. A contemporary journalist wrote that "the giant Tolstoy always had pygmies crawling at his feet, whether his contemporary authors or the crowds, the authorities or the admirers."[1] In one of the cartoons of this period, entitled "The Big and the Small Father," Tolstoy is portrayed next to a miniature figure of the Russian Emperor as a bearded giant, dressed in his signature Russian shirt and holding a scythe in his hand (Figure 4). Another cartoonist, alluding to the famous sixteenth-century Vatican sculpture of the god of the Nile River with his numerous children (allegories of the cubits of water by which the river rises for its floods), presented Tolstoy in the same pose, a giant surrounded by a dozen contemporary Russian writers (Figure 5). The cartoon emphasizes the huge difference between the titanic fatherly figure and his fellow authors, yet the image implicitly conveys the idea of Tolstoy as part of the Russian literary ecosystem. One cannot detach him from the constantly changing cultural milieu from which he originated, to which he belonged, with which he was in constant disagreement, and which he affected through writings published over almost sixty years of his literary career.[2]

Why is it important to know the Russian literary context (or contexts) of Tolstoy's oeuvre?

First, because such a contextualization helps us to understand the historical and ideological origins of the writer's works and literary beliefs as an integral part of Russian literature. The phenomenon of Tolstoy is deeply rooted in the formative period of Russian literary development, from the sentimental and didactic literature of Catherine the Great's age (Nikolai Karamzin's moving tales and Masonic allegorical confessional writings) to Vasily Zhukovsky's emotional Romanticism, Alexander

Figure 4   "The Big and the Small Father" (circa 1905). INTERFOTO / Alamy
Stock Photo.

Pushkin's "poetry of actuality" and "prosaic" historicism as exemplified in
Eugene Onegin (1823–31) and *The Captain's Daughter* (1836), and, in
particular, to Mikhail Lermontov's analytical psychologism as manifested
in his meditative elegies and the novel *A Hero of Our Time* (1840). The

Figure 5   "A giant and pygmies. Lev Tolstoy and contemporary writers" (1903). Matteo Omied / Alamy Stock Photo.

origins of Tolstoy's literary views also go back to the Romantic society tale (Alexander Bestuzhev-Marlinsky, Prince Fyodor Odoevsky, Pushkin), the genre of pastoral utopia (from Nikolai Gogol's "Old World Landowners," 1835, and Ivan Aksakov's patriarchal idylls, from 1846 on, to "Oblomov's Dream," 1849, by Ivan Goncharov) and the sentimental realism of the 1840s with its emphasis on the figure of the suffering peasant and the idea of the nobleman's social guilt (Dmitry Grigorovich's *Anton-Unfortunate*, 1847; Ivan Turgenev's *Sportsman's Sketches*, 1852).

Secondly, Tolstoy's literary context matters because his works not only emerged in concrete literary and historical circumstances, but expressed in their own ways shared concerns, ideas, fears, and aspirations characteristic of the respective periods. In particular, they are a product of the generation affected by the humiliating outcome of the Crimean War, the collapse of the decades-long isolationist conservative "scenario of power" of Nicholas I (1825–55), and a series of forthcoming profound social and political reforms that changed the emotional and ideological outlook of Russian culture. Tolstoy shares with the literary generation of the 1860s a fascination with (often accompanied by a suspicion of) natural and social sciences, such as physiology, physics, chemistry, biology, sociology, psychology, and history. He also shares a strong interest in the relationship between art and reality as manifested in the aesthetic manifestos of Pavel Annenkov, Nikolai Chernyshevsky, Apollon Grigoriev, Dmitry Pisarev, Dostoevsky, and Turgenev. Both Tolstoy and his contemporaries proclaimed and executed a move to "objective" prose as opposed to the "subjective" poetry favored by the preceding, idealistic generation. However, in many cases, Romantic poetry struck back, as seen in the numerous "nostalgic" references to Pushkin's, Zhukovsky's, and Lermontov's poems in Russian realist prose.

Among other characteristic features Tolstoy shared with the literary generation of the 1860s were bold attempts to exorcise the "specters of idealism" from readers' minds by means of frequent parodies and satires of Romantic genres and a radicalism of beliefs. On the emotional level, we witness a process of gradual morphing of the Russian intelligentsia's moral agitation and an early optimism, exemplified in Alexander Herzen's praise of the Emancipation Act, into frustration and eventually moral panic presented in Mikhail Saltykov-Shchedrin's gloomy satirical writings of the 1870s. Yet the most striking feature of the realist imagination of Tolstoy's age was a shared belief in the transformative mission of literature (regeneration or resurrection of the "fallen man") and the author's moral authority and responsibility, manifested in the semi-religious cult of Pushkin the prophet in the second half of the nineteenth century. From this noble (and utopian) vantage point, Russian writers of Tolstoy's age launched a severe critique of social institutions, ranging from the family to the official Church, while idealizing the life of lower ("humiliated and oppressed") classes, in particular peasants. They also introduced and passionately promoted a profound sociological and biological interest in the "Woman Question" (Alexander Herzen's *Who Is to Blame?*, 1846; Chernyshevsky's *What Is to Be Done?*, 1863) and gender and ethnic tensions (see Chapter 14). Symptomatically, in their "materialist" struggle with social ills, Tolstoy and writers of this period exposed a deep "metaphysical" attraction to the problem of physical decay (illness) and death (Nikolai Leskov's tales and novels; Saltykov-Shchedrin's *The Golovlyov Family*, 1875–80). Last but not least, Tolstoy and his fellow writers shared a passion for experimentation with literary forms, consciously relying on "monumental" and "all-embracing" artistic genres. One can say that Tolstoy's literary phenomenon was a materialization of the basic aspirations, fears, and tensions of the age of big issues and revolutionary "monstrous" literary forms.

Let us consider as an example Tolstoy's epic novel *War and Peace* (1865–9) within its actual literary and ideological contexts. In its ideological program, the monumental work about the age of the Napoleonic Wars of the early nineteenth century responds to fierce contemporary debates on the most pressing issues of the 1860s, unleashed in powerful, tendentious "thick" journals (periodicals which combined belles-lettres, literary criticism, politics, and science):

- What is the true (and false) representation of the "reality"?
- What is the role of historical leaders? of the masses?
- Does history have any meaning and direction (the idea of progress)?
- What is the national spirit?
- What is real (and false) patriotism?
- What are the limitations of sciences and rationalism?
- What is a woman's true role in society?
- What is freedom and what is necessity?
- How is our inner world (mind or soul) related to the material world?

Tolstoy's novel reflects an obsession with the past as manifested in the works of Russian historians of the 1860s and the boom of publications of archival documents and memoirs in journals. It also resonates with the "realist utopia" of the positivist resurrection of history in the flourishing genre of historical drama. Of the forty new historical plays put on in the 1860s, more than half were staged between 1865 and 1868, as *War and Peace* was appearing serially. A vivid manifestation of the distinctive pan-historicism of Russian culture of the time was also represented by the rapid development of the historical novel (Alexei Tolstoy's *Prince Serebrennyi*, 1861), historical painting (Vasily Surikov, Ilya Repin), and historical opera (Pyotr Tchaikovsky, Nikolai Rimsky-Korsakov, Modest Musorgsky, and, a little later, Alexander Borodin). It also conveys a contemporary obsession with the national theme and desire for a national epic. Last but not least, despite his intense critique of arrogant rationalistic thinking, in *War and Peace* Tolstoy strives to create a universal, systematic vision of life, ruled by certain natural laws and moving in a certain direction that is being investigated by the omniscient author. As Lydia Ginzburg wittily observed, "the Tolstoian hero" "exceeds the dimensions of his personality: that is, he functions not merely as a personality but also as someone in whom the laws and forms of life in general are manifest, and through whom they may be cognized."[3]

War and Peace exemplifies the creative motivations (stimuli) and monumental productions of the second half of the nineteenth century, the period when all these (mostly long-bearded) writers, artists, composers, folklorists, scientists, and social and religious thinkers embarked upon grand and largely unrealizable projects of "true" representation and "scientific" examination of "reality." What distinguishes the Russian projects of this period from their many ambitious counterparts in Western traditions is the fact that their creators claimed a special transformative (or, in the Symbolist lexicon, theurgical) status of these endeavors for their nation. The Russians emphasized a special sense of mission imposed upon them by some vaguely defined force, be it the people, science, history, language, or simply – as Tolstoy would have it – the Truth. It would not be an exaggeration to state that *War and Peace* should be considered within the context of such ambitious artistic projects as Nikolai Chernyshevsky's utopian novel *What Is to Be Done?*, which embraces the entire development of mankind through the lens of socialist doctrine (the "Fourth Dream of Vera Pavlovna"), the monumental historical paintings of Surikov and Repin, Musorgsky's *Boris Godunov*, and, say, Vladimir Dal's *Dictionary of the Living Great-Russian Language* (pub. 1863–6).

Thirdly, considering Tolstoy's works in their developing literary contexts allows us to feel and understand how Russian literature of the second half of the nineteenth century and early twentieth century operated *dialogically*. For example, Tolstoy's portrayal of the *muzhik* (whether it is Platon Karataev in *War and Peace* or Gerasim in *The Death of Ivan Ilyich*) is polemical to Turgenev's depiction of the peasant ("an unknown stranger" who haunts the author's imagination as manifested in *Sportsman's Sketches* and *Fathers and Children*, 1862), Dostoevsky's idealization of the Russian Orthodox peasant, as well as Slavophiles' and populist writers' utopian visions of the Russian peasants' communal way of life, Nikolai Nekrasov's sentimental mourning over unhappy and suffering peasants (*Who Lives Happily In Russia*, 1866–74, "The Railroad," 1865), or Nikolai Leskov's portrayal of peasants as dreamy wanderers and truth-seekers who symbolize the spiritual ordeals and long journey of the Russian nation toward a better world beyond the grave.

Tolstoy's contemporaries like Chernyshevsky, Konstantin Leontiev, and Apollon Grigoriev justly called him a master of portraying the last moments of life. Yet his deathbed scenes clearly reflect a paramount set of interests shared by artists of his "realist" generation: the literary examination of physical and emotional pain; the depiction of the "beautiful" or "ugly" death; an emphasis on the social and gender background (determinism) of the dying hero; and finally, the master theme of the tormented human soul entrapped both in a mortal body and in a corrupted society, futilely hoping for salvation. Thus, Tolstoy's treatment of the dying consciousness in *War and Peace* can act as a case study for his relationship to the literary and ideological context of the 1860s.

One can refer to numerous examples that serve as the cultural background for Tolstoy's famous death scenes. Suffice it to recall Dostoevsky's portrayal of Marmeladov's death in *Crime and Punishment* and Ilyushechka's death in *The Brothers Karamazov* (1880), Nekrasov's mesmerizing depiction of the death of a peasant woman in his narrative poem *Red-Nosed Frost* (1864), or the death of Leskov's gentle giant Akhilla in *Cathedral Folks* (1872). The theme is also widely presented in Russian realist painting and Russian music (cf. Modest Musorgsky's "Songs and Dances of Death," 1875–7). It was meticulously discussed in Russian "thick" journals (how do Russians die?) in connection with themes of social ills and the soul vs. body controversy. Clearly, Tolstoy's literary portrayal of dying characters' thoughts and emotions is strikingly individual, yet it can be better understood in dialogue with other realist writers' portrayals and interpretations of death and mourning.

Leskov read Prince Andrei's "awakening" from mundane life at his deathbed (the "truly beautiful and inimitable picture" of death) as an allusion to the mystical doctrine of the ascension of the individual along the ladder of being: having refused the "Old Testament Adam," Tolstoy's hero, according to Leskov, nearly enters the choir of angels.[4] In turn, the philosopher and critic Nikolai Strakhov juxtaposed Tolstoy's kind of psychological realism with the "photographic" or "critical" realism then dominant in Russian literature. Strakhov understood Tolstoy's artistic task as depicting the human soul and life "in its real sense, not in the incorrect forms bequeathed to us by antiquity." Strakhov's philosophical evaluation of Tolstoy's psychologism corresponds with his own understanding of man as the crowning achievement and central mystery of all of creation.[5] Ironically, this interpretation is completely alien to Tolstoy's rejection of a ladder of being that ascends from lower forms to the human individual: "Man is king over all creatures? How so? In the ranks of being there are no gradations. There is infinity, that is, obscurity" (48:128).[6] An even more radical summation can be found in his diary entry from November 17, 1873: "After death we may exist in a chemical, rather than our earthly physical form. In my Father's house are many mansions" (48:67).

In one of the scenes later excluded from *War and Peace*, Tolstoy relates a discussion between two characters who play chess on the eve of the bloody Battle of Schöngraben. They speak of Johann von Herder's idea of metempsychosis or the transmigration of souls. One might call the discussion a strikingly optimistic variation on Shakespearean themes of the decay and sleep of death placed within the materialist context of Russian literary debates on the soul and death. Staff Captain Tushin justifies Herder's ideas to his comrade: "I still believe that my soul was once in a worm, then a frog, then a bird, then in everything else. Now it's in a human body and later it will be in an angel somewhere." When his friend challenges him, he tries to clarify this idea, arguing that at death, people "just become a higher kind of organism." His friend counters: "But why does it have to be higher?" and points to the yellow worms devouring a recently killed bull. With some reflection, Tushin is convinced: "'You're right, why does it have to be a higher kind of organism? . . . Maybe it'll be better for us when we're made out of a million worms, or when we become grass. Maybe our lives will be brighter; maybe we'll be smarter. And I'll keep on living and enjoying life, whether I'm grass or a worm. If I become air, I'll rejoice and take flight like the air does. What do I know anyway, maybe it is better?" (13:369).

It is tempting to call the next part of this dialogue a Tolstoyan response to the scene in *Fathers and Children* where the nihilist Bazarov, lying in the shade of a haystack, talks about the burdock that will grow out of him after his death. Bazarov considers the "tiny bit of space" he occupies and the "period of time in which it is [his] lot to live" both infinitesimal compared to the universe and "the eternity in which I have not been and shall not be" and is deeply frustrated that "here, in this atom which is myself, in this mathematical point, blood circulates, the brain operates and aspires to something too . . . What a monstrous business! What futility!"[7] Tushin, by contrast, muses: "You remember how back in the day, when you'd lie in the grass and want to become the grass, or look at a cloud or some water, and it was as if you could become that grass or that cloud . . . you'd even want to become a worm." In response, his friend recounts a dream he had the day before about death.

> Then suddenly it appeared to me that I was standing behind a door and there's something trying to get in from the other side, and that thing is . . . my death. And I already don't have anything left to hold it back with. It shoved the door open, I fell, and I see that I'm dead. I got so scared that I woke up. I woke up. I said to myself, 'See, you ain't dead.' I was overjoyed.

Tushin expands on this, imagining a bullet in the head: "You'll just wake up a bunch of young and healthy worms" (13:369).

This dialogue obviously prefigures the future dream of Prince Andrei about the door and reawakening in death, which, in turn, can be interpreted as Tolstoy's "personal statement" in a dialogue with his contemporary writers. The materialist Bazarov's metaphysical yearning, which recognizes one's own worthlessness in an infinite world, is absent in Tolstoy, as is a Pushkinian vision of the beautiful but "indifferent nature" characteristic of Turgenev's treatment of death, or Dostoevsky's apocalyptic vision of a totally new world, or the tragic dead-end materialism of Saltykov-Shchedrin's novel *The Golovlyov Family*, where the reader is unable to imagine that in the world portrayed by the author "any kind of future is possible, that a door exists, through which one could emerge elsewhere" (13:250). As opposed to the tortured monologue of Shakespeare's Hamlet, whose "dread of something after death" Leskov juxtaposed with the triumphant death scene of Prince Andrei, Tolstoy's best characters are prepared to awaken to a new, unknown, state of existence, but one that is (probably) happier than earthly existence, in the form of a cloud, grass, air, rain, or even in the form of young and healthy yellow worms.

During his long literary career Tolstoy deliberately played the role of the lone wolf and *enfant terrible*, at war with many writers and popular ideas of his time. The "Zeus" of Russia's literary pantheon, he did not even show up at the highly symbolic Pushkin celebration in 1881, which was conceived as a solemn act of reconciliation between Russian writers with different ideological agendas. In the early twentieth century, after Turgenev's and Dostoevsky's deaths, it may have seemed as if Tolstoy was the only giant left among literary dwarfs. However, in the real multi-act Russian literary drama of the second half of the nineteenth century he was just one – albeit extremely influential – actor involved into a nonstop passionate conversation with fellow authors on issues of the utmost significance for their audiences.

To paraphrase Tolstoy's final sentence of *War and Peace*, the epistemological value of seeing Tolstoy in conversation with his contemporaries lies both in the renunciation of a vision of his "unreal immobility in space" (generally taken for granted) and concurrently in the recognition of his dependence on other writers and literary contexts "of which we are unaware." Gulliver is determined by his bonds.

Notes

1 V.I. Sreznevskii, *Tolstovskii muzei v S.-Peterburge* (St. Petersburg: Tip. Drekhlera, 1912), 139.
2 Tolstoy was not only a super-prolific writer but also a zealous reader, a bibliomaniac, and a kind of "literary cosmopolitan." His library in Yasnaya Polyana contains 22,000 books and journals in more than 30 languages.

3 Lydia Ginzburg, *On Psychological Prose*, trans. Judson Rosengart (Princeton University Press, 1991), 246–7.

4 N.S. Leskov, *Polnoe sobranie sochinenii v 30 tomakh* (Moscow: Terra, 1999–2007), vol. VI, 531.

5 As expressed in his book *Mir kak tseloe* (*The World as a Whole*), 1858–72.

6 All quotations from Tolstoy are translated by Timothy Portice.

7 Ivan Turgenev, *Polnoe sobranie sochinenii i pisem v 30 tomakh* (Moscow: Nauka, 1981), vol. VII, 119.

CHAPTER 20

European Literature

Priscilla Meyer and Melissa Frazier

In Russia the sudden importation of Western European culture and technology under Peter the Great (r. 1682–1725) was the impetus for a growing national self-awareness in which admiration of Western Europe conflicted with the desire to feel pride in Russia. Russian novels of the eighteenth and nineteenth centuries were in intense, ambivalent dialogue with the European tradition.

The eighteenth century in Russia began by assimilating French culture in its manners and literature and, with the help of European Romantic quests for national identity, ended by asserting the value of Russian culture. The publication of the six-volume Academy dictionary from 1789–94, of books of Russian folk songs and mythology, and of Nikolai Karamzin's *Pantheon of Russian Writers* (1800) and *History of Russia* (1811) set out Russia's native resources and became the basis for the call to make Western elements truly national, with Russian content; as Admiral Shishkov put it, "If we don't stop thinking in French, then we shall always lie, and lie in our own language."[1]

During the transition from eighteenth-century imitations of Europe to the next stage of intertextual dialogue with it, the Russian struggle with the distinction between imitation and true cultural adaptation of an original became the explicit topic of literary discussions. Russian writers of the nineteenth century, like many others of the period, were quite consciously creating a new national literature.

In the 1830s, ushered in by Victor Hugo's *Last Day of a Condemned Man* (1829), the French novel had turned toward an urban realism that was shocking to readers accustomed to the Romanticism of the preceding thirty years. For Russian writers, the naturalism of Hugo, Zola, and others defined the new Western European literature as decadent. The essential virtue of Russian otherness was its Orthodox Christianity, best embodied in the peasantry that had not been corrupted by exposure to Western Europe.

163

In "A Few Words Apropos of the Book *War and Peace*" (1868) Tolstoy declared his independence from "European forms," and certainly his Western European readers were struck by the formal originality and philosophical weight of his writing: where Henry James wrote disparagingly of "large loose baggy monsters," for Virginia Woolf, Tolstoy's use of detail was "alarming" in its very intensity.[2] Nineteenth-century Russian writers wrote in response to Western European literature, however, and Tolstoy was no exception. As Tolstoy's son Sergei later remembered, "he was always reading foreign literature, especially English and French novels."[3] The impact of this reading is readily apparent in his work.

Tolstoy's trilogy *Childhood* (1852), *Boyhood* (1854), and *Youth* (1856) betrays the influence of Sterne and Dickens as well as Rousseau, while *War and Peace* (1865–9) rests on the British tradition of the historical novel as invented by Scott in *Waverley* (1814) and continued in Thackeray's *Vanity Fair* (1848); his battle scenes reflect Stendhal's rendering of the same historical moment in *The Charterhouse of Parma* (1839). As Liza Knapp notes in her own contribution to this volume, Tolstoy's reading in religion took a British turn, and his great love for Dickens as well as more measured response to George Eliot was often expressed in moral terms (see Chapter 33); as Tolstoy wrote in 1904, "I think that Charles Dickens is the greatest novel writer of the 19 century [sic] and that his works, impressed with the true Christian spirit, have done and will continue to do a great deal of good to mankind."[4] French novels, on the other hand, represented for him the antithesis of the moral approach to the family novel, as in Flaubert's *Madame Bovary* (1856). In *Anna Karenina* (1875–8), Tolstoy draws on both traditions as he both questions and ultimately upholds a traditional view of marriage.

English Literature

While Tolstoy was exceptional in his ability to read English literature in the original, translations were also widely available in the Russian "thick journals" (book-length periodicals). Tolstoy's own editor M.N. Katkov in the *Russian Herald* (*Russkii vestnik*) alone published not just Dickens, Anthony Trollope, George Eliot, and Wilkie Collins, but also a host of lesser-known figures, as the Russian reading public in Tolstoy's day was introduced to the full spectrum of contemporary British writing, from the domestic novels of Charlotte Yonge to the racier, exposé style of Charles Reade. As Boris Eikhenbaum argues, *Anna Karenina* most strikingly reflects Tolstoy's reading in the British family novel.

In *Anna Karenina*, Tolstoy emphasizes the British underpinnings of his plot in his many references to the English: Anna reads an English novel, Vronsky's racehorse has an English trainer, Vronsky's estate is furnished in an English style, the novel's social elite are members of the English club, and even Kitty bears an English nickname until Levin intervenes. The barest hint of infidelity in the British family novel points to women's lack of agency in a patriarchal system, what Eliot in *Middlemarch* (1871) calls the story of "later-born" St. Theresas "struggling amidst the conditions of an imperfect social state."[5] While the adultery does not quite materialize in Trollope's *Can You Forgive Her?* (1865), for example, Lady Glencora marries at her family's insistence, and for much of the novel the possibility of an adulterous affair threatens her family happiness. The plea for forgiveness in Trollope's title nonetheless refers to another almost-transgression, as the mistake of his heroine Alice Vavasor, like that of Tolstoy's Kitty, is that she breaks an engagement with one man for another only to return to her original fiancé in the end. The limitations faced by women are still more obvious when the British novel casts adultery as bigamy.

As Maia McAleavey argues, the "bigamy plot" recurs with remarkable frequency across the Victorian novel.[6] It is also a notable feature of the novel of sensation as produced by two pioneers of the genre: Mary Elizabeth Braddon in *Lady Audley's Secret* (1862) and *Aurora Floyd* (1863), and Mrs. Henry (Ellen) Wood in *East Lynne* (1861). The British novel of sensation entailed both lurid plots and a particular approach to the reader. As D.A. Miller explains, the genre offered "one of the first instances of modern literature to address itself primarily to the sympathetic nervous system, where it grounds its characteristic adrenalin effects: accelerated heart rate and respiration, increased blood pressure, the pallor resulting from vasoconstriction, and so on."[7] While Tolstoy in *What Is Art?* (1897) carefully distances himself from what he calls the "physiological-evolutionary" approach, still his anxiety that art, including his own, might serve as a conduit for an unthinking and unbridled hedonism is apparent in his presentation of the adulterous effects of music in both *War and Peace* and *The Kreutzer Sonata* (1889), as well as in Levin's morally compromised response to Anna under the influence of her portrait. Despite that discomfort, Tolstoy was a vocal admirer of both Braddon and Wood, and in *Anna Karenina* he reiterates their emphasis on the difficulties faced by women in achieving and maintaining a much-desired marriage and a stable family life.[8]

It is no easy task for their heroines to reach the altar in the first place, as Braddon's Aurora Floyd and Lucy Audley and Wood's Lady Isabel, like Tolstoy's Anna and even Natasha Rostova in *War and Peace*, all struggle to navigate the treacherous waters of the premarital state in the absence of a mother's support. Still more decisive is the extent of their financial resources. Aurora survives her repeated attempts at self-determination not least because, like Kitty and Alice Vavasor, she is a considerable heiress in her own right. Lucy and Lady Isabel, on the other hand, like Anna, marry in the first place only under the pressure of sometimes dire financial need. Women's inequality also complicates marriage once achieved. In *Anna Karenina*, the Shcherbatsky sisters, like Anna, are pointedly not just beneficiaries, but also victims of their husbands' decisions, while in *East Lynne*, the tragedy that ensues is due in no small part to Archibald Carlyle's blindness to Lady Isabel's needs. In *Aurora Floyd*, after the disaster of Aurora's first marriage, the second succeeds largely because her truly exceptional husband acknowledges Aurora's autonomy. This repeated emphasis on the heroines' limited options in a still "imperfect social state" openly invites readers' understanding and even forgiveness of their adulterous acts. A shared reliance on the "bigamy plot" serves the same function.

If the heroines in these novels all engage in sex outside of marriage, it is only in the context of often highly involved extenuating circumstances. In *Aurora Floyd*, the admittedly less than demure Aurora commits bigamy in the mistaken belief that her first husband has died; in *Lady Audley's Secret*, Lucy's first husband deserts her. In *East Lynne*, Lady Isabel even after her affair and subsequent divorce continues to think of Carlyle as her husband, while Carlyle's first thought on realizing that his children's governess is his former wife in disguise is that "he must be a man of two wives." In *Anna Karenina* it is a problem of two husbands, or, as an apparently dying Anna herself notes, two men who bear the same name: Alexei. In *East Lynne*, Carlyle not only kisses his dying ex-wife, but declines to help indict her former lover for murder. As he explains, "I leave him to a higher retribution: to One who says 'Vengeance is mine.'"[9] By 1889 and *The Kreutzer Sonata*, Tolstoy will reject not just sex and "sensation," but marriage altogether along with his own literary art. In *Anna Karenina*, he still holds to an ideal of marriage and the kind of novel-writing that would support it. Even as early as 1878, however, Carlyle's biblical quote serves as his epigraph.

French Literature

For the Russian reader, French novels of adultery revealed that culture's decadence; Tolstoy takes up the erotic aspect of female transgression in *Anna Karenina* in a subtextual argument with it. He refutes the views of marriage contained in Émile Zola's *Thérèse Raquin* (1867) and *Madeleine Férat* (1868), Alexander Dumas' essay "L'Homme-femme" and play *Claude's Wife* (1872), Gustave Flaubert's *Madame Bovary* (1856), and Rousseau's *Émile et Sophie, ou, Les solitaires* (1781). Tolstoy replaces the superficial war of the sexes and trivialization of the institution of marriage that he finds in the French tradition (going back to *Dangerous Liaisons*, 1782) with a quest for the meaning of life. He reinfuses idealism into the realist novel, which he found distressingly naturalistic, by constructing the "scaffolding" of Levin's tale, to show the continuous approach to the Ideal in the everyday.

Zola's two novels contain the basest examples of adultery. *Thérèse Raquin* and *Madeleine Férat* present a powerful woman whose passions drive her to suicide and are sources for some dramatic moments in *Anna Karenina*. Thérèse and Laurent drown her husband in order to indulge in sensual passion and then have dreams of their victim – Laurent has a recurring nightmare and Thérèse "has seen the drowned man rise up before her," just as Vronsky and Anna have nightmares of the peasant who was killed by the train, a parallel which emphasizes Tolstoy's description of their adultery as a figurative murder. In the second novel, the tormented heroine Madeleine's delirious thoughts on her journey toward suicide are accompanied by the clanking sounds and rhythm of the railway wheels in an interior monologue resembling features of Anna's final train journey.

As late as 1906 Tolstoy was still inveighing against what he considered Zola's "indifferent, even contemptuous relationship to the basic questions of life" (35:569). In *Anna Karenina* he incorporates Zola's devices – the shared dream, the pre-suicide delirious interior monologue – into his own treatment of adultery to present the deep humanity of his adulteress. In contrast to Zola's simple heroines, Anna has the noble qualities of an ideal Russian aristocrat – generosity of spirit, maternal love for her son, a capable intellect, a Christian conscience – and Tolstoy's desire to tell her tale is motivated not by Zola's idea that human beings are inevitably governed by their animal nature, but by a search for the meaning of human existence in their higher nature.

Dumas' essay *Man-Woman* (*L'Homme-femme*), which recommends kill-ing the adulteress,[10] stimulated Tolstoy's thinking about the "Woman Question"; his polemical play on how to treat a guilty wife, *Claude's Wife* (*La Femme de Claude*), constructs the worst possible adulteress, Césarine, who abandons her husband and child for her lover. Tolstoy had told his wife he wanted to depict an adulteress who was "only pitiable and not guilty" in 1870, but after reading Dumas' essay in 1873, he began by making Anna not only unredeemably evil but unattractive as well. As he worked on the novel, however, while incorporating his response to Dumas, his initial impulse took precedence and Anna evolved into an attractive woman. In this third stage, Tolstoy is in dialogue with *Claude's Wife* as well, as he examines a woman's *understandable* adultery. Reading *Anna Karenina* alongside *Man-Woman* shows that Tolstoy not only rejects a husband's right to avenge himself by murder, but also contradicts the premise of Dumas' essay, that woman wins the grand struggle between the sexes that is marriage. Tolstoy refutes this in the story of Levin's marriage to Kitty. Agreeing with Dumas about the painful conflict between the masculine and feminine in marriage, he disagrees that the two are irrec-oncilable; he sees the intellect and instinct as complementary, not hostile forces.

Dumas maintained that prostitution and adultery were undermining faith in the sanctity of the marriage bond that is unbreakable by the law of the Church and State, a view of adultery close to Tolstoy's. Marriage, death, and childbirth are associated with the sacraments, and Levin is closest to accepting God at those mysterious transitions in his life. But Tolstoy, with his unusual ability to identify with women, answers Dumas' somewhat simplistic polemics with rich ambiguity. Tolstoy gives a more profound response to the adulteress than Dumas, or than Flaubert in *Madame Bovary*.

There are remarkable parallels between *Anna Karenina* and *Madame Bovary* not only in theme and plot line, but in character description, motifs, and central emblems, suggesting a carefully structured polemic. The unfulfilled young woman with small child and uninspiring husband who takes a passionate lover and commits suicide is the obvious point of contact between the two novels. But Tolstoy incorporates an array of details that show he had *Madame Bovary* in mind while writing *Anna Karenina*: the heroines' appearances, key moments (ballroom and opera scenes), motifs (horses with a bird association linked to the erotic; fog/haze/mist; green, velvet, cigars, manure, clanking metal), and two central emblems: the Hirondelle that takes Emma Bovary to Rouen (to the opera, and to her lover Léon) and the railway train that marks the key moments in Anna's affair with Vronsky (their first meeting, the beginning of Vronsky's courtship, Anna's suicide, and Vronsky's departure for the war in Serbia).

Anna is an ideal version of Emma. Emma admires and imitates luxury; Anna already has it. Emma wants a passionate aristocratic dashing lover but finds only imitations of one; Anna gets Emma's wish in Vronsky. Emma wants to be the heroine of a novel; Anna is seen as one by her peers. Emma fantasizes eloping to Italy with the pseudo-aristocrat Rodolphe (who clenches his teeth in predatory passion); Anna and the truly aristocratic Vronsky (of the "regular," "compact" teeth) actually do elope to Italy. In this way, Tolstoy isolates and distills the moral and psychological aspects of adultery for a young married woman, purifying it of the concern with social status and material luxury that obsesses Emma and positing an intelligent, self-aware heroine who is understandably dissatisfied in her marriage.

Tolstoy's antidote to the decadence he found in the French novel of adultery is made up of the ideals of Rousseau and the eternal authority of the Gospels; he needed both to answer the question that increasingly tormented him as he was writing *Anna Karenina* – the meaning of life, and how to live. Rousseau's little-known sequel to *Émile, Émile et Sophie, ou, Les Solitaires,* considers the moral questions faced by the husband when the wife is in all other respects an honorable woman. In all these novels but Rousseau's *Émile et Sophie,* the women are unredeemable, egotistical adulteresses and the men their victims. Tolstoy responds to the French works, and restores Rousseau's ideals, by creating in Anna a complex, sympathetic adulteress with a moral sense; the parallel story of Levin embodies the values she forsakes. To describe Levin's struggle toward new insight, Tolstoy draws from Rousseauian ideals and from the Gospels, which enable Levin to overcome his impulse to suicide; their absence from Anna's life makes her suicide inevitable.

Émile et Sophie, ou, Les Solitaires contributed to Tolstoy's depiction of Karenin's struggle with the problems faced by a betrayed husband. Rousseau's sketch analyzes these feelings: what will society think? how should he behave toward his wife? his son? what feeling can he have for the child of his wife's lover? Rousseau examines the moral basis for answering them; Tolstoy addresses Rousseau's judgments by adding a Christian dimension. He often agrees with Rousseau's analysis, but introduces the idea of the sacrament: a marriage is sanctified by God and it is not for the wife or the husband to dissolve it.

Answering both the French novels of adultery as well as the English family novels with Rousseau and the Gospels, Tolstoy reinfuses idealism into the realist novel, as his responses to Dumas, Zola, and Flaubert suggest. Viewing the foreign cultural world through the lens of their own national self-image, Russians construct the West in contrast with Russia's own moral codes. In *Anna Karenina*, Tolstoy implicitly opposes the Russian view of French "moral degradation"[11] to Russia's high religious morality, while affirming the value of family presented in the English novel.

Notes

1 A.S. Shishkov, *Rassuzhdenie o starom i novom sloge rosssiiskogo iazyka* (1803) (Moscow: Lenand, 2015), 8.
2 Henry James, *The Art of the Novel* (New York: Scribner, 1934), 84; Virginia Woolf, *The Common Reader*, first series (San Diego: Harcourt, 1984), 181.
3 Gareth Jones (ed.), *Tolstoi and Britain* (Oxford: Berg, 1995), 45.
4 Ibid., 54.
5 George Eliot, *Middlemarch* (London: Penguin, 1994), 3, 838.
6 Maia McAleavey, *The Bigamy Plot: Sensation and Convention in the Victorian Novel* (Cambridge University Press, 2015).
7 D.A. Miller, *The Novel and the Police* (Berkeley: University of California Press, 1988), 146.
8 Jones (ed.), *Tolstoi and Britain*, 45, 49.
9 Mrs. Henry Wood, *East Lynne* (New Brunswick, NJ: Rutgers University Press, 1984), 516, 421.
10 Lisa Knapp, "'Tue-la ! Tue-le!': Death Sentences, Words and Inner Monologue in Tolstoy's *Anna Karenina* and 'Three More Deaths,'" *Tolstoy Studies Journal* 9 (1999), 1–19.
11 D.I. Fonvizin, letter to Petr Aleksandrovich Panin, September 29, 1778, *Polnoe sobranie sochinenii D.I. Fonvizina* (S.-Peterburg: A.A. Kaspari, 1893), 904.

CHAPTER 21

European Philosophy

Jeff Love

Tolstoy found philosophy both fascinating and repugnant. The same man who wrote one of the most far-reaching investigations of the philosophy of history could also slyly mock Plato in *Anna Karenina* where a peasant named Platon has far greater impact on Konstantin Levin than any of the major philosophical figures he had studied and who were relevant in Russia in his youth, like G.W.F. Hegel (1770–1831) whose philosophy of history beguiled Russian intellectuals from Mikhail Bakunin to Alexander Herzen, or Arthur Schopenhauer (1788–1860) who captured the attention of other major Russian writers like Ivan Turgenev. Perhaps this divided attitude contributed to one of the most bloated and pernicious clichés of Tolstoy scholarship: that Tolstoy was a magnificent artist but paltry thinker, even a "crank." This cliché turns us to a far broader tradition, that of the ancient rivalry between the poets and the philosophers. After all, it was Aristotle, following Plato, who said in Book I of the *Metaphysics* that "poets tell many lies," and Plato's depiction of poets as inspired but ignorant finds its way to Tolstoy himself who mocks writers for thinking that they know enough to be teachers, wisdom figures of their time, whereas they know nothing.

I mention wisdom and teaching here because they are at the heart of Tolstoy's philosophical interests. While far more adept than he ever let on, Tolstoy was primarily interested not in the technical arguments of the philosophers, but in the general orientation of their teaching, the practical path for living they advocated. He often merely ignores the thicket of argument to get at the foundations of a philosopher's thinking, and, hence, he has been considered an amateur or neophyte by those who judge philosophical insight in terms of technical virtuosity. Those who judge him do so perilously because Tolstoy had, as all attest, an unusual ability to get to what he considered the "simple truths" that people avoid by constructing thickets of argument, fictions, diversions.

The simplest of these truths is that of death: that we, as individuals, die. One of the most death-haunted authors in the Western canon (see Chapter 2), Tolstoy preferred the company of rather pessimistic thinkers, and, while he constantly sought out those who could teach us about the best way to live, his thought was imbued with a sense that no manner of living could rob death of its sting. Thus, we find in Tolstoy a peculiar combination of a thinker who seeks to determine the best form of living, of community, for all human beings, but who is also supremely aware of how death threatens to undermine all communitarian hopes: we are the ironic social animal, at once creatures of the city and deeply alone, at once god and beast.

This chapter has three main parts. In the first, I look at two philosophers who had an impressive impact on Tolstoy: Jean-Jacques Rousseau (1712–78) and Arthur Schopenhauer (1788–1860). In the second, I turn to Immanuel Kant (1724–1804), whose thought is another crucial context for Tolstoy's principal "pure" work of social or moral philosophy, *On Life* (1886–7). In the third part, I engage with what I consider Tolstoy's most enduring contribution to philosophy, the philosophy of history set out in *War and Peace*. In particular, I examine the unexpected but significant affinity Tolstoy's fiction has with the thought of Baruch Spinoza (1632–77). While this section covers what is perhaps "merely" an affinity, it suggests that Tolstoy's longest fictional work is in fact one of the supreme artistic instantiations of a Spinozist account of the world.

While Plato is present, as inspiration and parodic foil, through much of Tolstoy's work, there are three philosophers with whom Tolstoy engaged extensively over a broad span of his life: Rousseau, Schopenhauer, and Kant. This engagement is telling because each of these philosophers presents a largely pessimistic view of human life with considerable skepticism regarding the possibility of attaining secure knowledge of the world through reason. Indeed, each of these philosophers presents a thorough-going critique of reason's capacity to know and thus to act as a reliable guide for practical action. Even Kant, whose critique of reason appears to serve practical ends, can appear to be primarily skeptical since he doubts the capacity of reason ever to govern human behavior fully.

There is little doubt concerning Tolstoy's deep appreciation of Rousseau. A commonplace of the biography is that the young Tolstoy wore a locket with an image of Rousseau, and he could recite passages of Rousseau's works that he had learned by heart until late in his life. While Rousseau is usually considered somewhat of an optimistic philosopher with his notion of the goodness of the state of nature and human perfectibility, there is another, far more somber current in Rousseau's thought that views society as a kind of fall, not only into the stifling conventions of social and political life, but, far more importantly, into the knowledge of death and the painful desire for permanence evinced by the claim for property and ownership. As Rousseau says in his celebrated *Discourse on Inequality*, "the knowledge of death and its terrors is one of man's first acquisitions in moving away from the animal condition."[1] Rousseau's thought more generally reflects a remarkably ambivalent attitude to society and socialization. A similar attitude emerges in Tolstoy's own work where society is often depicted as cruel and dull, a mere theater where the actors play their roles as if in an old – indeed ancient – play, suppressing their fear of death by immersing themselves in the labyrinth of diversions – status, intrigue, power – that society offers. And like Rousseau's own work, Tolstoy's fiction is filled with lonely "seekers" or "solitary wanderers" who do not fit into society's often facile categorizations. Usually born into society's highest levels, these wanderers try to find their way in the strange world of society, asking questions that no one in society has any wish to discuss – they are often like Pierre Bezukhov or Konstantin Levin, somewhat too large, too natural, and too awkward for society.

As seekers, these major characters are driven by forces they do not understand, and they do not understand what drives others to do the things they do. The thought of Schopenhauer was indeed a fashion in the Russia of the mid nineteenth century, and it is not hard to see why Tolstoy would be attracted to Schopenhauer's dark vision of the world. Tolstoy was apparently first introduced to Schopenhauer by his friend, the poet Afanasy Fet, at the end of the 1860s while he was completing *War and Peace*, and Schopenhauer's essay on freedom of the will, whose influence is quite evident in the major essay on history concluding that work, made a deep impression on Tolstoy. In the summer of 1869, Tolstoy read all of Schopenhauer's main work, *The World as Will and Representation*. His reaction to the work, recorded in a letter to Fet from August 1869, is worth quoting:

> Do you know what this summer has been like for me? Continuous astonishment about Schopenhauer, and a series of spiritual pleasures I've never experienced before. I have purchased all his works and have read and am reading them (I've read Kant too), and honestly no student in his course has learned and discovered as much as I have during this summer.
>
> I don't know whether I'll change my opinion, but at present I'm sure that Schopenhauer is the greatest genius among men. (61:31)

Later on, Tolstoy would change his opinion about Schopenhauer, but this immense praise should not be dismissed, and traces of Schopenhauer's thought are evident most notably in *Anna Karenina* but also in brilliant short works like "How Much Land Does a Man Need?" (1886), which James Joyce referred to as the best short work ever written. Its main character, Pakhom, is alight with the desire to acquire property. He travels to the land of the Bashkirs who offer him as much land as he can cover in a day. Pakhom tries desperately to cover as much land as he can and in the end he dies.

The parable is a blunt metaphor. The lust for acquisition of property is insatiable and irrational: it is a blind urge for individual sovereignty that unmakes one's life with the allure of protecting one against death by ownership itself. Here one sees the confluence of Rousseau's vain striving to free oneself of the knowledge of death through the illusion of sovereign ownership coupled with Schopenhauer's insistence on the primacy of the blind, irrational will that incessantly drives us and can only be countered by some resigned form of inanition. The more profound point of the story is that through social organization we give narrative form to the inherently selfish blind will to grant it a veneer of social purpose with a salubrious end that is nothing but illusion. Driven inexorably by the will, we create illusions that flatter and unite us, suggesting we have an agency and joint purpose that we cannot possibly have.

Tolstoy writes, in 1874:

> Having lived for close on fifty years, I am convinced that life on earth has nothing to give, and that the clever man who looks at life on earth seriously, its labors, fears, reproaches, struggles – *what for?* for madness sake? – such a man would shoot himself at once, and Hartmann and Schopenhauer are right. But Schopenhauer gave people to feel that there is something, which stopped him from shooting himself. What that something is is the purpose of my book. What do we live by? *Religion.*[2]

Recognizing the impasse created by such a position, Tolstoy looks to religion, but his culminating philosophical work, *On Life*, is an attempt to address this impasse philosophically, and it is in this work that Kant comes to the fore as a pivotal philosophical inspiration.

Immanuel Kant is generally considered one of the greatest philosophers. His three principal works, *The Critique of Pure Reason* (1781), *The Critique of Practical Reason* (1788), and *The Critique of the Power of Judgment* (1790), changed the direction of European philosophy. Kant investigates the conditions that permit our knowledge of the world, and his focus on these conditions as constitutive of human subjectivity turned the focus of philosophy away from nature or the whole as such to the knowing subject, a tendency that began a century before with René Descartes's (1596–1650) *Meditations on First Philosophy* (1641).

On Life is preoccupied with the individual subject and, in particular, with the discord created by the tension between the selfish inward impulsion that Schopenhauer interprets as the will and the sense of collective agency that is society and associated with reason. In simplest terms, Tolstoy decries the pathos of the individual, destined to die, and advocates the adoption of reason and the community created by reason as the proper venue of salvation from death.

The main thread of argument in *On Life* sets out an opposition between two kinds of life: what Tolstoy refers to as the "animal life" or our "animal personality," and the genuinely human life expressed by "rational consciousness" (*razumnoe soznanie*). The former relates to the life of the individual with all its immediate and self-interested concerns as a life that seeks the welfare of the individual as against others – the primary imperative of this kind of life is self-preservation. The latter relates to the reflective capacity that permits us to think about the good in itself or the proper end of human striving. The good has two basic characteristics: (1) that one place the general welfare over one's own; (2) that, in doing so, one may free oneself of the inordinate and ultimately vain concern to preserve and protect one's own body. To think the good is attempting to think from the perspective of others and the whole, to be rational by overcoming the influence of animal life with its focus on self-interest.

The equation of rationality with the good and freedom is Kantian. According to Kant's moral theory the inclinations of the body enslave us. They compel a complete dependence on the body's environment and immediate concerns. Various stimuli activate the body, and these impose themselves to the extent the body must react to them: the body is thus thoroughly reactive and initiates nothing of its own. Heteronomy is the term Kant uses to describe this reactive way of being. Rationality provides a contrast because rationality is active, following its own ends and directing action in accordance with these ends. A rational subject or agent is autonomous, setting its own rules for itself, regardless of the momentary enthusiasms of the body, and the laws by which such an agent acts are necessarily universal, capable of being adopted freely by all other rational agents. Universality is the primary condition for determining whether an action is rational or not; an action can only be universalized if anyone can perform it without contradiction, without inflicting harm on others or inviting destruction. Likewise, Tolstoy equates the good with rationality and universality. To seek the good is to seek the universal over the particular, the one over the many, rational principle over physical impulse.

On Life shows Tolstoy's very Kantian respect for autonomy or real freedom as coming from rational consciousness, the shared acceptance of universal principle over the vain pursuit of bodily self-preservation that can lead only to conflict and disappointment in death. Tolstoy thereby expresses an attitude of resistance to the pessimism of Schopenhauer and Rousseau by rejecting the governance of bodily impulse and the ambiguous attitude to society that one finds in Rousseau.

I have saved the best for last: Tolstoy's extraordinary philosophy of history and its contexts. There are few aspects of Tolstoy's philosophical work that have raised more questions or encouraged more polemics than Tolstoy's philosophy of history from *War and Peace*. Tolstoy has been called a skeptic, a nihilist, and many other things besides, based on this philosophy of history. He has been called Hegelian too (a curious claim given Tolstoy's pronounced antipathy to Hegel) as well as a disciple of Herder.[3] This latter finding strikes me as far closer to the mark: for behind Herder, one finds Spinoza, and I believe that there are few grander expressions of Spinoza's thought in fiction than *War and Peace*.

Baruch Spinoza developed an immensely influential monist philosophy of infinite substance in the *Ethics* (1677) that views human beings and human emotions as strictly natural beings determined by natural laws in the same way as animals, stones, and plants. The immediate unifying feature between Spinoza and Tolstoy is the affirmation of the infinite and the consequent relocation of the focus of thought from the human being to the infinite whole. *War and Peace* is constructed polemically to articulate this change of focus, and the novel culminates in a long essay that advocates the discovery of laws of history akin to Newton's laws of physics. The genuinely "Copernican turn" in the novel is reflected in a rejection of the thesis that great men make history and the affirmation of history as a kind of motion that shows certain patterns.

The Spinozan elements in this polemic are noteworthy. Not only does Tolstoy affirm that causation is infinitely complex, thus undermining the notion that one finite actor can be the generative efficient cause in an historical event, he also shows how our irrational attachment to our own freedom makes it difficult to overcome this view of our own agency. The polemic against this simple causal model whereby finite beings become efficient causes is a hallmark of Spinoza's thought, as is the notion that we are emotionally attached to our freedom and that this emotion (or, rather, affect) directs us to a far greater and more immediate degree than reason.

And, like Spinoza's, Tolstoy's concept of emancipation is oriented to liberating us from our emotional attachment to our own freedom – which causes us to create self-serving narratives with virtually endless virtuosity – and to embracing our proper place in the whole as a mere part of the latter. That this emancipation is unattractive, indeed intolerable, is witnessed by the behavior of several principal characters in the novel who try to free themselves of the illusion of freedom but are ultimately unable to do so. To the contrary, like Pierre Bezukhov at the very end of the novel, human beings are tempted by the illusion of agency almost inexorably, the fact of our lack of freedom being simply too hard to bear.

The positive "thesis" of *War and Peace* is hardly an aggressively skeptical one insofar as the freedom from illusions of agency is liberating not in the sense of freeing us from necessity but of encouraging us to leave our infantile attachment to freedom in favor of an acceptance of necessity. Only a being that cannot tolerate its own limitations can maintain such illusions in any case, and such a being must suffer from those illusions to the extent it cannot see fit to let them go. The very essence of this suffering is the same for Tolstoy throughout his vast work – it is the suffering of the lonely individual destined to die, a suffering that only relents to the extent that we may overcome a concept of individuality nested in an untenable concept of individual agency.

The struggle between individual inclination and the demands of society and nature never resolves itself in Tolstoy's work, neither in his novels, nor in his philosophical work, nor in his attempt to create a version of Christianity whose principal teaching consists of a virulent devotion to the renunciation of animal egotism in favor of the other, whether that other be a person or an animal or a plant. Tolstoy knew that this struggle could not issue in victory without suicide, for one lives at the cost of others for as long as one lives.

Notes

1 Jean-Jacques Rousseau, *The Discourses and Other Early Political Writings*, ed. and trans. Victor Gourevitch (Cambridge University Press, 1997), 142.
2 Leo Tolstoy, *Diaries*, vol. 1: *1847–1894*, ed. and trans. R.F. Christian (London: Faber and Faber, 2015), 462.
3 See Lina Steiner, "Herder's Russian Advocate: Tolstoy on the Vocation of Humanity," in Liisa Steinby (ed.), *Herder und das 19. Jahrhundert / Herder and the Nineteenth Century* (Conference Proceedings) (Heidelberg: Synchron Press, 2020), 427–43.

CHAPTER 22

Theater

Caryl Emerson

In the history of Russian theater, 1882 is a landmark year. The government finally ended its imperial monopoly over stage repertory, making commercial theater possible and encouraging amateur groups to experiment and professionalize under wealthy patrons.[1] To be sure, censorship remained in place, both secular and ecclesiastical. Plays were even censored twice: first for publication, then separately for performance. But lifting the monopoly was a huge boost for Russian-language drama. The Romanov court had imported classical theatrical genres from Western Europe in the early eighteenth century, and aristocratic taste continued to prefer – and thus the royal court generously funded – ballet and Italian-language opera. After 1882, the sheer explosion of venues and the new concentration on Russianness were welcomed by Tolstoy, for it accommodated his own spiritual realignment.

In the 1850s, as a contrary young man in the capitals, Tolstoy had delighted at comedies of exposure (Molière's satires and Gogol's *Inspector General*). But he was never infatuated with the theater – possibly due to his nearsightedness, a handicap that did not affect his deep appreciation of music. Tolstoy's relationship with staged art was anxious and passionate. Unlike the in-print prose word, which works on us privately, Tolstoy held that visual or audible stimuli, artistically shaped, could infect us irresistibly, unifying an audience around an abomination as easily as around a moral truth. He was harsh on playwrights who, in his view, abused the potential of the medium. Shakespeare he loathed, Chekhov's plays he disliked, and theatrical convention he routinely ridiculed or condemned. Yet from 1856 until the end of his life, Tolstoy tried his hand at a wide variety of dramatic genres: farce, social satire, comedy, folk tragedy, dramatized parable and didactic fable, skits against drunkenness with live speaking devils, even an enscenement of his own diaries.

Much of this output was published only posthumously. In drama as in prose, Tolstoy was self-consciously an outsider, either pushing back against the theatrical practices of his time or pushing in new directions further than others would go. The context that mattered to Tolstoy as creative writer was neither the prior canon nor the current market, but the work of art in relation to his own moral evolution. Since Tolstoy's evolving self was a highly public commodity, even false steps made news and the Tolstoyan influence seeped into unlikely venues. In 1895 the young Konstantin Stanislavsky, not yet having founded the Moscow Art Theater, began negotiating to stage Tolstoy's folk tragedy *The Power of Darkness*. Tolstoy was indifferent to the actual production in 1902. But a Tolstoyan disciple and amateur theater enthusiast, Leopold Sulerzhitsky, became one of Stanislavsky's closest friends and, from 1906, his personal advisor. In 1912, Stanislavsky appointed him director of the theater's First Studio. Tolstoy was no longer alive to comment on this collaboration, but Sulerzhitsky's holistic ideals of actor training, collective creativity, and art as communion were infused with his master's spirit.[2]

The Mystery Play and the Departure

Tolstoy's playwriting falls into two distinct periods separated by almost twenty years. His first dramatic fragments date from 1856 and stretch over ten years. All are merciless satires on fashionable ideas: liberated women, nihilists, the collapse of patriarchal country life. During this period Tolstoy finished only one full-length play, *The Infected Family* (1863), a parody of Chernyshevsky's "new people" and their doctrine of rational egoism. He was keen to see it staged. The great realist playwright Alexander Ostrovsky, whom Tolstoy admired, endured the fledgling playwright's recitation of the piece and then recorded in his diary: "a monstrosity" (*bezobrazie*).[3] Among the reasons, surely, is that Tolstoy presents all his characters (young and elderly, new and old) as ridiculous and deluded. Tolstoy soon abandoned the play, returning to drama only in 1886.

What might explain Tolstoy's two-decade hiatus in playwriting? One answer was offered by Mikhail Bakhtin in 1929, in his Preface to volume XI, the drama, of a new Collected Works of Tolstoy.[4] The early unsuccessful theater pieces are no more than ill-tempered pamphlets, Bakhtin avers, a record of Tolstoy's personal attitude toward the 1860s. At that time the fragmentation of voices required by the stage did not interest Tolstoy as an artist. He was busy working out his own confident, autonomous, unencumbered authorial word. What prompted the second playwriting period was Tolstoy's spiritual crisis, which was simultaneously a "crisis of the narrating epic word."[5] Only when his early epic confidence had collapsed could Tolstoy take dramatic form seriously and produce potent original art for the stage. Each of his dramatized "didactic shorts," as well as his three completed full-length plays – *The Power of Darkness* (1886), *The Fruits of Enlightenment* (1889), and *The Living Corpse* (1900) – displays unmistakably Tolstoyan features and final aims. Bakhtin divides the work of the fertile second period into two categories: folk or peasant dramas, which aspire to the medieval mystery play, and the autobiographical narratives (including the unfinished *A Light Shines in the Darkness*, based on Tolstoy's diaries), which aspire to an *ukhod*, a principled departure from one life to another (232). The intended audience varies: satire for the upper-class salon, art for the common people, personal confession.

The peasant dramas are written in folk vernacular, which Tolstoy knew and loved. In the spirit of his great contemporary Nikolai Leskov, Tolstoy worked from within native belief systems, in quest of a premodern wisdom. Bakhtin notes, however, that Tolstoy's peasant dramas do not occur in real developmental social time. Post-emancipation Russia was a complex, turbulent, rapidly changing place. New values were emerging, and new vices too; Ostrovsky documented this confusion in his plays about rich peasants and merchants, as did Alexei Pisemsky in his pre-emancipation tragedy *A Bitter Fate* (1859), whose grim plot of infanticide is echoed in Tolstoy's *The Power of Darkness*. Tolstoy as dramatist does not idealize the peasant. Lower-class life can be vicious and brutal. But, Bakhtin observes, morally this life is static and simple. The peasantry is Tolstoy's ahistorical site for "the 'universally human' and 'extra-temporal' struggle of good with evil."[6] Even the "magnificent, deeply individualized peasant language is no more than an immobile, unchanging background and dramatically dead shell for the internal spiritual deed of the hero."[7] Change and motion in real time are reserved for the autobiographical dramatizations of departure, which is to say, for the eternal seeker Lev Tolstoy, a singular agent speaking to the Divine within himself.

Four Dramatic Exemplars

As Victor Borovsky has noted, theater in Russia, borrowed from the West, "did not pass through all the natural stages of self-development, rooted in folklore and ritual forms of acting."[8] Tolstoy offered a simulacrum of native Russian theater with *The First Distiller* (*Pervyi vinokur*, 1886).[9] It was a dramatization of his own folktale "How the Demon Earned His Crust of Bread," which was in turn an adaptation of Belorusian and Tatar legends on the origin of drunkenness. A petty demon steals a poor peasant's chunk of bread, hoping to evoke a curse that will deliver the peasant into his power. But the peasant merely shrugs and wishes the hungry thief well. The Chief Devil, disgusted, gives his demon three years to seduce the peasant. The demon becomes the peasant's hired worker, makes him rich, and teaches him how to distill vodka from his excess grain. With addiction to alcohol come greed, flattery, frivolity, violence. The Chief is satisfied and the village is won.

What are the Tolstoyan features in this mystery playlet? Its necessary truth is that hard physical labor and poverty will make a person sober and generous. (A virtuous hard-working alcoholic or a philanthropic millionaire are not comfortable types for Tolstoy.) Thus alcohol must be an alien evil, introduced into the peasant's world from the outside. Tolstoy attached little artistic importance to this anti-vodka sketch, hoping merely to supplement the "worthless or harmful plays" performed during carnival season.[10] By July 1886, *The First Distiller* had indeed been snatched up by a people's theater in Moscow, where 3,000 workers attended the premiere in the pouring rain. But then the censor banned it.[11]

More substantial is our next exemplar, written the same year: the folk tragedy *The Power of Darkness* (*Vlast' t'my*). Its events were real, based on a criminal court case tried several years earlier in Tula. Its title, however, spoken by Jesus to his captors (Luke 22:53), suggests a mystery play. The plot is the familiar murder tale of lascivious hired hand and debauched master's wife, whose lust leaves a trail of victims (the most famous Russian variant is Leskov's 1865 "Lady Macbeth of Mtsensk District," turned into an opera by Dmitry Shostakovich in 1934). In Tolstoy's play, the womanizing Nikita conspires with his master's wife Anisya to poison the ailing master. Nikita and Anisya marry, but Nikita soon tires of her and takes up with her stepdaughter Akulina. In Act IV, just barely off stage and at excruciating length, Nikita crushes Akulina's whimpering newborn infant. Witnessing this horror are Nikita's parents, his scheming, utterly amoral mother Matryona and his saintly father Akim. In Act V, during Akulina's cover-up wedding, Nikita falls on his knees and confesses, begging forgiveness of all and insisting that "I did it all by myself, alone."[12] Nikita's rejection of all co-responsible criminal parties is characteristically Tolstoyan in its self-centeredness, but other themes are social and shared with *The First Distiller*. Wealth – especially when stored in banks – is denounced by Akim as "filthy"; drunkenness is rife (Akim drinks only tea).

One emphasis in this powerful tragedy is new: its attack on eloquence. The verbal hallmark of Matryona is to deliver a slick fine-sounding proverb

to cover every corrupt situation. Her husband Akim is the opposite: he is
inarticulate, a chronic stutterer. This stutter was precious to Tolstoy, who
never trusted clever or dazzling words. But incoherence on stage hardly
accorded with theatrical practice. Early in 1887, when *The Power of
Darkness* was in rehearsal at Petersburg's Alexandrinsky Theater, the actor
Pavel Svobodin, who was playing Akim, wrote to Tolstoy for counsel. You
must not mumble or stumble, Tolstoy replied. Akim is not a feeble man.
"His motions – movements – are vigorous; only nimble smooth speech
God did not grant him."[13] That same month the play was banned,
however, and the rehearsals cancelled; the premiere took place in Paris in
1888, encouraged by Émile Zola.[14] The imperial censor's ban was lifted
only nine years later.

In 1889, Tolstoy finished another play filled with peasants – but to
wholly different purpose. His five elder children had requested a theater
piece to perform with family guests and neighbors during the winter
holidays at Yasnaya Polyana. The result was *The Fruits of Enlightenment*,
spritely entertainment in the mold of an eighteenth-century French
drawing-room comedy (its sassy peasant-soubrette recalls Susanna in *The
Marriage of Figaro*). The cast is huge (over thirty speaking parts); the scenes
tiny and flexible. An enterprising peasant girl, Tanya, working as a maid in
the manor house, manipulates her master into finalizing a bill of sale for
some land sorely needed by her home village. She coaches her betrothed,
the butler's assistant Semyon, into faking a séance during which the
master, a convinced spiritualist, will sign the necessary legal papers. The
ruse works. So did the play; Tolstoy laughed heartily at every performance,
including (so Aylmer Maude reports) one charity venue in Tula where the
doorkeeper turned Tolstoy out, thinking he was a common peasant.[15]

As in our earlier exemplars, peasant realities and perspectives ground this
play. Much of Act II, for example, is taken up with the cook Lukerya's
comic complaints that the gentry do nothing but play cards or piano,
dance with one another naked, and sit down to eat ("they even eat in
bed"). But Maude insists that the play had a second serious aim beyond
embarrassing the "cultured classes" by juxtaposing their "empty, useless,
and expensive pastimes" to the need of laboring peasants for land (265).
This was to critique the pan-European fad for "scientific spiritualism."[16] In
Tolstoy's play, one Professor Krugosvetlov (modeled on real-life converts
to spiritualism at St. Petersburg University) delivers a pre-séance lecture.
But Tolstoy's parody, Maude explains, is not against science, or even faked
science; it is against the professor's confusion of matter and spirit. The
spirit realm may or may not exist, but we cannot investigate it or adduce

proofs of it by relying on the time-space of the five senses. In his cogent discussion of this comedy, the historian of science Michael Gordin notes its close connection with Tolstoy's treatise *On Life*, under composition at the same time, and Tolstoy's lifelong inquiry into appropriate scientific method.[17] The Tolstoyan truth here is that metaphysical inquiry and materialistic science are not incompatible. But each has its own way of knowing.

Our final exemplar is *The Living Corpse*, a "drama in twelve vignettes" published only posthumously, in 1911. When rumor of its existence reached the Moscow Art Theater early in 1900, Nemirovich-Danchenko visited Yasnaya Polyana, where Tolstoy told him: "When I die, you can play it."[18] (MAT mounted the play a year after Tolstoy's death, and by October 1912, 9,000 performances had taken place in over 200 theaters across Russia.[19]) The plot is of the departure, or *ukhod*, type – but without asceticism, self-display, or mournful righteousness. Chekhov had been one stimulus. "Went to see *Uncle Vanya* and was outraged," Tolstoy wrote in his diary at the end of January 1900. "Hankered to write up my drama *Corpse*."[20] There were other prompts and sources. Its gypsy theme was surely influenced by Tolstoy's older brother Sergei, for many years in a common-law marriage with a gypsy woman. As with *The Power of Darkness*, this play too parallels a celebrated court case – albeit not for murder, but bigamy. The central event, a faked suicide, parodies Chernyshevsky's utopian *What Is to Be Done?* (1863) and Sukhovo-Kobylin's satire *The Death of Tarelkin* (1869). A Dostoevskian aura hovers over the play: the opening vignette recalls, lopsidedly, Katerina Verkhovtseva and Dmitry Karamazov, and Act IV contains a Kirillov figure who plans a suicide out of principle. Unlike Dostoevsky, however, Tolstoy does not organize his characters around ideas but around personal habits. And the amiable but weak and dissolute Fedya Protasov, a habitual wastrel, wants only to avoid hurting others while remaining true to himself. Loyalty, confused love, and naïve honesty are more vital to this plot than ambition, jealousy, greed, or transgression.

The play opens on a crisis. Believing himself an unworthy drunkard who has squandered their fortune, Fedya has left his wife Liza and their infant son and taken refuge with the gypsies, announcing he will not return. Liza sends Viktor Karenin, a former suitor (still in love with her), to fetch Fedya back. But Fedya, now in a platonic love relation with Masha the gypsy singer, procrastinates. To obtain a divorce, he would have to lie and fabricate adultery, which he cannot do. He considers suicide but

Masha (who has read Chernyshevsky) talks him out of it; why not fake a drowning?

The sham drowning is accomplished. Not wanting to ruin Masha, Fedya abandons her too and disappears into taverns, a "living corpse." Viktor and Liza marry and are now expecting their own child. But then Fedya is recognized, blackmailed, and charges of bigamy filed. The final courtroom scenes resemble *The Power of Darkness*. Once confronted by the law, Fedya, like Nikita, bows low and begs forgiveness of all. The verdict, he is told, will be restoration of the original marriage and most likely exile to Siberia of the reunited couple. But here the ultimate guilty party unmasked by Tolstoy is not the defendant but the legal system. Fedya addresses the court: why do you meddle in other people's lives? Three people were struggling spiritually but we disentangled everything. Those two are now happy and think kindly of me – while you investigators and lawyers, for a few filthy coins, don your uniforms and make arrests. Then Fedya Protasov pulls out a gun and shoots himself in the heart. Curtain.

This gesture, reminiscent of the criminal trial that falsely condemned Dmitry Karamazov, is not Chekhov's. It is not Uncle Vanya's futile self-dramatizing gunplay against the professor, nor Konstantin's desperately lonely suicide off stage at the end of *The Seagull*. Those were private fates within petty private settings, whereas Tolstoy insisted on opening his dramas out at the last moment to transform a family, a village, a courtroom, the worldview of an audience. In 1908, in a discussion about theater with his one-time disciple the journalist Isaak Feinerman, Tolstoy remarked that the stage was sculptural. The playwright could not force characters to share themselves artificially in prepared monologues, they could only be prompted by deeds that the audience sees. And here Russia had recently been through such a caldron of events – war, revolution, rebellion in the streets. None of it had been captured dramatically, Tolstoy noted sadly, no serious tragedies or comedies had emerged, "the well of the stage is dry."[21]

Notes

1 Cynthia Marsh, "Realism in the Russian Theatre, 1850–1882," in Robert Leach and Victor Borovsky (eds.), *A History of Russian Theatre* (Cambridge University Press, 1999), 146–65, esp. 147–8.
2 See Maria Shevtsova, *Rediscovering Stanislavsky* (Cambridge University Press, 2020), esp. 32–6.

3 See Aleksei Zverev, "Dramaturgiia Tolstogo," essay appended to Aleksei Zverev and Vladimir Tunimanov, *Lev Tolstoi* (Moscow: Molodaia gvardiia, 2006), 729. To Tolstoy's impatience that the play was topical and should be staged immediately, Ostrovsky responded: "Are you afraid that people will smarten up too soon?"
4 L.N. Tolstoy, *Polnoe sobranie khudozhestvennykh proizvedenii*, ed. K. Khalabaev and B. Eikhenbaum (Leningrad: Pechatnyi dvor, 1929), vol. XI, iii–x. Translated by Caryl Emerson as Mikhail M. Bakhtin, "Preface to Volume 11: *The Dramas*," in Gary Saul Morson and Caryl Emerson (eds.), *Rethinking Bakhtin: Extensions and Challenges* (Evanston, IL: Northwestern University Press, 1989), 227–36.
5 Ibid., 228.
6 Ibid., 232.
7 Ibid., 233.
8 Victor Borovsky, "Russian Theatre in Russian Culture," in Leach and Borovsky (eds.), *History of Russian Theatre*, 6–17 (at 6).
9 Translated in Leo Tolstoy, *Plays*, vol. I: *1856–1886*, trans. Marvin Kantor and Tanya Tulchinsky (Evanston IL: Northwestern University Press, 1994), as "The First Moonshiner, or How the Demon Earned His Bread."
10 Related by Aylmer Maude in his Preface to Leo Tolstoy, *Plays: The Power of Darkness, The First Distiller, Fruits of Culture*, trans. Louise and Aylmer Maude (New York: Funk & Wagnalls, 1904), vii.
11 Zverev, "Dramaturgiia Tolstogo," 732.
12 Leo Tolstoy, "The Realm of Darkness, or 'If a Claw Gets Stuck, the Bird Is Lost,'" in *Plays: Volume One*, 1–90, here 90. *Vlast'*, political power, implies territory and sovereignty and thus can also be rendered "realm"; *t'ma* is not any ordinary darkness, but a moral abyss.
13 Letter to P.M. Svobodin, March 5, 1887, in *Tolstoy's Letters*, vol. II: *1880–1910*, ed. and trans. R.F. Christian (New York: Charles Scribner's Sons, 1978), 416. Translation adjusted.
14 For this history, see Justin Weir, "Violence and the Role of Drama in the Late Tolstoy: *The Realm of Darkness*," in Donna Tussing Orwin (ed.), *Anniversary Essays on Tolstoy* (Cambridge University Press, 2010), 183–98, esp. 185.
15 Aylmer Maude, *The Life of Tolstoy*, vol. II: *Later Years* (Oxford University Press, 1987; 1st edn 1930), 265. Further page references in text.
16 For background on the comedy's real-life models, see Ilya Vinitsky, *Ghostly Paradoxes: Modern Spiritualism and Russian Culture in the Age of Realism* (University of Toronto Press, 2009), chap. 7, "The (Dis)infection: Art and Hypnotism in Tolstoy," 136–55.
17 Michael D. Gordin, "Tolstoy Sees Foolishness, and Writes: From *On Life* to *Fruits of Enlightenment*, and Back Again," in Inessa Medzhibovskaya (ed.), *A Critical Guide to Tolstoy's On Life: Interpretive Essays* (DeLand, FL and Toronto: The Tolstoy Society of North America and *Tolstoy Studies Journal*, 2019), 105–33, esp. 110–13.
18 Zverev, "Dramaturgiia Tolstogo," 751.

19 Marc Slonim, *Russian Theater from the Empire to the Soviets* (Cleveland: World Publishing Company, 1961), 82.

20 Entry for January 27, 1900, in *Tolstoy's Diaries*, vol. II: *1895–1910*, ed. and trans. R. F. Christian (New York: Charles Scribner's Sons, 1985), 476. Translation adjusted.

21 S. Teneromo (Isaak Fainerman), "L.N. Tolstoi o teatre," *Teatr i iskusstvo* 34 (1908), 580–1 (at 580).

CHAPTER 23

Music

Emily Frey

Tolstoy's meetings with Russian musicians tended to be debacles. After a visit with Sergei Rachmaninoff, Tolstoy apparently felt compelled to apologize for offending the young pianist; a meeting with Nikolai Rimsky-Korsakov ended with Tolstoy proclaiming "Today [I've] come face to face with gloom."[1] Pyotr Tchaikovsky, who was deeply flattered by Tolstoy's interest in him and who (more to the point) possessed eminently diplomatic manners, fared better – but not by much. The two met at the Moscow Conservatory and a few times thereafter in Tchaikovsky's apartment in December 1876; no serious incidents ensued. But as Mikhail Ippolitov-Ivanov recalled:

> Though he bowed before L.N. Tolstoy as a writer of genius, Tchaikovsky had a very low opinion of his conversations on art in general and on music in particular, finding his judgments amateurish and shallow. Tolstoy's opinion that Beethoven was untalented deeply outraged Pyotr Ilyich, but he considered it pointless to argue and try to prove otherwise in light of Tolstoy's obstinacy and insistence. And so he did everything possible to avoid conversation with Tolstoy on the subject, and more than once did Tchaikovsky – as he himself confessed to me – avail himself of an intervening courtyard in order to escape a meeting and a conversation with Tolstoy on the street.[2]

Ippolitov-Ivanov's image of Tchaikovsky (by no means a petite, inconspicuous fellow) slipping between buildings to evade that famous beard is as emblematic as it is droll. For better or for worse, Tolstoy's personal relationships with his contemporaries among composers were not destined to be warm.

The reasons for these unpleasant encounters are easy to imagine. Whatever Russian composers had to say on the matter, Tolstoy was not a complete musical naïf: like most educated Russians of his time, Tolstoy often experienced music through the medium of amateur domestic performance, and he was himself a journeyman pianist. In his earlier years,

too, Tolstoy attended public concerts and operas, which were just beginning to proliferate in Russia by the middle of the nineteenth century. Yet
the author of *The Kreutzer Sonata* (1889) had a notorious love-hate
relationship with music, an art whose affective force he found irresistible
and therefore suspect.[3] For Tolstoy, music's singular, terrible (*strashnyi*)
power was its ability to imitate, access, and excite the emotions without
rational intermediaries such as words and images. That capacity to bypass a
person's mental defenses and act directly upon the soul, without the
subject's conscious participation and potentially even against her will,
was at the root of Tolstoy's moral misgivings about the art form. In
Tolstoy's mature theory of art, to stir the emotions without giving them
a proper outlet was a recipe for moral catastrophe. This was part of the
reason why, in Tolstoy's estimation, peasant music was the most whole-
some music of all: it provided just such an "outlet" in the form of a well-
defined social function, as in work songs, marching songs, and dances.
Peasant music also served a crucial unifying purpose; it was both accessible
to everyone (according to Tolstoy) and typically accompanied communal
activity. Such ideas would naturally rub against the professional pride of
any composer. For as much as Tchaikovsky, Rimsky-Korsakov, Modest
Musorgsky and others admired Russian folk music, and even used it as a
basis for their own compositions, they were still and all writing musical
works to be consumed by the educated classes in opera houses, concert
halls, and drawing rooms, not peasant huts. Moreover, Tolstoy's profoundly anti-operatic attitudes – on unabashed display in Book VIII of
War and Peace – were bound to vex his composing contemporaries, who
preferred to work in that genre above all others.

    As it happened, however, Tolstoy's musical contemporaries were a
uniquely literary bunch. In no other country did composers display such
a marked penchant for plucking operatic plots, and even wholesale libret-
tos, from the modern literature of their own nation. Nor were opera
composers of other nations so strongly disposed to adapt literary masterpieces. These high-minded predilections cut across all of nineteenth-
century Russian music's embattled rivalries and seemingly unbridgeable
gaps. Both radical autodidacts like Musorgsky and conservatory-trained
traditionalists like Tchaikovsky adapted the major works of Alexander
Pushkin, Nikolai Gogol, and Alexander Ostrovsky, and they tended to
do so in a way that preserved as much of the original text as possible. This
preference for textual conservation probably explains why Tolstoy's own
works did not often find their way onto nineteenth-century opera stages:
Tolstoy's prosy, rambling, unrhythmic lines do not bend easily to the

conventions of the operatic libretto, after all. (Not for nothing had the composer Alexander Dargomyzhsky chosen to base his pioneering litero-musical experiment of 1869 – a verbatim operatic setting of Pushkin's play *The Stone Guest* – on a work written in unrhymed iambic pentameter.)

However, if they rarely regarded Tolstoy's works as suitable objects of musical adaptation, nineteenth-century Russian composers did see them as "musical" in other ways. The special power Tolstoy ascribed to music, what we might call the power of emotional catalysis, was the very quality that distinguished Tolstoy's fiction in at least one composer's eyes. Several of Tchaikovsky's letters and diary entries, written for disparate audiences and over a span of some years, describe the composer's astonishment at tears provoked by a seemingly innocuous passage of Tolstoyan prose. "Reading [Tolstoy] … evokes in me a completely special, unique feeling that can only be called tenderness," wrote Tchaikovsky to one of his most exalted correspondents, the Grand Duke Konstantin Konstantinovich. "I feel this tenderness … [even] with episodes that would seem entirely prosaic, ordinary, and banal. For example, I remember that once, on reading that chapter where *Dolokhov* fleeces *Rostov* at cards, I burst into tears and couldn't stop them for a long time. How can this scene, where both characters' behavior is far from praise-worthy, call forth tears?"[4] Elsewhere Tchaikovsky speaks of Tolstoy's gifts in explicitly musical terms. In an 1887 letter to the pianist Yuliya Shpazhinskaia, Tchaikovsky declared – albeit in a backhanded and rather convoluted way – that the pre-*Confession* Tolstoy was in his way the most musical of all writers: "In an *artist* absolute truth is not found in a banal, perfunctory sense, but in a higher one, opening up to us some kind of unknown horizon, some inaccessible spheres, where only *music* is able to penetrate, and among writers no one has reached so far into those as the Tolstoy of earlier times."[5]

The relationship between Tolstoy and the music of his time is thus considerably richer and more complicated than his mutually unsatisfying meetings with composers might indicate. Consider, for example, one of Tchaikovsky's most famous statements about his own music, long taken as an artistic *profession de foi*. "Truth and sincerity," he wrote to Sergei Taneyev in 1891, "are not the result of a process of reasoning, but the inevitable outcome of our inmost feelings … I always choose operatic subjects in which I have to deal with real men and women, who share the same emotions as myself."[6] Tchaikovsky had first voiced this definition of his own brand of realism over a decade earlier, as he worked on the opera *Evgeny Onegin* in 1877, a few months after his meetings with Tolstoy.

Tchaikovsky's operatic turn toward "real people," his elevation of sincerity (*iskrennost*) and inner feeling over abstract reasoning and external effect, and his notion that art should be based on the artist's own emotional experience have often been understood as a reaction against the failures of Tchaikovsky's first three operas, which had all been written on historical or fantastical subject matter. But these same three elements – ordinariness, sincerity, and emotional self-portraiture – are also a veritable troika of Tolstoyan aesthetics. An 1877 letter to Nadezhda von Meck, worth quoting at some length, makes the Tolstoy connection explicit.

> It seems to me that [*Onegin*] is destined for failure and disregard by the public masses. The plot is very simple, there are no stage effects, the music is devoid of brilliance and bombastic effects. But it seems to me that perhaps a *select* few, listening to this music, will be touched by the same sensations that moved me when I was composing it. I don't want to say that my music is so good that it is inaccessible to the *despised crowd*. I generally don't understand how it is possible to write deliberately for the masses or for a select few; to me it's necessary to write obeying my own spontaneous impulse, not thinking at all about catering to this or that section of humanity. That is how I wrote *Onegin* ... [and] those who are able to seek in an opera the musical representation of things far from tragic, far from theatrical – ordinary, simple, universal human feelings – may (*I hope*) be left satisfied with my opera. In a word, it was written sincerely, and on this sincerity I rest all my hopes.
>
> If I have made a mistake in choosing this subject – that is, if my opera does not enter the repertory – this won't upset me much. This winter I had a few interesting conversations with the writer Count L.N. Tolstoy, which revealed and clarified a lot for me. He convinced me that an artist who does not follow internal inspiration, but instead calculates narrowly on *effect*, doing violence to his talent with the aim of pleasing the public and forcing himself to pander to them – such person is not fully an artist. His works will be slipshod, their success ephemeral. I have come to believe in this truth completely.[7]

This letter fairly rings with Tolstoyan ideas. Tchaikovsky's image of himself composing utterly unselfconsciously, spurred by inner feeling rather than considerations of effect, is a virtual synopsis, some twenty years avant la lettre, of the concept of sincerity that Tolstoy describes most famously in *What Is Art?* (1898). Likewise, in imagining a sympathetic audience who may "be touched by the same sensations that moved me when I was composing it," Tchaikovsky approaches Tolstoy's "infection" theory of art – an "infectious" work being one in which the author's state of soul is transmitted to the receivers, uniting artist and audience in the experience of shared emotion.

Further Tolstoyan resonances can be found throughout contemporaneous Russian opera, whatever the author's moral disdain for the art form. Following the example of *War and Peace*, as well as those of historical dramas of the period by authors such as Ostrovsky, Musorgsky and Rimsky-Korsakov created operas that were simultaneously works of art and lessons in historiography. Indeed, Musorgsky's *Khovanshchina* (begun in 1872 and left unfinished at the composer's death nine years later) matches *War and Peace* in its insistence that grand historical processes are impervious to the desires and actions of isolated individuals, no matter what their rank. Musorgsky's historical vision is even bleaker than Tolstoy's, however: while Tolstoy's characters may find domestic happiness despite their world-historical insignificance, in Musorgsky's most pessimistic opera even such limited bliss is a pipe dream. (As Richard Taruskin memorably described the moral of *Khovanshchina*: "Everyone plots and strives and everyone loses."[8])

Musorgsky and Rimsky-Korsakov belonged to a loose assemblage of St. Petersburg composers known as the Balakirev circle, or sometimes (usually by their detractors) as the *moguchaya kuchka* or "mighty little heap." This was a motley collection of artists with diverse styles and aims, and their close association as a group was relatively short-lived. They became famous by championing, passionately and self-consciously, the realist cause that engulfed the Russian arts during the 1860s. While the composers of the Balakirev circle were not the first or the only Russians to advocate for "truth" in music, they were certainly the loudest. Their brilliantly idiosyncratic and often impractical ideas about how to convey "truth" in tones have proven remarkably influential, at least in scholarly accounts of nineteenth-century music. Musorgsky and Alexander Dargomyzhsky in particular have come to be considered the paradigmatic "realists" among all nineteenth-century European composers.

Anglophone scholarship on Russian music has been largely preoccupied with the issue of nationalism. Thus, the Balakirev circle's "realist" musical innovations have usually been understood in nationalistic terms: as attempts to forge a distinctly "Russian" musical idiom that related directly to the Russian language, capturing the subtle connotations of individual words and even at times the musical characteristics of Russian speech. Likewise, the group's full-throated disavowal of conventional operatic form – the parceling of material into speech-like, plot-driving recitatives and lyrical, emotionally expansive arias – is usually considered an effort to

break away from Italian models of operatic dramaturgy, again for nationalistic reasons. But we may also see in these operatic renovations attempts
to realize a fundamentally Tolstoyan objective: the representation of
consciousness as a fluid, continuously evolving process. In a famous review
of 1856, the critic Nikolai Chernyshevsky (1828–89) had identified this
capacity to depict the minute movements of consciousness as Tolstoy's
"special talent," distinguishing him from the majority of authors who
present "only the two outermost links of [an emotional] chain, only the
beginning and the end of the psychological process."[9] This description of
non-Tolstoyan psychological representation hits on practically the raison
d'etre of the Italian *solita forma*, the backbone and organizing principle of
Italian operas from Rossini to middle Verdi. Sometimes called "double aria
form," *la solita forma* is built upon the juxtaposition of diverging emotional
states – the "two outermost links of an emotional chain," so to speak.
Emotional contrast, not emotional process, is the point of the Italian
double aria; the two musical "moods" are typically static, and the transition
between them is often accomplished instantaneously. By overthrowing the
formal aria in favor of a flexible "melodic recitative," and thus by dissolving
the conventional operatic separation of action and emotion, avant-garde
Russian composers of Tolstoy's time hoped to depict the progress of
feeling precisely, immediately, and continuously. The Balakirev circle's
melodic recitative was a style designed to convey through music "the subtle
developments of . . . inner life, changing from one to the next with
extraordinary rapidity and inexhaustible variety," just as Chernyshevsky
had written about Tolstoy's prose.[10]

Russian scholars have produced numerous studies linking Tolstoy with
the musicians of his time. Tolstoy and Tchaikovsky were an especially
popular scholarly pairing during the early Soviet period, when both
aristocrats needed to be politically rehabilitated, assimilated to Soviet
ideology. (Tolstoy proved more problematic in this regard than did
Tchaikovsky, despite the latter's closeness to the imperial family.)
Western scholars, however, have been less eager to pursue these "lateral"
connections, preferring instead to treat the relationship between music and
literature in Russia primarily from the standpoint of adaptation. As a
consequence, anglophone writers have very often studied the relationship
of nineteenth-century composers to Pushkin, who took his last breaths
before Tchaikovsky, Musorgsky, and Rimsky-Korsakov did their first.
They have much less frequently examined the relationships of those same
composers to Tolstoy, with whom the musicians shared time and, occa-
sionally, space. As their failed simpatico as human beings suggests,

relations between Tolstoy and his composing contemporaries were complicated: they revered some elements of each other's art while disregarding or even loathing others. But however disastrous their meetings, the creative dialogue between Tolstoy and contemporary Russian musicians continued long after their spoken dialogue ceased.

Notes

1 See Sergei Bertensson and Jay Leyda, *Sergei Rachmaninoff: A Lifetime in Music* (Bloomington: Indiana University Press, 2001), 89; and V.V. Yastrebtsev, *Reminiscences of Rimsky-Korsakov*, ed. and trans. Florence Jonas (New York: Columbia University Press, 1985), 199.

2 Mikhail Ippolitov-Ivanov, excerpt from *50 let russkoi muzyki v moikh vospominaniiakh*, in E. E. Bortnikova et al. (eds.), *Vospominaniia o P.I. Chaikovskom* (Moscow: Muzyka, 1973), 273.

3 On this topic, see Caryl Emerson, "Tolstoy and Music," in Donna Tussing Orwin (ed.), *Anniversary Essays on Tolstoy* (Cambridge University Press, 2010), 8–32; and Stephen Halliwell, "And Then They Began to Sing: Reflections on Tolstoy and Music," *COLLeGIUM* 9 (2010), 45–64.

4 Petr Il'ich Chaikovskii, *Polnoe sobranie sochinenii*, ed. Kseniia Yur'evna Davydova and Galina Ivanovna Labutina (Moscow: Muzyka, 1976), vol. xva: *Pis'ma* (1889), 204.

5 Petr Il'ich Chaikovskii, *Polnoe sobranie sochinenii*, ed. Natal'ia Sinkovskaia and Irina Sokolinskaia (Moscow: Muzyka, 1974), vol. xiv: *Pis'ma* (1887–8), 76.

6 Modeste Tchaikovsky, *The Life & Letters of Peter Ilich Tchaikovsky*, ed. Rosa Newmarch (London: J. Lane, 1906), 621.

7 Petr Il'ich Chaikovskii, *Polnoe sobranie sochinenii*, ed. Nina A. Viktorova and Boleslav Isaakovich Rabinovich (Moscow: Gosudarstvennoe muzykal'noe izdatel'stvo, 1961), vol. vi: *Pis'ma* (1866–77), 170–71.

8 Richard Taruskin, *Musorgsky: Eight Essays and an Epilogue* (Princeton University Press, 1993), 324.

9 Chernyshevskii, "Detstvo i otrochestvo," in S.P. Bychkov (ed.), *L.N. Tolstoi v russkoi kritike: sbornik statei* (Moscow: Gosudarstvennoe izdatel'stvo khudozhestvennoi literatury, 1952), 97.

10 Ibid.

CHAPTER 24

The Visual Arts

Maria Taroutina

On first reading Lev Tolstoy's *Anna Karenina*, the realist painter Ilya Repin (1844–1930) noted that the artist Mikhailov is "awfully similar to [Ivan] Kramskoi!"[1] In a memorable passage in the novel, the titular heroine, her lover Count Alexei Vronsky, and their friend the medieval specialist Golenishchev, visit Mikhailov's studio, where they view his unfinished painting *The Admonition of Pilate*. Although the aristocratic visitors praise Mikhailov's technical craftsmanship, they ultimately denounce his "materialist" portrayal of Christ and "the realism of the new school" (19:34–5, 42–3/Pt. 5, Chs. 9, 12).[2] This fictional episode was likely inspired by a series of real-life events, where controversial artworks by the likes of Repin, Kramskoi (1837–87), and Nikolai Ge (1831–94) were misunderstood, criticized, and even censored for their unflinching and at times irreverent visual "truth-telling" – an approach to art that Tolstoy valorized and promoted in his various novels, essays, and letters. Tolstoy took a keen interest in the visual arts and aesthetic debates of his time. In addition to Kramskoi, he formed close friendships with several of the most prominent artists of the day. This chapter examines Tolstoy's views on art, contextualizing and analyzing them in relation to the principal concerns and prevalent issues of the Russian art world of 1870–1900, and especially with reference to the theories and praxis of the Wanderers or Itinerants, henceforth referred to as the *Peredvizhniki*. It then closes with a brief discussion of how Tolstoy's aesthetic ideology was increasingly superseded at the end of the nineteenth century by alternative artistic philosophies, which subsequently paved the way for the twentieth-century Russian avant-garde.

The central tenets of Tolstoy's aesthetic theory are articulated most clearly in *What Is Art?* (1897–8), on which the author worked for nearly fifteen years. In Tolstoy's view, the first and arguably most important criterion of "good" art was the level of its "infectiousness" or the degree to which an artist could transmit to others "by means of movements, lines,

colors, sounds, images expressed in words" the same feelings and sentiments that he or she had initially experienced (30:65). Tolstoy maintained
that art was first and foremost a communicative – and not merely expres-
sive – medium and should therefore contain a "higher meaning" and a
"serious, fundamental idea."[3] More specifically, he believed that art had to
deliver a strong religious message or moral narrative, posing and answering
essential questions about lived experience, faith, and human progress:

> Art is not ... the manifestation of some mysterious idea of beauty or
> God ... it is not the expression of man's emotions by external signs; it is
> not the production of pleasing objects; and, above all, it is not pleasure; but
> it is a means of union among men, joining them together in the same
> feelings, and indispensable for the life and advancement toward well-being
> of individuals and of humanity. (30:66)

In other words, art should not be reduced to a mere pastime or entertainment for the elites, but instead ought to be beneficial and "accessible and
comprehensible to everyone" (30:109).

Tolstoy expressed a similar idea two decades earlier in *Anna Karenina*,
contrasting Anna's, Vronsky's, and Golenishchev's vacuous, superficial
tastes with Mikhailov's sincere dedication to uncovering a profound,
spiritual "revelation" in his painting (19:42–3, 434–5/Pt. 2, Ch. 12).
Although the artist's "elite" guests compliment his painterly craftsmanship,
they criticize his choice of religious subject matter, preferring a small,
casual genre scene of two boys fishing. Conversely, the "savage" and
inarticulate Mikhailov understood that the "mechanical ability to draw
and paint" could not be "independent of content ... as if one could draw
well something that was bad" (19:42, 434/Pt. 2, Ch. 12). Such a vision of
art was equally espoused by Kramskoi, who wrote that "the idea and the
idea alone creates technique and elevates it."[4] Lastly, the third key concept
in Tolstoy's aesthetic theory is that art must be fundamentally "sincere"
and should unite people around core Christian values, becoming "a means
by which humanity progresses toward unity and blessedness" (30:178).

Tolstoy lamented that these three crucial elements were "almost entirely
absent from our upper-class art, which is continually produced by artists
actuated by personal aims of covetousness or vanity" (30:150). According
to Tolstoy, the highly polished and technically accomplished paintings
produced by the students of the Imperial Academy of Arts in St.
Petersburg were ultimately false as they lacked any deeper meaning or
enduring message and instead depicted pastorals, "amorous" scenes, and
frivolous episodes from Greek mythology and Roman antiquity.

Figure 6   Henryk Siemiradzky, *Dance Amongst Daggers* (1881). Reproduced by permission
of the Tretyakov Gallery.

Indeed, popular academic artists such as Henryk Siemiradzky
(1843–1902) and Pavel Svedomsky (1848–1911) tended to closely adhere
to the established pictorial conventions of European Salon painting, producing artworks such as *Roman Orgy in the Time of the Caesars* (1872),
Dance Amongst Daggers (1881) (see Figure 6), and *Medusa* (1882), all of
which had little to do with high-minded spiritual or philosophical concerns and which depicted obscure subjects and exotic themes. As a result,
Tolstoy argued that such art was entirely foreign and largely inaccessible to
"the great majority of working-people" in Russia (30:83). Consequently,
rather than uniting Russian viewers around shared "feelings flowing from
the perception of our sonship to God and of the brotherhood of man," this
estranged "upper-class" art only sowed class divisions, "bewilderment and
contempt or indignation" (30:158).

Such views were not unique to Tolstoy and were widely shared by many
members of the progressive intelligentsia. For example, in 1863 the prominent critic Vladimir Stasov (1824–1906) wrote that "art should respond
only to real feelings and ideas, and should not be served up like some tasty
dessert one can well do without."[5] In place of "pretense and imitation,"
Stasov advocated that art should be "authentic, genuine, and not trivial."[6]
Almost a decade earlier, in his 1855 dissertation titled "The Aesthetic
Relation of Art to Reality," Nikolai Chernyshevsky (1828–89) similarly
argued that rather than concern itself with depicting the "fantastic," the
"ideal," and the "beautiful," art should offer profound insights into lived

reality and the character, behavior, and condition of human beings in society.[7] Much like Tolstoy, he believed that the supreme aim of art was to elevate and ennoble all humanity and not merely to reflect the tastes of the privileged classes.

The most scathing and urgent critique of the official art establishment was articulated by Ivan Dmitriev (1840–67) in 1863 and triggered a series of events that had important and long-lasting implications for the Russian art world. In an article published in the newspaper *The Spark* (*Iskra*), Dmitriev wrote that:

> Art has not been of any use to the people, has not given any kind of content, because it itself has been extremely insipid, and has not introduced any element of education into life. From the very beginning it has been here an entertainment for experts and the rich and remains entertainment still now. It is neither an activity, nor a genuine necessity, but just a harmful triviality... Art should be a benefit to the people, a necessity of the people, but it obviously will not attain these results with useless, ancient habits.[8]

A few weeks after the publication of Dmitriev's article, a group of fourteen art students, led by Kramskoi, officially withdrew from the Imperial Academy of Arts on the grounds that the assigned topic for the prestigious Gold Medal competition was too rigid and stunted their creative vision. They went on to form the St. Petersburg Artel, an independent artistic collective that was meant to ensure the professional and economic autonomy of its members. This dramatic secession came to be referred to as the "Rebellion of the Fourteen" and was soon followed by the establishment of the larger and more far-reaching Society of Traveling Art Exhibitions (*Tovarishchestvo peredvizhnykh khudozhestvennykh vystavok*) in September of 1870 with Kramskoi and Ge at its helm. The society operated for over five decades until 1923 and counted among its members some of the most prominent and respected artists of the day, including Repin, Vasily Polenov, Vasily Perov, Arkhip Kuindzhi, Ivan Shishkin, Vasily Surikov, Viktor Vasnetsov, Alexei Savrasov, Isaac Levitan, Valentin Serov, Nikolai Yaroshenko, Vladimir Makovsky, and Grigory Myasoedov.

Like the "Rebellious Fourteen," the *Peredvizhniki* challenged the artistic dictatorship and economic monopoly of the Academy and actively embraced Tolstoy's call for an art inflected with moral purpose that would be universally accessible to all. In its founding charter, the group stipulated that the principal reason for its formation was "to provide the inhabitants of the provinces with the opportunity to keep up with the achievements of Russian art."[9] In other words, their main goal was to make art readily available to people of all walks of life beyond the two capitals of Moscow and St. Petersburg. In addition, they also sought to "serve society" by building awareness of the most acute social problems plaguing Russia in the second half of the nineteenth century in the hopes of encouraging people to take action against such injustices.[10] Thus various *Peredvizhnik* paintings addressed highly polemical and controversial topics, such as revolutionary activism, bureaucratic and clerical corruption, drunkenness, poverty, and exploitation of the lower classes, as well as providing new, unorthodox interpretations of established religious narratives and historical events. Such an explicitly civic-minded project helped to ensure wide-spread support for the *Peredvizhniki* among the "thinking" Russian public, which felt that they represented the birth of a new national school of art, one that would no longer passively imitate the Western tradition.[11] The wealthy industrialist Pavel Tretyakov (1832–98) began to actively commission and collect *Peredvizhnik* artworks in order to create the first Museum of Russian Art, which later became known as the Tretyakov Gallery.

However, it would be naïve to assume that the *Peredvizhnik* enterprise was driven exclusively by such lofty, ideological objectives. In reality it was also fueled by more pragmatic considerations of finding new markets for their art beyond the nobility of the two capitals and expanding their buying public to the growing professional classes in the Russian provinces. This helps to explain why a large number of the works exhibited at the *Peredvyhznye* exhibitions did not represent contentious subject matter and instead depicted landscapes, domestic portraits, and neutral genre scenes. The works that did tackle more polemical topics often provoked vociferous public outcry and were censored and removed from exhibitions by state authorities. In multiple instances, Tolstoy would immediately come to the artists' defense, supporting and encouraging them in a private capacity, but also advocating for them more publicly through his various publications and correspondence with influential art world stakeholders such as Tretyakov and Stasov.

Thus, for example, at the time that Kramskoi's controversial realist masterpiece, *Christ in the Wilderness* (1872; Figure 7), was first displayed at the Second Peredvizhnik Exhibition in December of 1872, the artist was living on Tolstoy's estate and working on the latter's celebrated portrait (see Chapter 39). *Christ in the Wilderness* generated a number of negative responses both among the cultural elites and in the press at the time, with various commentators labelling Kramskoi's Christ "ugly," "heretical," and "infected by positivism."[12] Indeed, the work provocatively rejected the accepted pictorial norms of Orthodox iconography. In lieu of a noble, divine figure with a beautiful physiognomy, Kramskoi depicted a haggard, exhausted, and conflicted human Christ. Sitting on a boulder in the middle of a rocky, deserted landscape, Kramskoi's Christ is thin and hunched over, his hair is disheveled, his thin beard is unkempt, his clothes are ragged, and his eyes are sunken as he gazes blankly at the ground before him. It is no surprise that such an atypical portrayal of a sacred figure was almost immediately perceived by conservative critics as irreverent and intentionally subversive. By contrast, Tolstoy maintained that he "knew no better Christ" in the history of art.[13] Significantly, it was at Yasnaya Polyana that Kramskoi first conceived another work on the subject of Christ: *Laughter (Hail, King of the Jews)* (1870s; Figure 8) – a large-scale painting in which Christ is scorned by the people of Jerusalem in the presence of Pilate and which most probably inspired Mikhailov's fictional version of *The Admonition of Pilate*.

Figure 7   Ivan Kramskoi, *Christ in the Wilderness* (1872). Reproduced by permission of the Tretyakov Gallery.

Figure 8   Ivan Kramskoi, *Laughter (Hail, King of the Jews)* (1870s). Reproduced by
permission of the State Russian Museum.

Other leading *Peredvizhniki* such as Nikolai Ge and Ilya Repin were
likewise regular visitors at Tolstoy's estate and systematically engaged with
his aesthetic theories. Like Kramskoi, they also produced iconic portraits of
the writer and took his pronouncements on their art extremely seriously.
For instance, when Tolstoy criticized Repin's preparatory sketches for his
monumental painting of *The Zaporozhian Cossacks Writing a Letter to the
Turkish Sultan* (1880–91) during a visit to the artist's studio in October of
1880, the latter immediately abandoned work on this piece for over a
decade.

Similarly, Ge was deeply influenced by Tolstoy's newfound aesthetically
minimalist Christology, which the writer had developed in the 1880s.[14]
Ge created his own painterly equivalent with a cycle of large-scale paintings
devoted to the events of the Passion, such as the now iconic *What Is Truth?*
(1890; Figure 9), *Golgotha* (1893), and *Crucifixion* (1894). In these representations, Christ is shown with wild, disheveled hair, uncomely angular
features, sunken cheeks, and dark, beady eyes. Much like Kramskoi's
Christ in the Wilderness, Ge's *What Is Truth?* provoked a furor when it

Figure 9   Nikolai Ge, *What Is Truth?* (1890). Reproduced by permission of the
Tretyakov Gallery.

was first publicly displayed at the Eighteenth Peredvizhnik Exhibition in
1890. Tsar Alexander III called the painting "repulsive" and ordered it to
be immediately removed.[15] Tolstoy, however, actively defended Ge's
masterpiece both in his private correspondence and in the press, writing
that "the merit of the picture, in my opinion, consists in the fact that it is
true (realistic, as is now said) in the most authentic sense of the word.
Christ is not such as would be pleasant to look at but precisely as someone
must be who has been tortured all night and is still being tortured."[16]

While Tolstoy's authority with the *Peredvizhniki* – and in the Russian
art world more broadly – remained virtually unchallenged throughout the
1870s and 1880s, by the late 1890s a younger generation of artists and
critics began to actively question and reject the writer's theory of art, which
they increasingly viewed as inflexible, conservative, and retrograde. For
example, the Symbolist artist Mikhail Vrubel (1856–1910) claimed that

Tolstoy's dogmatic approach to art and his prescriptive religiosity resulted in the oppression of the human spirit and the creative impulse. Vrubel complained that "the agreeable herd (*milye skoty*), headed by Tolstoy" obstinately refused to accept new developments in and alternative approaches to art. On the contrary, "with rigid malice" Tolstoy "protects his half-vision from the bright light. Faced with the pathetic, he sighs after the commonplaces of blind naturalism."[17] Similarly, the aestheticist *World of Art* (*Mir Iskusstva*) group enthusiastically adopted an "art for art's sake" stance, insisting in their published manifesto that in "beauty [lies] the great justification of humanity" and the principal "strength of art consists precisely in the fact that it is an aim in itself" and need not embrace any social, political, or moral purpose, or be clear, sincere, and nationalist.[18]

Even within the ranks of the *Peredvizhniki*, a younger generation of artists such as Valentin Serov (1865–1911) and Isaak Levitan (1860–1900) began to progressively privilege aesthetic considerations over moralistic imperatives and embraced Impressionist painterly techniques and content, despite continuing to exhibit their works alongside their older colleagues. Finally, by the close of the century, Repin, who had been a great admirer and devotee of Tolstoy for much of his life, would come to criticize the writer's rigid views on art, writing in 1894 that there is "a disease among us, Russian artists, jammed with literature. We do not have a burning, childlike love of form ... Our salvation is in form, in the living beauty of nature, but we crawl to philosophy, to morality ... How tiring it is. I am sure that the next generation of artists won't give a toss about tendentiousness, about the search for an idea, about intellectualizing."[19] Ironically, by the time that Tolstoy published *What is Art?*, a tectonic aesthetic shift was already under way in the Russian art world, one that would dramatically alter the path of Russian painting, paving the way for twentieth-century Russian modernism and the historical avant-garde.

Notes

1 Ilya Repin, letter to Vladimir Stasov, April 12, 1878, in *Il'ia Repin – Vladimir Stasov: Perepiska 1871–1906*, ed. Andrei Lebedev, 3 vols. (Moscow: Iskusstvo, 1949), vol. 1, 29.

2 Lev Tolstoy, *Anna Karenina*, trans. Marian Schwartz (New Haven, CT: Yale University Press, 2014), 428, 434–5.

3 S.A. Tolstaia, *Moia zhizn'*, ed. V.B. Remizov et al., 2 vols. (Moscow: Kuchkovo pole, 2011), vol. 1, 323.

4 Ivan Kramskoi, letter to Ilya Repin, February 23, 1874, in Ivan Kramskoi, *Pis'ma*, 2 vols. (Moscow: OGIZ-IZOGIZ, 1937), vol. II, 240.

5 Vladimir Stasov, "Akademicheskaia vystavka 1863 goda," in *V.V. Stasov: Izbrannye sochineniia v trekh tomakh: zhivopis', skul'ptura, muzyka* (Moscow: Iskusstvo, 1952), vol. I, 120.

6 Ibid.

7 Nikolai Chernyshevsky, *Esteticheskie otnosheniia iskusstva k deistvitel'nosti* (Moscow: Gosudarstvennoe izdatel'stvo khudozhestvennoi literaturu, 1955), 108–29.

8 Ivan Dmitriev, "*Rassharkivaiushcheesia* iskustvo (po povodu godichnoi vystavki v akademii khudozhestv)," *Iskra* 5:37–8 (September 27 to October 4, 1863), 527.

9 "Draft Statutes of the Association of Traveling Art Exhibits," in Elizabeth Valkenier, *Russian Realist Art: The State and Society; the Peredvizhniki and Their Tradition* (New York: Columbia University Press, 1989), 226.

10 Valkenier, *Russian Realist Art*, 40

11 Ibid.

12 Ivan Kramskoi, letter to Fedor Vasilev, February 13, 1873 in *Pisma, Stat'i: Ivan Nikolaevich Kramskoi*, ed. Sofiia Noevna Gol'dshtein, 2 vols. (Moscow: Iskusstvo, 1965–6), vol. I, 155.

13 Lev Tolstoy, letter to Pavel Tretyakov, June 19, 1894, in *L.N. Tolstoi i khudozhniki: Tolstoi ob iskusstve. Pis'ma, dnevniki, vospominaniia*, ed. I.A. Brodskii (Moscow: Iskusstvo, 1978), 122.

14 For a detailed discussion of this subject, see Jefferson Gatrall, "Tolstoy, Ge, and Two Pilates: A Tale of the Interarts," in Rosalind P. Blakesley and Magaret Samu (eds.), *From Realism to the Silver Age: New Studies in Russian Artistic Culture* (Dekalb: Northern Illinois University Press, 2014), 79–93.

15 Alexander III, quoted in Nikolai Nikolaevich Ge, *Pis'ma, stat'i, kritika, vospominania sovremennikov*, ed. Natalia Zograf (Moscow: Iskusstvo, 1978), 352n57.

16 Lev Tolstoy, letter to George Kennan, August 8, 1890, in Ge, *Pis'ma, stat'i, kritika*, 149–50.

17 Mikhail Vrubel, letter to Ekaterina Ge, February 1902, in Vrubel', *Perepiska, vospominaniia o khudozhnike*, ed. E.P. Gomberg-Verzhbinskaia et al., 2nd edn (Leningrad: Iskusstvo, 1976), 95.

18 Sergei Diaghilev et al., "Slozhnye voprosy. Vechnaia bor'ba," *Mir Iskusstva* 1–2 (1899), 15.

19 Ilya Repin, letter to E.P. Antokol'skii, August 7, 1894, in Ilya Repin, *Izbrannye pis'ma, 1867–1930*, ed. I.A. Brodskii, 2 vols. (Moscow: Iskusstvo, 1969), vol. II, 74.

PART IV

Science and Technology

CHAPTER 25

The Mechanized World

Julia Vaingurt

Chekhov's well-known dictum that "there is more love for humanity in electricity and steam than in chastity and refraining from meat" implicitly categorizes Tolstoy's prescriptions for a good life as incompatible with technological progress. Indeed, Tolstoy often expressed skepticism about mechanical solutions to human problems. In *Anna Karenina* (1875–8), for example, he launches parallel critiques of Russia's hasty embrace of the Industrial Revolution and of the view of artistry as merely the acquisition of techniques; in "Progress and the Definition of Education" (1862) Tolstoy's critique of the concept of progress is central to his dim view of Western-style education; and, finally, in his *Diaries*, his disagreements with socialists center on his skepticism vis-à-vis the value of modern technology.

However, certain new technologies did elicit Tolstoy's appreciation. In particular, Tolstoy was quite enthusiastic about the bicycle, which he learned to ride at the age of sixty-seven; photography, of which he was both a subject and practitioner; and the phonograph, which he used on a number of memorable occasions. Tolstoy corresponded with Thomas Edison and even recorded several of his works on Edison's phonograph for posterity. He made plans for screen adaptations of his works, and was one of the first world celebrities to allow paparazzi to immortalize his image on film. Tolstoy's attitude toward his era's unprecedented technological advances might seem contradictory, but, as this chapter will propose, his acceptance of some modern technologies and rejection of others was in fact consistent with his philosophy of life and the place of creativity in it.

Tolstoy conceived of technology as applied science; and he conceived of science and art as two spheres of human creativity that could be used for good or ill. In "The End of the Century" (1905), Tolstoy asserted:

> Civilization's defenders make an unconscious and sometimes even a conscious mistake, treating civilization, which is only a means, as an end in

itself, and believing that it is always a blessing. But it will only be truly good when the forces governing society are good. Explosives are beneficial when used for laying tracks, but are deadly in bombs. Iron is useful in plows, but deadly in bullets or prison locks. (36:108)

In his evaluation of technology (and art), Tolstoy rejected instrumental rationality, that is, the application of such purely formal measures as efficiency, cost-effectiveness, or technical mastery. According to Tolstoy, any activity must serve – as measurable by time-tested, universal parameters – an end other than itself: first and foremost, the promotion of human betterment. He appreciated modern technologies that did not trumpet the forward march of time or illusory notions of progress, but, in fact, *marked* progress: ones that preserved the past and cultural memory, promoted spiritual connection, and recorded humanity's fumbling yet persistent striving toward the moral absolute.

The Menacing Poetics of Railways

Chekhov was not alone in deeming Tolstoy a foe to modernity. Other contemporaries – fervent believers in technology's potential to serve the common good – expressed their sometimes vehement disagreement with Tolstoy's teachings. For example, Nikolai Fyodorov, the father of Russian cosmism,[1] decried Tolstoy's proselytizing of "inaction" (*nedelanie*), while the engineer Pyotr Engelmeier, Russia's first major espouser of the positivistic "philosophy of technology" (the title of one of his monographs), devoted a whole pamphlet to *A Critique of the Scientific and Aesthetic Views of Count L.N. Tolstoy* (1898). There he debunked non-resistance to evil as foreclosing any technological intervention, and Tolstoy's theory of creativity as conflating *useful* with *good*, which, in Engelmeier's view, precludes the free choice and experimentation so crucial to any technological process.[2] Supporting this view of Tolstoy as a Luddite, scholars have since repeatedly adduced the pernicious role of the train, an agent of corruption, destruction, and social coercion, in such major texts as *Anna Karenina*, *Resurrection*, and *The Kreutzer Sonata*.

We in the twenty-first century believe we live in an age of unprecedented technological acceleration. But it was in the nineteenth century – much of it spanned by Tolstoy's long life – that technological advancement made its swiftest strides, yielding, according to the calculations of the sociologist P. Sorokin, more innovations and discoveries than all the preceding centuries put together (specifically, 8,527). Steamboats and

automobiles transformed the perception of time and space, while telephones, telegraphs, cinema, radio, and other modern uses of electromag-
netic energy completely altered the very texture of everyday life.[3] The most
transformative technology of the nineteenth century, however, was arguably the railway system, apotheosizing as it did the Industrial Revolution,
as both its spectacular product and its fearsome dynamo.

In Russia, the rapid development of the railway network was conditioned by the country's great size and the dissolution of its feudal system.
The train was not only a vehicle of progress, transporting people with
speed and convenience, disseminating ideas, and eroding local differences;
it also epitomized class mobility and antagonism. Tolstoy's use of the train
to symbolize inexorable, destructive modernity was hardly unique in this
period. Without question, Tolstoy shared with Dostoevsky the fear, con-
veyed so eloquently by Lebedev, *The Idiot*'s harbinger of "the age of vices
and railroads," that "carts bringing bread to all mankind without a moral
basis for their action, could in absolute cold-blood debar a significant part
of humanity from the enjoyment of that which they bring."[4] Tolstoy
would often express nearly the same thought, but his emphasis would be
different. When Dostoevsky in *The Idiot* (and elsewhere) foregrounds
equity, he does so to cast doubt on it as a concept; any materialist utopia
is doomed to fail, to forfeit on its unfeasible promise of universal emancipation and fulfillment. Tolstoy did not share this categorical rejection of
social restructuring.

What is, for Dostoevsky, a more or less ideological objection becomes,
in Tolstoy's rendering, a sociological or at least technical one – the
exacerbation of class inequality. In *What Then Must We Do?* (1884–6)
Tolstoy contends that modern conveniences satisfy the needs of the upper
classes at the expense of the great masses of the people:

> All these successes are very wonderful, but by some unfortunate accident
> admitted by scientists themselves – up to now these successes have not
> improved the condition of the labourer but rather have made it worse. If a
> workman instead of walking can go by train, on the other hand the railroad
> has consumed his forest, carried away the grain from under his nose, and
> brought him to a condition not far removed from slavery to those who own
> the railroad ... If there are telegraph stations which he is not forbidden to
> use but which his means do not allow him to use, on the other hand his
> produce, as soon as the price is rising, thanks to the telegraph system gets
> bought up from under his nose by capitalists before the labourer hears of
> the demand there is for it. (25:477)[5]

Tolstoy bemoans the fact that, despite creating as many problems as
solutions, technological advancements, nevertheless, encourage self-

congratulation, self-satisfaction, and complacency: "Raptures over ourselves are so often repeated, we are so overjoyed at ourselves, that we are
seriously convinced ... that science and art never made such progress as in
our time" (25:413).[6] For Tolstoy, however, real betterment comes only
from *dis*satisfaction with oneself. When Engelmeier sent Tolstoy his
manuscript *Inventions and Patents: A Guide for Inventors*, Tolstoy replied
with a brief positive review that emphasized self-criticism as the necessary
trait of any good creator: "Every year I am visited by several such inventors,
and I always feel sorry for the abnormal spiritual condition which most of
them have to endure ... Your book can be of benefit to those of them who
haven't lost their ability to approach their projects critically, and that's why
I wish it success" (70:118–19). Despite their disagreements, Engelmeier
published this response as the foreword to his book, in effect concurring
with Tolstoy on the importance of self-criticism. Ilya Kliger identifies this
imperative for perpetual discontent and reassessment, this need to ever
"envision another world," as central to Tolstoy's "alternative" modernity,
his "modernity of dissatisfaction and critique."[7]

Enhancement vs. Betterment

As a uniquely modern thinker, Tolstoy was not alien to two central
preoccupations of modernity: movement and improvement. He did, however, invest these terms with his own meaning in accord with his moral
philosophy. The ethically conceived life had to be distinguished from mere
"accidental" enhancements. Deconstructing the idea of historical or political progress, as well as Darwinian evolutionary theory, Tolstoy nevertheless contended that the essence of life is movement: "I see no necessity of
finding common laws for history, independently of the impossibility of
finding them ... The law of progress, or perfectibility, is written in the
soul of each human being, and is transferred to history only through error"
(8:333).[8] Here and in general, Tolstoy counterposes external, hence accidental improvements (*usovershentsvovaniia*) to internal growth or "perfection" (*sovershenstvovanie*);[9] the formal, mechanical, and accidental to the
substantive, organic, and lawful.[10]

Tolstoy thought it crucial to learn the difference between the realm of
appearances and the realm of essences, insofar as humanity's development
lay in the movement from the former to the latter. As he puts it in *What
Then Must We Do?*: "It only seems that mankind is occupied with
commerce, treaties, wars, sciences, and arts, only one thing is important
to humanity, and it is doing only that one thing: it is elucidating to itself

[*uiasniaet sebe*] the moral laws by which it lives"(25:130).[11] In one of his diaries, Tolstoy underscores that one's attuned presence in the world and the sharing of its benefits are two interconnected preconditions of inner development: "the temporary, spatial world, which has no meaning in itself . . . is necessary for the process of the elucidation of consciousness [*uiasnenie soznaniia*]. It was Mohammed, I think, who said: God did not want to enjoy the goodness of life alone, and so he gave it to beings like him" (56:60).

"True" science, including its applied forms, for Tolstoy serves this collective spiritual growth. In "Science and Art" (1890–1), this alleged hater of technological advancement confesses its necessity: "It is natural to think and say that it would have been better for sciences and arts not to exist at all than to be sustained by such sacrifices . . . It is natural to think and say so, but this would be unfair" (30:27). Tolstoy must give the arts and sciences their due: they may not contribute to historical or political progress, which does not exist, but they do contribute to that other, most essential movement, the process by which consciousness develops and unifies in its striving toward the moral absolute. First, Tolstoy credits technologies with embodying, without any conscious intent on their creators' part, the internal drive toward the unification of mankind: "The good lies only in the unity and brotherhood of all. This truth is unconsciously confirmed by the installation of methods of communication, telegraphs, telephones, the press, the ever-increasing accessibility of the benefits of this world to all people" (30:386).

Second, Tolstoy concedes that modern technologies do not just manifest the movement of humanity toward unification; they *enact* it by embodying the collection, preservation, and transmission of knowledge from generation to generation:

> Everything we live by, everything that gives us joy and pride, everything, from primitive huts and spades to railways, opera, and the Eiffel Tower, is nothing but the consequence of the transmission of knowledge. The most complex creation, like the Eiffel Tower, is nothing but knowledge that has been transmitted from generation to generation of how to dig, weld, forge, arrange iron into bars, nuts, screws, etc. . . . Everything that distinguishes . . . human from animal life is the result of the transmission of knowledge. (30:48)

Tolstoy admires the Eiffel Tower, the emblem par excellence of modernity and technological prowess, because he recognizes in it that which constitutes the essence of human life: solidarity and the concerted movement toward knowledge. Notably, Tolstoy's description omits whatever use-value the tower might have; in his view, it stands primarily as a visual record of movement and labor. Thus we find Tolstoy crediting the Eiffel Tower with the same beneficence he finds in good art: "art is a tool of communication, hence of progress, i.e., of the forward movement of humanity toward perfection" (30:321). Tolstoy's positive conception of technology, then, would see it merge with art: as a tool of human communication, art is technological; as the expression of this communication, the Eiffel Tower is artistic.

Tolstoy's insistence that only such technologies are beneficent as promote reflection on human communality anticipates Heidegger's distinction between thing and gathering, or the philosopher of technology Albert Borgmann's between thing and device. Tolstoy's appreciation for technology is tempered by his suspicion of the *division* of labor, which is hardly communal, and, as much to Tolstoy as to Marx, inherently alienating and exploitative. "I ought to use the products of others' labor as little as possible and labor myself as much as possible" (25:274). This would explain his simultaneous antipathy for the train and love of another revolutionary technology of the period – the bicycle, which you have to pedal yourself, which incorporates you into the natural environment, and which harbors, Tolstoy thought, a "natural holy foolishness" (*estestvennoe iurodstvo*, 53:24).

Collective Memory

Tolstoy had a certain sympathy for Fyodorov's dream of humanity coming together in the technological pursuit of a "common task," but not for the goal of physical resurrection he advocated. For Tolstoy, physical immortality would be redundant, since the transmission of knowledge, i.e. collective memory, already ensures functional immortality. This might explain Tolstoy's appreciation for the new recording technologies, the phonograph, photography, motion pictures: they make the interrelated functions of *techne* – the facilitating and registering of communication and the enhancement of memory – explicit.

Tolstoy was well aware of the awkwardness recorded by the phonograph, even complaining about it in his diary. And yet, when Edison sent him a phonograph and requested that he use it to record "some idea that would move humanity forward," Tolstoy threw himself entirely into the task. As Tolstoy's personal doctor, Makovitsky, describes in his diary: "Lev Nikolaevich was nervous for days before [the phonograph's arrival]; today he practiced before speaking into it. Spoke well in

Russian and French; but in English it did not come out too well, he stumbled in two places. Tomorrow will try again."[12] Tolstoy might have sought to diminish these stumbles and infelicities, but likely also appreciated them as markers of spontaneity and authenticity; after all, he found posed photographs distasteful, but admired the candid photographs his wife took of him. As registered in Edison's phonograph album, Tolstoy hailed the invention with a particular emphasis on its fixing of vocal *expression*:

> The greatest power of the world is thought. The more forms there are of expressing thought the more this power manifests itself. The invention of printing made an epoch in the history of humanity, another will be made by the telephone and especially the phonograph which is the most efficacious and striking form of fixing and immortalizing not only the words but also the expression of the voice which pronounces them.[13]

Tolstoy here harbors hope that record technologies might offer traces of interiority as transmitted in shades of voice; might reveal, retain, and communicate differences, unrepeatable and irreducible to symbolic language.

Tolstoy's choice of the fable "The Penitent Sinner" for his first-ever phonographic recording (February 1895) intimates the relationship between voice technologies and collective memory. In this story, a sinner finds himself at the locked gates of heaven and must use his power of speech to communicate with those on the other side, specifically, to stir memories that might move the hearts of saints. Appealing to John the Evangelist, the sinner reminds him of his teachings of love. Touched by this reminder, John opens the door to let the sinner in. It seems likely that the fable's dynamic of oral communication, "sight unseen," recommended itself to Tolstoy as a prototype for the moral use to which the phonograph might be put. Tolstoy's complementary pairing of the fable and the phonograph offers a succinct example of how to derive benefit from technology in general: invest it with a moral purpose, commune through it with others, use it to reflect upon and pass along the spiritual aims of humanity.

Notes

1 Russian cosmism was a philosophical movement that attempted to reconcile a Christian worldview and scientific thought. Central to its workings was the idea of active evolution, i.e., humans' intervention in their own evolution as well as organization and regulation of their natural environment in accordance

with the Christian ethics. Cosmists looked forward to the unification of humankind, physical resurrection of the dead, and abolishment of death, as well as free movement in cosmic space.

2 See M. Gel'fond, "N.F. Fedorov i L.N. Tolstoi: 'Obshchee delo' protiv 'ne-delaniia,'" https://cyberleninka.ru/article/n/n-f-fedorov-i-l-n-tolstoy-obschee-delo-protiv-ne-delaniya-grani-filosofskoy-kritiki-idei-nenasiliya-v-russkoy-duhov noy-kulture/viewer; V. Gorokhov, *Tekhnika i kul'tura: vozniknovenie filosfii tekhniki v Rossii i Germanii v kontse XIX–nachale XX stoletiia* (Moscow: Logos, 2010).

3 P. Sorokin, *Social and Cultural Dynamics: A Study of Change in Major Systems of Art, Truth, Ethics, Law and Social Relationships* (New York: Routledge, 2017), 244.

4 F. Dostoevsky, *The Idiot*, trans. Alan Myers (Oxford University Press, 1992), 244.

5 L. Tolstoy, *What Then Must We Do?*, trans. Aylmer Maude (Hartland: Green Classics, 1991), 131.

6 Ibid., 130.

7 I. Kliger, *The Narrative Shape of Truth: Veridiction in Modern European Literature* (University Park: Pennsylvania State University Press, 2011), 169.

8 L. Tolstoy, *Pedagogical Articles*, trans. Leo Wiener (Boston: Dana Estes, 1904), 163.

9 *Usovershentsvovanie* and *sovershenstvovanie* share the same Russian root denoting "perfection," but the former is used (and was used already in Tolstoy's time) to refer to improvement of a specifically technical, instrumental nature, often with regard to machinery – an "upgrade." Using it in this particular, commonly accepted meaning, Tolstoy is careful to sound a note of irony: "The artist of the future will not know the obscenity of technical improvements that conceal an absence of substance" (30:407).

10 "The railway is to adventure what a brothel is to love" – Tolstoy once quipped in a letter to Turgenev – "equally convenient, but also equally mechanistic and killingly monotonous" (60:170).

11 Tolstoy, *What Then Must We Do?*, 41.

12 Quoted in A. Sergeenko, "Perepiska Tolstogo s T. Edisonom," in *L.N. Tolstoi* (Izd-vo AN SSSR, 1939), kn. 11, 334.

13 "Extracts from the Edison Phonograph Album [Leo Tolstoy and Arthur Nikish]." Rodgers and Hammerstein Archives of Recorded Sound, New York Public Library, http://digitalcollections.nypl.org/items/91583395-e028-999e-e040-e00a18060d4e.

CHAPTER 26

The Natural World

Thomas Newlin

The earliest extant piece of writing by Tolstoy is a series of miniature portraits of various wild and domestic birds – eagle, falcon, owl, parrot, peacock, hummingbird, rooster – that he composed in 1835, at age six or seven. Assembled under the general rubric "Natural History," they were part of a joint literary venture that he had conjured up with his three older brothers. Laconic and factual, they display a nascent impulse toward didacticism ("The eagle is the tsar of birds. They say of it that a boy began to tease it. It got angry and pecked him to death," 90:93), and hint in form and tone at the animal fables that he would write in the early 1870s for his primers for peasant children. These youthful natural-historical vignettes mark the formal beginning of Tolstoy's lifelong engagement as a writer and thinker with the natural world.

Tolstoy could hardly be called a "naturalist" in a scientific or even an amateur sense: he kept no lists or notes of the birds he bagged or spotted; he pressed no flowers; he did not dissect anything, mount anything, or place anything under a microscope; he apparently never even bothered to read Sergei Aksakov's famous fishing or hunting notes. But he spent much of his life outdoors and was in constant and often charged "contact," to use Thoreau's term, with nature – as a hunter, a farmer, a forester, a would-be peasant, a beekeeper, an inveterate long-distance walker, a skilled horseback rider, and (according to Turgenev) a peerless horse whisperer. Tolstoy's bodily, day-to-day engagement with nature shaped who he was and how he conceived of himself; it is reflected, abundantly, in what he wrote. The natural world remained an essential touchstone for Tolstoy for the whole of his life – a reservoir and measure of what was authentic and good. Yet as he grew older this regard was tinged with ambivalence. He came to believe that not everything that was natural (war, violence, predation, sex) was necessarily good, and he apparently doubted whether humans could live in a way that was at once fully natural and fully moral. This is a central paradox of Tolstoy's thinking.

Green Origins

Tolstoy went to some lengths to fashion a "green" creation myth about himself. The ancestral estate where he was born bore the evocatively verdant name Yasnaya Polyana, or "Clear Glade" ("yasnaya" probably derived from the word for ash tree, *yasen*). This was the place that Tolstoy, for the whole of his life, considered home. "Without my Yasnaya Polyana," he wrote, "I am hard put to imagine Russia, or my relationship to her" (5:262). He later fetishized the exact spot where he came into the world – a green Moroccan leather couch – as a kind of originary *locus amoenus*, and insisted that his wife give birth to their thirteen children there as well. Although the wing of the house where he breathed his first breath was dismantled and carted off in the 1850s as payment for a gambling debt, Tolstoy turned this ignominious and uni-dyllic biographical detail to his own advantage, employing it as another subtle way to naturalize his birth: "You see that larch," he would remark to the uninitiated, "right over there where those branches are was the room where I was born."[1]

Two other childhood memories that Tolstoy first recounted in 1903 – the intertwined stories of the green stick and the ant brotherhood – involved a similar sort of mythopoetic and "green" self-fashioning. Both these constructs are manifestly biological, but at the same time bespeak a utopian desire on Tolstoy's part to transcend biology. When he was five, he claimed, his eldest brother told his siblings he was privy to a secret that would lead to universal love and happiness and make everyone "ant brothers." This secret was inscribed on a green stick buried in the ravine in the woods at Yasnaya Polyana. The three boys would play at being "ant brothers," and as an old man Tolstoy professed an abiding faith in "the ideal of the ant brothers clinging lovingly to each other – not just under two chairs draped with blankets, but under the whole canopy of the heavens that stretches over all the people of the world" (34:386–7). While the brothers did not unearth the green stick, it could be said that Tolstoy spent the better part of his life attempting to realize its fecund and revelatory potential – to fathom and express, in writing, the salvific if mute truth inherent in nature. He was laid to rest, in accordance with his wishes, at the site where the green stick was supposedly buried. Gazing at the grassy mound that marks Tolstoy's grave, we cannot help but be struck by the similarity between his birthplace and his final resting place: here, as a mythopoetic construct, his life in nature comes full circle.

Self and God in Nature

Tolstoy's fiction abounds in potent moments that feature a figure – almost invariably male, and typically a permutation of Tolstoy himself – in nature's midst: the young Nikolenka in *Childhood* (1852), absorbed in watching an army of ants and a fluttering butterfly while the din of the hunt echoes in the background; Olenin in the stag's lair in *The Cossacks* (1853–63), giving himself up in masochistic ecstasy to mosquitoes; in *War and Peace* (1865–9) Andrei Bolkonsky's fateful encounter with the oak tree, or Nikolai Rostov's exhilarating but vaguely disquieting face-off with a wolf, or the moment when the captive Pierre Bezukhov, sitting Buddha-like under the stars and taking in the vastness of the sky and forests and fields before him, begins laughing uproariously at the pretense of his confinement; in *Anna Karenina* (1875–8) Levin out mowing, in an imperfect but exhilarating communion with nature and his fellow men, or stretched out on an unmown patch of grass at the edge of an aspen wood, musing on the nature of goodness and absentmindedly helping a solitary bug move from one blade of grass to another. These scenes generally involve a positive suspension of self-consciousness that allows for a momentary dissolution or expansion of the solitary self into a greater "All" – into an all-encompassing and benevolent natural world that for Tolstoy is more or less synonymous with God. Tolstoy's conception of God, as Nikolai Berdiaev noted, is "a peculiar form of pantheism." The impersonal but animating and unifying force that he repeatedly evokes (but seldom invokes) in his fiction "is not a being, but rather a law, diffused through everything as a divine principle."[2]

In 1894 Tolstoy famously preached that "the kingdom of God is within you." But to find God in his works we almost always need to go outdoors. Indeed, those characters who have little contact with nature – the Kuragins in *War and Peace*, for instance – tend to be morally bereft, and are ultimately consumed by their own selfishness. It is worth noting that Tolstoy wrote relatively few works that take place more or less entirely indoors. Those that do, such as *The Death of Ivan Ilyich* (1886) or *The Kreutzer Sonata* (1889), feel acutely claustrophobic, and the strict confinement of these narratives to an artificial, man-made realm heightens and accentuates the spiritual agony of their protagonists. It is as if Tolstoy purposely and almost cruelly sought to deny his characters (and his readers) that psychic "safety valve" that plays such an important role in so many of his other works – that is, access to the redemptive, self-annihilating world of nature.

War and Peace in Nature

It would be misleading to suggest that Tolstoy's view of nature – or of those who live relatively "natural" lives – was fixed or uniformly sanguine. In "A Few Words about *War and Peace*" (1868), he mused darkly on the apparent naturalness of war itself, and signaled his ambivalence about the "zoological laws" driving human and animal behavior:

> Why did millions of people kill one another when it has been known since the world began that it is physically and morally wrong to do so? Because it was such an inevitable necessity that in doing it men fulfilled the elemental zoological law which bees fulfill when they kill one another in the autumn, and which causes male animals to destroy one another. One can give no other reply to that terrible question. (16:14)

It is unclear whether Tolstoy actually ever read Darwin's *On the Origin of Species* (1859), even though he was friends with Sergei Rachinsky, the book's first Russian translator. But even if they came to him second hand, Darwin's ideas (see Chapter 27 in this volume) were evidently unsettling and stimulating him in the 1860s as he wrote *War and Peace*. He would engage even more explicitly with Darwinian thinking – in particular the concept of "struggle for existence" – in later works such as *Anna Karenina* and *The Kreutzer Sonata*.

In *War and Peace* Tolstoy offered up an important – albeit abstracted – metaphor for life in nature as a realm of both ceaseless "struggle" (war) and overarching harmony (peace). This is the pulsating globe that Pierre sees in a dream during his captivity: "This globe was alive – a vibrating ball without fixed dimensions. The entire surface of the globe consisted of drops tightly packed together. And these drops all moved and shifted, and now merged from several into one, now divided from one into many. Each drop strove to spread out and take up the most space, but the others, striving to do the same, pressed it, sometimes destroying it, sometimes merging with it" (12:158/Vol. 4, Pt. 3, Ch. 15). As a representation of how life works the image is strikingly modern – and ecologically prescient. Here Tolstoy moves beyond the traditional "chain of being" paradigm – a static, hierarchical, Linnaean taxonomy of relationships – that Pierre propounds to Andrei during the memorable scene on the ferry. A distillation of Tolstoy's long-standing preoccupation with ceaseless interplay between the whole of nature – the unknowable totality of everything that exists – and its myriad parts, it may have had concrete, biological origins in the swarming bees that Tolstoy studied in his apiary at Yasnaya Polyana as he was writing his epic non-novel. As a figuration of life in nature it acknowledges struggle, but does not reduce existence to struggle.

For if Tolstoy was a realist, and accepted – begrudgingly, and with a sense of horror – the evidence of "struggle for existence" and of human participation in this struggle, he did not countenance passive acquiescence to this "elemental zoological law," and held humans, as higher animals, to a higher standard: he believed we must strive to transcend the "struggle for existence" through *existential struggle*. Certainly in his own life he "struggled" mightily in an effort to put into practice what he preached. In his fifties he gave up hunting (one of the primary ways through which he had engaged the natural world) and became a vegetarian. By age sixty he was advocating for universal sexual abstinence (*Kreutzer Sonata*) and attempting to maintain celibate relations with his own wife; soon afterward he also began to promulgate a philosophy of radical non-resistance to violence (*The Kingdom of God is Within You*, 1894). He does not appear to have fretted much, late in life, over the possibility that these kinds of radical self-control ran counter to certain natural impulses.

But in his earlier novels he had grappled productively – if inconclusively – with this paradox. They abound, on the one hand, with characters who struggle existentially. These characters – Olenin, Pierre, Levin – all tend to think too much, and like Tolstoy dream of de-intellectualizing and naturalizing themselves. They find moments of clarity and insight, and escape temporarily from the fetters of the mind and self, in nature. Then there are other characters who simultaneously fascinate and repulse Tolstoy – as well as his cerebral protagonists – because they live naturally but think very little. Eroshka in *The Cossacks*, for instance, is a quintessential "natural man," but is self-serving and amoral; in *War and Peace* the Kuragins, while exclusively urban creatures, are blithely natural in their amorality and animality, and seem exquisitely adapted to their particular environment. Pierre at one point says of Anatole: "Yes, there goes a true sage. He sees nothing beyond the enjoyment of the moment. Nothing worries him and so he is always cheerful, satisfied, and serene. What I wouldn't give to be like him" (10:362/Vol. 2, Pt. 5, Ch. 19). Pierre's envy is Tolstoy's, and is in some sense utterly genuine. Yet we know that neither Pierre nor Tolstoy really wants to be like Anatole. Paradoxically the Kuragins, who are riven by incest and idiocy, are from a biological (and social Darwinist) standpoint the least successful of the novel's various families. Their failure to "survive," and the relative biological prosperity of the Rostovs and Bezukhovs at the novel's end, are in keeping with the particular spin that Darwin's Russian interlocutors gave his theories:

altruism (Pyotr Kropotkin's "mutual aid," Tolstoy's "law of love") trumps brute struggle.

Tolstoyan Environmentalism

Tolstoy was less perturbed by the violence inherent in nature than he was by human violence against nature. But he was not an explicitly environmentalist writer. The last decade of the nineteenth century witnessed the emergence of a clearly articulated environmental consciousness in Russia, with other writers such as Anton Chekov sounding an unmistakable alarm about the accelerating degradation of the natural world. In the apocalyptically tinged "Reed Flute" (1887), for instance, or a decade later in *Uncle Vanya* (1896), Chekhov's characters bear anguished witness to nature's decline – to the ever more obvious effects of population growth, pollution, and deforestation, to the disappearance of various bird and animal species in the face of habitat loss and overhunting, and to mounting evidence of local and even global climate change.[3] Tolstoy echoed many of these same concerns, but from a more oblique angle.

Starting in the 1870s, he increasingly turned his attention to the destructive effects of industrialization, urbanization, and consumer-driven capitalism in Russia, and his radical views about nonviolence and "nonaction" reflected – and perhaps also stimulated – a broader awareness of environmental change. Jane Costlow has argued that in *Anna Karenina* Tolstoy began to articulate something resembling an anti-capitalist "land ethic" through a series of existential jousting matches between Levin and his best friend and opposite, Stiva Oblonsky; notably, these disputations are woven into two hunting scenes in which both characters bang away, with no apparent misgivings, at their prey.[4] His 1893 essay "Non-doing" ("*Nedelanie*") makes no direct mention of the natural world, but his seemingly perverse indictment of the manic "activity" or "busyness" of the modern age had enormous environmental implications: his Christian-Confucian prescription of non-action, were it realized, would bring about a massive reduction of humankind's ecological footprint.

By the century's end Tolstoy become more direct in his environmentally inflected critique of human "doing." His late novel *Resurrection* (1899) opens with a simple but searing description of the daily violence that modern society perpetrates, unthinkingly, against the natural world:

> No matter how hard the several hundred thousand people congregated in one small place tried to disfigure the land where they crowded together, no

matter how much they paved over the land with stones so nothing would grow on it, rooted out every last vestige of irrepressible vegetation, fouled the air with the coal and oil, cut down the trees and chased away the animals and birds – still spring was spring, even in the city. The sun shone, the grass revived and turned green and sprang up everywhere it wasn't scraped away … the birches and poplars and wild cherries put forth their sticky and fragrant leaves, bursting buds swelled on the lindens, the crows, sparrows, and pigeons, full of the joy of spring, prepared their nests, and the flies, warmed by the sun, buzzed along the walls. All were glad: plants, birds, insects, children. But humans – grown-up men and women – did not cease tormenting themselves and each other. (32:3)

For Tolstoy environmental desecration always reflects a broader spiritual crisis, and the violence humans inflict on nature is an extension of the violence they inflict on each other. This same diagnosis is implicit in the way he framed his last major work of fiction, *Hadji Murat* (1904). As he walks past a vast and "lifeless" ploughed field ("nowhere was there a blade of grass or any kind of plant to be seen"), the narrator's reflections on the destructiveness of modern, industrial-scale agriculture – and his discovery of a solitary thistle, mutilated but still clinging tenaciously to life – prompt his memories of a different (but related) kind of violence: Russia's brutal history of colonial conquest. But here, as in *Resurrection*, Tolstoy still seems to find a measure of hope in nature's extraordinary resilience. Unlike Chekhov, he never prognosticated a barren, post-human world – a world without us. Though scarred, like the thistle, by the onslaught of modernity, at his life's end he still held onto his abiding belief in the utopian, evergreen promise of the ant brotherhood and the green stick.

Notes

1 Aleksandra Tolstaya, *Otets. Zhizn' L'va Tolstogo*, 2 vols. (Moscow: Kniga, 1989), vol. 1, 9.
2 N.A. Berdiaev, "Vetkii i novyi zavet v religioznom soznanii L. Tolstogo," in *O religii L'va Tolstogo* (Moscow: Put', 1912), 181–2.
3 See Thomas Newlin, "Decadent Ecosystems in *Uncle Vanya*: A Chorographic Meditation," in Katherine Bowers and Ani Kokobobo (eds.), *Russian Writers at the Fin de Siècle: The Twilight of Realism* (Cambridge University Press, 2015), 215–32; David Moon, "The Debate over Climate Change in the Steppe Region in Nineteenth-Century Russia," *Russian Review* 69:2 (2010), 251–75.
4 Jane Costlow, "Imaginations of Destruction: The 'Forest Question' in Nineteenth-Century Russian Culture," *Russian Review* 62:1 (2003), 91–118 (at 109–10).

CHAPTER 27

Darwin and Natural Science

Michael D. Gordin

From the vantage point of the natural sciences, the world Lev Tolstoy was born into in 1828 and the one he passed from in 1910 were unrecognizable. He was born in the year Friedrich Wöhler synthesized urea from inorganic components, thus ushering in the massive synthetic chemistry industry as well as sparking a vigorous debate about the boundary between inorganic matter and the stuff of life. He died ten years after Max Planck inaugurated the quantum age. Born into a European intellectual culture that still debated the merits of atomism as an explanation for matter (revived famously by John Dalton in 1808), his passing was broadcast internationally on radio and via transoceanic cables, taking full advantage of the electromagnetism that was the hallmark of mid-century physics.

From a surface engagement with Tolstoy's life and thought, it would seem that this was of little interest. When compared with medicine (Chapter 28), on which the writer had famously critical and detailed things to say, or industrial technology (Chapter 25) as symbolized by the ubiquitous train that so shaped Anna Karenina's life and death, Tolstoy only rarely delved deeply into the substance of these transformations in the natural sciences. When juxtaposed with Fyodor Dostoevsky, this supposed diffidence is all the more striking. Dostoevsky cared about atomism, non-Euclidean geometry, thermodynamics and the heat death of the universe, and more. Tolstoy's most salient such intervention – his skepticism toward Charles Darwin's theory of biological evolution by means of natural selection – stands out as a surprising exception.

But this impression of a Tolstoy disengaged from the sciences is merely on the surface. Tolstoy was repeatedly confronted with the theories and hypotheses of contemporary scientists, and they shaped his understanding of his own moment even when he did not explicitly invoke them. This attention to science was especially noticeable (though not unique) during the 1870s while he was composing and publishing *Anna Karenina*, with occasional eruptions as he developed his religious thought. This essay traces three of the crucial contexts which repeatedly brought the world of the natural sciences to Tolstoy and vice versa: the academic sphere of university science; the coverage of scientific advances in "thick journals" (*tolstye zhurnaly*); and the domestic sphere of correspondence and family life.

Professors and Pedagogy

Before he was a novelist, a soldier, or a revered (and excoriated) philosopher-sage, Lev Tolstoy was a university student. In 1844, he enrolled at the University of Kazan, on the Volga River, to study oriental languages, a discipline he abandoned the following year in favor of the law. (He had a career in diplomacy in mind.) In 1847 he withdrew without a degree to embark on a frenzy of autodidacticism and a military life. With respect to natural science, Tolstoy's time at Kazan bears closer attention. Although he did not study in the science faculties, he was surrounded by signs of a major sea change in Russian intellectual life.

During Tolstoy's time there, science in Kazan was marked by two signal developments. The first was the development of a form of non-Euclidean geometry, a mathematics of lines and angles that does not adhere to the ancient Greek "parallel postulate." In 1826 Nikolai Lobachevsky, full professor of mathematics at Kazan, announced a version of geometry (now called hyperbolic geometry) which allowed for more than one parallel line through a point. Although at first largely dismissed by the mathematical community, by the 1870s the non-Euclidean geometries of Lobachevsky and others constituted the century's greatest mathematical innovation. Lobachevsky was a Kazan mainstay, and served as rector of the university. In 1846, when Tolstoy was a student, he was dismissed, supposedly due to failing health.

The second was the efflorescence of a remarkable group of organic chemists, first under the leadership of Nikolai N. Zinin and then under Alexander M. Butlerov, whose theories of organic chemical structure (think of the tinkertoy models of molecules from science class) were pivotal contributions to the dominance of that science across Europe. The Kazan chemical school was especially well situated for the transformation of university science in the 1850s and 1860s, seeding chemistry faculties at both the Petersburg and Moscow universities.

Both Lobachevsky and the chemists demonstrate two key features of the natural sciences in Tolstoy's context: that the universities had begun to displace the St. Petersburg Academy of Sciences (founded in 1724 by Tsar

Peter the Great) as the major engine of innovation; and that developments in Russia were no longer seen as derivative or irrelevant with respect to Europe. The Russians were part of a European story, and knowledge of European science flowed into Russia largely through this conduit of higher education.

It was a powerful mechanism. In 1855, Alexander II succeeded his father as Tsar in the midst of the Crimean War, the humiliating defeat that was interpreted by his coterie as indicative of Russia's military, economic, and technical backwardness. A slew of reforms (Chapter 6) followed, among which was a reform of university education in 1863 which expanded access to members of clerical and bureaucratic families (known as *raznochintsy*, "people of different ranks"). These new students flooded especially into the sciences. They not only produced research, but more often served as translators of Western ideas into Russian. They shaped what Tolstoy read and comprise some of the minor characters in his novels (though not to the degree visible in Dostoevsky).

Tolstoy rarely commented on this university world. He was deeply concerned with education (Chapter 17), but it was education of peasants in the fundamentals of literacy and his own interpretation of ethics, not the high ambitions of the professors. When he did, he disapproved of it. In his diary entry of August 24, 1906, Tolstoy observed of his reading of the educational and industrial manifesto of Dmitry I. Mendeleev – famous for his formulation of the periodic system of chemical elements in 1869 – entitled *Cherished Thoughts*: "I was reading in Mendeleev that the significance, the ideal of a person is reproduction. Horribly absurd. This is stupidity ... a consequence of self-confidence" (55:237). Mendeleev returned the compliment. When perusing one of Tolstoy's tracts and remarking upon the author's phrase "If I am not crazy," Mendeleev scrawled in the margins of his copy: "not crazy, but not aware of the methods of exact knowledge, a utopian, a fantasist, a poet."[1] Mendeleev's son-in-law, the gifted Silver Age poet Alexander Blok, used the contrast between the two bearded titans as an allegory for two different futures for Russia: the pastoral versus the industrial.

Periodicals and Polemics

The dominant way in which the Russian public encountered the latest findings in the natural sciences was through the medium of print. Tolstoy was no exception. Although there was a vigorous market in translations and monographs written originally in Russian (not to mention the smaller trade in foreign-language books, which Tolstoy was exceptionally well placed to consume), the bulk of this communication happened in the medium of "thick journals." These periodicals – *The Contemporary*, *The Russian Messenger*, *The Northern Bee*, etc. – generally appeared monthly or bimonthly, catering to specific audiences by political persuasion and aesthetic taste, and consisted of a mix of belles-lettres, social commentary, literary criticism, historical essays, and popular science. Just about every major novel in nineteenth-century Russia, including *Anna Karenina* and *War and Peace*, debuted as serials within their pages. Thick journals were a long-standing solution to the problem of Russia's scattered reading public, but they entered their prime in the 1860s.

As far as science was concerned, the timing was fortuitous. In 1859, Charles Darwin published *On the Origin of Species*, outlining in full the theory of evolution he had been developing since the early 1840s. He had been sparked to publish by a letter from a young naturalist, Alfred Russel Wallace, who had hit upon the same general mechanism: given that organisms reproduced at a faster rate than the resources able to sustain them, there was a constant struggle for both sustenance and mates, a struggle whereby the weak and unfit perished and those most adapted to their environment through chance variations survived. Wallace and Darwin published side-by-side in the *Journal of the Linnean Society* in 1858, with *Origin* following hard apace. The reactions both within Britain and then across the world proceeded fairly rapidly, as *Origin* and Darwin's later texts were summarily abstracted, extracted, translated, and debated in a variety of formats.

The Russian engagement with Darwin was swift. Sergei A. Rachinsky's translation of *On the Origin of Species* appeared in 1864, with a second edition the subsequent year. Ivan M. Sechenov, a noted physiologist and progressive thinker, translated Darwin's most sensational work, *The Descent of Man*, in 1871, the same year it appeared in English. That decade a slew of Darwiniana was published in Russian, including *The Expression of Emotions* and *Voyage of the Beagle*. Between 1907 and 1909, Tolstoy would have witnessed a Russian edition of Darwin's collected works by botanist Kliment A. Timiriazev, sometimes known as "Darwin's Russian Bulldog." Wallace had his own Russian moment in the 1870s. Extracts of and commentaries on all of this material made it to the thick journals, and Tolstoy read much of it.

In an interesting contrast to the prominent objections to natural selection in Britain and America, the early Russian response was relatively accepting. Russian naturalists vigorously debated natural selection, but not on the grounds of religious orthodoxy: they disputed the Malthusian hypothesis of overpopulation that undergirded Darwin's tropical data in favor of "mutual aid" theories more suited to the inhospitable steppe where they did their own fieldwork. Radicals of all sorts embraced the theory both as a vindication of materialism and as a convenient allegory through which they could discuss "revolution" under the guise of "evolution." (Nikolai Chernyshevsky, usually a bellwether of the radical intelligentsia, was unusual in his rejection of Darwin, largely because of the Malthusian assumption.) Even the Orthodox Church refrained from attacking Darwinism either officially or through proxies until 1884, two decades after its Russian debut.

The death of Charles Darwin on April 19, 1882, prompted the thick journals to closely analyze his legacy. This may have triggered the main salvo from Nikolai Danilevsky, a pan-Slavist ideologue, who in 1885 published *Darwinism: A Critical Study*, which deepened a building public dispute over the moral implications of Darwin's theory. Nikolai Strakhov, a polemicizing intellectual who fashioned himself as a scientific savant, had been sniping at Darwinian evolution for some years by now, but Danilevsky reinvigorated his interest. Strakhov brought the book to the attention of Tolstoy, who refined his own views on evolution by natural selection over the next few years. By 1890, Tolstoy's negative assessment of Darwin was essentially set: even if natural selection were true, it was irrelevant to the only important question of how to live; the trouble with Darwinism was the *social* Darwinism of intellectuals valorizing cruelty and struggle. This was more of an objection to British philosopher Herbert Spencer's social theory, which became imbricated with Darwin's ideas in Russia and elsewhere, than an attack on the biological theory itself.

Indeed, Tolstoy had begun to develop these ideas already in the 1870s in the context of *Anna Karenina*, serialized in the *Russian Messenger* from 1875 to 1877. The accompanying articles, ranging from reports on emergent hostilities with the Ottoman Empire to debates over materialist science, crept into the narrative. Prince Vronsky's friend Golenishchev – treated in the book as a shallow faddist who is tolerated by the protagonists because he continues to associate with the disgraced Anna and Vronsky – mentions "*évolution*, selection, struggle for existence" (19:36/Pt. 5, Ch. 9) in conversation with the couple. Needless to say, Golenishchev's endorsement is a mark of disapproval from Tolstoy. Likewise, Levin (Pt. 8, Chs. 8, 12) repeatedly returns to the topic of valorizing struggle in nature in order to reject it for the same ethical reasons Tolstoy does. Decades later, Timiriazev would single out Levin's musings by grumbling: "Did you read the book you are so eloquently denouncing?"[2] Interestingly, the word Tolstoy used to describe the theory was not "evolution" but rather "development" (*razvitie*), which is a mark of Tolstoy learning most of what he knew from the polemics in the journals rather than from reading the scientific monographs.

Pens and Parlors

A third important context for Tolstoy's engagement with natural sciences, and one common to many of the wealthier members of the nobility and intelligentsia, was the home and estate. Today one commonly thinks of science as actively produced in laboratories and only passively consumed in the home. In the nineteenth century, and certainly in a rural context like Yasnaya Polyana (or the English countryside, for that matter), this was far from the case. New scientific knowledge was eagerly sought after and deployed in these contexts as well, though sometimes with a critical edge.

For all the many things that Yasnaya Polyana meant to the Tolstoy family (Chapter 4), primary among them was that it was a farm. Tolstoy would sporadically focus his attention on agriculture and sought to deploy the knowledge of naturalists in this domain (Chapter 26). A case in point is beekeeping. In Tolstoy's calendar for April 1887, he endorsed setting up beehives following the instructions offered by Alexander Butlerov in a recent monograph on the subject (40:27). This was the same Butlerov who was a leading representative of the Kazan school of organic chemistry, spending the second half of his career in St. Petersburg at the Academy of Sciences and the University.

Butlerov provides an entry point to another mode in which natural science – although not perhaps as many would define it today – was present in the private worlds of correspondence and the home. Butlerov was a leading Russian representative of spiritualism (*spiritizm* in Russian), an immensely popular movement that originated in upstate New York in the 1840s and then crossed the Atlantic to set up offshoot traditions in London, Paris, Berlin, Petersburg, and beyond. Spiritualists would gather in darkened rooms, often parlors in private homes, in the presence of a person called a "medium," who mediated between the psychic world of departed souls and the physical world of levitating tables, rapping on furniture, and automatic writing. Dismissed frequently as superstition both now and at the moment (certainly Mendeleev and Dostoevsky both considered it such), in the 1860s and 1870s numerous scientists across Europe wanted to use the methods of the natural sciences to investigate the phenomena revealed during these séances.

Tolstoy did not care much for what he saw as the worst mix of reductionism in the realm of the spiritual and simultaneously almost a parody of the ills which had moved organized religion away from the ethical precepts that ought to guide Christian living. Strakhov, who disapproved strongly of scientists' involvement, was instrumental in drawing Tolstoy's attention to spiritualism in the 1870s, though the novelist would have found it even without Strakhov's mediation. The same issues of the *Russian Herald* which carried installments of *Anna Karenina* in 1875–6 also contained a vigorous polemic on spiritualism featuring Butlerov. Tolstoy incorporated a critique of this into his ongoing novel, depicting the weak and inauthentic Karenin as subservient to his medium, Landau (Pt. 7, Chs. 20–2).

Tolstoy continued to simmer over the errors presented by spiritualism. In 1886 his children asked him to pen a play for domestic production as a family activity, and he completed it in 1889, when it was first staged at Yasnaya Polyana on December 30. The result, *The Fruits of Enlightenment*, is a rural farce about clever peasants manipulating a deluded spiritualist landowner in the name of justice (Chapter 22). The butt of the comedy is a distinguished scientist named "Kutler" (originally Kutlerov, an even more transparent jab at the recently deceased Butlerov). The play is an exposé of what happens when "science" is brought inappropriately into the domestic space, while the play itself was the result of just such an incursion.

Lev Tolstoy was not dismissive of science. That does not mean that he necessarily agreed with it, and it also does not imply that he welcomed the new scientific theories that were buffeting his intellectual culture. Russia, no less than Western Europe, was in the throes of coming to terms with a new understanding of nature brought about by the professionalization of science and the proliferation of its methods, a transformation that reached into every corner of the culture. Tolstoy's engagement concentrated on a single axis: did this new understanding of nature alter the fundamental ethical precepts? If the tenets emerged unscathed, then the science was at best irrelevant; if they contravened them – as Tolstoy worried Darwinism might – then they were something to be taken very seriously indeed.

Notes

1 R.B. Dobrotin and N.G. Karpilo, "D.I. Mendeleev o L.N. Tolstom," *Priroda* 9 (1978), 11–13 (at 12).
2 K.A. Timiriazev, "Darvin, kak tip uchenogo," in *Charlz Darvin i ego uchenie: S prilozheniem nashi antidarvinisty* (Moscow, 1898), 36; translation from Anna A. Berman, "Darwin in the Novels: Tolstoy's Evolving Literary Response," *Russian Review* 72:2 (2017), 331–51 (at 350).

CHAPTER 28

Medical Science

Elena Fratto

Over the course of Lev Tolstoy's long life, monumental transformations of medicine as a discipline and of medical institutions took place in Russia and throughout Europe. In the late nineteenth century quantitative assessment methods, such as an overreliance on measurements and statistics, came to characterize the positivistic approach to the human body. Treatment became institutionalized, physicians began to coalesce around professional organizations, and great scientific discoveries, such as germ theory and pasteurization, resulted in a broader recognition of physicians' agency in the management of public health crises. Moreover, the numerous wars fought in Europe catalyzed developments in medicine and provided generations of physicians with an extreme testing ground for surgical techniques and newly discovered medications.

While Russia initially lagged behind Western Europe in medical advancements, Alexander II's liberal reforms of the 1860s reduced the gap significantly.[1] The Judicial Reform of 1864 instituted local self-government units, the zemstvos (*zemstva*), which were put in charge of managing public health. Far from the central bureaucracy, zemstvo doctors saw their autonomy increase, even at the time of Alexander III's counter-reforms of the late 1880s, while their cooperation during the numerous epidemic waves solidified their corporate consciousness. At mid-century, epidemics were still considered administrative emergencies. The bulk of physicians' work consisted in stressing prevention, improving hygiene, and limiting contagion through isolation and quarantine. With rapid advances in Western medicine, the etiology of fatal diseases like cholera became clear, and techniques to reduce their impact were discovered. As a result, physicians gained unprecedented visibility and undisputed authority as experts in anti-epidemic measures. Russian physicians were no longer seen as mere clerks. Cognizant of Western medical thought, they applied their knowledge at home while seeing their social status grow.[2]

Among the most fervent promoters of medical corporatism (*korporativnost*) was Nikolai Pirogov. The first person to use anesthesia in a field hospital, Pirogov established the practices of field surgery and was a founder of experimental surgery. He tested and developed the use of anesthetics, plaster casts, and enhanced methods of amputation. He also introduced five-stage triage on the battlefield of the Crimean War (1853–6), in which Tolstoy served as a young officer, and which inspired his *Sevastopol Sketches* (1855). Pirogov's anatomic atlas, *Topographical Anatomy of the Human Body*, published in four volumes with detailed drawings between 1851 and 1859, facilitated the work of surgeons immensely and became famous all over Europe. Between 1856 and 1890, the decades that saw the publication of Tolstoy's most famous works, Russian physicians doubled their ranks. The number of medical journals increased considerably, too, with *The Physician* (*Vrach*) being the most influential, while a reformed medical education enhanced physicians' competence. The first university clinic in Russia was established in 1884 by the Faculty of Medicine at Moscow University. The Society of Russian Physicians, named after Pirogov, held its first congress in 1885, and by the end of the century Moscow began hosting international conferences on medicine.

Tolstoy expressed his thoughts on medicine, illness, and death on many occasions, both in his private writings and in his literary works, such as *Childhood* (1852), *Sevastopol Sketches*, "Three Deaths" (1859), *War and Peace* (1865–9), *Anna Karenina* (1875–8), "Notes of a Madman" (1884), and *The Death of Ivan Ilyich* (1886). Undoubtedly a realist writer, Tolstoy nevertheless veered away from physiological sketches or naturalistic prose, which was in many respects the literary counterpart to determinism in medicine. He firmly rejected the positivistic medical approach on the basis of its scientific, procedural, and ethical shortcomings.

Numerous physician characters who appear in his works apply their rigid diagnostic categories to patients myopically and despotically, failing to understand the existential distress that lies at the basis of physical ailments. Tolstoy ruthlessly lays bare the empty rituals and theatricality of their gestures and procedures. This is true of the doctors who treat Natasha's illness in *War and Peace* and the renowned specialists who visit Ivan Ilyich, among other instances in Tolstoy's oeuvre. In *War and Peace*, the doctors cannot see that Natasha is suffering from emotional distress after her broken engagement and keep misdiagnosing her.[3] While the treatment they prescribe is useless, all the surface rituals they undertake with serious expressions prove immensely helpful to the patient's morale and her family's.

> Doctors came to see her singly and in consultation, talked much in French, German, and Latin, blamed one another, and prescribed a great variety of medicines for all the diseases known to them, but the simple idea never occurred to any of them that they could not know the disease Natasha was suffering from ... Their usefulness did not depend in making the patient swallow substances for the most part harmful ... but they were useful, necessary, and indispensable because they satisfied ... the eternal human need for hope of relief, for sympathy, and that something should be done, which is felt by those who are suffering ... What would Sonya and the count and countess have done ... if there had not been those pills to give by the clock, the warm drinks, the chicken cutlets, and all the other details of life ordered by the doctors, the carrying out of which supplied an occupa- tion and consolation to the family circle? How would the count have borne his dearly loved daughter's illness had he not known that it was costing him a thousand rubles, and that he would not grudge thousands more to benefit her ... and had he not been able to explain the details of how Métivier and Feller had not understood the symptoms, but Frise had ... ? What would the countess have done had she not been able sometimes to scold the invalid for not strictly obeying the doctor's orders? (11:66–8/Vol. 3, Pt. 1, Ch. 16)[4]

That same empty theatricality, accompanied by self-importance and a despotic attitude, characterizes Ivan Ilyich's doctors as well:

> It was all just as it was in the law courts. The doctor put on just the same air towards him as he himself put on towards an accused person ... [Ivan Ilyich] remarked with a sigh: " ... tell me, doctor, in general, is this complaint dangerous, or not?" The doctor looked at him sternly over his spectacles with one eye, as if to say: "Prisoner, if you will not keep to the questions put to you, I shall be obliged to have you removed from the court." (26:84)[5]

The emphasis on surface, hypocrisy, and gestures, in stark contrast with an absolute lack of meaning and intention, appears even in his last doctor's visit, when Ivan Ilyich is nearing his death and everyone knows but nobody admits it. "Ivan Ilyich knows quite well and definitely that [the doctor's examination] is all nonsense and pure deception," but he submits to the doctor's "various gymnastic movements over him ... just as he used to submit to the speeches of the lawyers, though he knew very well that they were lying and knew why they were lying" (26:101).[6] Right after the doctor's visit, the stage actress Sarah Bernhardt (1844–1923) is mentioned, as if to emphasize the theatrical façade even further. An element of insincerity and empty performance is pervasive in the novella and the only caregiver whose presence Ivan Ilyich enjoys is Gerasim, the butler's young assistant, a simple and honest peasant who does not engage in hypocrisy and unnecessary ceremonies.

In the heyday of neurology, Tolstoy explored mental health with great fascination, most famously in "Notes of a Madman" (1884). He condemned the reductionism and the classificatory methods in vogue in late nineteenth-century diagnosis and treatment of neurological conditions, which deprived patients of their uniqueness and humanity. At the same time, he deeply admired neurologist Sergei Korsakov, head of psychiatry at the Moscow University Clinic, because of the humaneness of his treatment methods. It is no surprise that Tolstoy failed to find common ground with famed psychiatrist and criminologist Cesare Lombroso, whose theories on atavism, heredity, biological determinism, and "born criminals" were highly influential all over Europe.

When Lombroso was invited to a medical conference in Moscow in the summer of 1897, he took the occasion to make a trip to Yasnaya Polyana to visit Lev Tolstoy. Lombroso had expected Tolstoy to follow the patterns he had outlined in his criminological works, that is, to show "a cretinous and degenerate look," as he had described the genius.[7] He had even chosen a portrait of Tolstoy to illustrate the physiognomic type of the genius in one of his books. When Lombroso arrived at Yasnaya Polyana, on August 15, he was stunned by 69-year-old Tolstoy's strength and well-built figure. He proved to be a sturdy, old peasant type of man – quite contrary to the prototype of the slender, sick-looking person Lombroso's theory would have him be. Lombroso saw Tolstoy play lawn tennis with his daughters for two hours. Then the writer invited his visitor for a horseback ride to a river for a swim. After fifteen minutes, Lombroso was exhausted and he expressed admiration for Tolstoy's strength, while complaining about his own weakness. At that point, Lombroso recalls, his host just "protracted his arm and lifted me up enough above the ground, as if I had been a small dog."[8]

Once they were back in Tolstoy's house, Lombroso started explaining his deterministic theory of the born criminal, and perhaps he also mentioned his idea of punishment, including the death sentence as social defense against the beastly behavior of underdeveloped born criminals: Tolstoy "remained deaf to my argument, knitting his frightening eyebrows, and casting menacing lightning bolts [on me] from his sunken eyes; in the end he responded: 'This is delirious.'"[9] Tolstoy remained thoroughly unconvinced by Lombroso's theories, and predictably so.

That evening, Tolstoy wrote in his journal: "Lombroso was here – a naïve little old man" (53:150). Tolstoy's library in Yasnaya Polyana contains most of the books by Lombroso with the pages still uncut.

Lombroso's visit came while Tolstoy was taking a break from writing *Resurrection* in order to complete *What Is Art?* He resumed *Resurrection* during the fall, and presumably his meeting with Lombroso had an influence on the novel. In *Resurrection* (published in 1899) Tolstoy ridiculed the theory of atavism and heredity, as well as the conclusions drawn by criminal anthropology. Through the figure of Breve, the public prosecutor in Maslova's trial, Tolstoy voiced his concerns about the new criminology and mocked Lombroso's theory, and probably Lombroso himself. Breve is a convinced positivist and in court he speaks about Maslova's degeneration, typical of the corruption of the times. Breve describes Maslova's accomplice, Kartinkin, as an atavistic product of serfdom, and his mistress, Bochkova, as a victim of heredity. Maslova is just a degenerate of unknown parentage, her lawyer claims. Still the public prosecutor maintains that "the laws of heredity were so far proved by science that we can not only deduce the crime from heredity, but heredity from crime" (32:75/Bk. 1, Ch. 21).[10] Prince Nekhliudov disagrees, remaining unsatisfied by the answers provided by criminal anthropology. He reflects on the new science in a Siberian prison, where he had followed Maslova after she was found guilty. Nekhliudov turns to the famous works everybody quotes, but he finds that they cannot explain "why all these very different persons were put in prison, while others just like them were going about free, and even judging them."

> He obtained the works of Lombroso, Garofalo, Ferri, Liszt, Maudsley, Tarde, and read them carefully. But as he read he became more and more disappointed ... Science answered thousands of other very subtle and ingenious questions touching criminal law, but not the one he was trying to solve. He asked a very simple question: 'Why, and by what right, do some people lock up, torment, exile, flog, and kill others, while they are themselves just like those whom they torment, flog, and kill?' And in answer he got deliberations on whether ... or not signs of criminality could be detected by measuring the skull; what part heredity played in crime; ... what madness is, what degeneration is ... and so on. (32:313/Bk. 2, Ch. 30)[11]

When Lombroso read *Resurrection*, he claimed in frustration that he had found "factual evidence that [he] had spoken to him [Tolstoy] in vain."[12]

In spite of Tolstoy's bold and dismissive statements on medicine, his relationship with it was more complex than it might seem, and at times even contradictory. In 1876, when his wife was ill, he wrote in a letter: "I do not believe in either doctors or in medicine or in the fact that remedies made by people should in the slightest way alter the state of health." However, in 1886 a wound on Tolstoy's leg became infected and he would have died of septicemia if a doctor had not arrived at the estate from Moscow to intervene and prevent that. Later in his life, despite writing in his diaries that "everything about medicine is immoral," he thought it essential to have a doctor permanently attached to the household.[13] He kept himself informed about medical and scientific developments by reading scholarly articles, and embraced some of the contemporaneous theories in physiology enthusiastically. He even challenged tradition and propriety by learning to ride a bicycle at the relatively old age of sixty-seven because he had read about its health benefits in a scientific journal.[14]

Although a man with a strong constitution, Tolstoy had numerous dealings with physicians, some of which proved deeply influential on his literary career, besides saving his life. In 1847, at the age of eighteen, he spent a few weeks in the clinic of Kazan University to be treated for venereal diseases, and there he started writing his diary, an activity he would never abandon and that would serve as a precious tool for him to hone his writing skills. While in the army during the Crimean War he went to a spa in the Northern Caucasus where he was operated on with the use of chloroform. Tolstoy's descriptions of Ivan Ilyich on morphine, including the surreal states of mind in which the dying character attempts to put his floating organs back into place, are presumably based on the author's own recollections. Tolstoy also witnessed the medical postmortem examination of Anna Stepanova Pirogova, who, blinded by jealousy, had thrown herself under a train. According to Sofia Andreevna, that experience offered the inspiration for Anna Karenina's character and fate.[15]

Tolstoy's obsession with death and his lifelong attempt to control the passing of time through his storytelling endeavor would require a standalone chapter.[16] However, the enduring relevance of *The Death of Ivan Ilyich* to the medical humanities and to modern debates on caregiving and on dignifying end-of-life medical procedures attests to the rich heritage of Tolstoy's reflections on illness and health care in our times.[17] Tolstoy's views on nutrition and diet, inseparable from his pacifism and religious beliefs, also rank among the longest-lived reflections that the writer and thinker formulated over a century ago on health, the body, and on being human.

Notes

1 See Nancy Frieden, *Russian Physicians in an Era of Reform and Revolution* (Princeton University Press, 1981), chaps 1, 3, 4; and Alexander Vucinich, *Science in Russian Culture, 1861–1917* (Stanford University Press, 1970), chaps. 2–3.

2 See Frieden, *Russian Physicians*, 5–11, 53–75, 105–20.

3 Doctors also misdiagnose Kitty's heartbreak in *Anna Karenina*. For an examination of lovesickness in Russian literature, see Valeria Sobol, *Febris Erotica: Lovesickness in the Russian Literary Imagination* (Seattle: University of Washington Press, 2009).

4 I am quoting from Lev Tolstoy, *War and Peace: The Maude Translation, Backgrounds and Sources, Criticism* (New York: W.W. Norton, 1996), 582–3.

5 I am quoting from *Tolstoy's Short Fiction*, ed. and trans. Michael R. Katz (New York: W.W. Norton, 2008), 103.

6 Ibid., 117–18.

7 Cesare Lombroso, *L'uomo di genio in rapporto alla psichiatria, alla storia ed all'estetica* (Turin: Bocca, 1888), 7.

8 Cesare Lombroso, "Mein Besuch bei Tolstoi," *Das freie Wort* 1 (1902), 391–7 (at 394), translation mine.

9 Ibid., 396.

10 I am quoting from Leo Tolstoy, *Resurrection*, trans. Louise Maude (Oxford University Press, 1999), 82.

11 Ibid., 340–1.

12 Lombroso, "Mein Besuch bei Tolstoi," 396.

13 Reported in Irina Sirotkina, *Diagnosing Literary Genius: A Cultural History of Psychiatry in Russia, 1880–1930* (Baltimore, MD: Johns Hopkins University Press, 2002), 85–6.

14 Reported in Henri Troyat, *Tolstoy* (New York: Grove Press, 2001), 511.

15 *The Diaries of Sophia Tolstoy*, trans. Cathy Porter (New York: Random House, 1985), 855.

16 Scholars have commented extensively on Tolstoy's obsession with death. See, among others, the works of Kathleen Parthé, Liza Knapp, and Hugh McLean. Tolstoy's own death, discussed in Chapter 2 of this volume, received extraordinary international media coverage, something unprecedented for Russian public figures.

17 Most notably, among others, cultural historian Philippe Ariès draws on Tolstoy's novella to analyze the tradition of the "good death" in *The Hour of Our Death: The Classic History of Western Attitudes toward Death over the Last One Thousand Years* (New York: Random House, 1981), chap. 12, "Death Denied"; surgeon-writer Atul Gawande discusses caregiving by examining the relationship between the character of Ivan Ilyich and that of Gerasim, the butler's young assistant, in *Being Mortal: Medicine and What Matters in the End* (Picador: New York, 2014), Introduction, 99–100, 144.

PART V

Beyond Russia

CHAPTER 29

Pacifism and the Doukhobors

Veronika Makarova

A visitor might be surprised to find statues of Lev Tolstoy located on the premises of two Doukhobor museums in Canada: Doukhobor Discovery Centre in British Columbia and the National Doukhobor Heritage Village (NDHV) in Saskatchewan. They symbolize the important role that Tolstoy played in Doukhobor history. Both statues were created by Russian sculptor Yury Chernov, and presented to the Doukhobor museums by the Rodina Society for Cultural Relations in 1987 through the Society of Canadians of Russian Descent. Other reminders of the connection between Tolstoy and Canadian Doukhobors in Saskatchewan are the Tolstoy Library filled with Tolstoy's works and photos in the NDHV, the Tolstoy cemetery nearby, and the building of an early twentieth-century school named after Tolstoy that was attended by local children of different backgrounds. This connection encompasses a common ground in their pacifistic thought (explored in this chapter) as well as in other views, Tolstoy's support of the Doukhobors and his positive representations of them in his works, communication with their leader Peter Verigin, and interactions between Tolstoyans and the Doukhobors. This chapter will explore the history of the Doukhobors, Tolstoy's views on pacifism, and then Tolstoy's connection with the Doukhobors around the issue of pacifism.

Doukhobors

Canadian Doukhobors are members of a group of religious dissenters that originated in Russia among peasants at the beginning of the eighteenth century. The group's origin is cloaked in legends that allegorically connect the Doukhobors to a biblical story (Daniel 3) of three youths, Hanania, Azaria, and Mishael, who walked out unscathed from a blazing furnace into which they were thrown for refusing to worship a golden statue of King Nebuchadnezzar. The Doukhobors originally called themselves

"God's people." The name "Doukhobortsy" (eventually simplified to "Doukhobors") first appeared in a 1786 report by Archbishop Nikifor. His successor Archbishop Ambrosius allegedly used this name to rebuke the "heretics" for fighting against the Holy Spirit.[1] The meaning of this compound word is derived from two components: the (Holy) Spirit (*doukh*) and fighters (*bortsy*), i.e. Fighters for the (Holy) Spirit.

In Russia, Doukhobors endured multiple waves of persecutions and exiles for their rejection of the Orthodox Church, as well as refusal of military duty. Pacifism based on the sacredness of human life has always been at the very core of Doukhobor beliefs and values. Doukhobors see the reflection of God in every human being; therefore killing another person is as unthinkable as killing God. These beliefs are manifested in their motto "Toil and Peaceful Life" and in their psalms known as *The Living Book* that constitute their sacred teaching. The Doukhobors consider pacifism and nonviolence as features of true Christianity: "Christ forbade to kill people, and I believe in Christ."[2]

In 1887 universal compulsory military service was introduced and enforced in the Caucasus (where most Doukhobors lived at the time). The Doukhobors stood up in opposition to militarism which they saw as organized murder. In 1891, five Doukhobor men refused military service.[3] In December 1893, from his exile in the Far North of Russia, the new Doukhobor leader Peter (Pyotr) Verigin, a young visionary sent by the government into exile in order to weaken the Doukhobor movement, called out to the community with a message of stronger adherence to the ancestral Doukhobor beliefs: "in our time, all the Doukhobors have a direct duty to free not only themselves, but also their descendants from militarism, that is not to join the soldiers."[4] This message also encouraged them to share wealth with the poor and to give up smoking, tobacco, and eating meat.

As Nicolas II ascended the throne in 1894, all soldiers were required to swear allegiance to the monarch. Peter Verigin reached out to the Doukhobors again saying that Doukhobors should not swear an oath to a mortal man, because this does not agree with the teaching of Christ. Furthermore, he suggested that Doukhobors already serving in the army should lay down their weapons, that new recruits should refuse conscription, and that all others were to burn all the weapons owned by the Doukhobors "as a sign of a non-resistance to evil with evil" and following the commandment "thou shall not kill."[5] Consequently, Doukhobor soldiers in the army refused to continue their military duty during Easter of 1895; and on the night of June 29/30, 1895, a massive Burning of the

Weapons was held in a few Doukhobor villages in the Caucasus. The government responded with Cossack raids on the villages, court-martials, brutal physical punishments, imprisonments, and exile of Doukhobor soldiers, recruits, and all held responsible to very remote areas of Siberia. All the families of Verigin's followers were subjected to property dispossession and dispersed resettlement in remote mountainous areas with unhealthy and dangerous conditions. At the end of the nineteenth century, there were other sectarian movements in Russia that rejected violence and war, such as the Molokans, the Baptists, the Seventh-Day Adventists, and the Pentecostals, but only the Doukhobors actively opposed military service in an organized and "sensational" way.[6]

The new wave of persecutions following these protests made it extremely hard for Verigin's followers to stay in Russia. Peter Verigin petitioned Empress Alexandra (wife of Nicholas II) for Doukhobors to be released from military service, or to allow their emigration to another country (such as England or America). In 1897, a letter supporting the emigration of Doukhobors was sent to Emperor Nicholas II by The Society of Friends (Quakers) from London. The Dowager Empress Maria Fyodorovna (Nicholas's mother) also received a similar petition from the Doukhobors while travelling in the Caucasus. In February 1898, Doukhobors received permission to leave Russia. In 1899, close to 8,000 Doukhobors moved from Russia to Canada, where they settled on a few reserves in the territory of modern-day Saskatchewan. However, due to cancellations of their land registries by the government, about two-thirds of the Doukhobors moved to British Columbia between 1907 and 1918.[7] As of 2021, there are about 3,000 individuals either belonging to Doukhobor organizations or self-identifying as Doukhobor, and up to 30,000–40,000 individuals of Doukhobor descent in Canada.[8]

Tolstoy's Pacifism

Tolstoy volunteered for active military duty in 1852, participated in three wars, and received commendations for bravery in the battlefield, but he became disillusioned with the army and resigned in 1855 (see Chapter 11). His evolution as a pacifist was also fueled by the experience of witnessing a public execution by guillotine in France. Around 1880, Tolstoy's spiritual quest resulted in the birth of his new philosophy and lifestyle, including pacifism, which for him was primarily religious in nature.[9] He renounced violence not only against humans but against animals as well, gave up hunting, and became a vegetarian.

The cornerstone of Tolstoy's pacifism was laid down in "My Faith" (1884), and the concept was further developed in *The Kingdom of God Is Within You* (1893) and in multiple subsequent works. His pacifism centers around the commandment *"resist not evil"* of Christ's Sermon on the Mount (28:2). Non-resistance is not just an expression, but "a rule, a law" and a "key to all" (23:315). Tolstoy placed non-resistance among what he considered to be major Christian principles – equality, brotherhood, and communal property (28:89). The doctrine of non-resistance to evil with violence did not prohibit resistance, as long as it was not violent. Tolstoy clearly explained the premises of Christ's commandment as being derived from love: "Resist not evil means: never resist evil, that is never commit violence; never act contrary to love" (23:313). According to Tolstoy, wars directly contradict Christianity, as a soldier has to kill people he is supposed to love as a Christian (28:105). He placed the blame for wars directly on national governments that "would never refuse having an army and using it for wars" (28:116) and employ military drafts as the utmost level of violence in order to support the very foundation of government rule (28:141).

Tolstoy also gave many examples of nonviolent resistance throughout his life, such as his support of the Doukhobors and of other pacifist sectarians. In 1881, he wrote a plea to the Emperor Alexander III not to execute the individuals who assassinated the Emperor's father, Alexander II.[10] He protested the death penalty in "I Cannot Be Silent" (1908) as well as in the last article of his life, "Working Remedy" (1911).[11] Tolstoy's "non-resistance" concept had a profound impact on many world leaders and peace activists, including Mohandas Gandhi, Martin Luther King, and Jane Addams, as well as on movements (such as American non-resistors and the Doukhobors).[12]

Tolstoy and the Doukhobors

Pacifism forged a strong link between Tolstoy and the Doukhobors. Tolstoy was notified about the Doukhobors' refusal to serve in the army in 1891. He first met with a group of three Doukhobors in December 1894.[13] This meeting was inspired by Peter Verigin, who was at that time being held in Moscow's Butyrskaya prison on his way to a new place of exile in Siberia. Tolstoy found that Doukhobor pacifistic beliefs were very similar to his own, since they also emerged from their understanding of the teaching of Jesus Christ.[14] In July 1895, "Tolstoy was struck with joy by the news of the burning of the weapons and the entire movement of the

Doukhobors in the Caucasus," in the words of his associate Pavel Biriukov.[15] Following Tolstoy's request, Biriukov spoke with some of Verigin's followers and wrote an article "Persecutions of the Christians in Russia in 1895" which was published in *The Times* along with Tolstoy's foreword. Tolstoy also wrote a letter to a military authority requesting compassion in treating conscientious objectors. Subsequently, Tolstoy became the most passionate protector of the Doukhobors, writing multiple letters and articles about them, commending them as heroes of the "war against wars" in his article "Two Wars" in 1898 (31:97). In 1897, when rumors started circulating that Tolstoy could be nominated for the Nobel Peace Prize, he wrote a letter to a Swedish newspaper proposing that the award should go to Doukhobors instead.[16]

Tolstoy was impacted by Doukhobor ideas, as shown in the peasant sectarian concepts in the novel *Resurrection* (1899) and in his unfinished play *And the Light Shineth in Darkness* (1911) which relates the story of a young conscript who refuses to swear an oath of allegiance. Doukhobors are also explicitly present in his political and philosophical writings. For example, in *The Kingdom of God Is Within You*, Tolstoy mentions Quakers, Mennonites, Doukhobors, and Molokans as examples of people who consider military service incompatible with Christianity (28:22). Tolstoy–Doukhobor influences were mutual, as reflected in one of Tolstoy's letters from 1896, which says that he and his followers "can borrow a good deal from them [the Doukhobors] . . . and they can borrow something from us."[17]

In turn, the Doukhobor leader Peter Verigin was interested in Tolstoy, and in 1896, from his Siberian exile, he asked for a copy of *The Kingdom of God Is Within You* as well as a complete edition of Tolstoy's works. Correspondence between Tolstoy and Verigin started in 1895 and continued until Tolstoy's death in 1910. They often addressed each other as "dear brother," and "dear friend."[18] This correspondence was mostly about spiritual and philosophical matters. Tolstoy "exerted a significant influence on the Doukhobor leader" and, through him, on the Doukhobor community,[19] although Verigin did not hesitate to disagree with Tolstoy's concepts if they did not suit his own visions. Verigin and Tolstoy met in person twice: once in October 1902, when Verigin was on his way from Siberian exile to Canada, and for the second time, in December 1906 during Verigin's visit to Russia. Peter Verigin's son and successor Peter Chistiakov-Verigin also advocated Tolstoy's ideas among the Doukhobors.

Tolstoy was a pivotal figure in organizing Doukhobor immigration to Canada. He wrote an afterword to the appeal "Help!" (1896) for financial

assistance to the Doukhobors and their resettlement, which was composed
by his followers Biriukov, Ivan Tregubov, and Vladimir Chertkov. Tolstoy
also donated his royalty for the novel *Resurrection* toward resettlement of
the Doukhobors in Canada. A whole international team negotiated the
move of Doukhobors to Canada, including a Quaker Committee, James
Mavor (a professor of political economics at the University of Toronto),
Aylmer Maude (an English businessman, translator, and follower of
Tolstoy), Dmitry Khilkov, Chertkov (both Tolstoyans), a few
Doukhobor families, and many others. On October 5, 1898, approval
was obtained for resettling Doukhobors in Canada; on December 6,
Doukhobors were exempted from military service, and on December 21,
1898, the Doukhobors started boarding the first of four ships that brought
them to Canada in early 1899.[20] Sergei Tolstoy (Lev Tolstoy's son)
accompanied the Doukhobors on their trip, and he wrote a book about
this experience.[21]

Lev Tolstoy and the Tolstoyans played a somewhat controversial role in
the early history of Doukhobor settlements in Canada, encouraging a
communal lifestyle and civil disobedience. In one of his letters to
Doukhobors in 1900, Tolstoy wrote: "love of neighbour entails rejection
of violence, the uttering of oaths, military service and property."[22] This
letter was printed and distributed among the Doukhobors, most of whom
decided to cultivate the land communally. In 1900, Anna Chertkova
(Chertkov's wife) published an English-language textbook for the
Doukhobors filled with anti-governmental propaganda. Moreover,
Alexander Bodiansky (a Tolstoyan) wrote a letter on behalf of all the
Doukhobors in which he informed the government that Doukhobors
would not comply with the land registry rules, as these rules violated the
law of God. In 1902, the Doukhobors received warnings that unless the
land were registered as individual property (homesteads), it would be
repossessed. Fear for their future motivated the Doukhobors to go on
marches of protest in Saskatchewan, and a radical movement known was
the Freedomites was formed. Tolstoy wrote letters to Verigin advising
against radicalism and for compliance with the government, while expressing his admiration for the Freedomites in other letters.[23] In 1907, the land
which had not been claimed as private property following the Homestead
Act was repossessed by the government and Verigin followers and his
Christian Community of Universal Brotherhood commune were removed
from these lands.

Throughout the difficult journey of the Canadian Doukhobors in the
twentieth century, Tolstoy remained an important figure for them, as their

benefactor, a great literary author, and a spiritual guide[24]. Besides pacifism, other features uniting the Doukhobors with Tolstoy include rejection of the Church and its institutions, and a preference for agrarian labour, a communal lifestyle, equality of people, extermination of the extremes of wealth and poverty, vegetarianism, and abstinence from alcohol and tobacco. Pacifism, however, is identified by contemporary Doukhobors as one of the most important parts of their beliefs. As one informant in a study by the author noted: "I do not want our grandchildren and great-grandchildren to ever take a gun into their hands."[25] According to another informant, "young people learned about computers, YouTube, and so on. And they will be telling others about peace, brotherhood, and friendship, and they will talk more and better than we could."

Lev Tolstoy saw in Doukhobor "pacifism and simple Christian approach to life a practical embodiment of his own ideals."[26] For both Tolstoy and the Doukhobors, pacifism and nonviolence are rooted in the teachings of Christ and his commandments "love one another," "resist not evil," and "thou shall not kill." The practice of these simple principles "demands the total transformation of society, a nonviolent revolution which would replace the law of violence presently prevailing by a new law of love."[27] Through this transformation, "the war to end all wars" (31:97) could eventually be won, and peace would prevail, just as in the world vision shared by Tolstoy and the Doukhobors.

Notes

1 A. Donskov (ed.), *Leo Tolstoy in Conversation with Four Peasant Sectarians Writers* (University of Ottawa Press, 2019), 197.

2 V. Bonch-Bruevich, *Zhivotnaia Kniga Duhobortsev* (Winnipeg: Regehr's printing, 1954), 84.

3 A. Donskov, *Leo Tolstoy and the Canadian Doukhobors: A Study in Historic Relationships* (University of Ottawa Press, 2019), 367.

4 G. Verigin, *The Chronicles of Spirit Wrestlers' Immigration to Canada: God Is Not in Might but in Truth*, trans. V. Makarova, ed. V. Makarova and L.A. Ewashen (Cham: Palgrave Macmillan, 2019), 44.

5 Ibid., 57–8.

6 P. Brock, *Pacifism in Europe to 1914* (Princeton University Press, 1972), 445.

7 K. Tarasoff, *Plakun-Trava: The Doukhobors* (Grand Forks: Mir, 1982).

8 V. Makarova, "Evolution of the contemporary Doukhobor sobranie practice in Saskatchewan," *Canadian Ethnic Studies* 52:1 (2020), 95–117.

9 C. McKeogh, *Tolstoy's Pacifism* (Amherst, NY: Cambria Press, 2009), 101.

10 V.B. Shklovsky, *Lev Tolstoy* (Moscow: Molodaia gvardiia, 1963), 843.

11 Ibid., 856.
12 McKeogh, *Tolstoy's Pacifism*, 123.
13 Donskov, *Leo Tolstoy and the Canadian Doukhobors*.
14 Verigin, *Chronicles of Spirit Wrestlers' Immigration to Canada*, xii.
15 Ibid., xv.
16 Donskov, *Leo Tolstoy and the Canadian Doukhobors*, 111–13, 370.
17 Donskov (ed.), *Leo Tolstoy in Conversation*, 214.
18 Donskov, *Leo Tolstoy and the Canadian Doukhobors*.
19 Donskov (ed.), *Leo Tolstoy in Conversation*, 213.
20 Tarasoff, *Plakun-Trava*.
21 A. Donskov (ed.), *Sergei Tolstoy and the Doukhobors: A Journey to Canada, Diary and Correspondence* (University of Ottawa Press, 1998).
22 S. Inikova, "Leo Tolstoy's teachings and the Sons of Freedom in Canada," *Religiovedenie* 3 (2002), https://doukhobor.org/leo-tolstoys-teachings-and-the-sons-of-freedom-in-canada.
23 Ibid.
24 Donskov, *Leo Tolstoy and the Canadian Doukhobors*.
25 The author would like to acknowledge SSHRC Canada for providing an Insight grant that allowed the gathering of some information quoted in this article. Many thanks also go to A. Donskov, L.A. Ewashen, and S. Forrester for their helpful comments as well as to the Doukhobor community and friends.
26 Donskov (ed.), *Leo Tolstoy in Conversation*, 197.
27 Brock, *Pacifism in Europe to 1914*, 458.

CHAPTER 30

America

Galina Alekseeva

From the mid-1880s until he left Yasnaya Polyana in 1910, Tolstoy maintained close ties with Americans. During this period, he received about 2,500 letters from America, as well as numerous books and periodicals and thus became acquainted with those American writers, philosophers, and public figures who were near to him in spirit. Tolstoy had a keen interest in things American: history, culture, religion, art, literature, and traditions. To him, the United States was "the most sympathetic country" (87:4).

Tolstoy discovered America for himself, but America, in turn, discovered Tolstoy for itself. Many publishers brought out his works; literary magazines competed for his novels and philosophical and religious tracts. So many translations of Tolstoy's works were published across America in 1886 that people called it the "Tolstoyan year." On June 21, 1900, Tolstoy addressed the American people in a letter to Edward Garnett that was intended for publication in *Harper's Magazine*. "If I were to address the American people," he wrote, "I would try to express my gratitude for the enormous help I received from American writers who flourished in the '50s. I would mention Garrison, Parker, Emerson, Ballou and Thoreau – not as the greatest writers, but as those whom I think of as having particularly influenced me. Others would include: Channing, Whittier, Lowell, Walt Whitman – a brilliant galaxy of the kind one rarely encounters in world literature" (72:397).

Inspired by Tolstoy's ideas, his meditations on the meaning of life and on ways for humanity to evolve, American pilgrims – scholars, writers, journalists, diplomats, pastors, scientists, politicians, farmers – journeyed to Yasnaya Polyana. In the words of the publisher and journalist Lucy Mallory, Tolstoy "became immortal in his own lifetime."[1] To most visitors, meeting with Tolstoy was a profound, unforgettable event. After reading *On Life*, the lawyer, diplomat, and poet Ernest Crosby visited Tolstoy at Yasnaya Polyana in 1894, and then gave up his career and became an ardent preacher of Tolstoy's ideas in America. In early December of 1903, the Democratic politician William Jennings Bryan visited Tolstoy at Yasnaya Polyana. The following year, he wrote an essay about his visit and called it "The Apostle of Love." Bryan included the essay in his book *Under Other Flags* (1904), which was sent to Yasnaya Polyana. The lecturer and journalist George Kennan published a detailed description of his 1886 visit to Tolstoy in *The Century Magazine.* People of all convictions and views came to see Tolstoy, among them the Episcopal Minister William Newton, medical doctor Alice Stockham, journalist Henry George Jr., writer and translator Isabel F. Hapgood, diplomat Andrew White, and many others, some of whom recorded their recollections. Tolstoy's popularity was such that Theodore Roosevelt even wrote an article criticizing Tolstoy for his philosophy and warning young American writers not to be influenced by him. Because of *Anna Karenina* and *The Kreutzer Sonata*, Roosevelt found Tolstoy's philosophy "profoundly immoral" and called him a "sexual moral pervert."[2] Though in general Roosevelt recognized the greatness of Tolstoy's art, he was strongly against his religious, philosophical, and social views. Tolstoy read about Roosevelt's article in a 1909 essay in *The Russian Word,*[3] and commented in his diary: "Roosevelt's article about me. The article is stupid but it is pleasant for me" (57:70).

Tolstoy's profound interest in American writers could be explained by the general ethical and religious tendency of their eighteenth- and nineteenth-century ideas. In his early years, he most likely understood this tendency only intuitively, but later in life he would use it as the theoretical grounds for his articles and tracts. The conclusions he arrived at there were well prepared by his long engagement with American literature, philosophy, and religion, from keeping his "Franklin Journal" in the early 1850s – where he tried in his own way to imitate Benjamin Franklin's system of moral self-perfection described in his *Autobiography* – to finishing his famous address to the American people of June 21, 1900. It is interesting that Tolstoy was drawn not to the German Romantics, but to the eighteenth-century literature of reason and common sense. In his later years, he was especially interested in literature with a strong moral message. American nineteenth-century writers, as the true representatives of the New World, tried to collect knowledge and traditions from all across the globe. Their literature, which privileged ethics over intellectualism and aesthetics, appealed to Tolstoy because it continued the traditions of eighteenth-century ideals and was connected with the traditions of antiquity, with Eastern religious and philosophical systems, and with German classical philosophy. Tolstoy often spoke and wrote of parallels between Russian and American literature that derived from peculiarities in the two countries' histories.

In the 1880s to 1890s Tolstoy became particularly interested in American "practical Christianity" as he called it (65:144), which was part of the American utopia movement. With the help of his friends, he attempted to accumulate all the information he could on "practical Christianity," American communes, and the American idea of utopia. Tolstoy had a special interest in American religious communities in part because of his intention to write an essay "About 1000 Faiths." In one of his letters, he noted about American religious movements: "I very much want to write about what I know and how I interpret it" (64:314). He was drawn to numerous American communes – Shakers, Quakers, Christian Scientists, universalists, spiritualists, perfectionists, the commune of the Christian Commonwealth, the Brotherhood of the New Life of Thomas Lake Harris. Tolstoy believed they offered a model for others to emulate. The idea of a commune had been important to Tolstoy since his childhood when his beloved brother Nikolai told a mysterious legend about a "green stick" on which was written the secret to living in love, peace, and brotherhood. For many American writers as well as for Tolstoy himself, "building up a city on the hill" – the Kingdom of God on Earth – seemed to be quite real, the harmony of a person and God a clear reality. Like the American writers he admired, Tolstoy thought about the state as a temporary form of life and shared the view that the mission of a writer was similar to the mission of a prophet.

Tolstoy's personal library demonstrates his great interest in American literature, philosophy, and religion. The books of almost all the writers mentioned in his 1900 address have been preserved there. The shelves of his library contain works by Mather, Prescott, Cooper, Beecher-Stowe, Poe, Longfellow, Garland, London, Glasgow, Twain, Markham, and others, as well as the authors who influenced him most: Emerson, Thoreau, Whitman, Bellamy, Sinclair, Garrison, Ballou, George, and Hunter. Some of the books were sent to Yasnaya Polyana signed by the authors, some bear Tolstoy's marginalia and were used as sources for his work.

Tolstoy had *his own* America and cherished many writers whose names sometimes meant little to Americans. William Lloyd Garrison (1805–79), an American abolitionist and organizer of the Non-Resistance Society, is a prime example. Tolstoy subscribed to Garrison's ideas of non-resistance at a time when Garrison's name was virtually forgotten in America. He called

Garrison "the greatest man" and "the great prophet" (74:205–6) and mentioned his name many times in his diaries, letters, essays, and in *The Kingdom of God Is Within You*. In his address to the American people (June 21, 1900), Tolstoy named Garrison first among the authors who influenced him. He owned a copy of Garrison's biography in four volumes and warmly praised it.[4] Tolstoy found his own views had much in common with Garrison's doctrine of nonviolence. He translated Garrison's "Declaration of Sentiments" about universal peace and began to work on an introduction, which grew into his tract *The Kingdom of God Is Within You*. Thanks to *The Kingdom of God Is Within You*, which was translated and published in America in 1893, Garrison, who had been almost completely forgotten in his own country, acquired his popularity.

Besides Garrison's "Declaration of Sentiments," Tolstoy also included Adin Ballou's "Catechism" in *The Kingdom of God Is Within You*. In 1889, Lewis Wilson, a Unitarian pastor and one of Ballou's disciples, sent Tolstoy several books on the nonviolence and pacifism of his teacher, who was a Unitarian minister and founder of a utopian commune in Hopedale, Massachusetts. All those books have been preserved in Tolstoy's personal library. Ballou read Tolstoy's *What I Believe* in 1886, and thanks to Wilson, they began a correspondence about the theory and practice of nonviolence. There were grounds for both agreements and disagreements in their written dialogue, but they each respected the other and only Ballou's death in 1890 brought an end to their inspiring dialogue. Tolstoy felt great sympathy for Ballou's activities as a preacher of nonviolence and practical Christianity. Ballou's *Autobiography* (1896) includes a section on his relationship with Tolstoy (the autobiography appeared in Tolstoy's library after Ballou's death).

Tolstoy was profoundly interested in the works of New England writers, from Beecher-Stowe's *Uncle Tom's Cabin* (1852) and Channing's sermons, to Walt Whitman's *Leaves of Grass* (1855). However, he directed special attention to the life and works of Ralph Waldo Emerson and Henry David Thoreau. Though Tolstoy became aware of Emerson's writings in the 1850s and there was a note about Emerson in his diary of March 24, 1858 (48:11), he began reading Emerson in May–June of 1884 with great enthusiasm: "Emerson – self-reliance delight" (49:92). In June of 1884, Tolstoy read Emerson's *Representative Men* (1856), which has been preserved in Tolstoy's personal library. Tolstoy was particularly attracted to Emerson's essay on Napoleon and was satisfied with his perception of the French Emperor.

Almost at the same time, Tolstoy was discovering Thoreau, another leading transcendental philosopher and poet. Tolstoy quoted both

Emerson and Thoreau widely in his essays, diaries, letters, and his *Circle of Reading, Thoughts of Wise Men for Every Day*, and *Path of Life*. Tolstoy's personal library includes *Labour Prophet* (December, 1893), *Philosophy of Natural Life* (1903), and *Walden* (1904), which Tolstoy read in the 1890s to 1900s. Tolstoy was thrilled to read Thoreau's *Civil Disobedience* and immediately initiated its Russian translation and publication in the *Free Word* in England. Tolstoy's and Thoreau's understanding of nonviolence and civil disobedience had many parallels. In a fascinating chain of influence, Thoreau influenced Tolstoy, who influenced Gandhi, who founded "The Tolstoy Farm" in South Africa (see Chapter 31). Gandhi, in turn, influenced Martin Luther King, who spent a month in India to study Gandhi's nonviolent activities. Thus, Thoreau's ideas of the late 1840s were relayed across the world and then came back to America in the movement of Martin Luther King in the 1960s.

Tolstoy often compared the situation in America at the time of the Civil War and the abolitionist movement with the situation in Russia after the abolition of serfdom, which had been preceded by the Crimean War. He noted the appearance of the "brilliant galaxy" of writers both in the United States and in Russia at that time. He always mentioned Walt Whitman among the American writers he greatly respected. They both experienced a real war on the battlefield and in the hospitals. By the beginning of the Crimean War, Tolstoy was famous for his *Childhood* and some war stories. By the beginning of the Civil War, Whitman was known as the author of *Leaves of Grass*. Tolstoy's copy of this work contains his penciled notes indicating his deep appreciation of the American poet, whom he called "a philosophic poet" (1907).[5] In their depictions of war, both Tolstoy and Whitman destroyed accepted stereotypes, presenting not the glory of military genius or the parade of uniforms and epaulets, but war in its "true expression," an approach highly unusual among their contemporaries. In his *Sevastopol Stories*, Tolstoy captured the idea of war in general while also depicting the specificities of the Crimean War in particular. Whitman's *The Drum-Taps* shares this combination of universality and specificity. In their diaries, letters, and essays, both Tolstoy and Whitman created a panorama of war that integrated real events and people and captured the suffering war created. In their later years, the horrors they had witnessed would lead both men to completely reject war.

Tolstoy was sure that the abolition of private property would eventually free humanity, and in this connection, he paid special attention to the American political economist Henry George, with his ideas of "single tax" land reforms. According to George, people should own only the value they produce themselves. Economic value obtained from land must belong to all members of society equally. For Tolstoy, Henry George's philosophy was the economic foundation for his own religious and ethical doctrine. On February 22, 1885, Tolstoy wrote to his wife about reading an "important book" by Henry George (he was reading *Progress and Poverty* and *Social Problems* at that time). When Henry George learned of Tolstoy's interest in his concept of land reforms, he sent him his books, some autographed. Tolstoy developed the ideas of Henry George in his own essays and tracts, and made the protagonist of *Resurrection* (1899) a practical follower of George's reforms. Tolstoy recommended George's books to Russian prime-minister Pyotr Stolypin, Grand Duke Nikolai Mikhailovich, and Emperor Nicholas II, insisting that following George's reforms in Russia was the way to the country's salvation.

The book *Siberia and the Exile System* (1891) by George Kennan, a famous traveler, writer, and journalist, was another important source for *Resurrection*. In June 1886, Kennan arrived at Yasnaya Polyana from Siberia (via Moscow) to interview Tolstoy on behalf of *The Century Magazine*. Their conversation touched on Tolstoy's belief in nonviolence. The political exiles Keenan had met in Siberia had asked him to convince Tolstoy to speak out in their defense, but Tolstoy rejected their revolutionary method: violence. The discussion at Yasnaya Polyana found its reflection in Kennan's essay *A Visit to Count Tolstoi*.[6] Kennan was profoundly impressed by Tolstoy's personality; Tolstoy found Kennan a "pleasant and sincere man." He wrote to Kennan on August 8, 1890 about his "wonderful essays" and how through them he was in "spiritual communication" with him (65:138). He also mentioned Kennan in his diaries and letters, and Kennan probably served as the prototype for the Englishman in the third part of *Resurrection*. Kennan never lost his interest in Tolstoy either. He collected materials about Tolstoy from the Russian and foreign media, and in September 1909 he wrote an essay, *Count Tolstoy and the First Russian Duma*, for *Outlook*, in which he defended Tolstoy from Theodore Roosevelt's accusations about his moral doctrine.

In June 1889, the famous American translator Isabel F. Hapgood gifted Tolstoy a book by the recognized American writer Edward Bellamy, *Looking Backward: 2000–1887* (Boston, 1888). Tolstoy immediately began to read it with a pencil in his hand, noting in his diary: "Looking backward wonderful" (50:101). Deeply impressed by Bellamy, Tolstoy mentioned him in *The Kingdom of God Is Within You*, "The Slavery of Our Times," and *The Meaning of the Russian Revolution*. Tolstoy was well read in some of Bellamy's predecessors like Thomas More, Francis Bacon, and William

Morris. He both agreed and disagreed with Bellamy's version of utopia and expressed some critical remarks about it in a number of his works, but he still encouraged the well-known publisher and journalist A.S. Suvorin to publish this "remarkable" book (64:335).

Upton Sinclair (1878–1968), another American socialist writer who belonged to the Southern aristocracy, was one of the young writers warned by Roosevelt not to be influenced by Tolstoy. In March 1906, Sinclair sent an autographed copy of *The Jungle* (New York, 1906) to Yasnaya Polyana: "To Lyof Tolstoi with the sincerest regards of Upton Sinclair. Princeton, New Jersey, USA March 24th, 1906."[7] Tolstoy read this book very attentively, and as he had done in the book of Bellamy, marked some passages as he attempted to understand the author's ideas. He discussed it with his family members and friends.[8] Tolstoy obviously traced certain parallels with the situation in Russia, and understood that the socialist slogans in the novel were undoubtedly connected with the violence the characters experienced. In a way, Tolstoy was prepared for Sinclair's novel, as in 1905 he had read *Poverty* (1904) by the American sociologist Robert Hunter (Hunter visited Tolstoy in 1903 and joined the Socialist Party of America in 1905).[9] There are some parallels between Hunter's book and Tolstoy's *On the Census in Moscow* (1882) and *What Then Must We Do?* (1884–6). Tolstoy knew the phenomenon of poverty very well and judged Hunter's book as a professional. According to D.P. Makovitsky, Tolstoy thought that it was scrupulously researched. He wrote to Hunter about *Poverty*: "The theme of it has always been and remains of the greatest interest to me" (76:19). Tolstoy's personal library includes another copy of *Poverty* and one more of Hunter's books, *Socialists at Work* (1908).

In 1908, Thomas Edison sent one of his first phonographs to Tolstoy to record his voice (see Chapter 25), and two Americans arrived with that machine, which has been preserved in Tolstoy's study intact. Tolstoy's voice can still be heard, and his death did not stop the stream of American pilgrims to Yasnaya Polyana. Succeeding generations in search of moral and aesthetic ideals continue to look to Tolstoy. Frank Norris, Hamlin Garland, Stephen Crane, Ellen Glasgow, Ernest Hemingway, William Faulkner, Lillian Hellman, William Saroyan, Kurt Vonnegut: innumerable American writers continue to feel drawn to Tolstoy's genius.

Notes

1 Quoted in P. Sergeenko (ed.), *O Tolstom, K 80-letiyu L. N. Tolstogo, Mezhdunarodny Al'manakh* (Moscow: Kniga, 1909), 108.

2 Arthur G. Sharp, *The Everything Theodore Roosevelt Book: The Extraordinary Life of an American Icon* (Avon, MA: Adams Media, 2011). Roosevelt's article was published in *The Outlook* 92 (1909).

3 V. Kruglyak, "Roosevelt o Tolstom," *Russkoe Slovo*, May 19, 1909.

4 W. Ph. Garrison and Fr. J. Garrison, *William Lloyd Garrison, 1805–1879*, 4 vols. (New York: The Century, 1885–9).

5 Dushan Makovitsky, *U Tolstogo. 1904–1910: "Yasnopolyanskie zapiski,"* 4 vols. (Moscow: Nauka, 1979–81), vol. II, 587.

6 *The Century Magazine*, 34 (June 1887), 253–65.

7 *Biblioteka L.N. Tolstogo v Yasnoi Polyane: Bibliographicheskoe opisanie* (Tula: Izdatel'skii Dom Yasnaya Polyana, 1999), vol. III: *Books in foreign languages*, Pt. 2: M-Z, А-Я, 362.

8 Dushan Makovitsky described Tolstoy's correspondence with Sinclair in his *Notes*. See *U Tolstogo*, vol. II, 320–1, 329, 335, 338.

9 The book has been preserved in Tolstoy's personal library with his penciled marks on pages 334–5 and 337 of chap. 7, "Conclusion."

CHAPTER 31

India

Suvij Sudershan

In August 2019, many prominent Indian newspapers reported how, amidst a court case involving charges of sedition, scholar and activist Vernon Gonsalves had been asked by the Mumbai High Court to explain why he possessed a copy of Lev Tolstoy's *War and Peace*.[1] The judge later declared that he was misquoted, for he had sought an explanation not for the possession of the Russian classic (which, he claimed, he knew well enough), but rather, of another work: *War and Peace in Junglemahal: People, State and Maoists*. But this mistake, at worst a case of media sensationalism, also revealed the political power that Tolstoy's name carries in India.[2]

In India, Tolstoy's life and works have been interpreted in myriad ways, which can be divided into two broad categories: one linked with Gandhi and the other with Lenin. This split image arises from a duality of anti-colonial resistance movements in the first half of the twentieth century, which was the historical backdrop to Tolstoy's dissemination in South Asia. The first of these streams, the well-known Gandhian variety of nonviolent resistance, was predominantly rooted in a series of letters exchanged by the Indian anarchist and independence activist Mohandas Karamchand Gandhi (1869–1948) and the Russian writer. The active presence of this side of Tolstoy's legacy is visible in a number of works, discussed below, which focus on the saintly qualities held in common by, and passed in priestly confidence between, Tolstoy and Gandhi. The lesser-known strand of Tolstoy's Indian legacy is the leftist way of under-standing the Russian writer's works, forged within the circles of the progressive writers and activists who championed a more radical approach to the struggle against British colonialism. The ideological origin of this strand is located in the popularization of the Russian Bolshevik revolu-tionary Vladimir Lenin's (1870–1924) multiple writings on Tolstoy.

This chapter traces the development of these two Tolstoyan lineages in India: the Gandhian and the Leninist. Cultural and political actors in the

country – both before and after Independence and Partition in 1947 –
have consistently used the figure of the writer to enable and lend authority
to their actions and ideological positions. Due to the exceptional position
occupied by Gandhi, as "Father of the Nation," within the Indian socio-
political scheme, the Gandhian claims to Tolstoy have been more popu-
larly remembered. Gandhi also had multiple personal linkages to Tolstoy,
which were forged while the Russian writer was still alive. Simultaneously,
the Leninist interpretations of Tolstoy, which occupied a somewhat
peripheral position until Gandhi's assassination in 1948, also thrived in
the postcolonial nation. My overview will be tempered by the extreme
multiplicity of linguistic and literary traditions in South Asia, which exceed
the capabilities of any individual scholar. While the chapter provides a map
of the many ways in which Tolstoy has moved in the region, a deeper,
more specific understanding of the routes of this movement must await the
work of experts with specific knowledge of more of South Asia's different
linguistic and cultural traditions.

Near the end of his life, Tolstoy had become an internationally well-
known and controversial opponent of state oppression, both within and
outside tsarist Russia.[3] Tarak Nath Das, a radical Indian publicist, was
among the many anti-colonial activists and writers who reached out to
Tolstoy to publicize the oppression faced by Indians under British colonialism. The Das–Tolstoy correspondence was published as "Letter to a
Hindu" in October 1909. The publication of this correspondence in the
Indian press was accompanied by an introduction written by none other
than Gandhi himself.[4]

The multifarious links between Gandhi and Tolstoy span the fields of
literature, politics, and ethics. When he reworked *Ivan the Fool* into
Gujarati in 1922, Gandhi became one of the first Indian translators of
Tolstoy's creative works.[5] He also sent a copy of his own work, *Indian
Home Rule* (1909), to the Russian writer.[6] In 1910, Gandhi, along with
others, established a commune near Johannesburg in South Africa, which
was named "The Tolstoy Farm" and which operated on Tolstoyan principles of self-help, physical labor, and nonviolence.[7] These ideas, especially
nonviolent resistance, appealed immensely to Gandhi. The organizational
tactics he developed from them went on to determine the character of anti-
colonial politics under the Indian National Congress until 1947.[8] Even
after Gandhi's assassination in 1948, Gandhian leaders like Vinoba Bhave
and Jayaprakash Narayan would position themselves, and be understood
as, political Tolstoyans.[9] No wonder then that in her seminal work on

Tolstoy's multiple linkages to India, Radha Balasubramanian remarks that Gandhi was "in a sense Tolstoy's political-spiritual heir."[10]

Along with Tolstoy, Gandhi considered many other international thinkers and writers important to his development, including Henry David Thoreau and John Ruskin. However, the Tolstoy–Gandhi link is the best known, in part because several important commentators elaborated on the connection between the two men. In the USSR, A.V. Lunacharsky, the People's Commissar of Education, published an article called "Indian Tolstoi" (1923), which, while somewhat critical of Gandhian methods, ultimately lauded the importance of the Indian nationalist movement.[11] Gandhi also wrote letters to Tolstoy's widow in 1913 over "the question of [Tolstoy's] manuscripts," as well as to the prominent Tolstoyan V.G. Chertkov in 1929 explaining his stances on pacifism.[12] Furthermore, Gandhi ensured the preservation of this lineage for posterity by emphasizing Tolstoy's impact on his works to his biographer Joseph Doke as well as by cataloguing it himself in his booklet *Indian Home Rule*.[13] Another important and early commentator on the link between the two men was the Bengali writer and Nobel Laureate Rabindranath Tagore, who applauded Gandhi's astute understanding and utilization of Tolstoy's principles.[14]

These proclamations of proximity between the two men, combined with Gandhi's statements that painted Tolstoy as his guru, propelled the latter into an orbit unheard of for a foreign writer in India. This association was adopted and developed in other translations and adaptations of Tolstoy's work. Many of the early biographies and short-story collections through which Tolstoy was introduced in India described him, quite explicitly, as a saint. The appellations attached to his name in these works range from the Bengali monograph *Sage Tolstoy* (*Rishi Tolstoy*, 1912), to the Gujarati *Russia's Saint* (*Russia-no-Sadhu*, 1935), a Hindi collection which calls him "Mahatma Tolstoy" (1926), and the 1934 Tamil book *Mahatma Gandhi's Guru Tolstoy's biography* (*Mahatma Gandhiyin Guru Tolstoy saritham*).[15] While the introduction of foreign figures to the Indian reading public through invocations of sainthood or sagely knowledge is not peculiar to Tolstoy's case, it can certainly be admitted that, working in tandem with "Mahatma" (noble soul) Gandhi's already saintly image, and his statements of alignment with the Russian writer, Tolstoy's canonization in the Indian discourse was more total than that of others.

Mudda Viswanathan subtitled his 1950 Telugu adaptation of *Ivan the Fool* (*Chitra Seema*) "the Tolstoy story which inspired Mahatma Gandhi." The preface of this same text carries an illustration of Gandhi accompanied by a short contextual discussion of the importance of physical self-labor.[16] The Kannada writer D. Javare Gowda admits the importance Gandhi held for popularizing Tolstoy's works and, as an educator, actively used linkages between the two to introduce the Russian writer to Indian students.[17] The right-wing politician and writer Giriraj Kishore's play *Hang Gandhi!* (*Gandhi ko Phaansi Do!*, 2009) depicts Gandhi having visions of Tolstoy, who appears at crucial moments to guide Gandhi's actions as the latter begins his activist work in South Africa.[18]

Invocations of the saintly Tolstoy strengthened associations between him and Gandhi, much to the detriment of the Leninist vision of the writer. For instance, introducing his translation of *Social Evils and Their Remedies,* Madhav Prasad Mishra uses religious ideas and images to bring together the figures of Gandhi and Tolstoy, while chastising Lenin for his emphasis on that which is only material. For Mishra, Tolstoyan ethics would lead to a "spiritual communism" which was, crucially, very different from the "political communism" of Lenin.[19] He goes on to explain that this "spiritual communism" would be closer to "Ram Rajya" or "Kingdom of Ram" (the Hindu deity). "Ram Rajya" was the term (for the most part vaguely used) with which Gandhi described his ideal of post-Independence Indian society. Grounded in ideas of trusteeship – the rich act benevolently as trustees for the poor – "Ram Rajya" was a utopian vision of society in which class and caste differences could be abolished through fiduciary relationships between former oppressors and those exploited by them.[20] In this way, Mishra underscores Tolstoy's influence on both Gandhi and Lenin, but simultaneously undermines the latter in favor of the former. As Mishra points out, Gandhi's vision of society organically evolved from Tolstoy's, as opposed to Lenin's "grossly materialistic" conception of social relations, an apostasy for these Gandhian interpretations.

At the same time, and just as often, Lenin's closeness to Tolstoy was registered through the same glowing terms with which Mishra paints the Gandhi–Tolstoy relationship. For while Tolstoy's introduction to the Indian scene was accompanied by the rise of the Indian National Congress and Gandhian ideologies, in the international context, it was often received as a part and parcel of the events in Russia between 1905 and 1917, i.e. the First Russian Revolution and the Bolshevik Revolution. However, this leftist perspective on Tolstoy is often obscured through recourse to Gandhi's interpretations of the Russian writer, and their shared doctrine of "humane" nonviolence, which is opposed to an assumed implicit violence in the Leninist tradition.

The celebrated Urdu-Hindi writer Munshi Premchand (1880–1936) acted as a mediating figure between the Gandhian and Leninist interpretations. Premchand translated many of Tolstoy's stories, retaining the plot and purpose, but changing the names, cultural traditions, and occupations, so as to suit Indian realities, such as the presence of the caste system. Due to his prominence, his localized versions of Tolstoy's stories were very important for the promulgation of the Russian writer's works through pre-1947 India. At the same time, Premchand was profoundly influenced by Gandhian thought during the late 1910s and the 1920s (the period when he translated Tolstoy). Therefore, because of his well-known proximity to both Tolstoy and Gandhi, those influenced by Premchand and his ethos have been painted as Gandhians as well.[21]

However, this derivation ignores the development of Premchand's ideological influences. Premchand's politics evolved, and later in his life, they were marked by an admiration for socialism and the Bolshevik Revolution.[22] Premchand even disagreed with many of Gandhi's ideas, especially the aforementioned utopia of the "Kingdom of Ram," which the writer considered naïve, sectarian, and condescending toward the oppressed castes (legally categorized under the rubric of "Dalit," which means "broken").[23] Premchand's son and biographer, Amrit Rai, has sought to distance Gandhi from his father's translations of Tolstoy by pointing out how Premchand's translations were coterminous with Gandhi's own Tolstoy translations, i.e. at that time there was no mutual influence.[24]

A Gandhian understanding of the Premchand–Tolstoy relationship effectively neutralizes the existence of a separate and distinct history of writers whose interpretations of Tolstoy invoke Lenin and the Bolsheviks rather than Gandhi. Once Gandhi is taken out of this equation, a different way of seeing Tolstoy emerges. This tradition is largely rooted in the works of the All Indian Progressive Writers' Association (AIPWA), a group of socialist writers who had grown up admiring Premchand, and even invited the older writer to deliver their founding speech on April 9–10, 1936. Many writers who fell into the orbit of the AIPWA went on to adapt or translate Tolstoy's life and works through a leftist perspective. They focused a little less on nonviolence, and, instead, took their cue from other Tolstoyan principles like the abolition of private property.

Much like the Gandhian trend, here too writers and thinkers sometimes embellished Tolstoy's image to make him seem closer to Lenin's worldview, and, at times, to even inaccurately paint the Russian writer as a communist and a Bolshevik himself. In this context the Bengali activist-writer Mahashweta Devi included Tolstoy when listing her favorites: "the literature of famous communist writers – Ilya Ehrenburg, Tolstoy, Kataiyev."[25] Along the same lines, the Assamese literary historian Ismail Hossain dismissed the Nobel Prize committee, whose anticommunist attitudes he located in their antipathy toward *both* Maxim Gorky *and* Tolstoy and "the smell of socialist realism" in their works.[26] The same linkage appears in the Kannada writer U.R. Ananthamurthy's short poem "Lenin and Tolstoy":

> As if about to rise
> the uniformed Lenin lies in state
> undecayed
> in a shining stone mausoleum.
>
> Wanting to become nothing and failing,
> ripening, loosening, dropping, withering
> Tolstoy became earth
> becoming grass
> under a tree on a slightly risen mound.
>
> Long live the revolution[27]

The long cycle of poems by the Malayalam writer K. Satchidanandan titled *Snow* also contains two consecutive poems: "Tolstoy Is Not Here," dedicated to the Soviet Avar poet Rasul Gamzatov, and "Indian Lenin," also about Tolstoy.[28]

The history of this leftist Tolstoy tradition is highly variegated, comprised of positions taken and interpretations provided by all stripes of progressivists. One of the first female writers in the Odia language, Narmada Kar (1893–1980), published an adaptation of Tolstoy's "The Coffee-House of Surat" as "Dilemma" ("Dwanda," 1926).[29] The anti-caste activist and writer Pandurang Sadashiv Sane's (1899–1950) Marathi translation of *What Is Art?* in the 1930s (at a time when Sanskrit was still the traditional literary language) played a crucial role in the literary development of the Marathi language.[30] The Kashmiri playwright Ali Mohammad Lone (1927–87), in an act of resistance against the Indian occupation, adapted one of Tolstoy's works as a radio play in the 1960s.[31] The Tamil writer Su. Samuthiram (1941–2003) wrote path-breaking novels on the lives of the LGBTQ community in India, as well as a play on Tolstoy's life in the 1990s.[32]

It is this *duality* of Tolstoy's legacy in India, as opposed to a simply Gandhian formulation, which formed the backdrop to the "*War and Peace* episode" in the August 2019 trial of Vernon Gonsalves. Criticized by many as a part of the right-wing Indian government's crackdown on liberal lawyers and activists, the event also reveals the politically charged position that Tolstoy has occupied in modern India.[33] Indeed, among the many translators of Tolstoy is the Bengali peasant leader and communist activist Saroj Dutta (1914–71), who was assassinated by police forces for his political activities.[34] So, while initially, one might wonder what associations could enable *War and Peace* to even be *considered* (by the press, if not by the courts) a plausible accessory for those accused of "seditious Maoist tendencies," the anxiety it inspired in the contemporary moment reveals the latent anti-authoritarian associations Tolstoy's figure continues to carry. That Tolstoy had once been so relevant to such diverse political agents shows the pertinence that his works had to the historical moment of decolonization. That Tolstoy could still be seen as a threat to power in India highlights the continuation of that historical moment.

Notes

1 Swati Deshpande, "'Knew Tolstoy Book Was a Classic': Judge," *The Times of India* (Mumbai Edition), August 30, 2019, 1.
2 Ibid. I use the term "India" to designate the region in South Asia colonized by the British Empire before 1947 and the postcolonial state of the Republic of India after 1947.
3 Ernest J. Simmons, *Tolstoy* (London: Routledge, 2014), 222–3.
4 Radha Balasubramanian, *The Influence of India on Leo Tolstoy and Tolstoy's Influence on India: A Study of Reciprocal Receptions* (Lewinston, NY: Edwin Mellen Press, 2013), 120–7.
5 Masoodul Hasan, "Some Aspects of Tolstoyana in India," in T.R. Sharma (ed.), *Essays on Leo Tolstoy* (Meerut: Shalabh Prakashan, 1989), 6.
6 Alexander Shifman, *Tolstoy and India*, trans. A.V. Esaulov (New Delhi: Sahitya Akademi, 1969), 109–10.
7 Balasubramanian, *Reciprocal Receptions*, 132.
8 E.N. Komarov, "Mahatma Gandhi and the Russian Revolution," in *Gandhi through Soviet Eyes, Lenin through Indian Eyes* (New Delhi: Indo-Soviet Cultural Society Publications, 1971), 16–20.
9 Jayaprakash Narayan, "Reconstruction of Indian Polity," in Bimla Prasad (ed.), *Socialism, Sarvodaya, and Democracy* (New Delhi: Asia Publishing House, 1964), 226; Simmons, *Tolstoy*, 235.
10 Ibid., 128.
11 The article was published in *Krasnaya Niva* 1 (Moscow, 1923). A.H. Vafa, "Study of Gandhi's Views and Activities in Soviet Union," in *Gandhi through Soviet Eyes, Lenin through Indian Eyes*, 43–4.
12 Shifman, *Tolstoy and India*, 109–10.
13 Ibid.

14 Annada Ray Shankar, "Tolstoy and Tagore," *Indian Literature* 4:1–2 (Oct. 1960/Sept. 1961), 75.

15 Hasan, "Tolstoyana," 4–9; Balasubramanian, *Reciprocal Receptions*, 191.

16 Mudda Viswanathan, *Chitra-Seema: Adaptation of Tolstoy's "Ivan the Fool"* (Madras: Jaya Niketan, 1950).

17 Balasubramanian, *Reciprocal Receptions*, 138.

18 Giriraj Kishore, "Hang Gandhi!," trans. Prajapati Shah, *Indian Literature* 55:4 (264) (July/August 2011), 147–81.

19 Madhav Prasad Mishra, *Tolstoy's Social Evils and Their Remedies: A Translation* (New Delhi: Sasta Sahitya Mandal, 1947), 5–8.

20 Qamar Rais, "The Relevance of Prem Chand's Heritage," in Bhisham Sahni and C.P. Paliwal (eds.), *Prem Chand: A Tribute* (New Delhi: Premchand Centenary Celebrations, 1980), 24.

21 Amrit Rai, "The Contemporary Relevance of Prem Chand," in Sahni and Paliwal (eds.), *Prem Chand*, 74.

22 Ibid., 78.

23 Ibid., 74.

24 Ibid.

25 Mahashweta Devi, Amar Mitra, and Sabyasachi Deb, "Mahashweta Devi: In Conversation," *Indian Literature* 40:3 (179) (May–June 1997), 171.

26 Birinchi Kumar Das, "Socialist Realism in Mikhail Sholokhov's Novels: A Cross-Cultural Study," PhD thesis, Gauhati University (2009), 200–1.

27 U.R. Ananthamurthy, "Lenin and Tolstoy," *Indian Literature* 35:3 (149) (May–June 1992), 28–9.

28 K. Satchidanandan, "*Snow*," *Indian Literature* 32:1 (129) (Jan.–Feb. 1989), 25–32.

29 Narmada Kar, "'Dwanda' (Dilemma)," in Sachidananda Mohanty (ed.), *Early Women's Writings in Orissa, 1898–1950: A Lost Tradition* (New Delhi: Sage, 2005).

30 Megha Pansare, "Lev Nikolayevich Tolstoy in Marathi Polysystem," *Critic: A Journal of the Centre for Russian Studies* 2:12 (2014), 62–5.

31 Ali Mohammad Lone, "The Kashmiri Radio-Play," *Indian Literature* 16:1–2 (Jan.–June 1973), 302.

32 "Su. Samuthiram: Meet the Author," *Sahitya Akademi*, April 19, 1998.

33 Sonam Saigal, Vijaita Singh, "Teltumbde, Navlakha surrender to NIA," *The Hindu*, April 15, 2020, 1.

34 "The Dauntless Droplet, Ocean's Fervour in the Heart," *Liberation: Central Organ of CPI(ML)*, June 2014, n.p.

CHAPTER 32

Eastern Religion

Jeff Love

Tolstoy had a pronounced interest in a number of religions other than Christianity. This interest became urgent and comprehensive in the 1880s after his so-called conversion. In this chapter, I give a brief account of Tolstoy's relation to Daoism, Buddhism, and Hinduism regarding the crucial question about the nature of the good life that preoccupied the later Tolstoy. Indeed, I suggest that Tolstoy turned to these other religions precisely because of his concern with identifying a universal human wisdom about the good life.

Tolstoy has been referred to as a universalist, and there is little doubt that the breadth and depth of his interests in other cultures are far greater than that of any other Russian writer of his time. Tolstoy's universalism is of a rather conventional stamp, however: he asserts that all religions say essentially the same thing, a statement which could be considered wildly reductive or chauvinist since the measure of the essential remains Christianity.

If it is somewhat unfair to reproach Tolstoy in this manner – he has long been criticized for reductive generalizing under the baleful influence of the hedgehog and fox distinction[1] – I think it is appropriate to recognize that in speaking of the "East" in this essay, I am being even more reductive, referring only to modes of thought that developed within the context of two immensely complex cultures which held Tolstoy's interest for many years: China and India. Moreover, application of the term "religion" to modes of thought developed in widely different cultures is problematic as well, perhaps not so much in Tolstoy's case because Tolstoy is concerned, above all, with religion as a comprehensive view of life and compendium of wisdom. As a consequence, in what follows I narrow the focus of this essay to consider these three "Eastern" traditions in terms of Tolstoy's quest to identify a universal wisdom about what constitutes the good life.

Tolstoy's concern with universal wisdom is arguably nowhere more evident than in the major "philosophical" work of his later career, *On*

Life (1886–7). Tolstoy's syncretic attitude emerges in the work's defiance of generic boundaries – philosophy and religion are grouped together as expressions of a common quest for wisdom, and this wisdom emerges as fundamentally the same across many cultures. A typical passage from the treatise:

> 'The life of a person, as an individual merely pursuing his own happiness among an innumerable multitude of other such individuals, each destroying the other and destroying itself, is evil and nonsense. True life cannot be thus.' Man has said this to himself since remotest antiquity. This inner contradiction of human life has been expressed with unusual force and clarity by Hindu, Chinese, Egyptian, Greek and Hebrew sages. Human reason has been directed, since remotest antiquity, at comprehending a human happiness that cannot be destroyed by strife among creatures, by suffering or by death. Ever since we have been aware of life, all forward movement of humanity has consisted of an ever-greater illumination of this happiness, free from doubt and impervious to strife, suffering, and death.
>
> Since remotest antiquity, and in the most diverse of nations, the teachers of humanity have revealed to people ever-clearer definitions of life that try to resolve life's inner contradiction. They have directed people toward the true happiness and true life that are natural for people. The human condition in the world is everywhere the same, and therefore the contradiction of a man's pursuit of individual happiness, and the realization of its impossibility, is also the same for everyone. All definitions of true happiness – and therefore all definition of true life – that have been revealed to people by the greatest minds of humanity are thus essentially the same. (26:327)[2]

This passage introduces in terms of the "inner contradiction of life" the primary elements of Tolstoy's thought for which he seeks confirmation in other traditions of thought. He does so in order to prove the veracity of his own view by appealing to its universality – the underlying (and highly debatable) assumption being that what all people hold to be true must be true.

Briefly put, the "inner contradiction of life" consists in the attempt to find happiness in the life of the embodied individual, a life that cannot give happiness because it is bound for termination in death. On the contrary, the only life that can give happiness is one that is not terminated, and Tolstoy locates this life outside the body. While this "outside" may vary according to the relevant cultural tradition, it nonetheless expresses a common conviction that the good life is not that of the individual but rather one that renounces the individual in favor of a greater principle animating a collective or community. This principle may be God or the Dao or Brahman, but all of these have in common the fact that they are absolute and eternal, not subject to coming into being and passing away, as is the life of the embodied individual.

With this in mind, I now turn to Tolstoy's specific engagements with Daoism, Buddhism, and the Hindu tradition.

Of all the non-Western sages, Tolstoy was most fascinated by Laozi and the *Daodejing* (simplified: 道德经) conventionally translated as the *Classic of the Way and Virtue*. Laozi means "old teacher" and the school he founded (the "dao-jia") constitutes one of the major religio-philosophical traditions of Chinese civilization. The principal focus of Daoism is "dao," the path or way of things, and Daoism's teachings explore the meaning of the path and of our relation to it. While some have identified Daoist elements in Tolstoy's fiction, particularly in *War and Peace*, Tolstoy did not grapple explicitly with Laozi and Daoism until the 1880s. His engagement with Daoism only increased thereafter, the affinity with Daoism so much in evidence in *War and Peace* becoming intense enough to lead Tolstoy to work on a translation of the *Daodejing* with his disciple E.I. Popov. Let me consider both Tolstoy's affinity for Daoism in *War and Peace* and then his direct involvement with Daoist texts.

One of the most famous aspects of *War and Peace* is the notion of "wise passivity" or wise restraint from action or "non-action." This notion appears most polemically in General Bagration's behavior of restraint at Schön Graben and in Mikhail Kutuzov's refusal to engage the French or to give credence to military action as the execution of the plan or will of one human being:

> "... and yet my dear boy, there's nothing stronger than those two warriors, patience and time; they'd do it all, but the advisers *n'entendent pas de cette oreille, voilà le mal*. Some want it, others don't. What can we do?" he asked, evidently expecting an answer. "Yes, what would you have us do?" he repeated, and his eyes shone with a profound, intelligent expression. "I'll tell you what to do," he went on, since Prince Andrei still gave no answer. "I'll tell you what to do, and what I do *dans le doute, mon cher*," he paused, "*abstiens-toi*." (11:174/Vol. 3, Pt. 2, Ch. 16)[3]

A wise passivity also appears in "civilian" characters like Platon Karataev whose action is marked by a seemingly effortless skill.

Some scholars have identified this passivity with the Daoist notion of *wu-wei* (無爲), a term that is notoriously difficult to translate: non-action, inaction or, somewhat more complexly, non-volitional or effortless action. Tolstoy himself translated the term with "non-doing" (*nedelanie*). And while it is precarious to suggest that Laozi influenced *War and Peace*, there is no doubt a rather pronounced affinity between the sages of that novel, like Kutuzov and Karataev, and the Daoist sage who, as Tolstoy would later suggest, wisely refrains from action or intervention in the way of things.

As I cautioned above, however, what is most evident in Tolstoy's later engagement with Daoism is that Tolstoy finds confirmation of his insistence that individual life and, in particular, the sense we have that, as individuals, we can act intentionally and influence the way of things, is false, an illusion. To the contrary. The one who is wise recognizes the futility of such action and submits to a greater law, be it that of God or the right path. Tolstoy in fact translates "dao" (道) in both ways, as God or path, and thereby stresses his understanding of Daoism as saying the same thing as Christianity, as Tolstoy saw it; namely, that one must submit to God or the "law of God" and, in doing so, one frees oneself of both the illusion of individual agency and the pain of death that accompanies those who live only for their individual existence.

Tolstoy's concern with non-action in Daoism is thus anchored in his reading of Christianity and, more than that, in his conviction that the individual is the locus of two widely-held but illusory beliefs: that we have the power to influence our destiny and that our individual life does not have to end in utter destruction. According to Tolstoy, these stubborn beliefs are the perpetual wellsprings of violence against other human beings and nature. They are inherently destructive. Where the individual rules, discord rules because the individual cannot achieve the freedom he or she seeks. The "inner contradiction of life" assures that the individual can only fail.

Wisdom is to recognize the inevitability of this failure and accept the yoke or discipline of the greater whole, of God or the path. For Tolstoy, Laozi realizes this aim preeminently in the doctrine of non-action that saves us from the pain and violence of illusion by counseling us not to act or to recognize the futility of all action that does not respect the whole and the other, whether that be other human beings or nature. Here one can see with some clarity the basic elements of Tolstoy's most powerful moral and political idea – the non-resistance to evil or, in the terms set out here, the refusal to assent to the illusion of individual agency and power with its inevitably destructive consequences.

The evacuation of the individual one sees in Tolstoy's turn to Laozi is likely the primary reason he grew interested in Buddhism, though in the case of Buddhism, the influence narrative may well be a good deal more complicated. Tolstoy seems to have come across Buddhist ideas at a fairly young age. In 1847, while recuperating at a hospital in Kazan, Tolstoy apparently made the acquaintance of a Buddhist monk, and there is speculation about how this meeting may have encouraged Tolstoy to investigate Buddhism. And there is the fascination with the thought of Arthur Schopenhauer that began in earnest in 1869 and ended with the rejection of Schopenhauer's pessimism much later on. These two influences (one perhaps apocryphal, the other reliable) are helpfully emblematic of Tolstoy's reaction to Buddhism insofar as Tolstoy admired the Buddhist respect for self-renunciation and the monastic life but expressed distrust regarding the extremity of self-renunciation. In this respect Tolstoy tends to view Buddhism ultimately not as a way of life but as a way of escaping from life: with the renunciation of self comes not the enrichment but rather the extinguishment of life.

The metaphor of extinguishment may well have had an impact on *Anna Karenina* where the death of the eponymous heroine is likened to a candle going out. But Tolstoy is far franker elsewhere. In *The Kreutzer Sonata*, the main character, Pozdnyshev, says:

> "You say, how will the human race go on?" he said, sitting down again across from me, with his legs spread wide and his elbows resting low on them. "Why should it go on, this human race?" he said.
>
> "Why? If it didn't we wouldn't exist."
>
> "And why should we exist?"
>
> "Why? In order to live."
>
> "And why live? If there's no goal at all, if life is given for the sake of life, there's no need to live. And if so, then the Schopenhauers, and the Hartmanns, and all the Buddhists are perfectly right. Well, but if there is a goal in life, it's clear that life should come to an end once that goal is achieved. And that's how it turns out," he said with visible excitement, obviously cherishing his thought greatly. "That's how it turns out. Note that if the goal of mankind – goodness, kindness, love, as you wish – if the goal of mankind is what is said in the prophecies, that all men will be united by love, that spears will be beaten into pruning hooks, and so on, what is it that hinders the achieving of that goal? Passions hinder it. Among the passions the strongest, and most evil, and most stubborn is sexual, carnal love, and therefore, if the passions are annihilated, including the ultimate, the strongest of them, carnal love, then the prophecy will be fulfilled, people will be united, the goal of mankind will be achieved, and it will have nothing to live for." (27:29–30)[4]

This attitude emerges in *A Confession* as well, where Tolstoy retells the well-known story of the Buddha's encounter with suffering, the result of which is the Buddha's determination to help free others of suffering:

> And Shakyamuni could find no comfort in life, and he decided that life is the greatest evil and he used all the powers of his spirit to free himself from it and to free others – to free them so that after death life would not somehow be renewed, to destroy life completely, at the root. That is what all Indian wisdom says. (23:26)[5]

Here Buddhism stands for "all Indian wisdom," and it is expressly identified with the desire to "destroy life completely" so as to be freed of the cycle of suffering (*samsāra*) by dying definitively rather than being reborn. In this interpretation of the Buddhist view, salvation consists in being able to die definitively rather than to be continuously reincarnated or returned to the world of suffering – the highest liberation or freedom then is precisely the liberation from the cycle of birth and death.

While reincarnation may have held little interest for Tolstoy, the effect of this radical idea of extinction on practical life seems to have produced a very ambivalent response. Tolstoy no doubt admired the purity of the view: the only way to be truly free of nature is to die once and for all and to do so intentionally. In other words, true liberation comes from suicide, and Tolstoy speaks positively of suicide in *A Confession* in the sense that he attributes to the notion of suicide a sober and courageous attitude to life. He also regrets his own inability to commit suicide.

If one applies this thinking to human beings as a whole, one comes back to Pozdnyshev's question: "Why should we exist?" Tolstoy can find no response adequate to this question. If Laozi recommends restraint, the Buddha recommends a more radical form of restraint, not by abstaining from action, but from life itself as forcing action, as requiring us to act and thereby revealing our lack of freedom, our inability not to do violence: the material needs of the body render us predators and destroyers, no matter what.

These themes emerge prominently in one of the great texts of the Hindu tradition that made a strong impact on Tolstoy: the *Bhagavad Gita*. Tolstoy had an abiding fascination with Indian culture and Indian religion in particular. It seems tolerably clear that he was familiar with some of the primary texts in the Hindu tradition, including the *Rigveda* and some of the *Upanishads* as well as the two major "epic" poems of classical Indian culture, the *Rāmāyana* and the immense *Mahābhārata*.

Tolstoy was also familiar with the writings of Śankara, perhaps the seminal thinker in the Hindu tradition, and with Swami Vivekananda, a remarkable nineteenth-century thinker whom Tolstoy quotes in his correspondence with Mohandas Gandhi. Given that this correspondence is so well known and significant in that Gandhi is one of the key representatives of Tolstoyan thought in the twentieth century along with Martin Luther King, Jr. (see Chapter 31), I focus this brief account on Tolstoy's interest in the *Bhagavad Gita* and, especially, in the speeches of Krishna.

The *Bhagavad Gita* or Song of God appears at a crucial point in the *Mahābhārata* and consists of a dialogue between Krishna and Arjuna, the leader of an army ready for battle. The dialogue interrupts the battle and Krishna speaks for God. While the *Bhagavad Gita* expresses the basic metaphysical foundations of Hindu thought – the focus on the absolute, the infinite and perfect deity or Brahman – Tolstoy's reading is typically practical, shorn of metaphysics:

> The truth that the principle of all that exists we cannot otherwise feel and understand than as Love and that the soul of man is an emanation of this principle, the development of which is what we call human life – is a truth that is more or less consciously felt by every man and therefore accessible to the most scientifically developed minds as well as to the most simple. This truth is the foundation of the religion of Krishna and of all religions. (77:81)

In yet another example of Tolstoy's syncretism, he regards the absolute as love and sees in this identification another expression of a basic universal principle: God, the path, the absolute all express the same thing – love. This love frees us from the narrow confines of the "inner contradiction of life" by having us appreciate ourselves as a drop of water in an ocean that is love – if we cling to ourselves, we avoid love, the universal, that which is one and all, and confine ourselves to the suffering futility of the individual.

Love is Tolstoy's response to extinction and it is a characteristic reading of Christian thinking for Tolstoy insofar as love is active self-renunciation, not for the sake of freedom per se but for the other, for people and nature. Love is the very principle of the surrender of oneself to the service of the whole; and this surrender has nothing of the rejection that Tolstoy identifies in Buddhism, nor the non-action of Laozi – rather, love is an active practice of opening oneself to the other, to the absolute by renouncing any selfish claims to them, whether sexual, commercial, or spiritual.

Notes

1 This distinction, derived from a fragment of the Greek poet Archilochus (seventh century BCE) and made famous in the case of Tolstoy by Sir Isaiah Berlin's essay, "The Hedgehog and the Fox," describes for Berlin the difference between one who sees one "big" thing in the multiplicity of appearances, the hedgehog, as opposed to one who sees only multiplicity, the fox. Berlin claims that Tolstoy was by nature a fox who wanted to be a hedgehog.

2 Leo Tolstoy, *On Life: A Critical Edition*, ed. Inessa Medzhibovskaya, trans. Michael Denner and Inessa Medzhibovskaya (Evanston, IL: Northwestern University Press, 2019), 64–5.

3 Leo Tolstoy, *War and Peace*, trans. Richard Pevear and Larissa Volokhonsky (New York: Vintage, 2007), 550.

4 Leo Tolstoy, *The Kreutzer Sonata*, in *The Death of Ivan Ilyich and Other Stories*, trans. Richard Pevear and Larissa Volokhonsky (New York: Knopf, 2009), 247–8.

5 Leo Tolstoy, *A Confession*, in *The Death of Ivan Ilyich and A Confession*, trans. Peter Carson (New York: Liveright, 2014), 166.

CHAPTER 33

English Varieties of Religious Experience

Liza Knapp

As he worked through his religion and wrestled with his conscience, Tolstoy did it his own way. What he believed and how he lived had to be right for him. Still, he drew on a variety of sources, including Russian Orthodoxy, folk piety, ancient and world religions, and philosophy. Figuring among these sources was religious experience emanating from England.[1]

Tolstoy was on English soil only once, in 1861, when he spent two weeks in London. Using a letter of introduction by Matthew Arnold (from his post in the Department of Education), Tolstoy visited schools for the working class in order to observe pedagogical practices that he might apply – or avoid – in his own schools for peasants back home (see Chapter 17). He also reported having attended a reading by Charles Dickens.

Tolstoy's exposure to English religious life came from reading and largely through fiction. It has been argued that the novel is a secular genre, or, in Georg Lukács's formulation, "the epic of a world that has been abandoned by God."[2] Still, the English novel is noted for its religious dimension, for how it novelizes spiritual life, ethics, and religious experience. Tolstoy's reading of English novels began early (see Chapter 20). That what he read in these novels left its mark in his religious imagination, as well as on his development as a novelist, is evident in his fiction, his life-writing, and in his treatises. Tolstoy continued to read English novels even after he started disparaging the novel as a sin-sick genre.

English Protestantism, the Bible, and the English Novel

The English novel from its origins through its "rise" in the eighteenth century and into its heyday in the nineteenth century is intimately inter-twined with Protestant religious life and with the Bible.[3] English novels are laced with the language of the Bible. And the Bible figures in a variety of ways in the plot, where it is read, interpreted, alluded to, quoted from. The action often becomes or is perceived as a novelization of biblical stories and paradigms. These novels often show how hard it is "to live Gospel-wise" in the here and now of England.

John Bunyan's *Pilgrim's Progress* (1678) was, after the Bible, one of the most powerful influences on the English religious imagination. It is also regarded as a forerunner of the English novel. There were two copies in Tolstoy's library at Yasnaya Polyana and he would most likely also have known Pushkin's "The Wanderer" (1836), a verse translation, with poetic license, of Bunyan's opening.

Pilgrim's Progress, composed while Bunyan was in prison for religious dissent, critiques the way of the world that its pilgrim, Christian, abandons as he sets off for the Celestial City. Christian is compelled to leave home and family by his reading of "a book," namely, the Bible. Tolstoy himself left home shortly before his death, in what may be seen as a (delayed) response to his own reading of the Bible.

Before setting off, Bunyan's pilgrim looks up from his Bible to ask, "What shall I do?" This question echoes those posed in the Gospels (of John the Baptist in Luke 3:10; of Jesus in Matthew 19:6). It was also a favorite Tolstoyan question: his fictional heroes often ask it, directly or indirectly, and Tolstoy titled his major treatise on social injustice *What Must We Then Do?* (1886). Tolstoy's answer, like John the Baptist's, Jesus's, and Bunyan's, is that what Tolstoy in his translation of the Gospels calls "true" life (instead of "eternal" life) requires a radical break from the way of life of the person asking the question.

Tolstoy's questions about what should be done hark back to the Gospels. But his attempts at an answer resonate with those of Bunyan, that forerunner of English novelists. Tolstoy's appropriation of these questions further supports William James' suggestion in *Varieties of Religious Experience* that Bunyan and Tolstoy were similar in how they experienced religious feeling and how they suffered from "divided selves" and "sick souls": "neither Bunyan nor Tolstoy could become what we have called healthy-minded. They had drunk too deeply of the cup of bitterness ever to forget its taste."[4]

In a key moment in *Pilgrim's Progress*, when Faithful, one of the pilgrim's fellow travelers, is put on trial by the locals in the town called Vanity, the accusations against him are that he "affirm[ed] that Christianity, and the customs of our town of Vanity were diametrically opposite, and could not be reconciled."[5] Faithful gets the death penalty. Bunyan's Faithful sounds like an early English prototype of Tolstoy, who, from early on in his fiction, and more directly in his later works, indicates that what the nominally Christian society of his fiction and his world promotes and celebrates is "diametrically opposite" to what he regards as true Christianity.

From *Pilgrim's Progress* to *Vanity Fair*

Scholars note the impact of Bunyan's allegorical *Pilgrim's Progress* on the English novel. From its title page on, William Thackeray's *Vanity Fair* (1848) conjures up both *Pilgrim's Progress* and the Book of Ecclesiastes.[6] (In Ecclesiastes, which Tolstoy responds to in his *Confession*, 1880, the Preacher laments the vanity of all earthly endeavors in the face of death.) Tolstoy read *Vanity Fair* and other works by Thackeray in 1855. And, in "Sevastopol in May," in an overt reference to Thackeray, he bemoans the ubiquity of vanity "even on the brink of the grave."

Thackeray christens *Vanity Fair* after a stop on Christian's way to the Celestial City. Here, all manner of crime is on view and pretty much everything, including land, honors, preferments, husbands and wives, is for sale. In *Vanity Fair* and other works, Thackeray questions the masterplots that drive so many novels (courtship, adultery, social ambition). Tolstoy does the same when, for example, he hints in his novels at what he drives home in *The Kreutzer Sonata*: that courtship is goods for sale at a market. And the more they take to heart "the angel of death" hovering over us all, the more Tolstoy's heroes lose their stomach for courtship plots, family happiness, dreams of glory, imitation of Napoleon, and strategies for earthly success. Thackeray provided a model for *novelizing* these truths about vanity and death.

Varieties of Piety in England

From its break from the Catholic Church in the sixteenth century, the Church of England was subject to criticism and dissent, starting with the Puritans, who wanted a purer and truer form of Christian piety and experience. After a period of what has been seen as stagnation of religious life among Anglicans, in the second half of the eighteenth and first half of the nineteenth centuries evangelical and nonconformist movements flowered within and outside of the Church of England. This prompted some change in Church and state, and non-Anglican Protestants, Catholics, and Jews were granted civil and political rights in the nineteenth century.

John Wesley (1703–91), one of the founders of what became Methodism, set out to awaken religious feeling, working at first from within the Church of England. Wesley preached Christ's love and mercy, salvation by faith, and the importance of reading and responding to the Bible. As Wesley indicated in an early sermon on Luke 4:18–19 (and Isaiah 61:1–2), Jesus had come "to preach the gospel to the poor, to heal the broken-hearted, to preach deliverance to captives ... and to set at liberty them that are bruised."[7]

Evangelical movements spoke to the poor and working-class, neglected by the Church establishment and those in power. Elie Halévy and others have argued that these movements in England offered an outlet for unrest that elsewhere, such as in France, resulted in revolution. Religious dissent took other forms: Congregationalists, Baptists, Unitarians, and Quakers asserted their right to exercise religious freedom, to interpret and act on the Bible as they saw fit, to break with tradition and hierarchy. The established Church was challenged to stand its ground. And counter-movements, such as the Oxford Movement, advocated a conservative return to ritual and tradition.

Questions of faith, piety, and religious life were woven into the reality that nineteenth-century English novels represent. Doctrines and affiliations are often not explicitly delineated. Many of the novels feature the failure of religion, unfulfilled religious seeking, or secular substitutes. As they depict what Thomas Carlyle called the "condition of England," the plight of the working class, and other issues of social justice, these works address questions about the human condition, about love of God and neighbor, and the meaning of life in the face of death. Scholars of the English novel have argued that its concern with religious life contributed to the inward turn of the English novel, to its focus on conscience, on introspection.[8]

Tolstoy associated English novels with the family saga and happy endings: "all's well that ends well." He was also attuned to how they depicted religious life. The novels he read presented a variety of perspectives. They included, for example, those by Charlotte Yonge, which promoted the Oxford Movement.

George Eliot captured Tolstoy's imagination when he was a fledgling writer and God-seeker. He praised her *Scenes of Clerical Life* as a "Christian book," declaring "blessed" those "who, like the English, imbibe with their milk Christian teaching, and in such a lofty, purified form as evangelical Protestantism." Eliot's heroes – like Tolstoy – sought a religion that felt right to them. In *Middlemarch*, Dorothea Brooke declares: "I have always been finding out my religion since I was a little girl." Virginia Woolf wrote that this was true of all Eliot's heroes: "that is their problem. They cannot live without religion" – even when they "no longer know . . . to whom to pray." In her quest, Dorothea examines "all the different ways in which Christianity is taught" in search of the ones "that make a wider blessing."[9] Eliot did not confine herself to Christian religious experience: in *Daniel Deronda* she explores Judaism and Jewish identity.

Charles Dickens provided a model for revealing the hypocrisy of religious institutions, movements, and individuals. In *Bleak House*, which Tolstoy read in 1855, Dickens satirizes do-gooders of all stripes, "high church," "low church," or "no church," for *doing* nothing for the poor (ch. 46). Dickens ridicules Mrs. Jellyby's "telescopic philanthropy" (engaging in long-distance charitable missions while ignoring the misery under one's nose). In "Lucerne" (1857), Tolstoy targets "telescopic philanthropy" when he criticizes English tourists in the Swiss resort for refusing to give to a beggar and then lambasts the English for colonialist missionary activity. Tolstoy became a master of showing how Russian institutions (including the Orthodox Church), movements, and individuals violate Jesus' teachings and fail to practice what they preach.

English Evangelicalism on Russian Soil

Tolstoy encountered facets of English religious culture in the context of real life. The English had been involved in efforts to translate the Bible into Russian and to distribute copies. In the 1870s, Lord Radstock (Granville Waldegrave, 1833–1913), an English missionary, created what Nikolai Leskov called a "schism in high society" in Russia, when he converted many Russian Orthodox to an English-style evangelical faith. Vasily Pashkov and other prominent Russians devoted themselves to the movement. It became threatening to the establishment – to Church and autocracy – when it began to reach beyond "high society" to the Russian people. That evangelicals had this impact was taken as a sign that the Russian Orthodox Church was not answering the needs of many (would-be) believers. It was prompted to act to keep control and/or to reinvigorate faith.

Tolstoy observed the Radstock movement. As *Anna Karenina* reveals, he was skeptical of it, yet, at the same time, unsettled by the religious feeling it aroused.[10] Tolstoy scoffed at the quick conversions, especially since finding his religion was such an arduous process. He objected to evangelical faith in Christ as *savior*, and he dismissed what he saw as their "faith alone" mindset. Where, he wanted to know, was the action? He complained that these Radstockists did not change their lives. And yet, as he knew, Radstockists were very active in charitable and evangelizing social work for peasants, prisoners, and others in need. Some divested themselves of their fortunes. Radstockists disseminated religious literature to the Russian folk, including Bibles, translations of *Pilgrim's Progress*, and religious tales. This action was similar to what Tolstoy and his followers did to write and publish "for the people." Tolstoy, however, distanced himself from Radstockists.

English Religious Experience in *Resurrection*

In Tolstoy's final novel, *Resurrection* (1899), Nekhliudov, the hero, visits prisons as he follows a convoy of prisoners on their way to the penal colonies of Siberia. (Tolstoy thus moved into territory that Dostoevsky, an ex-convict, had covered in his *Notes from a Dead House*.) As Nekhliudov acts as an advocate for Katiusha Maslova and other prisoners, he follows the Gospel calls to preach prisoners' deliverance (Luke 4:18–19) and to visit and care for them (Matthew 25:34–46). And he follows in the Methodist footsteps of George Eliot's Dinah Morris. In *Adam Bede*, we are informed that "Methodists are great folks for going into prisons" – the implication being that this is not what Anglicans do. Dickens was another advocate for prisoners. He novelized prison life in *Little Dorrit*, *A Tale of Two Cities*, and elsewhere. He wrote sketches describing his visits to prisons in the United States. In *Resurrection*, Tolstoy takes on the chronotope of the prison, treated by Dostoevsky, Eliot, and Dickens. In fact, Dostoevsky's *Dead House*, Eliot's *Adam Bede*, and Dickens' *A Tale of Two Cities* are among the handful of novels that Tolstoy singles out in *What Is Art?* as examples of good art, by which he means art that unifies people and that promotes love of God and love of neighbor.

Resurrection shows Tolstoy emerging as a prison abolitionist. His view was rooted in his interpretation of Jesus' teaching on mercy and forgiveness: for Tolstoy, "judge not" meant abolishing courts and penal systems. *Resurrection* ends with Nekhliudov taking up a Bible he had gotten from an English evangelist, who had been observing prison conditions and distributing Bibles to the prisoners. Tolstoy pays tribute to English religious culture, which (unlike Russian Orthodox religious culture) was very focused on individual reading and interpretation of the Bible. But, in typical Tolstoyan style, he also shows that the English evangelist, if not a Mrs. Jellyby, was nevertheless out of touch with the Russian prisoners he visited. Tolstoy's Nekhliudov will find faith in his own unorthodox way, as Tolstoy himself did.

Tolstoy's Religious Views, on English Soil and among English Subjects

As he became known worldwide as a religious seeker and a moral authority, Tolstoy had connections with – and influence on – English religious culture. England became an important hub in the dissemination and examination of Tolstoy's work. Tolstoy had both critics and followers. Thus, he went from responding to English sources to active exchange with British subjects – in print (his work was widely translated, read, and reviewed in the English press), by letter, and in person, when he engaged with his English visitors.

Active in promoting Tolstoy's views in England was John Kenworthy. Kenworthy visited Tolstoy (1896), was involved in setting up Tolstoyan colonies and enterprises in England, and wrote a *Life and Works* of Tolstoy (1902). Kenworthy compares Tolstoy to both Bunyan and Wesley, suggesting that he "touches the same springs" in English readers hungry for social and religious inspiration and action. And he credits Tolstoy's appeal in England to Tolstoy's return to the Bible as his source: "the heart of our people has always concerned itself with the Bible as a repository of truth."[11] Thus, while he appreciates Tolstoy's Russianness and his uniqueness, Kenworthy draws attention to elements in Tolstoy's religious experience that are kindred to the English. These elements are likely to have been influenced, however indirectly and partially, by Tolstoy's exposure to English religious experience.

Notes

1 What follows draws on my work in *Leo Tolstoy: A Very Short Introduction* (Oxford University Press, 2019); *Anna Karenina and Others* (Madison: Wisconsin University Press, 2016); "Tolstoy's Unorthodox Catechesis: English Novels," in Predrag Cicovack (ed.), *Tolstoy and Spirituality* (Brighton, MA: Academic Studies Press, 2018), 53–76; and "Tolstoy's Sevastopol Tales: Sentiment, Sermon, Protest, and Stowe," in Elizabeth Cheresh Allen (ed.), *Before They Were Titans: Early Works of Tolstoy and Dostoevsky* (Brighton, MA: Academic Studies Press, 2015), 211–65.

2 Georg Lukács, *Theory of the Novel*, trans. Anna Bostock (Cambridge, MA: MIT Press, 1971), 88.

3 See Ian Watt, *The Rise of the Novel: Studies in Defoe, Richardson, and Fielding* (Berkeley: University of California Press, 2001; 1st edn 1957).

4 William James, *Varieties of Religious Experience: A Study in Human Nature* (New York: Longmans, 1917), 185.

5 John Bunyan, *The Pilgrim's Progress* (Harmondsworth: Penguin, 1965), 130.

6 Kirsty Milne traces this link in *At Vanity Fair: From Bunyan to Thackeray* (Cambridge University Press, 2015).

7 John Wesley, *Works*, vol. 1 (London: Wesleyan Conference, 1872, reprint), 185.

8 On introspection and the religious novel, see Kathleen Tillotson, *Novels of the Eighteen-Forties* (Oxford University Press, 1962), 131 and *passim*.

9 George Eliot, *Middlemarch: A Study of Provincial Life* (London: Penguin, 2003), 392 (chap. 39), 495 (chap. 50); Virginia Woolf, "George Eliot," in *The Common Reader*, ed Andrew McNeillie (New York: Harcourt Brace, 1984), 171.

10 On Tolstoy's response to English evangelical piety in *Anna Karenina*, see my *Anna Karenina and Others*, 122–69.

11 John Coleman Kenworthy, *Tolstoy: His Life and Works* (London: Walter Scott, 1902), 37–8.

PART VI

Tolstoy's Afterlife

CHAPTER 34

Tolstoy's Complete Works

Inessa Medzhibovskaya

At 9.5 by 7 inches in a calico binding of royal purple with an elegant gray touch and gold embossing, each of the ninety volumes of Tolstoy's *Complete Collected Works*, Jubilee Edition – the hero of this entry – features Tolstoy's bearded silhouette on a sturdy khaki-colored dustjacket and two more of these silhouettes facing each other on the front pastedown and flyleaf.[1] This edition is, to this day, the standard reference and citation source for Tolstoy in professional publications and transactions of scholars (the current volume being no exception).[2] Projected to be released over a maximum of eleven years after its launch in 1928 for Tolstoy's centennial (hence its nickname), the edition ended up being published over thirty years (1928–58) that coincided with the gravest period of Stalinism. The changes that appear in the lists of editors on the title pages, and the eventual removal of the name of the founding general editor, Vladimir Chertkov, are the result of changes in Soviet politics, frequent reshuffling of cadres, and silent termination of work contracts during the purges. What is the secret of its longevity, barring the idea that its burden might be the continued projection of Stalinism?

Finding the Principle for "Complete Works"

On Tolstoy's death, two people were left in charge of his literary legacy: his literary executor, Vladimir Chertkov, and his daughter, Alexandra Lvovna, holder of the copyright legalized by the Regional Court of Tula a few days after Tolstoy's passing. To initiate the publication process of his complete works in accordance with Tolstoy's will, the two were eager to ensure that all posthumous publications of both finished and unfinished works being republished or appearing for the first time would never be anyone's property. They worked together with interruptions and in very hard material conditions on the available portions of the manuscripts from 1911 until 1917, and then apart from 1918 to 1927. Alexandra Lvovna worked on the manuscripts written before 1881, assisted by a team of devoted volunteers: members of her family and scholars and critics from the older generation of philologists like Vsevolod Sreznevsky, Aleksei Gruzinsky, Liubov Gurevich, Mstislav Tsiavlovsky, Pavel Sakulin, and Nikolai Piksanov. Chertkov dedicated himself to the manuscripts written after 1881, with the aid of Tolstoy's closest disciples like Nikolai Gusev, Pavel Biriukov, and Konstantin Shokhor-Trotsky, as well as the newly joined, like Nikolai Rodionov. Their differences notwithstanding, the common goal that united Alexandra Lvovna, Chertkov, and their team members was to attract the attention of appropriate funders willing to abide by the conditions of Tolstoy's spiritual will and to support a non-commercial, nonprofit edition on an unheard-of scale.

The trial editions in the period 1911–27 made valiant efforts to overcome the "mechanical" approach of the first twelve editions of Tolstoy's collected works, the last of which was being prepared when the writer was still alive. This mechanical principle consisted in adding a volume or two to the existing number from the previous reprint of collected works whenever the right number of newer writings would appear. The posthumous editions of Tolstoy before 1928 introduced elements of commentary and genre distribution, and some included variants, but unsystematically. Until the canonical standard of Tolstoy texts could be developed, establishing a central organizing principle, an editorial concept for the work, was crucial. Daunting as their mass can be, with a few exceptions, Tolstoy's manuscripts are very well preserved. But they were disunited until 1939, when all known deposits of the manuscripts within the Soviet Union were ordered to be moved to the famed "Steel Room." The Steel Room was a space suitable for archival storage located in the mansion of the former magnate Savva Morozov, a few hundred yards from the State Tolstoy Museum (GMT) in Moscow at Kropotkinskaya 11 (Prechistenka 11 before 1918 and after 1991). The room received its name for its heavy stone vaults, high security rules, and several sets of fireproof doors necessary for entry and exit.

At the end of 1918 Chertkov found the right funding source at last and secured Lenin's verbal consent to the publication of everything that Tolstoy had ever written. But seven years of negotiations with the Soviet powers were necessary to bypass the stumbling block of state monopoly and declare that the bequest of the greatest of writers was the publication of his entire creative legacy as the nation's property (*vsenarodnoe dostoianie*). Thanks to the negotiations with the State Publishers (Gosizdat), Chertkov and Alexandra Lvovna made sure that the verso of the title page in all volumes published before 1949 bears an inscription in Russian, "Reproduction is permitted for free" (*Perepechatka razreshaetsia bezvozmezdno*), and, right below, in French, "Free reproduction for all countries" (*Reproduction libre pour tous les pays*). Only the Russian inscription remained in the volumes published from 1950 to 1958. After Chertkov had reached the compromise making Tolstoy's works national property, the State Publishers and the Council of the People's Commissars (SNK) signed a resolution on June 23, 1925, and then Stalin's key administrator, Viacheslav Molotov, worked out the funding details for implementing the edition within the framework of the first Five-Year Plan (1928–33). The recalcitrant old specialists and Tolstoyans on Chertkov's editorial board (Redkom) were to be supervised by a State Editorial Commission (Gosredkom), headed through 1933 by "good" Bolsheviks: the Commissar of Enlightenment Anatoly Lunacharsky and Vladimir Bonch-Bruevich (an old friend of Chertkov's) as well as their prominent deputies from the cream of the communist academy (Lev Kamenev was one of them, from 1931–4).

After the replacement of the "good" Gosredkom with apparatchiks in 1934, everything would become more problematic, but initially there was great excitement when volume 1, containing Tolstoy's *Childhood* and juvenilia, appeared in 1928. The first five years of the Jubilee Edition proceeded on a high note: one million rubles invested in the publication immediately after the signing of the first round of contracts; the appointment of thirty-two lead editors and many more proofreaders and copy-editors, typists, and service personnel placed on the payroll; an alleged 32 tons of metal to mold fonts for a single volume. The work groups for the three series into which the Jubilee Edition was divided (Tolstoy's works, Tolstoy's diaries, Tolstoy's letters) compared themselves to strike brigade workers of Turksib, Magnitogorsk, and Dneproges. Ironically, the vast majority of the volumes published at this tempo between 1928 and 1939 (thirty-eight in all) had been edited by the Old Guard scholars of Alexandra Lvovna's team who defected in 1929, never to return, or by formalists like Boris Eikhenbaum, Alexander Nikiforov, and Leonid Grossman and writers with strongly anti-Soviet reputations or names, like M.V. Muratov and V.S. Shokhor-Trotskaya. The volumes released through 1939 contained work written before 1881 as well as Tolstoy's three long novels: *War and Peace*, *Anna Karenina*, and *Resurrection*. The latter two included variants edited by the young scholar Nikolai Gudzy, the rising star of Soviet literary science. Chertkov was seventy-four in 1928, when the first volumes were released. His wife's death a year earlier had devastated him. He had enough strength to make sure that by the year 1934, when he turned eighty, Gusev and his protégé Nikolai Rodionov would be in charge of editing the diaries and letters. When he died in 1936, all of the Tolstoy/Chertkov correspondence but volume 82 of Tolstoy's letters to Chertkov, had been published.

The Jubilee Edition and Its Peculiar Character

The structure Chertkov chose for his edition, with the major participation of Tsiavlovsky and Piksanov, organized all writings into three categories: (1) artistic and theoretical material (the eventual volumes 1–45); (2) diaries (volumes 46–58); and (3) letters (volumes 59–89). In accordance with this plan, the edition was initially projected at ninety-five volumes, but it ended up being ninety, the final volume accommodating the surplus that did not make it into the series volumes on time. For the correspondence, each letter in each volume received an identification number and date, followed by editorial commentary ranging from several lines to several pages. As regards the diaries, not only did they cover the entire period of Tolstoy's composition, from 1847 to 1910, but they were the fullest versions ever published, with some clipped passages here and there (in observance of Tolstoy's will) for as long as Chertkov or his designee Rodionov could influence their editorial process. Each of the diary volumes also included Tolstoy's daybooks paralleling the period. Each volume was supplied with its own index and a bullet-style chronology of Tolstoy's life for the years covered by the volume. These were the most striking features of the Jubilee Edition.

The Jubilee Edition had initially relied on the structure designed in 1918–20 by Pavel Biriukov (who permanently left Russia in 1924). Without access to a fuller set of manuscript variants, Biriukov had proposed seven categories in fifty-six volumes, separating not only letters and diaries but also genres of Tolstoy's works; for example, writings on religious-philosophical and moral questions would have been separate from pedagogical works and writings on social topics. In addition, artistic works were to be separated not just by their genres but also by chronology, that is, the works written before and after 1881. His structure, if accepted, would have made the content of the Jubilee Edition, which radicalizes quickly from the mid-1870s onward, vulnerable to close ideological scrutiny by the Leninism-versus-Tolstoyanism watchdogs. Therefore the genre principle was sacrificed for what may be called an "overlapping" and "interlocking" principle: volumes 1–45 watered down any dangerous content by adopting a neutral subtitle, such as "Works Written in 1891–94" of volume 29 (published in 1954).

Such vulnerability was a special problem for volumes destined to be released at the height of the purges in 1936 and 1937. Therefore, the tract *What Then Shall We Do?* in volume 25 (published in 1937) was "hidden" among the folk and popular tales. The tract *On Life* and its addenda in volume 26 (published in 1936) were cloaked by *The Death of Ivan Ilyich* and the drama from peasant life, *The Power of Darkness*. The commentators alleged that these contemporaneous "works of social criticism" were written to criticize the horrors of the old regime, which could alone have given birth to such idealistic spiritualist deliria as *On Life*. Another protective measure adopted from the start was for the commentaries and variant descriptions to remain ideologically and politically neutral and extremely brief, especially for so-called theoretical and topical works in response to political events and for letters and diaries written during peak moments of political activity, these holy of holies of Tolstoy's search for justice and freedom.

In all, eighty volumes of the Jubilee Edition were completed before World War II, although only thirty-eight were published. The process had slowed down for several reasons. Volumes 13 and 15, with variants to *War and Peace*; 21, with Tolstoy's alphabet readers; 34 and 35, with works from 1900–3 and 1902–4; diary volumes 48, 49, and 50; and volume 84, with Tolstoy's letters to Sofia Andreevna from 1884 to 1910, were ordered to be revised after negative responses from external reviewers. (Normally, these were the party-minded gatekeepers contracted by Gosizdat to take a targeted swipe.) Among the criticisms: the apolitical and ideologically disengaged spirit of the prefaces and the commentaries and the outsized philological portions of the commentaries. By 1939, Gudzy, Gusev, and Rodionov were the most active editors, with younger scholars like Lydia Dmitrievna Gromova-Opulskaya (a disciple of both Gudzy and Gusev) joining in the early 1950s. This team lead the project through to the end.

From 1939 until 1949, the publication of volumes stalled. But in the thickening climate of the Cold War, the battle to finish the Jubilee Edition resumed. The work in 1946–9 was to restore the corrected proofs of the thirteen volumes lost during the Siege of Leningrad. The new motto governing the edition was "Economy versus arduous expansionism," which established the practice of twinned volumes (e.g., 15–16, 39–40, 50–1, 68–9, 70–1, 73–4, 81–2) that were published in a single book. With reduced commentary, the entire ninety volumes could now fit into seventy-eight books, despite the imposition of long prefaces of quotable

Lenin commissioned for twenty-one volumes after 1949. The Soviet reader who was able to obtain a coveted volume was well trained in the art of "skipping the ad" and getting to the factual points, especially in the better prefaces, such as those by Elizaveta Kupreianova, Lydia Opulskaya, Suzanna Rozanova, and Mark Shcheglov. Of the remaining volumes, twelve appeared before Stalin's death in March 1953, seven afterward, and the remainder were issued rather quickly between 1954 and 1957. The supplementary volume 90 – the last one – appeared in 1958, and a general index volume to the entire Jubilee was published only in 1964.

The Jubilee Edition in Hindsight and the New Edition of the Complete Tolstoy

As the edition was being completed, multiple errors were discovered in the indexes of individual volumes: the attribution of years to fragments and letters, personalia identifications and descriptions, and foreign spellings. The fact that unrelated and undated texts kept surfacing – of which only some made their way into the supplementary volume 90 – undermined trust in the edition's authoritativeness and completeness. It was clear that a separate, fundamentally academic edition of Tolstoy was necessary. A new generation of scholars focused on checking the Jubilee Edition against the manuscripts and raising the quality of the commentary. This eventually paved the way for Opulskaya's seminal sesquicentenary 1978 edition in twenty-two volumes. Some of the best Soviet scholarship was summoned and Rozanova served as one of the key commentators.[3] This is the most reliable published version of Tolstoy's main fiction to date, and includes *A Confession, What Then Shall We Do?, On Life*, and a good selection of his dramas, writings on aesthetics and education, diaries, and letters.

With the support of the foremost textologist, Galina Galagan, and a touching blessing from Tolstoy's family, on March 25, 1997, Opulskaya convened the first session of the editorial board to discuss the possibility of launching a new academic edition of Tolstoy's complete writings. Thus began in 2000 the 100-volume academic edition under the auspices of the Institute of World Literature in Moscow (IMLI).[4] For this new edition, whose audience is scholarly and research-oriented, the main drivers are authoritative accuracy and exhaustive completeness (*ischerpyvaiushchaia polnota*). The distribution of content is different from that in the Jubilee Edition, recalling Briukov's principles of 1913–18. Strictly chronological instead of overlapping within each of its categories, and going by the year of completion rather than the starting date, the new edition eschews the tactic of twinned volumes but opts for an extended designation on the spine for parts, variants, and addenda, e.g. an extension of the *War and Peace* variant publication version in volume 8 (part 1) also cross-lists as volume 25 (part 1). Series I in eighteen volumes includes artistic works (finished and unfinished); series II in seventeen volumes includes all variants and redactions to works in series I, with a cross-listed volume number of the definite final version from series I; series III consists of twenty volumes of essays, didactic tracts, and collections of nonfiction; series IV is thirteen volumes of diaries and notebooks; series V is thirty-two volumes of letters. In addition to the aforementioned volume 25 (part 1), volumes 1, 2, 3, 4, 9, 19, and 21 have been published. Slow and methodical as the work should be, it has been slowed down further by the deaths of its founding figures and essential experts: Opulskaya (2003), Galagan (2012), Pyotr Palievsky (2019), and Nina Burnasheva (2020). Whereas the ninety volumes of the Jubilee Edition took thirty years to complete, work on the 100-volume edition promises to be ongoing well into the twenty-first century. The project is now (2021) headed by Alexander Vadimovich Gulin of IMLI.

For the foreseeable future, the Jubilee Edition remains the most complete available edition of Tolstoy's work in any language. Only twenty years ago, finding a full set was not a guarantee even at better research libraries and even though the Kraus-Thomson Organization (Nendeln, Lichtenstein) reprinted it in 1972. Unlike the Jubilee Edition, whose print run of 5,000 copies proved insufficient and increased to 10,000 copies in 1934, Kraus reprinted solely for large libraries. Kraus' is an austere product in plain navy cloth, its font small and pale. Still, lucky is the library that has it. In 1992, the Russian company Terra issued a luxury reprint in heavenly blue with gilded borders on the cover. In 1999–2000, the Russian State Library scanned the Jubilee Edition into a non-searchable pdf format. Following the centennial of Tolstoy's death in 2010, Tolstoy's great-great-granddaughter Fekla Tolstaya called on all of Russia for volunteers to manually retype all ninety volumes. Taking the principle of free reprinting into the era of searchable text, the newest digitized version in the OCR format is on the landing page of the GMT in Moscow. The index volume is more than simply digitized: stored at index.tolstoy.ru, it provides thematic tags and instant links to all instances of a given name, place, institution, or work in the entire edition. And yet nothing compares to pulling a real Jubilee tome off the shelf, the imprint of all that unimaginable tonnage of metal within its pages, a monument to an incredible epoch, chock-full of historical and political horror, fabulous discoveries, and decades of hard work.

Notes

1 This essay summarizes key points of my original research into the archival history of the Jubilee Edition and other posthumous publications of Tolstoy. Please refer to Medzhibovskaya, *L.N. Tolstoy* (Oxford Bibliographies, 2021) and *Tolstoy and the Fates of the Twentieth Century* (forthcoming) for fuller discussion of the major editions of Tolstoy from 1864 onward, and of the archival collections used, and to the Suggested Further Reading section below for additional guides and information.
2 L.N. Tolstoy, *Polnoe sobranie sochinenii*, ed. V.G. Chertkov et al., 90 vols. (Moscow: Gosudarstvennoe Izdatel'stvo Khudozhestvennoi literatury, 1928–58).
3 L.N. Tolstoy, *Sobranie sochinenii v dvadtsati dvukh tomakh*, ed. L.D. Opulskaia et al. (Moscow: Khudozhestvennaia literatura, 1978–85).
4 L.N. Tolstoy, *Polnoe sobranie sochinenii*, ed. G.Ia. Galagan, A.V. Gulin, L.D. Gromova (-Opulskaia), et al., 100 vols. (Moscow: Nauka, 2000–).

CHAPTER 35

Tolstoy in English Translation

Carol Apollonio

Tolstoy's medium is the Russian language. His productivity in that medium is awe-inspiring. Translations of his works into the many languages of the world follow the rule of entropy, expanding in all directions from Tolstoy's time and place, with no sign of abating on the eve of the writer's third century. Considering the pathways of his two great novels, *War and Peace* and *Anna Karenina*, into English can give a sense of the history of Tolstoy's reception throughout the world, and also of the unique role that translators play in this process.

Tolstoy appreciated translation; he learned languages easily and was fluent in the major European languages and proficient in many others, including Turkish, Tatar, Ukrainian, and Bulgarian, not to mention classical languages. At the time of his death in 1910, his library of 22,000 volumes included 5,000 books in over 30 foreign languages.[1] He wrote parts of his fiction (famously, long passages in *War and Peace*) in French, and his knowledge of foreign languages influenced his writing style. Translation can serve writers as a form of apprenticeship; indeed, one of Tolstoy's earliest literary projects was a partial translation of Laurence Sterne's *A Sentimental Journey* (1851). During his period of religious and philosophical exploration in his later years, he studied Greek and Hebrew, and produced a unique translation and "harmonization" of the Four Gospels in 1880–1.

Evaluating Tolstoy Translations

Readers naturally want to know which Tolstoy translation or translator is "the best," but there is no absolute standard. Translation is an art, not a science, a complex matrix of literary interpretation and creation. Institutions (publishers, universities, censors) and individuals (editors, agents, marketing experts) play a role in a translation's reception, which may have nothing to do with its quality. The most primitive, and yet

common, form of criticism provides a short list of lexical errors or infelicities as grounds for condemning a translation. Evaluating the degree to
which a translation's words match those in the original is merely the
starting point, however. It is much more challenging, and crucial, to
consider the work as a whole, its spirit and tone as a work of literature
in its new context.

   An additional consideration for readers of the English Tolstoy has to do
with textual issues. Translators have worked with different versions of his
works; the new, definitive Academy collection (see Chapter 34) will
undoubtedly introduce changes, which future translators will have to
incorporate. In some cases, incautious critics have blamed translators for
variant wording that is editorial in nature and has nothing to do with the
fine art of translation. In 2007, with much fanfare, an "original version" of
War and Peace came out in a translation by Andrew Bromfield. The book's
marketing experts touted it as not only Tolstoy's authentic original, but
also shorter and easier to read than the existing versions, and free of
philosophical ballast and other verbiage. Without going into the intricacies
of the text's origins and history in the Russian scholarly and publishing
world, and of the frenzied critical debate that ensued, it should be noted
that Bromfield himself deserves no blame for what was essentially a fine
professional translation of the text that was provided to him. That said,
readers hoping to engage with the *War and Peace* that generations have
come to know and love should choose a different translation. Similar
criticism has been aimed at preeminent Tolstoy translators Louise and
Aylmer Maude (and others), who worked from Russian originals that
predated the scholarly editions now recognized as definitive.

Tolstoy's Language Challenges

Translators are faced with two contradictory mandates: to reach new
generations of readers in new cultural contexts, on the one hand, and to
respect the work's original time and place, on the other. Recent translation
theory has advocated for "foreignizing" translation strategies that maintain
the distinctive features of the original text, even at the expense of forcing
readers out of their comfort zone. A more traditional approach values
qualities that conform to the norms of the receiving language, offering a
pleasant reading experience. The battle often rages around vocabulary.
Here translators stake their territory, either committing, like the prolific
modern American translating team of Richard Pevear and Larissa
Volokhonsky (PV), to using words only from the work's original time

period, or unabashedly updating its vocabulary and deploying colloquialisms to appeal to new generations of readers, like Anthony Briggs in his 2006 version of *War and Peace*, or David Magarshack, with his 1961 *Anna Karenina*.

Constance Garnett (CG, 1861–1946), whose over seventy translations of the classics created an English voice and identity for the Russians, claimed that she would like to be judged for her work on Tolstoy, whose "simple style goes straight into English without any trouble."[2] Others quibble over the statement, noting the intricacies and peculiarities of Tolstoy's writing and criticizing Garnett's style as overly fluent or "Victorian," but the fact is, she was a literary artist of genius who rendered her predecessors and contemporaries obsolete and whose work has entered its second century without ever going out of print. Her Tolstoy sets a high standard against which all subsequent translators must measure themselves.

Russian grammatical structure differs radically from that of English; translating entails more than simply moving vocabulary over. Tolstoy's literary language presents specific challenges: at one extreme, he has a tendency to repeat key words, straining the limits of good style; at the other extreme, he can write monstrously long sentences, and his syntax can be quite extraordinarily complex. Importantly, these two features figure prominently in his most famous works. Tolstoy's penchant for repetition is particularly evident in morally loaded passages; his convoluted syntax predominates in descriptions of the natural landscape or in mass scenes like the battles in *War and Peace*. Difficulties relating to the former have to do with the relative intolerance of English, in comparison with Russian, for repetition – over and above its prominence in Tolstoy's writing. As for the latter, the precision of each element and its place in the whole – reflected in the grammar as well as the vocabulary – is almost impossible to duplicate in another language.

In coping with Tolstoy's repetitions, translators can take a stand for lexical literalism and commit to using one English equivalent throughout; alternatively, they can opt to vary the vocabulary. Both strategies have value; in the former case the English feels more alien; in the latter, it reads fluently, but the moral message or structural resonances can be muted. In *Anna Karenina*, adulterous Stiva Oblonsky chastises himself for his moral failing. Some translators retain the repetition: "I'm the guilty one in it all – guilty, and yet not guilty" (PV 2); alternatively: "I am to blame ... I am to blame and yet I am not to blame" (Rosemary Edmonds 14). Others substitute synonyms: "all my fault – all my fault, and yet I'm not to blame" (CG 4); "it's all my own fault, I'm to blame, though I'm not really to blame either" (Joel Carmichael 2). It is important to note that the original Russian word (*vinovat*) supports all of these lexical variants (guilt, blame, fault) in English – one is not necessarily more accurate than the other.

A related challenge has to do with Russian's tolerance for omissions. As a highly inflected and precise language (compare to Latin or Greek), Russian sentences can leave out important words, which readers can deduce based on context. Early in *Anna Karenina*, Dolly's mother asks her, literally, "how are your?" (*kak tvoi*), leaving out the noun "children." At the literalist extreme, the translator can opt for "How are all yours?" (PV 121), at the risk of baffling the English reader, when "How are the children?" as in David Magarshack's version, is perfectly acceptable and true to the original meaning (134). Russian verbs are clearly identifiable as either transitive or intransitive, unlike many English verbs, which could be either. A Russian writer can leave out the direct object of a transitive verb, where an English reader demands one. In English one must provide the object for the verb "to tell": "Stepan Arkadych started telling" (65) leaves PV's reader hanging, unlike, say, Marian Schwartz's: "And Stepan Arkadyevich began to tell his story" (62). One way of looking at the problem is to suggest that literalist translators omit the last couple of drafts, where the focus turns to polishing the English style.

As for Tolstoy's epic descriptions, here the translator is challenged to manipulate the syntax and draw deeply from the vocabulary of the English language, which is richer and more diverse than that of Russian. Tolstoy's descriptions exemplify his philosophy of history, which addresses the interrelationship between the smallest elements – the individual soldier (the words) – and the great sweep of history (the whole novel). Here, lexical accuracy is only the first step; the rest is up to the translator's ear, taste, and sense of style. Bartlett, Edmonds, and Garnett come closest to achieving this elusive standard.

Tolstoy's novelistic style is also unique in its integration of philosophical and historical argumentation into the text. Very different challenges face the translator of this more abstract style. Most Tolstoy translators are not specialists in philosophy or history, which complicates the task. Similar issues are at work in the Four Gospels project, where the text reflects not merely Tolstoy's linguistic translation choices, but also his engagement with the original Greek biblical text, with translations into other languages, and with a vast body of theological writing.

War and Peace and *Anna Karenina*

Trends in literary translation are often intertwined with politics. Revolutionary tensions seethed in Russia in the late nineteenth and early twentieth centuries, sparking a surge in interest in Russian literature among anglophone readers, particularly after the 1905 revolution.[3] The post-Soviet period has also seen a boom in Russian translation.

Tolstoy's prose fiction was just part of the large body of his writings that reached anglophone readers and fueled the expansion of the Tolstoyan movement. His shorter works had begun to appear in English as early as the 1860s; a single-volume *Childhood* and *Youth* came out in London in 1862, and *The Cossacks* in New York in 1863.[4] The early English translations of the Russian realists were often made from French versions. Such was the case with the first English *War and Peace*, Clara Bell's, which came out in 1886. Shortly thereafter, the American translator Nathan Haskell Dole published *Anna Karenina* (1886; 1887) and *War and Peace* (1889) on both sides of the Atlantic as part of his multi-volume Tolstoy series. Indeed, Tolstoy translations have flowed in parallel streams in England and the United States from the very beginning. The first decade of the twentieth century saw the publication of eighty-six English-language editions of individual works and at least six complete editions of collected works plus two more in progress.[5] Garnett's *Anna Karenina* appeared in 1901, followed in 1904 by her *War and Peace*; 1904 also saw versions of *Anna Karenina* and *War and Peace* by American translator Leo Wiener, also, like Dole's, in a multi-volume set. The productivity of this generation of translators is astonishing, paralleled in our age only by American translator Marian Schwartz's impressive and growing corpus (including *Anna Karenina*, 2014), which weighs in at some eighty volumes.

Louise and Aylmer Maude are the most knowledgeable and prolific of Tolstoy's many translators. Louise was born into an expatriate family in Moscow in 1855; she met Aylmer after he came to Russia in 1874 to study. Soon after their marriage in 1884 they met Tolstoy and established a relationship with the writer that continued after the couple returned to England in 1897. The Maudes produced the most sustained and authoritative body of Tolstoy translations in English. As can be the case with translators at the scholarly end of the spectrum, their *Anna Karenina* (1918) and *War and Peace* tend to a cautious strategy with respect to the original Russian text.

Until the 1950s, when Penguin initiated its Classics series, the Maudes and Garnett had been for several decades the acknowledged voices of

Tolstoy in the anglophone world. Their influence continues to this day, in revised versions (Garnett's *Anna Karenina* by Leonard J. Kent and Nina Berberova in 2000; the Maudes' *War and Peace* in Amy Mandelker's 2010 Oxford Classics edition). These updated versions may be the ones most widely used in classrooms, due to the overall quality of the translation and the critical apparatus. Two other editions are also superb for classroom use. Pevear/Volokhonsky's *War and Peace* (2007) is the most "foreignizing" version of the text, and is unmatched as a physical book, with abundant reference materials and unsurpassed production quality. Rosamund Bartlett's 2014 version of *Anna Karenina* is both meticulous in its style and authoritative and generous in its scholarly apparatus.

Penguin's Tolstoy speaks in the voice of Rosemary Edmonds (1905–98), a former translator for General de Gaulle who studied Russian at the Sorbonne after the War.[6] Her renditions (*Anna Karenina*, 1954; *War and Peace*, 1957) feature an elegant, fluent English style and a sensitive ear for dialogue. David Magarshack, who is best known for his Penguin Dostoevsky novels, published his colloquial and bumpy version of *Anna Karenina* for Signet in 1961. Signet also brought out Ann Dunnigan's *War and Peace*, in 1968. The Briggs version appeared almost forty years later, in 2006. As for *Anna Karenina*, there have been more translations into English, probably because of its relatively moderate length: Joel Carmichael's (1960), Margaret Wettlin's – the only version published in Russia (1976) – and a 2008 Oxford Classic by Kyril Zinovieff and Jenny Hughes. 2014, when Bartlett and Schwartz published their translations, was a big year for *Anna Karenina*.

The State of the Art and the Future of Translation

For Tolstoy readers, three important trends mark the present moment. (1) Readers of Russian literary translation can find just about any classic online for free. The reliability of these versions can vary, but some, such as those in Project Gutenberg, are serviceable. All of Garnett's versions are easily available, as are some other older translations. (2) Institutional support in Russia for translation of Russian literature has been robust, with many new translations, including of the classics, receiving funding from entities like the Institute of Translation and the Prokhorov Foundation. (3) The new academic complete collected works is sure to spark authoritative new translations – though it is hard to predict whether these can match the high artistic standards set by the translators discussed here.

English Translations of Tolstoy's Novels

War and Peace

1 trans. Nathan Haskell Dole, 4 vols. in 2 (New York: Walter Scott, 1889)
2 trans. Leo Wiener, *The Complete Works of Count Tolstoy*, vols. 5–8 (Boston: Dana Estes, 1904; London: Dent, 1904)
3 trans. Constance Garnett, 4 vols. (London: Heinemann, 1904)
4 trans. Aylmer and Louise Maude (New York: Norton Classics, 1966) [1920/1930s]; ed. and rev. Amy Mandelker (Oxford World's Classics, 2010)
5 trans. revised by Princess Alexandra Kropotkin, ed. W. Somerset Maugham (Philadelphia and Toronto: John C. Winston, 1949)
6 trans. Rosemary Edmonds, 2 vols. (Harmondsworth: Penguin, 1957)
7 trans. Ann Dunnigan (New York: Signet Classics, 1968)
8 trans. Anthony Briggs (New York: Viking Penguin, 2006)
9 "Original Version," trans. Andrew Bromfield (New York: HarperCollins, 2007)
10 trans. Richard Pevear and Larissa Volokhonsky (New York: Alfred A. Knopf, 2007)

Anna Karenina

1 trans. Clara Bell (from the French) (New York: Harper, 1886)
2 trans. Nathan Haskell Dole, 2 vols. (New York: Thomas Y. Crowell, 1886)
3 trans. Constance Garnett (London: William Heinemann, 1901); rev. Leonard J. Kent and Nina Berberova (New York: Modern Library, 2000)
4 trans. and ed. Leo Wiener, *The Complete Works of Count Tolstoy* (Boston: Dana Estes, 1904), vols. 9–11
5 trans. Rochelle S. Townsend, 2 vols. (London: J.M. Dent & Sons, 1912; New York: E.P. Dutton, 1912)
6 trans. Louise and Aylmer Maude (Oxford University Press, 1918); 2nd edn rev. and ed. George Gibian, Norton Critical Edition (New York: W.W. Norton, 1995)
7 trans. and intro. Rosemary Edmonds (Harmondsworth: Penguin, 1954; repr. with revisions, 1978)

8 trans. Joel Carmichael, with an introduction by Malcolm Cowley (New York: Bantam, 1960).

9 trans. and with a foreword by David Magarshack (New York: Signet Classics, 1961)

10 trans. Margaret Wettlin, 2 vols. (Moscow: Progress Publishers, 1976)

11 trans. Richard Pevear and Larissa Volokhonsky (London: Penguin, 2000)

12 trans. Kyril Zinovieff and Jenny Hughes (Oxford: Oneworld Classics, 2008)

13 trans. with intro. and notes by Rosamund Bartlett (Oxford University Press, 2014)

14 trans. Marian Schwartz, ed. and intro. Gary Saul Morson (New Haven, CT: Yale University Press, 2014)

Notes

1 Galina Alekseeva, "Lichnaia biblioteka L.N. Tolstogo," https://ypmuseum.ru/data/pdf/sciencelibrary_-statya-lichnaya-biblioteka_69_ru.pdf (ccessed June 24, 2020).

2 Constance Garnett, "The Art of Translation," conversation recorded in *The Listener*, 942 (January 30, 1947), repr. in Daniel Weissbort and Astradur Eysteinsson (eds.), *Translation: Theory and Practice: A Historical Reader* (Oxford University Press, 2006), 292–3, 292.

3 Rachel May, *The Translator in the Text: On Reading Russian Literature in English* (Evanston, IL.: Northwestern University Press, 1994), 30–1.

4 Rebecca Beasley, *Russomania: Russian Culture and the Creation of British Modernism, 1881–1922* (Oxford University Press, 2020), 98.

5 Harold Orel, "The Victorian View of Russian Literature," *Victorian Newsletter* 51 (Spring 1977), 1–51 (at 4).

6 Catherine McAteer, *Translating Great Russian Literature: The Penguin Russian Classics* (London: Routledge, 2021), 23–6.

CHAPTER 36

Film Adaptations

Alexander Burry

Lev Tolstoy was unique among major nineteenth-century Russian writers in that he lived to see the advent of film, critique the medium, and even serve as a subject for it.[1] Films of Tolstoy's works began to appear toward the end of his life and in the 1910s, beginning a long history of cinematic adaptation of his oeuvre. Along with his contemporary Fyodor Dostoevsky, Tolstoy has attracted the most attention from filmmakers of any Russian writer. The popularity of his works for film arises in part simply from his cachet: throughout the history of cinema, directors have sought to capitalize on the prestige of literary classics. However, Tolstoy's works in particular also contain several features that encourage cinematic transformation: their plots are highly eventful, often engage historical material, and abound in dramatic romantic encounters. At the same time, the length, vast canvas, and huge number of plot events in *Anna Karenina* and especially *War and Peace* create difficulties for filmmakers attempting to transform Tolstoy's novels into standard-length films. Moreover, as a psychological novelist, Tolstoy includes frequent interior monologue, a type of narrative that notoriously challenges cinematic directors attempting to convey his particular brand of realism.

Tolstoy's works have generated a wide variety of cinematic adaptations, from films that transmit his texts as closely as possible to those that use them as mere starting points. In many cases, the films go far beyond simply replicating a given work in a new medium, creating dialogues not only with their source texts, but also with other literary, cinematic, and cultural texts that shape the adaptations.[2]

Films of *War and Peace*

War and Peace was a popular subject for film in the years immediately following Tolstoy's death. Several versions of it appeared during the silent era: Pyotr Chardynin's 1912 *War and Peace*, with Ivan Mozzhukhin as

Pierre, Vladimir Gardin and Yakov Protazanov's co-production *War and Peace* (1915), and Chardynin's *Natasha Rostova* of the same year. However, only four decades later did the first sound film of the novel emerge: King Vidor's 1956 Italian-American production. Vidor's film, starring Audrey Hepburn as Natasha, Mel Ferrer as Prince Andrei, and Henry Fonda as Pierre, was designed for commercial success. Fitting Tolstoy's 1,400-page novel into just three and a half hours compelled Vidor and the screenwriters to cut enormous swaths of the text, creating what appears to be more an illustration of the main passages and characters of *War and Peace* than a thorough, detailed transposition of the novel. The film was released in the US in 1956, to mixed reviews, and in the USSR in 1959, where it was generally well received by Soviet audiences.

This release prompted a sense of competition in the Soviet film industry, which believed that an American version of *War and Peace* needed to be bettered by Tolstoy's compatriots. Denise Youngblood calls Sergei Bondarchuk's film, whose production spanned the years 1961–6, "arguably the major artifact of the cultural Cold War waged by the USSR against the United States."[3] Bondarchuk's stated intention was to direct a film that, by contrast with Vidor's *War and Peace*, was faithful to Tolstoy's novel, and which demonstrated Soviet superiority to the US in cinema and culture. In keeping with the monumentalism of the Brezhnev era, Bondarchuk – generously financed by the Soviet government – in many ways succeeded in outdoing his cinematic predecessor. The film's war scenes in particular are masterfully done, capturing the sprawling, chaotic quality described by Tolstoy, where Vidor's battles tend to be too neat and well-orchestrated. Bondarchuk, whose film totals seven hours in length, also includes more scenes from Tolstoy's novel overall than does Vidor, and transfers generous amounts of dialogue and internal monologue directly from the text. And yet, despite all these successes, it is debatable whether the film accomplishes the director's goal of fidelity to Tolstoy's novel. Bondarchuk's major omissions include Pierre's involvement with Freemasonry, all of Tolstoy's philosophical sections, and the entire epilogue; these passages contain important ideas on the novelist's part. It would thus be more accurate to describe Bondarchuk's film as a dialogue with Tolstoy, one in which the director interprets patriotism – out of Tolstoy's various foci – as the dominant theme of the novel. This interpretation reflects the Soviet ideology of the Brezhnev period, which celebrated the collective over the individual, and thus corresponded with Tolstoy's characterization of the role of the Russian national spirit in the defeat of Napoleon.[4]

In addition to these two feature films, *War and Peace* has been televised four times, including two series by the BBC. The 1972 series, a mammoth twenty-hour affair, outdoes Bondarchuk's film in its inclusion of all parts of the plot, and in Anthony Hopkins' winningly eccentric, clumsy, and heart-warming performance as Pierre. The last episode of the series provides the viewer with a transposition of Tolstoy's epilogue, including Pierre's involvement in a secret society, which Prince Andrei's son Nikolai looks upon with admiration. The more recent 2016 series, scripted by Andrew Davies and directed by Tom Harper, similarly includes Freemasonry and other elements of Pierre's ideological peregrinations that are omitted in Bondarchuk's film.

Films of *Anna Karenina*

As of 2022, more than twenty films and TV series have been based on *Anna Karenina*, making it second only to Dostoevsky's *Crime and Punishment* among Russian literary classics in terms of frequency of screen adaptation. If creators of *War and Peace* adaptations go to great lengths to encompass as much of Tolstoy's material as possible, directors of *Anna Karenina* films, by contrast, tend to take a looser approach to text-setting. This can be seen in such features as their portraits of the heroine, the degree of their inclusion of Levin in the narrative, their depiction of nineteenth-century Russia, and their gradual adoption of a new screen language not rooted in *Anna Karenina* itself.

From the beginning, *Anna Karenina* bore a special relationship with cinema, because of Tolstoy's use of the train, an important source for early film, as a major locus of his narrative. Art critic Vladimir Stasov draws this connection in a letter on the Lumières' 1895 *Arrival of a Train at La Ciotat Station*, with its famous shot of a train that appeared to early audiences to be about to enter the auditorium: "All of a sudden a whole railway train comes rushing out of the picture towards you; it gets bigger and bigger, and you think it's going to run you over, just like in *Anna Karenina* – it's incredible."[5] This picture in turn influenced subsequent adaptations of *Anna Karenina*, such as Julien Duvivier's 1948 version, which similarly shoots the death scene with a train approaching Anna. Of the silent films, Gardin's 1915 *Anna Karenina* is noteworthy. Although most of the footage of it is lost, sketches and reviews reveal a film of unparalleled length for the period (nearly 150 minutes), featuring various innovations for its time, including lengthy scenes, a slow tempo, and a psychological focus.

Greta Garbo became associated with the character of Anna through the two films in which she performed the role. The first, Edmund Goulding's 1927 silent film *Love*, in keeping with the appetites of viewers, substituted for Anna's tragic suicide a happy ending in which she reunites with her lover Vronsky and her beloved son Seryozha. The second, Clarence Brown's 1935 *Anna Karenina*, preserves Anna's tragic death. Directed right after the passage of the 1934 Motion Picture Production Code, Brown's film transformed *Anna Karenina* in part by omitting elements of the novel that could be considered "objectionable"; scenes such as Anna and Vronsky's consummation of their affair and her pregnancy with Annie were excised. It also reduces the Levin plotline to a few short scenes. At the same time, Brown provides scenes of military gaiety and drunken revelry in an attempt to render Russia relatable by emphasizing its past imperial culture at a time, in the mid-1930s, of tense Soviet–US relations.

Since Brown's *Anna Karenina*, several directors have attempted to incorporate Levin more thoroughly into their films. Duvivier endeavors to develop Anna's and Levin's stories in parallel, but the former, as Irina Makoveeva puts it, "retains its encompassing function."[6] Alexander Zarkhi's 1967 Soviet film also includes numerous scenes involving Levin. However, these are allotted limited time in a two-and-a-half-hour film and lack sufficient depth to convey Levin's spiritual struggle. Zarkhi eschews the use of voice-over, which might have communicated Levin's insights during such episodes as the mowing scene, relying instead solely on a peasant song tracking over Levin's mowing to convey his spiritual bliss. He also omits Part VIII, perhaps because it centers on Levin's religious revelation, although Levin does pass along some of his insights to Anna during their meeting late in the film. Despite the general Soviet acceptance of Tolstoy as a writer, cultural authorities disliked his religious preaching, and this may have affected the degree to which Zarkhi could represent this aspect of the novel. Bernard Rose and Joe Wright, in their respective 1997 and 2012 films, make an effort to address this lacuna, with small degrees of success. Rose has Levin report some of his revelations to Vronsky as the latter heads off to war; Wright includes a scene of Levin being struck by the insight of his peasant Theodore (Fyodor) that his choices are based on feeling and instinct rather than reason. But overall, the oeuvre of *Anna Karenina* adaptations still awaits a film that successfully integrates the Levin–Kitty plotline with the Anna–Vronsky line, since the scenes of Levin's ordinary, everyday family life presumably lack the interest for audiences that Anna's adultery plot holds. The most recent adaptation of the novel, Karen Shakhnazarov's 2017 *Anna Karenina: Vronsky's Story*, takes an entirely opposite approach; Vronsky narrates the adultery plot to a grown-up Seryozha via flashbacks as both fight in the Russo-Japanese War. Levin's plot is completely omitted.

Several critics have noted that *Anna Karenina* films have taken on a language of their own, as directors become increasingly aware of the growing tradition of filming the novel. Certain scenes find their way into the adaptations particularly often: these include Anna and Vronsky's initial meeting, the consummation of their love, Vronsky's horse race, Anna's visit to her son Seryozha on his birthday, and her suicide. These scenes create a common language among filmmakers that privileges adultery as a romantic myth of a fated love that outlasts death.[7] Another line in the development of a film language specific to *Anna Karenina* adaptations involves highlighting the eye in depicting Anna's suicide. This element, found not in Tolstoy's novel but in avant-garde cinema such as Dziga Vertov's *Man with a Movie Camera* and Luis Buñuel's *Un chien andalou*, becomes a part of the history of *Anna Karenina* adaptations. As Yuri Leving writes, "a new cinematic hypertext has emerged with visual references to Vertov and Russian avant-garde cinema that make us reimagine the scene [of Anna's suicide] in Tolstoi's novel."[8] Presumably, we can expect these new hypertexts to develop in further, unexpected ways as *Anna Karenina* continues to travel through world cinema.

Films of *Resurrection*

Tolstoy's 1899 novel *Resurrection*, despite being banned in Russia, achieved great popularity in the US and the UK, and stage productions and silent films of the novel soon appeared. The first cinematic adaptation was D.W. Griffith's 1909 film. For this one-reel, thirteen-minute film, there could be no question of reproducing Tolstoy's novel with any degree of accuracy, so Griffith abridges Tolstoy's material in order to focus on the most crucial scenes of the novel: nobleman Dmitry Nekhliudov's seduction of the peasant Katiusha Maslova, her descent into prostitution, and her Siberian sentence, during which he rejoins her. Griffith centers the film on a cycle of fallenness and redemption, and an opposition of the physical and the spiritual, matching exchanges (Katiusha giving Nekhliudov a flower before he seduces her and Nekhliudov giving her a Bible, which leads to her spiritual regeneration) and mirroring scenes (Katiusha's bedroom, where the seduction takes place, and the scene of their encounter in Siberia), suggesting Tolstoy's message of the power of Christian forgiveness and spiritual growth.[9]

Perhaps the most well-known adaptation of *Resurrection* is Rouben Mamoulian's 1934 film *We Live Again*, which substitutes a "happy ending" for Tolstoy's conclusion. In the novel, Maslova refuses Nekhliudov's marriage proposal, which he makes to repent for his role in her downfall; she instead chooses to marry the revolutionary Simonson. Mamoulian, however, has Katiusha accept Nekhliudov's offer, and the film's final shot shows them walking off together, arm in arm, an ending clearly designed – like the aforementioned ending of Goulding's *Love* – to satisfy Hollywood audiences. In Kenji Mizoguchi's 1937 *Straits of Love and Hate*, the Japanese director achieves a genuine dialogue not just with Tolstoy but also with earlier Japanese melodramatic adaptations of *Resurrection* by presenting Maslova as a heroine who resists the patriarchy rather than sentimentalizing the novel by making it about unrequited love. Lastly, Soviet director Mikhail Shveitser directed *Resurrection* in two parts, in 1960 and 1962 (before the major adaptations of *War and Peace* and *Anna Karenina* in that decade discussed above). Shveitser's focus on Tolstoy's narrative of cruel imprisonment and a corrupt legal system reflects the Thaw era in which the film was produced; Soviet audiences could be expected to view the prison scenes in light of the Gulag system that Premier Nikita Khrushchev had critiqued.[10]

Films of Other Works by Tolstoy

Arguably, Tolstoy's shorter works have inspired even more diverse and creative responses in film than his novels. His novella *The Death of Ivan Ilyich* (1886), with its depiction of the gradual death of a civil servant and his discovery of the meaninglessness of the life he has led, is notably difficult to reproduce straightforwardly in film. Even Alexander Kaidanovsky, who in his 1985 *A Simple Death* comes closest to presenting the novella in its entirety, announces from the beginning that it is "based on motifs from Tolstoy's *Death of Ivan Ilyich*," and mixes its basic narrative with recordings of Tolstoy making other pronouncements. Several other directors have developed Tolstoy's central idea of discovering the meaning of life through the experience of death in remarkable directions. The greatest of these films is Japanese director Akira Kurosawa's 1952 *Ikiru* (*To Live*). Kurosawa, an avowed lover of Russian literature, adapted three Russian works directly for film: Dostoevsky's *The Idiot* (1951), Maxim Gorky's *The Lower Depths* (1957), and Vladimir Arseniev's *Dersu Uzala* (1975). In his looser adaptation of *The Death of Ivan Ilyich*, Kurosawa's protagonist, bureaucrat Kanji Watanabe, realizes that his life has been meaningless, and persistently cuts through red tape to facilitate the construction of a children's playground to replace a cesspool. This departs from Tolstoy's Ivan Ilyich, who realizes the pointlessness of his life, but dies without being able to do anything concrete to redeem it.

Other directors have similarly taken a creative approach to setting Tolstoy's novella. Bernard Rose, in *Ivan Xtc* (2000), transposes the plot loosely to contemporary Hollywood, announcing the death of a drug-addicted talent agent named Ivan Beckman at the beginning of the film and then following recent episodes of his life: his recruiting of an important actor to the agency, his interactions with a girlfriend and prostitutes, and his lung cancer diagnosis, which he tries to come to terms with in the course of the film. Rose creatively makes *The Death of Ivan Ilyich* part of a larger dialogue with other intertexts, including the real life of agent Jay Moloney, who committed suicide at the peak of his career.[11] More recently, in 2012, Iranian director Ali Mosaffa's film *The Last Step* transposes James Joyce's story "The Dead" along with Tolstoy's novella.

Other shorter works of Tolstoy have also inspired remarkable films. Notable adaptations of *Father Sergius* include Yakov Protazanov's 1917 silent film and Paolo and Vittorio Taviani's 1990 *Night Sun*. *The Kreutzer Sonata* has been transposed to cinema a dozen times, with films by Eric Rohmer (1956), Shveitser (1987), and Rose (2008) as standouts. Several other shorter works have been successfully adapted. Robert Bresson, a director whose career was shaped in large part by adaptations of Dostoevsky's works, turned to Tolstoy's *Forged Coupon* (1904) in his last film, *L'Argent* (1983). He sets the first part of Tolstoy's novella, in which the forging of a coupon starts a chain of events leading to murder, in modern-day Paris, but omits Tolstoy's second part, in which the protagonist finds redemption by turning to Christianity. In 1996, Sergei Bodrov updated the story "Prisoner of the Caucasus" (1872) into *Prisoner of the Mountains*, creatively adapting the plot to the then-current Chechen War; the film received a Golden Globe award and an Oscar nomination. Such films, along with the more recent adaptations of Tolstoy's works, underscore his enduring popularity for filmmakers, which is likely to continue for decades to come.

Notes

1 For a discussion of Tolstoy's views on film, see Michael A. Denner, "Introduction," in Lorna Fitzsimmons and Michael A. Denner (eds.), *Tolstoy on Screen* (Evanston, IL: Northwestern University Press, 2014), 3–20.
2 On such dialogical intertextuality, see Robert Stam, "Beyond Fidelity: The Dialogics of Adaptation," in James Naremore (ed.), *Film Adaptation* (New Brunswick, NJ: Rutgers University Press, 2000), 54–76.
3 Denise Youngblood, *Bondarchuk's War and Peace: Literary Classic to Soviet Cinematic Epic* (Lawrence: University Press of Kansas, 2014), 1.
4 See Stephen M. Norris, "Tolstoy's Comrades: Sergei Bondarchuk's *War and Peace* (1966–7) and the Origins of Brezhnev Culture," in Fitzsimmons and Denner (eds.), *Tolstoy on Screen*, 155–78.
5 Yuri Tsivian, *Early Cinema in Russia and Its Cultural Reception*, trans. Alan Bodger (University of Chicago Press, 1998), 3.
6 Irina Makoveeva, "Visualizing Anna Karenina," PhD thesis, University of Pittsburgh (2007), 66.
7 Irina Makoveeva, "Screening *Anna Karenina*: Myth via Novel or Novel via Myth," in Fitzsimmons and Denner (eds.), *Tolstoy on Screen*, 275–97.
8 Yuri Leving, "The *Eye*-deology of Trauma: Killing Anna Karenina Softly," in Alexander Burry and Frederick H. White (eds.), *Border Crossing: Russian Literature into Film* (Edinburgh University Press, 2016), 114.
9 See Vance Kepley, "'A Free Adaptation of Leo Tolstoy's Powerful Novel': D.W. Griffith's *Resurrection* (1909) and American Commercial Cinema," in Fitzsimmons and Denner (eds.), *Tolstoy on Screen*, 45–58.
10 See David Gillespie, "Mikhail Shveitser's *Resurrection* (1960, 1962): Film Adaptation as Thaw Narrative," in Fitzsimmons and Denner (eds.), *Tolstoy on Screen*, 75–90.
11 On this film, see Amy Mandelker, "Out of Breath: Bernard Rose's *ivans xtc.* (2000) and Tolstoy's 'The Death of Ivan Il'ich'," in Fitzsimmons and Denner (eds.), *Tolstoy on Screen*, 217–43.

CHAPTER 37

Musical Adaptations

Tony H. Lin

Musical adaptations of Lev Tolstoy's works span a wide range of genres and were already being composed during his lifetime (see appendix). With the exception of Sergei Prokofiev's *War and Peace* (1942), however, few of these musical offspring have entered the international canon in the way transpositions of Alexander Pushkin's works have (the opera *The Queen of Spades*, for example, has arguably overshadowed its source text). This difference may be due largely to the different genres in which the originals were written; sprawling prose texts like Tolstoy's present greater challenges than poetry or short story when set to music. This chapter samples various musical adaptations – including instrumental music, ballets, musicals, and operas – and considers them as variations on Tolstoy's source texts. While none of the adaptations quite outshines the original, they represent continuous engagement with and popularization of Tolstoy's texts beyond the literary realm.

Turning Literature into Music

When asked about turning *Crime and Punishment* into a play, Fyodor Dostoevsky succinctly stated that "one idea cannot be expressed in another non-corresponding form."[1] In reshaping and reconceptualizing the source text for musical adaptations, composers and librettists need to consider the properties unique to their medium vis-à-vis literature. For example, qualities fundamental to music – such as tempo, dynamics, and timbre – are largely absent in other media. Music transcends the boundaries of language and can depict unnamable and unclassifiable emotions. By contrast, literature uses words to convey directly what music can only suggest. Intangible and complex human phenomena such as contemplation and retrospection may be musically evoked, but not narrated.

Tolstoy's works are particularly challenging for musical adaptations. With poetic works, each syllable can be set to a musical note, but in prose adaptations, the number of characters and scenes is often reduced, and individual words and paragraphs are often sacrificed or rewritten to create a different, sometimes unrecognizable, entity. Tolstoy's omniscient narrator often focuses on minute details and nuanced feelings that do little to advance the plot. While these details are important to Tolstoy's aesthetics and philosophy, they are hardly suitable for adaptations. Furthermore, listening to a musical performance and reading a novel involve different modes of perception; one lasts a single evening, while the other can spread over days or months.

Musical adaptations of Tolstoy's works cover both vocal and non-vocal genres. For those works that do not employ the human voice, a transmedial concern immediately emerges: how can instrumental works convey what is verbally expressed in texts, considering musical notes do not carry semantic meaning like words? "Program music" – music based on a written text or "program" – bridges music and texts, endowing abstract musical notes with meaning. In *Anna Karenina* (1875–8), Levin attends a concert featuring Mily Balakirev's *King Lear* and, not having read the program, he is left baffled by what he hears.

Musical adaptations of literature are akin to variations on a theme; some variations closely resemble the theme, while others are hardly recognizable. What is hidden or briefly mentioned in one medium may, per the creative license of the transposer, be emphasized or altered in another. For example, Tolstoy's matter-of-fact description of Anatole Kuragin's roguish behavior and his plotting of Natasha's abduction becomes a jolly scherzo in Prokofiev's opera. Additionally, General Kutuzov's first aria begins with Tolstoy's words "a wonderful, a matchless people" but then continues with a patriotic pronouncement not found in Tolstoy. Despite Tolstoy's ambivalence toward music (discussed in Chapter 23), his works contain much musical potential. For example, *Anna Karenina* prominently features dances and operas, and Tolstoy consistently describes the characters' voices in detail, including dynamics, register, and texture.

Instrumental Music

While "musical adaptations" most commonly refer to musical works based on literary texts, I am using the term more broadly to encompass pieces *inspired by* Tolstoy's works as well. Czech composer Leoš Janáček (1854–1928), perhaps the most prolific non-Russian composer to set Russian literary texts to music, wrote his String Quartet No. 1 (1923),

"Kreutzer Sonata," inspired by Tolstoy's 1889 novella.[2] The choice of a quartet matches the number of traveling interlocutors in the beginning of the story, which takes places on a train. A member of the gentry, Pozdnyshev, recounts how he murdered his wife, whom he suspected of having an affair with the violinist with whom she had performed Beethoven's "Kreutzer" Sonata, Op. 47. As Janáček explained: "I had in mind the pitiable woman who is maltreated, beaten, and murdered."[3] Numerous interjections coupled with episodes of ephemeral lyricism characterize the piece, which features frequent shifts of mood and tempi. Each of the four movements includes the marking *con moto* ("with movement") and numerous dialogue-like passages, such as the alternating *adagio* and *con moto* in the first movement. The dialogue-like passages echo Beethoven's work, and the triplet ostinati in the first two movements resemble a train in motion. The largely tonal piece opens with an upward melody (tonic→subdominant→dominant) that becomes a motif throughout the quartet, and its inversion concludes the piece. The quartet is intense and passionate, fraught with moments of rupture akin to Beethoven's music and Pozdnyshev's mannerisms – for instance, he makes sounds like a sharply broken-off laugh (*oborvannyi smekh*) and answers sharply (*rezko*).[4]

In 1930, the Ukrainian composer Sergei Bortkevich (1877–1952) wrote a collection of fourteen piano pieces, Op. 39, based on Tolstoy's *Childhood*. These character pieces are mostly named for chapters in Tolstoy's novella. In the "innocent" key of C major, the opening piece carries the same title as Tolstoy's first chapter, "The Teacher, Karl Ivanovich," and contains overt references to Tolstoy's text. Measure 8 includes a "program" in parenthesis, "[Karl Ivanovich] kills a fly," which is illustrated by accented Neapolitan chords. Bortkievich's pieces musically portray characters and episodes in Tolstoy's novella. For example, "Papa" carries an unusual marking of *Allegro deciso* ("determined"), and "Iurodivyi" ("Holy Fool") Grisha is written like an Orthodox chant. Mirroring Tolstoy's ending of *Childhood*, Bortkevich concludes his set with "The Mother's Death." Marked *Andante dolente* ("sorrowful"), the piece quotes "Maman" and "Grisha" from earlier in the cycle and ends with a chant-like coda – recalling the cantor chanting the Psalms in Tolstoy's story – marked *morendo* ("dying") and to be played *una corda* (using the soft pedal). These relatively simple pieces, very much in the Romantic style, may call to mind Robert Schumann's *Album for the Young* or *Kinderszenen*.

Ballets

Using ballet to portray a narrative has similar limitations to other non-vocal adaptations; as an inherently visual medium, it relies on the synthesis of body movements and music to convey meaning. Several dance works based on *Anna Karenina* have premiered recently, such as Boris Eifman's 2005 production (with music by Pyotr Tchaikovsky) in St. Petersburg, and Angelica Cholina's 2012 production (with music by Alfred Schnittke, Tchaikovsky, and Gustav Mahler) in Moscow's Vakhtangov Theater.[5] Because neither contains music composed specifically for the production, I will instead discuss Rodion Shchedrin's (b. 1932) original *Anna Karenina* ballet score. Shchedrin has consistently derived his musical inspiration from literature, transposing Nikolai Gogol's *Dead Souls* (1976) and Vladimir Nabokov's *Lolita* (1994) into operas, as well as Anton Chekhov's *The Seagull* (1980) and *The Lady with a Dog* (1985) into ballets. His ballet music for *Anna Karenina* first appeared in the eponymous 1967 film by Alexander Zarkhi before premiering in Margarita Pilikhina's film-ballet at the Bolshoi Theater in 1972 (libretto by Boris Lvov-Anokhin). Subtitled "Lyrical scenes in three acts," the ballet was dedicated to his wife, ballerina Maya Plisetskaya (1925–2015). Its genesis may have been a 1962 meeting with the Kennedys at the White House, where the First Lady greeted and complimented the Bolshoi dancer Plisetskaya: "You're just like Anna Karenina."[6]

Shchedrin's music captures the diversity of moods and the complex psychology of the novel, ranging from ballroom dance and march to the forceful horserace scene and chaotic denouement of Anna's suicide. In the prologue, Shchedrin introduces several motifs that are heard throughout the ballet; for example, the opening two bars, featuring a downward tritone, constitute the Anna motif. In several instances in the score, Shchedrin quotes Tolstoy's text, such as the line "I am like a tightened string that's about to snap."[7] Some of these lines are to be recited, including Anna's final interior monologue (albeit not verbatim, as some words are omitted). In many ways, Shchedrin's score reads like a musical map to the novel, as short explanatory texts accompany many musical passages. That said, he took major artistic liberties, leaving out Levin's plot entirely, including diegetic music during Anna's theater visit (Bellini's *I Capuleti e i Montecchi*, never specified by Tolstoy), and bringing to the fore a character who is peripheral in the novel: the peasant (*stantsionnyi muzhik*) who dies as Anna arrives in Moscow. The peasant appears in four of the twenty-one tableaux of the ballet, underscoring the relentless nightmarish mood.

Musicals

Musicals – a hybrid genre that puts roughly equal emphasis on songs, spoken dialogue, acting, and dance – have become, perhaps surprisingly, instrumental in revitalizing some classics of Russian literature, such as Gogol's *Dead Souls* (Ekaterinburg premier, 2008) and Mikhail Bulgakov's *The Master and Margarita* (St. Petersburg premiere, 2018). These musical productions continue the long-standing tradition of setting Russian classics to music, while at the same time adapting them to a new era. *Anna Karenina* (music by Roman Ignat'ev) premiered at Moscow's Operetta Theater in October 2016 and has enjoyed ongoing popularity since then. Like Shchedrin's ballet, the musical mostly focuses on the heroine's plotline, although it also includes Levin and duly covers most major scenes in the novel. There are nonetheless oddities necessitated by stage performance: namely, the ice skating scene is replaced with roller skating and the horserace features only the spectators. The libretto by Yuly Kim transforms Tolstoy's sophisticated text into simple, singable lyrics. Some critics have pointed out that the musical overemphasizes the aspect of spectacle, which does not align with Tolstoy's aesthetics. Musicals, like operas, convey interiority externally, demanding heightened emotion and drama, which makes them incongruous with the Tolstoyan idea of the significance of the ordinary.

Musicals bridge high art and more popular genres. *Anna Karenina* co-producer Alexei Bolonin addresses the strengths of the genre but also concedes: "Tolstoy's novel like no other is suited for a musical because it has all the necessary ingredients, most importantly, a love story. We, of course, cannot address his philosophical ideas, as this is not the right genre for that. But some things that were important for Tolstoy are reflected in the sets or in the lyrics, and there are some direct quotes from the novel, too."[8] With amplified music, projected images, and bright lights (particularly memorable are the wheels in Anna's suicide sequence), the audience is immersed in a total-art experience. As the musical captivates the audience and sustains its attention, its relationship with the novel is symbiotic. The musical's advertising slogan, "World masterpiece in one breath" (*Mirovoi shedevr na odnom dykhanii*), captures the essence of the musical vis-à-vis the novel. While the latter invites one to read closely, as well as to ponder the relationships and interrelationships, the former focuses on entertaining the audience. This has not always been a recipe for success, however. A 1992 musical of *Anna Karenina* (music by Daniel Levine) closed on Broadway after just forty-six performances. As a reviewer in *The*

New York Times quipped: "Every unhappy musical is unhappy in its own way, but no musical is more unfortunate than *Anna Karenina*" (August 27, 1992).

More recently, Tolstoy has met with Broadway success in Dave Malloy's 2012 "electropop opera" *Natasha, Pierre & the Great Comet of 1812*, based on *War and Peace*. The work's title makes no pretense of fully preserving the source text, a fact evident in its omission of such key characters as General Kutuzov, Napoleon, and Platon Karataev. The composer of the book, music, and lyrics, Malloy did not expect American audiences to be familiar with the novel, so he simplified the lyrics considerably to better facilitate tuneful singing. Besides illustrating a classic Russian novel in a distinctly non-Russian genre, both musicals, *The Great Comet* and *Anna Karenina*, feature racial diversity that challenges preconceptions about the work and its characters. Similar to the recent hit *Hamilton*, *The Great Comet* introduces a multiethnic cast: Okieriete Onaodowan (who played Madison in *Hamilton*) briefly played Pierre, and Denée Benton played Natasha Rostova. In the 2016 Moscow production of *Anna Karenina*, Vronsky was played by a Korean-Ossetian Sergei Li. The cast's diversity, combined with the musical genre, helps Tolstoy's novel become a living document, keeping up with the changing times.

Operas

Combining many art forms into one *Gesamtkunstwerk*, opera is the genre to which transposers of Tolstoy's works have most often turned, though not always with success. Janáček and Benjamin Britten each attempted to set *Anna Karenina* to opera but abandoned their efforts. In the Soviet period, both Shostakovich and Prokofiev contemplated setting *Resurrection* (1899) as an opera, yet neither realized this objective.[9] Successfully completed adaptations, such as Hungarian composer Jenő Hubay's (1858–1937) *Anna Karenina* (1920), often rearrange, and sometimes alter, the storyline. Hubay's opera underscores Anna's tragedy and places her reunion with Seryozha shortly before her concluding suicide scene. One notable opera based on Tolstoy has achieved international success and recognition: Prokofiev's *War and Peace* (1942).

Prokofiev turned to Tolstoy's masterpiece just two months before the 1941 Nazi invasion of the Soviet Union. Since the composition overlapped with (and outlived) the "Great Patriotic War," Prokofiev's personal endeavor turned into a national project, which he carried out while in evacuation. Unlike Malloy's musical, Prokofiev's opera retains all the key characters (with the notable exception of Nikolai Rostov) while adopting the familiar approach of writing "scenes"; ironically, the scene of Natasha at the opera is omitted. With his eventual second wife, Mira Mendelson, Prokofiev worked on the libretto, a genre drastically different from the novel for its succinctness and absence of omniscient narration. Despite the librettists' pruning efforts, the opera was criticized for having superfluous (*izlishnii*) details and "too many conversations" (*obilie razgovorov*), and it was never performed in its entirety during Prokofiev's lifetime.[10]

Tempting though it is to discuss how the opera deviates from Tolstoy's novel, doing so presumes the superiority of one medium and neglects how adaptations can guide us to view a familiar text anew. Take, for example, the musical rendering of Anatole Kuragin's seduction of Natasha; Natasha's fear of being seized is made manifest as her singing becomes absorbed by Anatole's. She reproduces his melody when reading his love letter; thus, her singing of "*ia pokhishchu vas*" ("I will kidnap you") musically enacts his takeover of her will. The scene of Andrei Bolkonsky's dying, which initially attracted Prokofiev to writing the opera, also illustrates the power of transforming a two-dimensional text into a three-dimensional performance. While the text tells the reader that Andrei is half delirious, the opera shows it. When Andrei sings the gibberish *pi ti* sound (which the censors found ridiculous) and thus enacts delirium on stage through music, the audience gains access to Andrei's inner state with an immediacy that effectively breaks the fourth wall.

Conclusion

Like variations on a theme, musical adaptations, with their varying degrees of resemblance to Tolstoy's source texts, are no substitute for the originals. However, for many people, especially outside Russia, these musical versions become a first point of exposure to Russia's literary classics. While the successful adapters of Tolstoy's works have spanned many countries – Russia, the Czech Republic, Italy, Germany, Hungary, Poland, and the United States – there are fewer musical adaptations of Tolstoy than one might expect for such a giant of Russian literature. That only a handful of these musical adaptations have become standard repertoire should not obscure the fact that his works continue to inspire composers, who in turn produce their own Tolstoyan offspring, revealing hidden facets that enrich our appreciation of the originals.

Musical Adaptations

War and Peace

- Sergei Prokofiev: *War and Peace,* Op. 91 (opera, 1942)
- Boris Blacher: *War and Peace* (musical, 1955)
- Nino Rota: *War and Peace* (film music, 1956)
- Erwin Piscator, Alfred Neumann, and Guntram Prufer: *War and Peace* (musical, 1967)
- Dave Malloy: *Natasha, Pierre & the Great Comet of 1812* (musical, 2012)

Anna Karenina

- Edoardo Granelli: *Anna Karenina: Lyrical Scenes in Six Tableaux* (opera, 1910)
- Jenő Hubay: *Anna Karenina,* Op. 112 (opera, 1920)
- Igino Robbiani: *Anna Karenina* (opera, 1924)
- Iulii Meitus: *Anna Karenina* (opera, 1970)
- Rodion Shchedrin: *Anna Karenina* (ballet in 3 acts, 1971)[11]
- Iain Hamilton: *Anna Karenina* (opera in 3 acts, 1981)
- Daniel Levine: *Anna Karenina* (musical, 1992)
- Tibor Kocsák: *Anna Karenina* (musical-opera, 1994)
- Vladislav Uspenskii: *Anna Karenina* (musical drama in 2 acts, 2000)
- David Carlson: *Anna Karenina* (opera in 2 acts, 2007)
- Hermann Reutter: Epigraph of Count Tolstoy to the novel *Anna Karenina* for mixed chorus (2008)
- Roman Ignat'ev: *Anna Karenina* (musical, 2016)

Resurrection

- Albert Roussel: *Résurrection,* Op. 4 (symphonic prelude, 1903)
- Franco Alfano: *Resurrection* (opera in 4 acts, 1904)
- Ján Cikker: *Resurrection* (opera in 3 acts, 1962)
- Aleksander Tansman: *Resurrection* (ballet in 4 tableaux, 1962)
- Tod Machover: *Resurrection* (opera, 1999)

Other

- Leoš Janáček: String Quartet No. 1, inspired by Tolstoy's *Kreutzer Sonata* (1923)
- Sergei Bortkevich: *Childhood*, Op. 39 (14 easy piano pieces based on Tolstoy's novel, 1930)
- Oreste de Maurizi: Romance à Tolstoï (1952)
- Bohuslav Martinů: *What Men Live By* (pastoral opera in one act based on *Where Love Is, God Is*, 1953)
- Günther Kretzschmar: *The Old Man Planting Apple Trees* (musical scene for children's choir and piano, 1972); *The Tsar and the Shirt* (cantata for three voices, youth choir, solo and small orchestra, 1984)
- Peter Michael Hamel: *The Living Corpse* (1994 music to 1924 silent film by Fedor Ozep)

Notes

1 Quoted in Alexander Burry, *Multi-Mediated Dostoevsky: Transposing Novels into Opera, Film, and Drama* (Evanston, IL: Northwestern University Press, 2011), 3.
2 Besides the string quartet, Janáček also composed music based on texts of Zhukovsky, Lermontov, Gogol, Ostrovsky, and Dostoevsky. He planned to write two operas based on Tolstoy's texts – *Anna Karenina* and *The Living Corpse* – but never finished.
3 Quoted in Michael Beckerman, *Janáček as Theorist* (Stuyvesant: Pendragon Press, 1994), 112.
4 Perhaps it is no accident that this particular quartet is used extensively in the movie *The Unbearable Lightness of Being* (1988), based on Milan Kundera's eponymous novel. Besides the fact that both Kundera and Janáček are Czech, there are many affinities between Kundera's novel and Tolstoy's *The Kreutzer Sonata*, such as jealousy and disillusion with marriage. Kundera's novel also explicitly quotes Beethoven's last string quartet, Op. 135.
5 Cholina's production, which uses actors as dancers, advertises itself as "choreographic spectacle on the motifs (*po motivam*) of Tolstoy's novel." See https://vakhtangov.ru/show/anna_karenina.
6 Maya Plisetskaya, *I, Maya Plisetskaya* (New Haven, CT: Yale University Press, 2001), 222.
7 See the piano reduction score in R. Shchedrin, *Anna Karenina* (Moscow: Muzyka, 1974), 94.
8 As quoted in www.rbth.com/arts/theatre/2016/11/12/leo-tolstoys-anna-karenina-turned-into-a-musical_646637 (last accessed June 14, 2020).

9 See Anna A. Berman, "Scripting Katyusha: On the Way to an Operatic Adaptation of *Resurrection*," *Slavic and East European Journal* 55:3 (2011), 396–417.

10 Quoted in Irina Medvedeva, "S.S. Prokof'ev i S. I. Shlifshtein v perepiske 1940-kh godov," in *S.S. Prokof'ev: K 125-letiiu so dnia rozhdeniia* (Moscow: Kompozitor, 2016), 180.

11 There is also a piano transcription by Mikhail Pletnev: "Prologue and Horseracing."

CHAPTER 38

Biographies

Caryl Emerson

Tolstoy lived a very long, very loud life. But it lacked the catastrophic coercive outer events that drive the biographical plots of his more persecuted compatriots Pushkin, Dostoevsky, even Chekhov. The healthy, wealthy, highborn Tolstoy was largely in charge of his own life. Its most celebrated events were not imposed on him by the tyrannies of nature, bodily illness, social convention, or oppressive government, but resulted from his own freely offered verbal acts: acts of inventing, recreating, and eventually condemning the ideas and institutions that others live by. By the time he was put under permanent government surveillance in 1883, Tolstoy was famous enough to turn such constraints to his advantage.

In addition to eventlessness, another problem faces the biographer. Censored or banned, public, private, or printed abroad, Tolstoy authored more words about himself than any outside person could ever hope to do: diaries, letters, quasi-autobiographical fiction and drama, public confessions, highly subjective treatises. Yet this self-referential word was of a peculiar lacerating sort. Routinely and in full sincerity Tolstoy would disown his prior deeds and writings. With age he grew ever more insistent that the experience of his lived life did not matter; what mattered was the Truth that shone through his ideas. Nevertheless, Tolstoy willingly participated in his own visual self-mythologization, tirelessly sitting for portraits, photographs, sculptures, newsreels, sensing that the newly revolutionized media, armed with his image, would circulate this Truth. Scandals and inconsistencies could even increase its authority, keeping Tolstoy's outrage in the public eye. How should a biographer relate to this huge supply of self-cancelling material?

This chapter discusses five exemplary 'Lives of Tolstoy' shaped by these factors. At one end of the spectrum is the comprehensive life, conventionally divided into periods framed by Tolstoy's attempts to find his most perfectible self: worldly competitor, family man, spiritual seeker. At the other end is the genre of the brief glimpse, always truncated, often eccentric. In between (but not covered here) is the "middleweight" Tolstoy biography, over the past few years artfully realized by Pavel Basinsky, Donna Orwin, and Andrei Zorin.[1] Tolstoy as novelist and moral thinker is such a global icon, however, that another and more 'aestheticized' mode of biography – Tolstoy in the portraiture, novels, and films of other creative artists – is discussed in this volume in its own entry, by Margarita Vaysman (Chapter 39).

The Comprehensive Biography

The long form presumes development and completeness. Each of our three exemplars, separated by half a century, meets this expectation with different strengths: that of eyewitness, fellow European novelist, and chronicler of a global phenomenon. Aylmer Maude (1858–1938), English clergyman's son and business manager in Moscow, is the Boswell model, the biographer who lives and converses alongside his subject. Introduced to Tolstoy in 1888, Maude quickly became his close friend, chess and tennis partner, and trusted translator. Maude's wife Louise, born in Moscow in 1855 into a British commercial family with Quaker sympathies, was perfectly bilingual; she specialized in translating Tolstoy's fiction, her husband the philosophical tracts. In 1902 Tolstoy authorized Aylmer to write his biography. With input from both Tolstoy and Sofia Andreevna, Maude's *Life of Tolstoy* appeared in 1908. By that time the Maude family had repatriated to England, but they remained deeply invested in Tolstoyan causes; Aylmer had accompanied the Doukhobors to Canada in 1898.

In 1930 Aylmer revised and enlarged the biography, hoping to dispel the myths around Tolstoy's final tragic years. "I wrote this book," he states in his preface, "because so many people are interested in Tolstoy and so few seem to understand him."[2] Important, however, is that Maude's thousand-page narrative, which makes ample use of letters, diaries, memoirs, and remembered discussions, is not the usual "authorized biography" – if by that we mean a defense or apology. Maude makes it clear throughout that he is a friend, not a disciple. He has high respect for the integrity of Tolstoy's Russian biographers, but when he disagrees with them, "the difference probably arises chiefly from the fact that I am English while they are Russian" (viii). While never doubting Tolstoy's sincerity and courage, he insists on his right to pass judgment, noting with wonder how Tolstoy "ignores, or totally condemns, what the Western world has done" in taming nature and creating wealth (vol. II, 199). Art too is fair game. Citing a letter to Tolstoy in 1857 from the journal editor Alexander Druzhinin, exasperated by the young author's "super-refinement of analysis" and "ungrammatical long sentences," Maude confides that "as a translator I can testify that Tolstoy never fully learned the lesson" the editor was trying to teach him (vol. 1, 175).

Maude's biography is still unsurpassed for its critical independence and objectivity at close quarters. By the time Maude died, Tolstoy had been canonized selectively in the USSR and a ninety-volume collected works undertaken (1928–58; see Chapter 34 on this heroic, harrowing feat). Thirteen of those volumes were diaries; thirty-one were personal letters. Taking full advantage of this now-public trove and working free of Soviet censorship, Henri Troyat published his *Tolstoi* in French in 1965 and in English two years later.[3] Troyat (born Lev Aslanovich Tarasov in Moscow) was eleven when his family, having fled the Revolution, settled in Paris in 1920. A prolific writer, Troyat eventually produced biographies of Dostoevsky, Chekhov, Gogol, Ivan the Terrible, and Rasputin alongside dozens of his own novels. If Maude's interest had been the friction caused by Tolstoy's moral ideas, the texture of Troyat's biography more resembles a society novel. Maude recorded philosophical conversations; Troyat makes bold to supply Tolstoy's thoughts in free indirect discourse. Troyat is not easily awed. With aplomb he demystifies as a "masquerade" Tolstoy's second pilgrimage to Optina Pustyn monastery in 1881, dressed as a peasant but with bodyguards and a valet trudging behind carrying clean clothes ("Tolstoy was in seventh heaven," 429). And what about Troyat's home readership? France had been Imperial Russia's alter ego and most immediate cultural other. When discussing *War and Peace*, Troyat remarks that Tolstoy might have "invented nothing" in his portrait of Napoleon, but he certainly selected from memoirs only those details "that would make the emperor of the French appear ridiculous . . . Chauvinism gives him a heavy hand" (325–6). In the *New York Review of Books* (February 21, 1971), Edmund Wilson called Troyat's biography a "depressing but absorbing narrative," akin to a novel one cannot put down. This is novelistic in Bakhtin's sense of the term: no epic distance, but also no epic respect.

In 2010, the centennial of Tolstoy's death, Rosamund Bartlett published her *Tolstoy: A Russian Life*.[4] Neither Maude's overheard conversations nor Troyat's biographical novel, it adopts the outer perspective on Tolstoy as a world-scale human event. Her tripartite chapter-titles resemble epithets cast at her subject by astonished onlookers: "Husband, Beekeeper and Epic Poet"; "Pilgrim, Nihilist, Muzhik"; "Sectarian,

Anarchist, Holy Fool"; "Elder, Apostate and Tsar." Knowledge of Tolstoy's literary worlds is taken for granted. A welcome addition to biographical convention is a page providing the Behrs' family tree in addition to Tolstoy's (xiv). Bartlett, also a Chekhov scholar and translator, deftly highlights differences between these two great writers: we learn that Chekhov too worked as a census-taker in Moscow in 1882 – but as a poor medical student, not a celebrity, and Chekhov wrote a humorous sketch about it, not a furious denunciation (296).

Bartlett ends her Epilogue, "Patriarch of the Bolsheviks," in 2009, deep into the Putin era. By that year, already two decades after the eclipse of communism, the "long Tolstoy biography" in Russia had undergone a seismic shift. The secularized and progressive image of Tolstoy made congenial by Viktor Shklovsky in 1963 had been superseded in 2006 by a massive, meticulous re-examination by Alexei Zverev and Vladimir Tunimanov, which aimed at reconciling Tolstoy with Russia's spiritual – read: Christian – legacy.[5] Bartlett expertly sorts out these competing claims. She traces the anguished twentieth-century history of the divided Tolstoy family; the fate of Yasnaya Polyana through revolution and two world wars; the paradoxical but misleading overlap between Bolshevism and Tolstoy's radical anarchism; the government's eventual decision to "separate Tolstoy from Tolstoyanism" (435) – to reprint his word, then hide that word, then stamp out the deed (that is, the Tolstoyan communes). These followers became the martyrs that Tolstoy himself was never permitted to be. But Bartlett notes that the reconfirmation, in 2001, of the original "separation" [*otluchenie*] of Tolstoy from the Church, again closely allied with the Russian state, has assured that the thorn of the living Tolstoy will continue to irritate all organized political power.

The Brief Glimpse

The current vogue for compact lives of famous people – glimpses, "short introductions," "Simply X" – has served Tolstoy well. Two biographies in the short form will be sampled here, from 2019 and 2010, with an eye to what fuels the Short Life. Something must organize it other than the slow year-by-year crawl along a wide road, piling up details with cumulative explanatory force. Since all biographical subjects die, one convenient focal point for comparing life-stories is how they end.

For the lengthy biography, especially when both page-count and life-span are very long, closure comes naturally with death. (Bartlett's Epilogue is so good precisely because she grasps the conflictual nature of Tolstoy's immortality; his dying resolved nothing.) The short form, in contrast, is freer from the inertia of years and events. Closer to a free-form creative sculpture than to a chronicle, the brief portrait is severe in its narrative contour. Helpful here is H. Porter Abbott's distinction, in his *Cambridge Introduction to Narrative*, between "closure at the level of expectations" and "closure at the level of questions."[6] The comprehensive biography ends when the expectations raised by its vast texture of documentation are reasonably satisfied. Death is a relief; suspense and wonder are put to rest with epic calm. But a brief glimpse, often from an unexpected angle and with an appealingly fresh (if partial) take on the biographical subject, can keep suspense, surprise, and urgent questions alive by the very boldness of its organizing principles and the huge gaps in its explanatory fabric.

Liza Knapp's *Leo Tolstoy: A Very Short Introduction* (2019) announces its thesis on the second page. Whatever other great writers might say, from Turgenev and Flaubert to Mark Twain and Hemingway, "Tolstoy's art and thought aren't separable" – and this fusion enriches the fiction, it does not obscure or impoverish it.[7] The reason, Knapp intimates, is that Tolstoyan thought is not abstract or technical (what can I know?) but embodied, ethical, and applied (what should I *do*?). Creative fiction for Tolstoy was always a testing-ground for incipient moral precepts. Thus the so-called *Perevorot* or "turning point" of 1877–83 was a shift in emphasis but not a biographical break. Knapp concentrates on those rapturous energizing moments, fictive and nonfictive, that reflect Tolstoy's "dream of universal Ant-Brotherly love" (7): Pierre meeting Platon Karataev, Konstantin Levin's moral resuscitation, Tolstoy's advice to reigning tsars to behave like Jesus. A two-page chronology at the end (121–3) frees up Knapp to tuck equally weighted scenarios from real life, fiction, and philosophy into chapters organized largely by theme (Tolstoy On War and Peace, On Love, On Death, What Tolstoy Believed, What Then Must We Do, Tolstoy Cannot Be Silent). Near the end of her book Knapp relates one episode from the American Tolstoyan Ernest Howard Crosby's 1894 visit to Yasnaya Polyana (79–80). Tolstoy's youngest daughter Alexandra was hit hard by a stick while playing with a peasant boy. She ran to her father, hoping the boy would be punished. Tolstoy explained that punishment would only cause him to hate them both, and suggested that instead they offer the boy some jam, answering violence with love. Crosby did not know how this experiment turned out, but back home in New Jersey, when he related this anecdote, one gentleman remarked: most likely the next day the peasant boy hit her hard on the other arm.

And there you have it, said Crosby – the gentleman from Russia and from New Jersey. Which is better versed in human nature, and which is the better civilizer, "the jam or the stick?" Tolstoy's buried green stick of universal happiness, the bit of symbolic sculpture that organizes Knapp's opening chapter and inspires the Tolstoy siblings to become Ant Brothers, could not have been given better closure at the level of questions.

Our second example of the short biography is by Anthony Briggs, *Brief Lives: Leo Tolstoy* (2010).[8] Like Bartlett's long text, it was timed as a death-centennial tribute. But unlike Bartlett, who commemorates Tolstoy by broadening his scope and range of influence, Briggs narrows in on flawed personal psychology. In so doing he does not diminish Tolstoy's energy or genius, nor does he declare Tolstoy's philosophizing foolish, didactic, contradictory, or feeble (Briggs admires the Second Epilogue to *War and Peace*, considering it "full of striking ideas," 53). His judgments on the great fiction are controversial, but hardly scandalous. We read that the real success story in *War and Peace* is the "unintellectual, unspiritual, altogether untheoretical" pragmatist Nikolai Rostov (48); *Resurrection*, unexpectedly for a didactic narrative, is full of zany humour and "half-hidden comic technique" (98) that highlights the brutality elsewhere. An experienced translator (his version of *War and Peace* appeared in 2007), Briggs pays welcome attention to the intricate non-linear structure of a Tolstoyan novel as an interlocking mesh of tiny scenic cells. But Briggs is firm on one character defect of his subject: Tolstoy's susceptibility to three "appalling male figures" who became his intellectual-spiritual mentors, his "monstrous alter-egos" (8). If Knapp shows us a Tolstoy fused in art and thought, a moral maximalist inspired from childhood to deathbed by that green stick, Briggs sees a darker energy at work. Furthermore, he identifies specific culprits and proceeds to weaponize them: Jean-Jacques Rousseau, Arthur Schopenhauer, and Vladimir Chertkov.

The first mentor governed Tolstoy's youth and early adulthood; the second, his midlife loss of faith in the human species. The third became his ally and ice-cold conscience after he had outgrown the family. Briggs has neither space nor inclination to discuss the two philosophers in any depth, nor to situate Tolstoy's complex devotion to his disciple. He sculpts his Brief Life around Tolstoy's relations to this triad of men not so much for their philosophical thought as for their personal nastiness. Briggs' final pages sum up its "guiding principle": "At the deepest level of his psyche Leo Tolstoy seems to have been an unhappy, unpleasant man attracted to other unhappy, unpleasant men ... This made him, like his three masters, angry, intolerant and uncongenial" (110–11). Tolstoy – a master at exaggerating his own sins – was now beaten at his own game. As intended, Briggs jolted some pious Tolstoy-lovers, and provoked others. In 2017, Darya Eremeeva, tour guide at the Moscow Tolstoy Museum, produced a little book on her subject with the engaging title *Count Leo Tolstoy: How the Genius of Yasnaya Polyana Joked, Whom He Loved, What Enraptured Him and What He Condemned*, documenting Tolstoy's personal courtesy, resilience, and frolicking good humour even during serious illness.[9] Eremeeva insists that it was Sofia Andreevna who was mournful, melancholic, unable to flex or find jokes funny – and she knew it, and suffered over it (42).

We might give the final word to this most experienced, least naïve biographer of Tolstoy: his wife. As primary interlocutor and portal in day-to-day living, she bore the brunt of all intimacy and distance. Halfway through her thousand-page-long *My Life*, Sofia Andreevna remarks: "When I think back on it now, I am amazed at how much there was that aroused Lev Nikolaevich's displeasure! And I feel a sense of unbearable agony and pity for him … He could not and did not want to spend his time on the family, and as an artist and thinker he was right."[10] Like Aylmer and Louise Maude, Sofia Andreevna was an eyewitness and participant in the mortal life. Since her investment was total, however, we can only marvel at the generosity of that judgment, that in the end Tolstoy, immortal artist and thinker, was right.

Notes

1 Pavel Basinskii, *Lev Tolstoi – Svobodnyi chelovek* (Moskva: Molodaia gvardiia, 2016); Donna Tussing Orwin, *Simply Tolstoy* (New York: Simply Charly, 2017); Andrei Zorin, *Leo Tolstoy* (London: Reaktion, 2019).

2 Aylmer Maude, *The Life of Tolstoy*, containing both vol. I: *First Fifty Years*, and vol. II: *Later Years*, separately paginated (Oxford University Press, 1987), vii.

3 Henri Troyat, *Tolstoy*, trans. from the French by Nancy Amphoux (New York: Doubleday, 1967).

4 Rosamund Bartlett, *Tolstoy: A Russian Life* (London: Profile, 2010).

5 V. Shklovskii, *Lev Tolstoi* (Moscow: Molodaia gvardiia, 1963); English translation by Olga Shartse as Victor Shklovsky, *Lev Tolstoy* (Moscow: Progress Publishers, 1978). Aleksei Zverev and Vladimir Tunimanov, *Lev Tolstoi* (Moscow: Molodaia gvardiia, 2006).

6 H. Porter Abbott, *The Cambridge Introduction to Narrative*, 2nd edn (Cambridge University Press, 2008), 58–61.

7 Liza Knapp, *Leo Tolstoy: A Very Short Introduction* (Oxford University Press, 2019), 2.

8 Anthony Briggs, *Brief Lives: Leo Tolstoy* (London: Hesperus Press, 2010).

9 Darya Eremeeva, *Graf Lev Tolstoi: Kak shutil, kogo liubil, chem voskhishchalsia i chto osuzhdal yasnopolianskii genii* (Moscow: Boslen, 2017).

10 Sofia Andreevna Tolstaya, *My Life*, trans. John Wordsworth and Arkadi Klioutchanski, ed. Andrew Donskov (University of Ottawa Press, 2010), 610.

CHAPTER 39

Tolstoy as the Subject of Art: Painting, Film, Theater

Margarita Vaysman

When Lev Tolstoy died in 1910, he was a literary celebrity, famous well beyond the borders of his native Russia. Toward the end of his life, photographers – today we would call them paparazzi – would camp out on the lawn outside of the Yasnaya Polyana estate, following Tolstoy's every move. His first posthumous photograph, taken on his deathbed in Astapovo, appeared in leading global media from New York to Bombay, and the newsreel documenting his funeral drew such crowds that its screenings had to be banned. Tolstoy's death became one of the first truly international media events of the twentieth century (see Chapter 2). But the public hunger for images of the great man was already prominent much earlier in his life, when both commissioned and unsolicited portraits and photographs proliferated, creating an international Tolstoy iconography. Throughout the twentieth century, artists, filmmakers, and writers attempted to create their own vision of Tolstoy, either embracing or opposing, but always engaging with, this visual canon. This chapter will discuss Tolstoy as a subject of art in painting, cinema, and the theatre, exploring the impact of celebrity-generated images on his representation in these media.

Portraits

From framed prints to pictures in textbooks, portraits of Tolstoy remained ubiquitous in Soviet classrooms throughout the twentieth century. Today, portraits by Ivan Kramskoi (1837–87), Nikolai Ge (1831–94), and Ilya Repin (1844–1930) are printed on the covers of government-issue school notebooks and on iPhone cases, passing the baton between generations. As Tolstoy's popularity was growing during his lifetime, so did the need for an appropriate portrait of the modern genius. Painters, sculptors, and photographers flocked to Yasnaya Polyana, in the hope that they would be allowed to capture Tolstoy's likeness while he was at work. Pavel Tretyakov

Figure 10   Ivan Kramskoi, *Portrait of the Author Lev Nikolaevich Tolstoy* (1873).
Reproduced by permission of the Tretyakov Gallery.

(1832–98), patron of the arts and the owner of the largest private gallery in
Russia at the time, specifically commissioned a number of portraits of
Tolstoy, including the by now iconic painting by Kramskoi (Figure 10).
However, both Kramskoi's painting (Tolstoy in his forties, intensely
looking out from under furrowed brows, 1873) and Ge's portrait
(Tolstoy hard at work at his desk, 1884) are eclipsed in the public
imagination by Ilya Repin's two famous images. His *Tolstoy with a Book*
(1887, Figure 11) shows Tolstoy in a chair, looking up at the viewer from a
book he is holding in his lap, whereas the even more immediately recognizable *Ploughman* (1888, Figure 12) depicts Tolstoy driving a plough out
in the fields.

In the course of his career, Repin created twelve portraits, twenty-five
sketches, and three sculptural representations of Tolstoy, but none of them
achieved the same iconic status. It was these two 1880s paintings that both
originated *and* perpetuated what would become Tolstoy's enduring public

Figure 11   Ilya Repin, *Tolstoy with a Book* (1887). Reproduced by permission of the
Tretyakov Gallery.

image: that of a writer, philosopher, and prophet, either resting, deep in
thought; or working outside, in direct contact with nature.

Both portraits started their life as a series of sketches Repin worked on in
1882 in Moscow, and then developed five years later during his short stay
in Yasnaya Polyana in August 1887. Unlike the earlier 1873 portrait of
Tolstoy by Kramskoi, Repin's work had not been directly commissioned
by Tretyakov, and yet it pleased him so much, that the art collector
snapped up the *Ploughman* immediately after it was exhibited in 1888.
Repin had created, Tretyakov noted in a personal letter, exactly the kind of
portrait that "future generations" would want to have as a reminder of
Tolstoy's genius, down to specific compositional details: he is "such a
major personality, that this figure's full stature should be captured for
posterity, and definitely outside, in the summer, in full length."[1]

Later, Vladimir Chertkov's photographs of Tolstoy – we would now call
these promotional images – would reference Repin's paintings, by both

Figure 12   Ilya Repin, *Ploughman* (1888). Reproduced by permission of the
Tretyakov Gallery.

documenting Tolstoy at work in his study and capturing him outside, in
the fields. The composition of these photographs followed the general
fashion of contemporary portraiture, but the recurrence of certain settings,
angles, and colours testified to the intermedial endurance of Repin's work.
Ploughman in particular enjoyed a fascinating afterlife of commercial
reproduction, used to decorate a range of objects: plates and tear-off
calendar stands, perfume bottles and pen-knives. It was this prominence
across different media, from postcards to chocolate wrappers, that would
propel Repin's image into the twentieth and twenty-first centuries and
keep the image of Tolstoy anchored in the public consciousness. Recently,
Repin's 1887 portrait was wielded as a weapon of visual soft power at the
closing ceremony of the 2014 Winter Olympics in Sochi. There, it
featured in the gallery of Russian writers, alongside Mikhail Lermontov,
Nikolai Gogol, and Ivan Turgenev, used in exactly the kind of way
Tretyakov would have wished.

Commissioned portraits and authorized photographs represent the
image of Tolstoy that was, to a degree, controlled by its subject, allowing
us to debate the measure of his involvement in the process of their
production. But some of the most interesting representations of Tolstoy

Figure 13   Fresco from Tazovo, *The Last Judgement*. Reproduced by permission of the
State Museum of Religion.

come from a large pool of unsolicited artistic depictions, including not one
but several church murals showing Tolstoy's descent into hell. After the
Russian Orthodox Church excommunicated Tolstoy by special decree in
1901, a fresco titled *Last Judgement* (Figure 13) was painted in a small
church in Tazovo, a village near Kursk, some 500 kilometers south of
Moscow. In this mural, violently red fire separates the devil, holding
Tolstoy in his clutches, from salvation and the Church, represented by
the figures in gilded robes. The background of the mural shows a group of
laymen onlookers, all of whom have evidently given up any hope of saving

Figure 14   Fresco from Orel, Perm Region, *Tolstoy in Hell*. Reproduced by permission of
the Bereznikovsky Museum.

Tolstoy's immortal soul. Another mural on the same subject (Figure 14)
has been restored in a small church in Perm region as recently as 2015.

A less sinister subset of unauthorized images included various caricatures, in magazines and special editions, a few of which specifically refer-
enced Tolstoy's celebrity status and the crisis of authenticity it engendered.
The nature of fame, creating a mediated image of the public figure
seemingly separate from the person behind it, was at odds with Tolstoy's
lifelong struggle for truth and sincerity. In his personal life, this contradiction became the catalyst for bitter conflicts with his family, but it was
also reflected in the treatment he received from the press. The *Razvlechenie*
(*Entertainment*) magazine put a satirized version of Repin's *Ploughman* on
one of its 1901 covers, and included further pictures inside. Tolstoy was
shown standing in the middle of the field, trying to continue ploughing,
despite a horde of photographers armed with bulky early camera-
contraptions attacking from the right, and a painter, clearly resembling

Figure 15   Yan Styka, *Leo Tolstoy Embracing Jesus* (1910). Reproduced by permission of
Mary Evans Picture Library.

Repin, busy working at three portraits at the same time on the left.
A whole compendium of "portraits, paintings, etchings, and caricatures"
was published in 1903.[2]

More benevolent, but equally highly stylized, images of Tolstoy arrived
at Yasnaya Polyana by post from abroad, produced by the Polish artist Jan
Styka (1858–1925). Styka never met Tolstoy and was creatively interpret-
ing publicly available photographs in his devotional paintings, exhibited in
Paris in 1910. One painting, *To Infinity*, depicted Tolstoy's flight from
home; another portrayed him in conversation with Christ (Figure 15).
A sketch for a panorama titled *Humankind* showed the following:

"Humankind is restrained by chains. Nearby, one can see a group of thinkers ... A powerful figure of Tolstoy stands out, showing him at the plough, ploughing up the furrow of the future fair life, without chains."[3]

In time, depicting Tolstoy in a group with other thinkers and religious figures would become a visual cliché as ubiquitous as his peasant shirt or gray beard. In this vein, Philip Glass' 1979 minimalist opera *Satyagraha* examined the role Tolstoy, Rabindranath Tagore, and Martin Luther King Jr. played in the life of Mahatma Gandhi. An artwork of high late-Soviet kitsch, *Russia Eternal: A Hundred Centuries* (1988) by Ilya Glazunov (1930–2017), showed Tolstoy in a peasant robe, walking in the first row of an eternal church procession, a step behind Russia's canonized martyred rulers, holding a sign that reads "nonviolent resistance."[4] But just ten years later, an installation by the performance artist Oleg Kulik (b. 1961) would question this kind of indiscriminate appropriation of Tolstoy as a subject of art (Figure 16). An ironic take on the iconography of Tolstoy, *Tolstoy and the Chickens* (1997–2004) consisted of a life-size wax figure of Tolstoy, complete with the beard and peasant attire, sitting at his writing desk. The desk was positioned under a raised platform on which live chickens walked around, and, notably, defecated on the writer's head. The entire installation was enclosed into a wood and glass cage, resembling an old-fashioned museum display. According to Kulik, it depicted the relationship between Tolstoy and modern Russian thinkers, who, here represented by chickens, proclaimed themselves to be Tolstoy's intellectual heirs.

Films

The first film reels featuring Tolstoy appeared as early as 1908, shot by the Russian documentary film pioneer Alexander Drankov (1886–1949). Tolstoy, due to his celebrity status, was Drankov's second subject after the Russian royal family, and the *kinokhronika* from 1908–10 showed Tolstoy in his natural habitat: at home with his family, at work in the fields, and with the "chief" Tolstoyan Chertkov. Tolstoy's flight from home and his death soon after in 1910 provoked further public interest, and two years later Yakov Protozanov and Elizaveta Thiman's *Departure of a Grand Old Man* (1912) answered that call. Following the phenomenal popularity of footage showing Tolstoy's funeral, this early biopic mixed documentary images with staged scenes featuring professional actors in such a way that it was difficult for the contemporary audiences to tell one from the other. The opening images – Tolstoy walking toward the

Figure 16   Oleg Kulik, *Tolstoy and the Chickens* (1998). Photo: Vaida Budreviciute.
Reproduced by permission of the Collection du Frac des Pays de la Loire.

camera – were carefully modelled to resemble Drankov's famous reels.
Shot in authentic locations, they invited the viewers to notice and revel in
the combination of these hitherto separate visual realities. Alarmingly for
Tolstoy's family, who were rapidly losing control over how their famous
relative was presented on screen and threatened to sue, *Departure* heralded
a new stage of Tolstoy's fame – posthumous celebrity. As *Russkoe slovo*
reported, according to the rightful heirs of Tolstoy's image, the film
"depicted absolutely unbelievable scenes, and those that were believable,
in many cases were presented in an unacceptable and false light. Countess
S.A. Tolstaya, V.G. Chertkov and other people, close to Lev Nikolaevich,

were represented on screen as caricatures, in scenes that were insulting to them."[5] As a result, the film was never widely released in Russia.

In the USSR, it was mainly Tolstoy's fiction, rather than his biography, that inspired lavish costume dramas, such as Sergei Bondarchuk's 1969 *War and Peace* (discussed in Chapter 36). The story of Tolstoy's life had to wait until 1984, when Sergei Gerasimov, a leading Soviet filmmaker, released his last film, *Lev Tolstoy*. Gerasimov both directed and played the part of Tolstoy in this deeply personal drama in two parts, *Insomnia* and *Escape*, that explored Tolstoy's alienation from his family toward the end of his life. The moral conundrum of mediated celebrity persona troubles Gerasimov's Tolstoy, too: one scene features Tolstoy playing a recording of his own voice to the village children, pronouncing "I will be gone one day, but the record will be there to remind you to behave yourselves!" Gerasimov's Tolstoy lives in the world of modern technology: audio and video recordings (Drankov features as a character), train travel, global telegraphic communication. At the centre of this connected world, Tolstoy presides over a Yasnaya Polyana microcosm, the heart of the fin-de-siècle Russian world, where visitors come for advice and blessings while his family suffers through one sage announcement after another (all made at a dinner table). Aerial shots zoom out, the estate fading into the landscape, aiding the creation of just such an illusion. The meetings in Gaspra with visitors like the writer Maksim Gorky (1868–1936) are also clearly modeled on existing photographs and official Soviet iconography, like the 1953 painting by A.I. Kirillov, *Tolstoy and Gorky in Gaspra in 1902*. Portraits and photographs of Tolstoy are a part of this film's visual DNA: the interior sets are often shot from an angle that resembles Ge's and Repin's paintings, and several close-ups of Tolstoy's face and body reproduce not just the poses he held in them but also the lighting. In Astapovo, the camera shows Tolstoy receiving visitors on his deathbed from exactly the same angle as in the famous first photograph of Tolstoy's corpse. Faithfully reproducing the existing Tolstoy iconography, Gerasimov problematizes the crisis of authenticity such reproduction engenders. As a result, his film offers a nuanced take on the effect that countless representations of Tolstoy as a subject of art have had on our perception of his personality.

Michael Hoffman's 2009 film *The Last Station* similarly focused on Tolstoy's final years. This time, the story of Tolstoy's rift with his wife and his flight to Astapovo is told from the perspective of his secretary, Valentin Bulgakov. The film inherits this decentred focalization from Jay Parini's 1990 novel of the same name that it adapts for the screen. Another central character is Sofia Tolstaya, which allows Hoffman to create an almost sacrilegiously intimate image of the writer (the film includes several scenes in the Tolstoys' marital bed). Celebrity, and the damage it incurs, become a dominant theme in the film. The opening title introduces Tolstoy as a "celebrated writer," and the first scenes show Sofia picking up a newspaper from a carriage pulling into Yasnaya Polyana – all under intense observation by a camp of photographers, representatives of Tolstoy's global fandom. The subject of the first discussion we witness between the couple is celebrity gossip.

The film also incorporates Tolstoy's many mediated selves in photographs, film reels, and gramophone records. Tolstoy's doctor, Makovitsky, jots down every word Tolstoy utters, and the sound of his scribbles accompanies many scenes in the film. Paul Giamatti's charismatic Chertkov is shown actively managing Tolstoy's public image: staging the photographs, editing Tolstoy's speeches, and, most importantly, granting or withdrawing access to the great man. Following the lead of the first Tolstoy biopic, *The Last Station* also mixes documentary and fictional narratives of Tolstoy's life, but makes a deliberate point in disrupting the visual iconography that Gerasimov used so emphatically. Many scenes are set in locations familiar from photographs and paintings, but are deliberately shot from a different angle, or repurposed to focus on other members of the Tolstoy family. Attempting to show an intimate portrait of Tolstoy, Hoffman breaches the calcified façade of the writer's public image in an assured and revealing manner.

The only other Russian film to feature Tolstoy as a fully developed character, Avdotya Smirnova's 2018 *The Tolstoy Defence, or A History of One Appointment*, also pursued an iconoclastic approach. The film tells a tragic but predictable story of a young nobleman's moral corruption and the role Tolstoy comes to play in his life. One of Tolstoy's recent biographers, Pavel Basinsky, consulted on the script, and the story itself was based on an actual court case Tolstoy once intervened in as a defense lawyer. Throughout the film, even in scenes shot on location, Smirnova follows Hoffman in deliberately contesting the Tolstoy iconography. Most startlingly, Smirnova's Tolstoy, played by Evgeny Kharitonov, is young, and resembles the much less commonly reproduced portrait by Kramskoi rather than Repin's bearded wise old man. Mostly shot on location, scenes in Yasnaya Polyana include not just the interior of the dining room and the bedrooms, but also pigsties and stables. Smirnova crafts a new Tolstoy for a modern audience in a way that is echoed in Andrei Zorin's 2020 biography: as a nineteenth-century writer, who struggled with very contemporary moral dilemmas.

Postmodern Afterlives

In Viktor Pelevin's 2009 novel *t.* the reader is introduced to a Russian superhero: Count T., who left Yasnaya Polyana to travel the world and search for truth and wisdom. T. practices martial arts, challenges Dostoevsky to a duel with axes, and discusses the crisis of authorship with his own literary creator. This treatment of Tolstoy as a disembodied avatar of his ideas is echoed in one of the most popular recent Russian comedies, *What Else Are Men Talking About?* (2011, dir. D. Diachenko). In this film, Repin's *Ploughman* comes to life and the ghost of Tolstoy follows the characters around in contemporary Russia, preaching on morality. This postmodernist Tolstoy of Russian popular culture is far removed from any historical context and is not much different from the image his international celebrity had crafted worldwide. Unexpected parallels include Tolstoy's appearance as a character in a Lucasfilm TV series, *Young Indiana Jones: Travels with Father* (1996, dir. M. Schultz, D. Mehta). The young Indiana meets an old man called Lev in a field in Russia – the boy has run away from home, and so, he discovers to his surprise, has Lev. Lev and Indiana bond over this shared experience, and Tolstoy gives Jones a crash-course in property distribution by eating all of the boy's apples. In these representations, the mediated celebrity self gradually takes over the actual historical person of Tolstoy, until he disappears altogether.

This absence, rather than presence, of Tolstoy, is a shared characteristic of modern representations of Tolstoy in various media, from novels, like Vladimir Sorokin's *Manaraga* (2017), to contemporary drama. *Tolstoy Is Not Here* (2014), a play by Olga Pogodina-Kuzmina, examines the life of Tolstoy's family (Tolstoy himself is not among the characters) in the shadow of his departure, and has enjoyed a successful run in both Moscow and St. Petersburg since 2017. Marius Ivashkyavichus' award-winning play *Russian Novel* (2016), staged at the Mayakovsky Theatre in Moscow, also explores the duality of Tolstoy's presence/absence in contemporary Russian culture. Tolstoy's legacy – his family, friends, and writings – is literally center stage in this production, whereas Tolstoy himself, as in Pogodina-Kuzmina's play, is simply not there anymore.

Notes

1 Ilya Repin, *Pis'ma I.E. Repina. Perepiska s P.M. Tret'iakovym. 1873–1898* (Moscow and Leningrad: Iskusstvo, 1946), 120.

2 *Graf Lev Tolstoi. Velikii pisatel' zemli Russkoi v portretakh, graviurakh, zhivopisi, skul'pture, karikaturakh i t. d.* (St. Petersburg, 1903).

3 "Za granitsei," *Russkoe slovo* 267 (November 19, 1910), 10.

4 For other prominent examples, alongside the cases I discuss here, see A. Tulyakova, "Lev Tolstoy kak geroi pop-kul'tury," *Arzamas*, https://arzamas.academy/mag/444-tolstoy (accessed April 30, 2020).

5 "V Yasnoy polyane," *Russkoe slovo* 225 (October 4, 1912), 7.

Suggested Further Reading

This guide to further reading is organized by chapter, with some chapters combined where there is a great deal of overlap between the sources. Most sources are only listed once, even though they may be relevant to multiple contexts.

Introductions

Knapp, Liza. *Leo Tolstoy: A Very Short Introduction*. Oxford University Press, 2019.

Love, Jeff. *Tolstoy: A Guide for the Perplexed*. London: Continuum, 2008.

Orwin, Donna Tussing. *The Cambridge Companion to Tolstoy*. Cambridge University Press, 2002.

Simply Tolstoy. New York: Simply Charly, 2017.

The Man

Tolstoy's Life and Death

Bartlett, Rosamund. *Tolstoy: A Russian Life*. London: Profile, 2010.

Basinsky, Pavel. *Leo Tolstoy: Flight from Paradise*. Trans. Huw Davies and Scott Moss. London: Glagoslav, 2015.

Chertkov, Vladimir. *The Last Days of Tolstoy*. London: Heinemann, 1922.

Maude, Aylmer. *The Life of Tolstoy*. Oxford University Press, 1987.

Nickell, William. *The Death of Tolstoy: Russia on the Eve, Astapovo Station, 1910*. Ithaca, NY: Cornell University Press, 2010.

Shklovsky, Viktor. *Lev Tolstoy*. Trans. O. Shartse. Moscow: Progress, 1978.

Tolstoy, Alexandra. *The Tragedy of Tolstoy*. New Haven, CT: Yale University Press, 1933.

Troyat, Henri. *Tolstoy*. Trans. Nancy Amphoux. Garden City, NY: Doubleday, 1967.

Wilson, A.N. *Tolstoy*. New York: W.W. Norton, 1988.

Zorin, Andrei. *Critical Lives: Leo Tolstoy*. London: Reaktion, 2020.

Tolstoy's Family and Ancestry

Donskov, Andrew (ed.). *Tolstoy and Tolstaya: A Portrait of a Life in Letters*. Trans. John Woodsworth et al. University of Ottawa Press, 2017.

Tolstaya, Sofia Andreevna. *My Life*. Trans. John Woodsworth and Arkadi Klioutchanski; ed. and intro. Andrew Donskov. University of Ottawa Press, 2010.

Tolstoi, Count Léon L. *The Truth about My Father*. London: John Murray, 1924.

Tolstoy, Alexandra. *Tolstoy: A Life of My Father*. London: Gollancz, 1953.

Tolstoy, Nikolai. *The Tolstoys: Twenty-Four Generations of Russian History*. London: Hamish Hamilton, 1983.

Tolstoy, Oleg. *The Tolstoys in the 21st Century*. London: Merrell, 2015.

Tolstoy, Sofia. *The Diaries of Sofia Tolstoy*. Trans. Cathy Porter. Rev. and abridged edn. Richmond: Alma, 2009.

Estate Culture and Yasnaya Polyana

Cavender, Mary W. *Nests of the Gentry: Family, Estate, and Local Loyalties in Provincial Russia*. Newark: University of Delaware Press, 2007.

Nikitina, Nina. *A Tour of the Estate with Lev Tolstoy*. Trans. Katharine Judelson. Tula: Izd. Dom Iasnaia Poliana, 2004.

Roosevelt, P.R. *Life on the Russian Country Estate: A Social and Cultural History*. New Haven, CT: Yale University Press, 1995.

Russian Social and Political Contexts

Peasants and Folklore

Donskov, Andrew (ed.). *Leo Tolstoy in Conversation with Four Peasant Sectarian Writers: The Complete Correspondence*. University of Ottawa Press, 2019.

Figes, Orlando. *Natasha's Dance: A Cultural History of Russia*. New York: Picador, 2002.

Olson, Laura J. "Russianness, Femininity, and Romantic Aesthetics in *War and Peace*." *Russian Review* 56:4 (Fall 1997), 515–31.

Tolstoy, Alexandra. "Tolstoy and the Russian Peasant." *Russian Review* 19:2 (1960), 150–6.

Emancipation and the Great Reforms

Hruska, Anne. "Love and Slavery: Serfdom, Emancipation, and Family in Tolstoy's Fiction." *Russian Review* 66:4 (2007), 627–46.

Lincoln, W. Bruce. *The Great Reforms: Autocracy, Bureaucracy, and the Politics of Change in Imperial Russia*. DeKalb: Northern Illinois University Press, 1990.

Lounsbery, Anne. "On Cultivating One's Own Garden with Other People's Labor: Serfdom in Tolstoy's 'Landowner's Morning.'" In Elizabeth

Cheresh Allen (ed.), *Before They Were Titans: Early Tolstoy and Dostoevsky.* Brighton, MA: Academic Studies Press, 2015. 267–98.
Moon, David. *The Abolition of Serfdom in Russia, 1762–1907.* New York: Longman, 2001.

Nobility and the Russian Class System

Antonova, Katherine Pickering. *An Ordinary Marriage: The World of a Gentry Family in Provincial Russia.* Oxford University Press, 2013.
Grigoryan, Bella. *Noble Subjects: The Russian Novel and the Gentry, 1762–1861.* DeKalb: Northern Illinois University Press, 2018.
Reyfman, Irina. *How Russia Learned to Write: Literature and the Imperial Table of Ranks.* Madison: University of Wisconsin Press, 2018.
Schönle, Andreas, Zorin, Andrei, and Evstrativ, Alexei (eds.). *The Europeanized Elite in Russia, 1762–1825: Public Role and Subjective Self.* DeKalb: Northern Illinois University Press, 2016.
Smith, Alison K. *For the Common Good and Their Own Well-Being: Social Estates in Imperial Russia.* Oxford University Press, 2014.
Wirtschafter, Elise Kimerling. *Structures of Society: Imperial Russia's "People of Various Ranks."* DeKalb: Northern Illinois University Press, 1994.

Orthodox Church

Gustafson, Richard. *Leo Tolstoy: Resident and Stranger.* Princeton University Press, 1989.
Kenworthy, Scott M., and Agadjanian, Alexander S. *Understanding World Christianity: Russia.* Minneapolis: Fortress Press, 2021.
Kolstø, Pål. "Leo Tolstoy, a Church Critic Influenced by Orthodox Thought." In Geoffery Hosking (ed.), *Church, Nation and State in Russia and Ukraine.* London: Macmillan, 1991. 148–66.
Medzhibovskaya, Inessa. *Tolstoy and the Religious Culture of His Time: A Biography of a Long Conversion, 1845–1887.* Lanham, MD: Lexington, 2008.
Michelson, Patrick Lally, and Kornblatt, Judith Deutsch (eds.). *Thinking Orthodox in Modern Russia: Culture, History, Context.* Madison: University of Wisconsin Press, 2014.

Law and Politics

Borisova, Tatiana. "The Digest of Laws of the Russian Empire: The Phenomenon of Autocratic Legality." *Law and History Review* 30:3 (2012), 901–25.
Borisova, Tatiana, and Burbank, Jane. "Russia's Legal Trajectories." *Kritika: Explorations in Russian and Eurasian History* 19:3 (2018), 469–508.

Burbank, Jane. "An Imperial Rights Regime: Law and Citizenship in the Russian Empire." *Kritika: Explorations in Russian and Eurasian History* 7:3 (Summer 2006), 397–431.

Hamburg, G.M. *Russia's Path toward Enlightenment: Faith, Politics, and Reason, 1500–1801.* New Haven, CT: Yale University Press, 2016.

Leatherbarrow, William J., and Offord, Derek. *A History of Russian Thought.* Cambridge University Press, 2010.

Lieven, Dominic (ed.). *The Cambridge History of Russia*, vol. II: *Imperial Russia, 1689–1917.* Cambridge University Press, 2008.

Pravilova, Ekaterina. *A Public Empire: Property and the Quest for the Common Good in Imperial Russia.* Princeton University Press, 2015.

Wortman, Richard. *The Development of a Russian Legal Consciousness.* University of Chicago Press, 2010.

  Russian Monarchy: Representation and Rule: Collected Articles. Brighton, MA: Academic Studies Press, 2013.

War and the Military

Curtiss, John Shelton. *Russia's Crimean War.* Durham, NC: Duke University Press, 1979.

Fuller, William C., Jr. "The Imperial Army." In D. Lieven (ed.), *The Cambridge History of Russia*, vol. II: *Imperial Russia, 1689–1917.* Cambridge University Press, 2008. 530–53.

  Strategy and Power in Russia, 1600–1914. New York: Free Press, 1992.

Keep, John. "The Military Style of the Romanov Rulers." *War & Society* 1:2 (1983), 61–84.

McPeak, Rick, and Orwin, Donna (eds.). *Tolstoy on War: Narrative Art and Historical Truth in "War and Peace."* Ithaca, NY: Cornell University Press, 2012.

Orwin, Donna. "Leo Tolstoy: Patriot, Pacifist, and *Molodets.*" In Orwin (ed.), *Anniversary Essays on Tolstoy.* Cambridge University Press, 2010. 76–95.

Reese, Roger R. *The Imperial Russian Army in Peace, War, and Revolution, 1856–1917.* Lawrence: University of Kansas Press, 2019.

Stone, David R. *A Military History of Russia from Ivan the Terrible to the War in Chechnya.* Westport, CT: Praeger Security International, 2006.

Tolstoyans

Alston, Charlotte. *Tolstoy and His Disciples: The History of a Radical International Movement.* London: I.B. Tauris, 2014.

Brock, Peter. "Russian Sectarian Pacifism: The Tolstoyans." In Brock, *Pacifism in Europe to 1914.* Princeton University Press, 1994. 442–70.

Edgerton, William. "The Artist Turned Prophet: Leo Tolstoy after 1880." In *American Contributions to the Sixth International Congress of Slavists*, vol. II. The Hague: Mouton, 1968. 61–85.

(ed.). *Memoirs of Peasant Tolstoyans in Soviet Russia.* Bloomington and Indianapolis: Indiana University Press, 1993.

Gordeeva, Irina. "The Evolution of Tolstoyan Pacifism in the Russian Empire and the Soviet Union." In Christian Peterson et al. (eds.), *The Routledge History of World Peace since 1750.* London: Routledge, 2018. 98–108.

Clothing

Bliven, Naomi. "Tolstoy's Dress Code: A Moral Schema, in which the Impossibly Chic Are Hung by a Thread." *New York Times Magazine,* May 1, 1994, 66.

Newlin, Thomas. "Peasant Dreams, Peasant Nightmares: On Tolstoy and Cross-Dressing." *Russian Review* 78 (October 2019), 595–618.

Ruane, Christine. *The Empire's New Clothes: A History of the Russian Fashion Industry 1700–1917.* New Haven, CT: Yale University Press, 2009.

The "Woman Question"

Cruise, Edwina Jannie. "Women, Sexuality, and the Family in Tolstoy." In Donna Tussing Orwin (ed.), *The Cambridge Companion to Tolstoy.* Cambridge University Press, 2002. 191–205.

Herman, David. "Stricken by Infection: Art and Adultery in *Anna Karenina* and *Kreutzer Sonata.*" *Slavic Review* 56:1 (Spring 1997), 15–36.

Marrese, Michelle Lamarche. *A Woman's Kingdom: Noblewomen and the Control of Property in Russia, 1700–1861.* Ithaca, NY: Cornell University Press, 2002.

Murav, Harriet. "Law as Limit and the Limits of the Law in *Anna Karenina.*" In Liza Knapp and Amy Mandelker (eds.), *Approaches to Teaching Tolstoy's Anna Karenina.* New York: MLA, 2006. 74–82.

Stites, Richard. "M.L. Mikhailov and the Emergence of the Woman Question in Russia." *Canadian-American Slavic Studies* 3:2 (Summer 1969), 178–99.

  The Women's Liberation Movement in Russia: Feminism, Nihilism, and Bolshevism, 1860–1930. Princeton University Press, 1978.

The Family

Berman, Anna A. *Siblings in Tolstoy and Dostoevsky: The Path to Universal Brotherhood.* Evanston, IL: Northwestern University Press, 2015.

Engel, Barbara Alpern. *Breaking the Ties That Bound: The Politics of Marital Strife in Late Imperial Russia.* Ithaca, NY: Cornell University Press, 2016.

  Mothers and Daughters: Women of the Intelligentsia in Nineteenth-Century Russia. Cambridge University Press, 1983.

Freeze, Gregory L. "Bringing Order to the Russian Family: Marriage and Divorce in Imperial Russia, 1760–1860." *Journal of Modern History* 62:4 (1990), 709–46.

Tovrov, Jessica. *The Russian Noble Family: Structure and Change.* New York: Garland, 1987.

Wagner, William G. *Marriage, Property, and Law in Late Imperial Russia.* Oxford: Clarendon Press, 1994.

Literature, the Arts, and Intellectual Life
Tolstoy's Oeuvre

Bayley, John. *Tolstoy and the Novel.* University of Chicago Press, 1988.
Berlin, Isaiah. "The Hedgehog and the Fox." In Berlin, *Russian Thinkers.* London: Penguin, 1994. 22–81.
Eikhenbaum, Boris. *The Young Tolstoy.* Trans. G. Kern. Ann Arbor, MI: Ardis, 1972. *Tolstoy in the Sixties.* Trans. D. White. Ann Arbor, MI: Ardis, 1982. *Tolstoy in the Seventies.* Trans. A. Kaspin. Ann Arbor, MI: Ardis, 1982.
Feuer, Kathryn. *Tolstoy and the Genesis of War and Peace.* Ed. Robin Feuer Miller and Donna Tussing Orwin. Ithaca, NY: Cornell University Press, 1996.
Medzhibovskaya, Inessa. *L.N. Tolstoy.* Oxford Bibliographies, 2021. https://www.oxfordbibliographies.com/view/document/obo-9780190221911/obo-9780190221911-0104.xml?rskey=t8usJQ&result=1&q=Medzhibovskaya#first Match
Morson, Gary Saul. *Hidden in Plain View: Narrative and Creative Potentials in "War and Peace."* Stanford University Press, 1987.
Orwin, Donna Tussing. *Tolstoy's Art and Thought, 1847–1880.* Princeton University Press, 1993.
Paperno, Irina. *"Who, What am I?": Tolstoy Struggles to Narrate the Self.* Ithaca, NY: Cornell University Press, 2014.
Wasiolek, Edward. *Tolstoy's Major Fiction.* University of Chicago Press, 1978.

Peasant Schools and Education

Blaisdell, Robert (ed.). *Tolstoy as Teacher: Leo Tolstoy's Writings on Education.* Trans. Christopher Edgar. New York: Teachers & Writers Collaborative, 2000.
Hans, Nicholas A. *The Russian Tradition in Education.* London: Routledge, 2012.
Moulin, Daniel. *Leo Tolstoy.* London: Bloomsbury, 2014.

Russian Philosophy

Bykova, Marina F., Forster, Michael N., and Steiner, Lina. *The Palgrave Handbook to Russian Thought.* New York: Palgrave Macmillan, 2021.
Emerson, Caryl, Pattison, George, and Poole, Randall A. (eds.). *The Oxford Handbook of Russian Religious Thought.* Oxford University Press, 2020.
Hamburg, G.M., and Poole, Randall A. (eds.). *A History of Russian Philosophy, 1830–1930: Faith, Reason, and the Defense of Human Dignity.* Cambridge University Press, 2010.
Leatherbarrow, William, and Offord, Derek (eds.). *A History of Russian Thought.* Cambridge University Press, 2010.
Medzhibovskaya, Inessa. *Tolstoy's On Life: From the Archival History of Russian Philosophy.* DeLand: FL and Toronto: Tolstoy Studies Journal, 2019.
Poole, Randall A. "Tolstoy and Russian Idealism." In Inessa Medzhibovskaya (ed.), *A Critical Guide to Tolstoy's On Life: Interpretive Essays.* DeLand, FL

and Toronto: The Tolstoy Society of North America and *Tolstoy Studies Journal*, 2019. 27–64.

Walicki, Andrzej. *A History of Russian Thought from the Enlightenment to Marxism.* Trans. Hilda Andrews-Rusiecka. Stanford University Press, 1979.

Zenkovsky, V.V. *A History of Russian Philosophy.* Trans. George L. Kline. 2 vols. New York: Columbia University Press, 1953.

Zernov, Nicolas. *The Russian Religious Renaissance of the Twentieth Century.* New York: Harper & Row, 1963.

The Russian Literary Scene

Allen, Elizabeth Cheresh (ed.). *Before They Were Titans: Essays on the Early Works of Dostoevsky and Tolstoy.* Brighton, MA: Academic Studies Press, 2018.

Eikhenbaum, Boris. *Tolstoy in the Sixties.* Trans. D. White. Ann Arbor, MI: Ardis, 1982. *Tolstoy in the Seventies.* Trans. A. Kaspin. Ann Arbor, MI: Ardis, 1982.

Ginzburg, Lydia. *On Psychological Prose.* Trans. Judson Rosengart. Princeton University Press, 1991.

Orwin, Donna Tussing. *Consequences of Consciousness: Turgenev, Dostoevsky, and Tolstoy.* Stanford University Press, 2007.

Todd, William Mills (ed.). *Literature and Society in Imperial Russia, 1800–1914.* Stanford University Press, 1978.

Vinitsky, Ilya. "The Worm of Doubt: Prince Andrei's Death and Russian Spiritual Awakening of the 1860s." In Donna Tussing Orwin (ed.), *Anniversary Essays on Tolstoy.* Cambridge University Press, 2011. 120–37.

European Literature

Blumberg, Edwina Jannie. "Tolstoy and the English Novel: A Note on *Middlemarch* and *Anna Karenina.*" *Slavic Review* 30:3 (1971), 561–9.

Buckler, Julie. "Victorian Literature and Russian Culture: Translation, Reception, Influence, Affinity." In Lisa Rodensky (ed.), *The Oxford Handbook of the Victorian Novel.* Oxford University Press, 2013. 206–26.

Goubert, Denis. "Did Tolstoy Read 'East Lynne'?" *Slavonic and East European Review* 58:1 (1980), 22–39.

Mandelker, Amy. *Framing Anna Karenina: Tolstoy, the Woman Question, and the Victorian Novel.* Columbus: Ohio State University Press, 1993.

Meyer, Priscilla. *How the Russians Read the French: Lermontov, Dostoevsky, Tolstoy.* Madison: University of Wisconsin Press, 2008.

European Philosophy

Barran, Thomas. "Rousseau's Political Vision and Tolstoy's *What Is Art?*" *Tolstoy Studies Journal* 5 (1992), 1–13.

Becker, David. "Tolstoy and Schopenhauer and *War and Peace*: Influence and Ambivalence." *Canadian-American Slavic Studies* 48 (2014), 418–47.

Kvitko, David. *A Philosophical Study of Tolstoy.* New York: Columbia University Press, 1927.

Medzhibovskaya, Inessa. *Tolstoy and the Religious Culture of His Time: A Biography of a Long Conversion, 1845–1887.* Lanham, MD: Lexington, 2008.

Orwin, Donna. *Tolstoy's Art and Thought 1847–1880.* Princeton University Press, 1993.

Walsh, Harry Hill. "Schopenhauer's 'On the Freedom of the Will' and the Epilogue to 'War and Peace.'" *Slavonic and East European Review* 57:4 (1979), 572–5.

Music, Theater, and Visual Arts

Brunson, Molly. *Russian Realisms: Literature and Painting, 1840–1890.* DeKalb: Northern Illinois University Press, 2016.

Donskov, Andrew. *Essays on L.N. Tolstoj's Dramatic Art.* Wiesbaden: Otto Harrassowitz, 1988.

Emerson, Caryl. "Tolstoy and Music." In Donna Tussing Orwin (ed.), *Anniversary Essays on Tolstoy.* New York: Cambridge University Press, 2010. 8–32.

Gasparov, B. *Five Operas and a Symphony: Word and Music in Russian Culture.* New Haven, CT: Yale University Press, 2005.

Halliwell, Stephen. "And Then They Began to Sing: Reflections on Tolstoy and Music." *COLLeGIUM* 9 (2010), 45–64.

Jackson, David. *The Wanderers and Critical Realism in Nineteenth-Century Russian Painting.* Manchester University Press, 2006.

Leach, Robert, and Borovsky, Victor (eds.). *A History of Russian Theatre.* Cambridge University Press, 1999.

Shabanov, Andrey. *Art and Commerce in Late Imperial Russia: The Peredvizhniki, a Partnership of Artists.* New York: Bloomsbury Academic, 2019.

Slonim, Marc. *Russian Theater from the Empire to the Soviets.* Cleveland, OH: World Publishing Company, 1961.

Taruskin, Richard. "Chaikovsky and the Human: A Centennial Essay." In Taruskin, *Defining Russia Musically.* Princeton University Press, 1997. 239–307.

Tolstoy, Alexandra. "Tolstoy and Music." *Russian Review* 17:4 (1958), 258–62.

Tolstoy, Leo. *Plays,* vol. I: *1856–1886*; vol. II: *1886–1889*; vol. III: *1894–1910.* Trans. Marvin Kantor with Tanya Tulchinsky; intros. by Andrew Baruch Wachtel. Evanston, IL: Northwestern University Press, 1994–8.

Valkenier, Elizabeth. *Russian Realist Art: The State and Society: The Peredvizhniki and Their Tradition.* New York: Columbia University Press, 1989.

Science, Technology, and the Natural World

Baehr, S. "The Troika and the Train: Dialogues between Tradition and Technology in Nineteenth-Century Russian Literature." In J. Douglas Clayton (ed.), *Issues in Russian Literature before 1917*. Columbus, OH: Slavica, 1989. 85–106.

Berman, Anna A. "Darwin in the Novels: Tolstoy's Evolving Literary Response." *Russian Review* 72:2 (2017), 331–51.

"Of Phagocytes and Men: Tolstoy's Response to Mechnikov and the Religious Purpose of Science." *Comparative Literature* 68:3 (2016), 296–311.

Blackwell, William L. *Beginnings of Russian Industrialization, 1800–1860.* Princeton University Press, 2016.

Brooks, Nathan M. "Alexander Butlerov and the Professionalization of Science in Russia." *Russian Review* 57:1 (January 1998), 10–24.

Costlow, Jane. "Imaginations of Destruction: The 'Forest Question' in Nineteenth-Century Russian Culture." *Russian Review* 62:1 (2003), 91–118.

Fratto, Elena. *Medical Storyworlds: Health, Illness, and Bodies in Russian and European Literature at the Turn of the Twentieth Century.* New York: Columbia University Press, 2021.

Frieden, Nancy. *Russian Physicians in an Era of Reform and Revolution.* Princeton University Press, 1981.

Gerstein, Linda. *Nikolai Strakhov.* Cambridge, MA: Harvard University Press, 1971.

Gordin, Michael D. "Tolstoy Sees Foolishness, and Writes: From *On Life* to *Fruits of Enlightenment*, and Back Again." In Inessa Medzhibovskaya (ed.), *A Critical Guide to On Life: Interpretive Essays*. DeLand, FL and Toronto: The Tolstoy Society of North America and *Tolstoy Studies Journal*, 2019. 105–38.

Jahn, G. "The Image of the Railroad in *Anna Karenina*." *Slavic and East European Journal* 25:2 (1981), 1–10.

McLean, Hugh. "Claws on the Behind: Tolstoy and Darwin." *Tolstoy Studies Journal* 19 (2007), 15–32.

Miller, Robin, "Tolstoy's Peaceable Kingdom." In Donna Tussing Orwin (ed.), *Anniversary Essays on Tolstoy*. Cambridge University Press, 2010. 52–75.

Newlin, Thomas. "Swarm Life and the Biology of *War and Peace*." *Slavic Review* 71:2 (2012), 359–84.

Sirotkina, Irina. *Diagnosing Literary Genius: A Cultural History of Psychiatry in Russia, 1880–1930.* Baltimore, MD: Johns Hopkins University Press, 2002.

Sobol, Valeria. *Febris Erotica: Lovesickness in the Russian Literary Imagination.* Seattle: University of Washington Press, 2009.

Todes, Daniel P. *Darwin without Malthus: The Struggle for Existence in Russian Evolutionary Thought.* New York: Oxford University Press, 1989.

Vinitsky, Ilya. *Ghostly Paradoxes: Modern Spiritualism and Russian Culture in the Age of Realism.* University of Toronto Press, 2009.

Vucinich, Alexander. *Darwin in Russian Thought*. Berkeley: University of California Press, 1988.

Beyond Russia

Pacifism and the Doukhobors

Breyfogle, Nicholas B. *Heretics and Colonizers: Forging Russia's Empire in the South Caucasus*. Ithaca, NY: Cornell University Press, 2005.

Donskov, Andrew. *Leo Tolstoy and the Canadian Doukhobors: A Study in Historic Relationships*. University of Ottawa Press, 2019.

Ewashen, Larry A. Larry's Desk (website). www.larrysdesk.com.

Kalmakoff, Jonathan. Doukhobor Heritage (website). http://doukhobor.org.

Sanborn, Josh. "Pacifist Politics and Peasant Politics: Tolstoy and the Doukhobors, 1895–99." *Canadian Ethnic Studies* 27:3 (1995), 52–71.

Woodsworth, John. "Attitude and Character Transformation as Revealed in the Correspondence of Tolstoy and Verigin." *Canadian Ethnic Studies* 27:3 (1995), 245–51.

America

Sokolow, J.A., and Roosevelt, P.R. *Leo Tolstoi's Christian Pacifism: The American Contribution*. Carl Beck Papers in Russian and East European Studies 604. Pittsburgh, PA: University of Pittsburgh Center for Russian and East European Studies, 1987.

Stockham, Alice. *Tolstoi: A Man of Peace*. Chicago: A.B. Stockham, 1900.

Walsh, Harry. "The Tolstoyan Episode in American Social Thought." *American Studies* 17:1 (1976), 49–68.

India

Balasubramanian, Radha. *The Influence of India on Leo Tolstoy and Tolstoy's Influence on India: A Study of Reciprocal Receptions*. Lewinston, NY: Edwin Mellen Press, 2013.

Foster, John Burt. "From Tolstoy to Premchand: Fractured Narratives and the Paradox of Gandhi's Militant Non-violence." *Comparative Critical Studies* 10 (2013): 57–74.

Green, Martin. *Tolstoy and Gandhi, Men of Peace: A Biography*. New York: Basic Books, 1983.

Eastern Religions

Bodde, Derk. *Tolstoy and China*. Princeton University Press, 1950.

Denner, Michael. "Tolstoyan Nonaction: The Advantage of Doing Nothing." *Tolstoy Studies Journal* 13 (2001), 8–22.

Ignatovich, Alexander. "Echoes of the Lotus Sutra in Tolstoy's Philosophy." *Dharma World* 25 (1998), 20–2.
Milivoyevic, Dragan. *Leo Tolstoy and the Oriental Religious Heritage*. Boulder, CO: East European Monographs, 1998.

English Varieties of Religious Experience

Heier, Edmund. *Religious Schism in the Russian Aristocracy 1860–1900: Radstockism and Pashkovism*. Dordrecht: Springer Netherlands, 1970.
Jones, W. Gareth (ed.). *Tolstoy and Britain*. Washington, DC: Berg, 2005.
Knapp, Liza. *Anna Karenina and Others: Tolstoy's Labyrinth of Plots*. Madison: University of Wisconsin Press, 2016.
Medzhibovskaya, Inessa. *Tolstoy and the Religious Culture of His Time: A Biography of a Long Conversion, 1845–1887*. Lanham, MD: Lexington, 2008.

Tolstoy's Afterlife

Publication History

Croskey, Robert. *The Legacy of Tolstoy: Alexandra Tolstoy and the Soviet Regime in the 1920s*. Seattle: Herbert J. Ellison Center for Russian, East European, and Central Asian Studies, University of Washington, 2008.
Gulin, A.V. "L.N. Tolstoy in the Twenty-First Century and the Academic Complete Edition." Trans. Inessa Medzhibovskaya. *Tolstoy Studies Journal* 22 (2010), 79–85.
Popoff, Alexandra. *Tolstoy's False Disciple: The Untold Story of Leo Tolstoy and Vladimir Chertkov*. New York: Pegasus, 2014.

Tolstoy in English Translation

Beasley, Rebecca. *Russomania: Russian Culture and the Creation of British Modernism, 1881–1922*. Oxford University Press, 2020.
Garnett, Richard. *Constance Garnett: A Heroic Life*. London: Sinclair-Stevenson, 1991.
May, Rachel. *The Translator in the Text: On Reading Russian Literature in English*. Evanston, IL: Northwestern University Press, 1994.
McAteer, Catherine. *Translating Great Russian Literature: The Penguin Russian Classics*. London: Routledge, 2021.
Tolstoy Studies Journal regularly publishes superb articles about Tolstoy translations.

Musical and Film Adaptations

Burry, Alexander, and White, Frederick H. (eds.). *Border Crossing: Russian Literature into Film*. Edinburgh University Press, 2016.

Denner, Michael, and Fitzsimmons, Lorna (eds.). *Tolstoy on Screen*. Evanston, IL: Northwestern Univesity Press, 2014.

Goscilo, Helena, and Petrov, Petre (eds.). *Anna Karenina on Page and Screen*. Pittsburgh, PA: Department of Slavic Languages and Literatures and Center for Russian and East European Studies, University of Pittsburgh, 2001.

Seinen, Nathan. "Kutuzov's Victory, Prokofiev's Defeat: The Revisions of 'War and Peace.'" *Music & Letters* 90:3 (2009), 399–431.

Tsivian, Yuri. *Early Cinema in Russia and Its Cultural Reception*. Trans. Alan Bodger. University of Chicago Press, 1998.

Wachtel, Andrew (ed.). *Intersections and Transpositions: Russian Music, Literature, and Society*. Evanston, IL: Northwestern University Press, 1998.

Youngblood, Denise. *Bondarchuk's War and Peace: Literary Classic to Soviet Cinematic Epic*. Lawrence: University Press of Kansas, 2014.

Tolstoy as Subject of Art: Painting, Film, Theater

Reischl, Katherine Hill. "Photography and the Crisis of Authorship: Tolstoy and the Popular Photographic Press." *Jahrbücher für Geschichte Osteuropas*, Neue Folge, 60:4 (2012), 533–49.

Index

Printed in the USA
CPSIA information can be obtained
at www.ICGtesting.com
LVHW082159221123
764744LV00006B/30

9 781108 479240